Perspectives on Input, Evidence, and Exposure in Language Acquisition

Language Acquisition and Language Disorders (LALD)
ISSN 0925-0123

Volumes in this series provide a forum for research contributing to theories of language acquisition (first, second and additional; child and adult), language learnability, language attrition and language disorders.

For an overview of all books published in this series, please see
benjamins.com/catalog/lald

Series Editors

Roumyana Slabakova
University of Southampton and
The Arctic University of Norway

Lydia White
McGill University

Editorial Board

Kamil Ud Deen
University of Hawaii at Manoa

Katherine Demuth
Macquarie University

Naama Friedmann
Tel Aviv University

Heather Goad
McGill University

Barbara Höhle
University of Potsdam

Nina Hyams
University of California at Los Angeles

Jürgen M. Meisel
University of Calgary

Mabel Rice
University of Kansas

Luigi Rizzi
University of Siena

Petra Schulz
Johann Wolfgang Goethe-Universität

Bonnie D. Schwartz
University of Hawaii at Manoa

Antonella Sorace
University of Edinburgh

Ianthi Maria Tsimpli
University of Cambridge

Volume 69

Perspectives on Input, Evidence, and Exposure in Language Acquisition
Studies in honour of Susanne E. Carroll
Edited by Lindsay Hracs

Perspectives on Input, Evidence, and Exposure in Language Acquisition

Studies in honour of Susanne E. Carroll

Edited by

Lindsay Hracs
University of Calgary

John Benjamins Publishing Company
Amsterdam / Philadelphia

The paper used in this publication meets the minimum requirements of the American National Standard for Information Sciences – Permanence of Paper for Printed Library Materials, ANSI z39.48-1984.

DOI 10.1075/lald.69

Cataloging-in-Publication Data available from Library of Congress:
LCCN 2024016051 (PRINT) / 2024016052 (E-BOOK)

ISBN 978 90 272 1486 7 (HB)
ISBN 978 90 272 4686 8 (E-BOOK)

© 2024 – John Benjamins B.V.
No part of this book may be reproduced in any form, by print, photoprint, microfilm, or any other means, without written permission from the publisher.

John Benjamins Publishing Company · https://benjamins.com

Table of contents

Preface   VII
    Lindsay Hracs

CHAPTER 1. Introduction   1
    Lindsay Hracs

Theory in language acquisition research
CHAPTER 2. Linguistic approaches to language acquisition: Looking back at the formative years of a unified language acquisition theory   16
    Jürgen M. Meisel

Gender in bilingual and heritage language acquisition
CHAPTER 3. Acquisition of morpho-syntactic features in a bilingual Italian child: An integrated approach to gender   54
    Laura D'Aurizio, Johanna Stahnke & Natascha Müller

CHAPTER 4. Gender assignment in German as a heritage language in an English-speaking context: A case study of acquisition and maintenance   88
    Tanja Kupisch & Roswita Dressler

Input and exposure in the classroom
CHAPTER 5. Acquisition of 3PL verb markings by (very) advanced FSL learners and bilingual Francophone students   118
    Raymond Mougeon, Françoise Mougeon & Katherine Rehner

CHAPTER 6. L2 intonation perception in learners of Spanish   144
    Angela George

Evidence in controlled first exposure language learning
CHAPTER 7. Isolated and combined effects of models and corrective feedback in the acquisition of the Turkish locative morpheme   162
    Yucel Yilmaz, Senyung Lee & Yılmaz Köylü

CHAPTER 8. First exposure to Russian word forms by adult English speakers: Disentangling language-specific and language-universal factors   191
    Natalia Pavlovskaya, Nick Riches & Martha Young-Scholten

Input and evidence in the acquisition of syntactic structure

CHAPTER 9. Speech modifications and the Processability Theory hierarchy: Some observations on word order in Swedish L1 and L2 input   226
Gisela Håkansson

CHAPTER 10. Varieties of DP recursion: Syntax, semantics, and acquisition   245
Ana T. Pérez-Leroux, Yves Roberge, Diane Massam, Susana Bejar & Anny Castilla-Earls

Proper name index   267

Subject index   271

Preface

With profound admiration and gratitude, this volume has been assembled to celebrate the remarkable contributions of Dr. Susanne E. Carroll. Throughout a career marked by unwavering dedication to scientific inquiry, Susanne has not only significantly advanced our understanding of input in language acquisition, but has also inspired countless colleagues and students along the way. When Susanne's retirement was officially announced, messages began pouring in detailing her impact on the field and on those who were fortunate enough to get to know her. In lieu of a *tabula gratulatoria*, some of the volume contributors have chosen to include their messages here:

> Your research inspired us and gave rise to a new approach to gender in the Romance languages. We want to thank you for that and we hope that more will come. Tu n'as jamais oublié la terre, qu'il faut la soigner pour faire évoluer. Tu as cultivé ton jardin. Merci!
>
> Laura D'Aurizio, Johanna Stahnke, and Natascha Müller

> Looking back, I think we first met when I was working on my Master of Arts in German. You taught a LANG designated course on Grammatical Gender that laid the groundwork for my research with Dr. Tanja Kupisch featured in this Festschrift. I appreciated your insights into German and French, two languages we both share. I was enthusiastic about having you on my committee when I pursued my PhD in Education as my interest in bilinguals in schools included investigating their linguistic competence in both languages. You supported me with reference letters for my SSHRC application and job search, for which I am very grateful as they contributed to my success in both. Interestingly, when I discovered that teachers struggled to find appropriately leveled reading materials for their Bilingual Program classrooms, you suggested that I consider that area for future research, a project which I have now been able to begin. I wish you all the best in your retirement – your legacy lives on.
>
> Roswita Dressler

> I contributed to this volume as a way to offer my acknowledgement and gratitude for a professor who has paved the way for scholars in language acquisition. Even though our research is in different subfields, I have learned a lot from Dr. Susanne Carroll. We combined our research in the article titled *What absolute beginners learn from input: From laboratory to classroom research*, published in 2018 in a special issue of the journal *Instructed Second Language Acquisition 2(2): Second Language Teaching and Generative Linguistics*. I have appreciated the time

Dr. Susanne Carroll has taken to meet with me and offer advice on how to succeed as a professor. In addition, she taught a course on assessment taken by a graduate student I supervised and to this day, I am still hearing about how much the student learned in this course. This is further evidence that Dr. Susanne Carroll's knowledge is extending to current and future scholars. I will be forever grateful for her wisdom and knowledge that will live on well after her retirement. It is in this spirit that I offer my chapter to this Festschrift. Angela George

It feels very difficult to associate such an energetic person with retirement.
Gisela Håkansson

I still remember us meeting in Hamburg when I was about to leave for Calgary and you introduced me to the details of winters in Calgary. Our paths have crossed many times since. I admire your work and I am grateful for the support and advice you have given me. Tanja Kupisch

Il me semble que ce n'est qu'hier que nous nous sommes côtoyés à UBC puis à UofT et que nous avons collaboré à OISE au projet de recherche sur l'effet de la correction des erreurs chez les apprenants L2. Tout au long de ta carrière tu as représenté pour moi un modèle à suivre pour la rigueur et à la profondeur de tes analyses ainsi que pour ta résolution à t'attaquer à des questions complexes. Je te souhaite tout le bonheur qui te revient à l'occasion de ta retraite. Profites-en bien!
Yves Roberge

It is a great pleasure to congratulate you on your retirement and to take the opportunity to thank you for all the support I received from you during my year in Calgary. The opportunity to do a post-doc under your supervision in the Language Research Center was a great chance that opened new doors for me in academia. I would also like to thank you for writing *Input and Evidence*, which, in my opinion, is the most theoretically sophisticated treatment of negative feedback to date and has been a big source of inspiration for my work. I wish you the best in your retirement. Yucel Yilmaz

I know I am capturing the opinion of so many others when I write that I have been extremely fortunate to have a mentor, colleague, and collaborator that supports me and pushes me to excel while insisting I pursue answers to my research questions with the utmost scientific rigor. I am beyond pleased to have had the opportunity to organize this volume in Susanne's honour.

Lindsay Hracs

CHAPTER 1

Introduction

Lindsay Hracs
University of Calgary

1. Preliminary perspectives

In celebrating the distinguished career of Dr. Susanne E. Carroll, this volume serves as both a tribute to her scholarly achievements and a testament to the profound effect she has had on the field of linguistics. The contributions within comprise research from scholars who have had an impact on Carroll's career in terms of formative experiences, eventual trajectory, and/or collaborative efforts, as well as from scholars who have been impacted by Carroll's influential work. Accordingly, this volume brings together a diverse collection of viewpoints and insights that collectively illuminate the intricate landscape of the field of language acquisition.

A brief inspection of titles on Carroll's list of publications reveals that she is well-versed in a variety of topics—the current discussion touches on only a subset of that list. First and foremost, Carroll is a trained syntactician. After completing her dissertation on French dislocations and topicalizations at the Université de Montréal in 1981, she went on to publish on *for-to* infinitives (Carroll 1983) and reflexives in French (Carroll 1986a) and English (Carroll 1986b). Carroll's commitment to integrating theoretical perspectives with language acquisition research is especially apparent in her papers on formalizing the relationship between language acquisition studies and grammatical theory (Carroll 1989a); the strength and weaknesses of a structural universals-only approach to second language acquisition (SLA) (Carroll & Meisel 1990); the difficulties parameter-setting approaches have with solving the representational problem of language acquisition (Carroll 1996); features and primitives in SLA (Carroll 2009); and more recently, embedding a theory of conceptual representation in language acquisition studies (Carroll & Hracs 2024a). In fact, a major motivation for Carroll has been developing an explanatory theory of SLA (see Carroll 2001 for her work on the *Autonomous Induction Theory*). Carroll will be the first to tell you that before anything else, she is (and always will be) a linguist, and that for her, SLA research is not a matter of testing theories, but instead, SLA research must make use of linguistic theories to define learning problems. Carroll (2017a: 3)

https://doi.org/10.1075/lald.69.01hra
© 2024 John Benjamins Publishing Company

argues that little progress can be made toward understanding how language acquisition takes place in the absence of precise claims about how particular learning problems are solved.

A central thread running through Carroll's work is input in language acquisition, focusing on the psycholinguistic processes that take learners from linguistic stimuli to knowledge of a language. From an empirical perspective, Carroll has examined the acquisition of gender (Carroll 1989b, 1995, 2005) and the role of feedback and correction in SLA (Carroll 2001; Carroll & Swain 1993; Carroll et al. 1992). Carroll has also conducted a variety of controlled first exposure language learning (CFELL) studies in which participants with no prior exposure to the language under investigation are exposed to a finite set of linguistic stimuli that have been carefully designed, and in many cases constructed from scratch, to examine the acquisition of a particular phenomenon (see Carroll & Hracs in press for a survey of CFELL research). Carroll's work on CFELL covers topics such as segmentation and word learning (Carroll 2012, 2013, 2014), number (Carroll & Widjaja 2013), cognates (Carroll & Windsor 2015), classifiers (Carroll & Hracs 2024b), and visual information processing (Carroll & Hracs 2024a). CFELL studies allow researchers to be precise about the linguistic properties they are testing while measuring how much exposure is needed for learning to take place. Moreover, these studies provide insight into how adult learners apply knowledge of their first language (L1) to solve learning problems in their second language (L2).

There are three main themes found within this collection: *input, evidence,* and *exposure*. Readers of Carroll's work will notice her careful and intentional distinction between *input* and *exposure*. Building on perspectives from learnability theory, Carroll defines input as the information which is relevant to solving a particular learning problem (Carroll 2017a: 5). Further, based on work from Fodor (1998a, 1998b), Carroll (2001, 2017a) argues for a distinction between *input-to-language-processors* (i.e., linguistic stimuli fed into language processors and analyzed based on the learner's grammar) and *input-to-language-acquisition-mechanisms* (i.e., information that learning mechanisms need to create novel representations). She maintains that "unnecessary confusion" has resulted from the assumption that the input needed to solve a learning problem is found in a learner's environment (Carroll 2017a: 12), when in fact input is better thought of as mental representations that are analyzed by a processor during language development (Carroll 2001: 16). In other words, for Carroll, input-to-language-acquisition-mechanisms is not a measurable property of the speech signal. Furthermore, Hracs (2021) argues that distinguishing between types of input is necessary because what constitutes input can shift over the course of acquisition as changes in the state of the learner's grammar occur in tandem with cognitive development.

In contrast, *exposure* is what is observable in a learner's environment, e.g., child-directed speech (Carroll 2017a: 4). The quality and quantity of exposure are factors that can be measured, but Carroll (2001: 15–16) argues that we cannot fully understand how language development happens simply by analyzing measurable properties of exposure. However, because exposure is something that can be measured, it can be used to draw conclusions about what learners have attended to and mentally represented (Carroll 2017a: 4). For Carroll, this is the primary motivation for CFELL studies. It is important to note that even within the following chapters, the terms input and exposure are defined in different ways and are often used (somewhat) interchangeably. With that being said, the crucial thing to keep in mind is that we cannot make claims about input and exposure independently of a theory of perception and processing as well as a detailed characterization of the learning problem.

Finally, *evidence* with respect to the current volume can be thought of observations used in support of a particular conclusion. Broadly speaking, we can take this to mean evidence that learning has taken place. More narrowly, *positive evidence* can be thought of as the "stimuli which provide evidence for a particular analysis" (Carroll 2001: 18). Alternatively, *negative evidence* is not found in the mental representation of a stimulus nor is it provided once a stimulus has been processed, but nevertheless it supplies information to the language acquisition mechanisms (Carroll 2001: 18–19). In her discussion of evidence, Carroll puts forth that acquisition takes place when input causes a parsing failure. That is to say, the lack of evidence for a particular analysis corresponds with an activation of the learning mechanisms (Carroll 2001: 18). Under this approach, discussions of evidence cannot take place independent of discussions of input and learning mechanisms.

While highlighting the importance of theory-driven acquisition work, the studies included in this volume attempt to make explicit the types of structures available to L1 and L2 learners and how they are used to solve a variety of learning problems. Thus, a goal of this volume is to underscore the necessity of being precise about what mental representations of linguistic structure are and how they change over time. Relatedly, over the past few decades, there have been increasing calls for language acquisition research to be informed by linguistic theory. The studies outlined below work toward filling that gap by providing a counterpoint to research that does not provide a formal characterization of the knowledge driving linguistic behaviour over the course of development. To that end, this volume will be of particular interest to those studying language acquisition from the perspective of generative linguistics, especially those whose research centres on issues of input, evidence, and exposure.

2. An overview of the volume

A comprehensive picture of Carroll's substantial research output is reflected in the variety of contributions found in the following sections: Theory in language acquisition research; Gender in bilingual and heritage language acquisition; Input and exposure in the classroom; Evidence in controlled first exposure language learning; and Input and evidence in the acquisition of syntactic structure. The breadth of the studies in this volume are an indication of how far-reaching Carroll's impact on the field of language acquisition has been and continues to be.

Section 1. Theory in language acquisition research

Beginning the volume with a discussion of the formation of a unified acquisition theory, Meisel's chapter examines the path of establishing linguistics as a domain of cognitive science. In particular, Meisel focuses on the study of language development as a significant part of linguistic theorizing and explores how investigations of language development have changed over the past 50 years. He starts with a discussion of the cognitive turn which resulted from the advent of generative linguistics in the 1960s. Meisel notes that at this point, the ideal speaker-hearer became the object of linguistic research, ultimately altering the course of linguistic theorizing. In the 1970s, the systematic study of language learning in individuals became more widespread and the discipline of developmental psycholinguistics emerged. As Meisel points out, during this time, researchers began to seriously consider the nature of a learner's mental grammar and ask questions about its properties and how those properties are acquired, as well as its transition from the initial state to the final state. Meisel argues that the shift from studying language as a product of speech communities to the study of the implicit knowledge of individual language users prompted the development of a unified acquisition theory. Although it took some years for the field of SLA to integrate the notion of innate mental grammars into the research, the author suggests that the study of whether the characteristics of L1 and L2 are the same began to flourish at this time.

Following the survey of the evolution of linguistic theorizing, Meisel further explores the nature of linguistically informed approaches to language acquisition with an in-depth investigation of German verb placement. Essentially, a detailed characterization of this learning problem allows the author to better explore the role of exposure, input, and innate knowledge in both the L1 and L2 acquisition of German verb placement. He ultimately argues that linguistically motivated research can explain the properties of early grammars and how they are acquired and adds that theoretically motivated empirical research has resulted in success in uncovering the nature of L2 learners' knowledge and development as well.

Meisel concludes the chapter by stating that despite the progress made in late 20th and early 21st centuries, the developmental problem has not been solved, arguing that this is at least in part due to the fact that linguists and psychologists are still not giving it the attention it deserves. In particular, while changes in learners' grammars are systematic, researchers still cannot explain the uniformity of change across all learners. Additionally, Meisel highlights that our theoretical analyses are only ever approximate models of what is taking place in the mind, and that we must also focus on how properties of linguistic grammars are processed and learned if we hope to understand more about mental grammars. As mentioned in the previous section, this has been a pervasive topic in Carroll's work over the course of her career. Fittingly, Meisel contends that more input analyses could make a significant contribution to linguistic theorizing.

Section 2. Gender in bilingual and heritage language acquisition

The study by D'Aurizio, Stahnke, and Müller investigates acquisition of gender and declension class features in Italian. Specifically, they present a case study of a bilingual child from the age of 2;0.11 to 5;0.8 who is acquiring Italian and German. The chapter starts with an overview of gender, number, and declension class features in Italian, paired with the authors' assumptions regarding the structure of the DP in Italian. From this, they suggest that Italian exhibits a morphological gender system whereby the gender of a noun can be inferred from its class. D'Aurizio et al. subscribe to the parameter-setting approach taking parameters to be emergent from the interaction of universal grammar (UG), linguistic input, and domain-general processing. Additionally, they assume that declension class in Italian represents a parameterized feature that is part of the inflectional system. Drawing on acquisition data, their first research question explores whether or not the Italian nominal system is marked, maintaining that languages with more features present in the nominal system are marked and thus should be acquired later than if the system exhibits only one of the features. Secondly, D'Aurizio et al. ask whether gender interacts with declension class in Italian, and if so, whether the gender feature follows from the class feature.

To answer their questions, the authors identified the declension class of every noun in their dataset by coding on the basis of the number of referents for every form produced by the child, allowing them to use singular and plural suffix marking to determine the class. Furthermore, they coded the gender and number marking on determiners, and following Kupisch (2006), also coded for article omissions. Results show that gender errors are rare in their corpus, but that determiner omission is frequent until age 3;0. The authors reason that these determiner omissions are evidence for the markedness of the Italian nominal system. However, they ultimately argue that the morphological gender system in Italian is unmarked and acquired early on. Finally, D'Aurizio et al. conclude by emphasizing the essential role that language acquisition studies play in linguistic theorizing.

In a second case study involving the acquisition of gender, Kupisch and Dressler examine the development of German as a heritage language in a learner who is growing up in an English-speaking environment. They analyzed naturalistic, longitudinal data at age 1–2, age 4–5, and age 7 in order to determine whether development follows the same trajectory as monolingual German children, or whether there are indications of delay and stagnation similar to that observed in heritage speakers of other languages. The chapter begins with an exploration of German gender, centering on the interaction of number, gender, and case along with potential phonological, morphological, syntactic, and semantic cues to nominal gender. Like D'Aurizio et al. in the previous chapter, Kupisch and Dressler draw attention to the role that the acquisition of articles plays in the acquisition of gender, suggesting that while the development of gender happens quite early in monolingual children, the children use strategies such as article omission or underspecification of forms to avoid gender marking in early stages. The authors point out that in some cases, early sequential bilingual acquisition and simultaneous bilingual acquisition appear to be slower than monolingual acquisition and can exhibit qualitative differences from monolingual acquisition that are more L2-like in nature.

Kupisch and Dressler extracted instances of DPs from free speech video recordings in both German and English that were taken at the three different time periods. They coded for the presence or absence of a determiner, grammatical number (singular or plural), and whether the DP occurred inside a prepositional phrase. Results show that error rates decrease over time, but that they are rather low (i.e., $\leq 6\%$) from very early on; by age 2;5.15, the child consistently used most articles, article omission has ceased, and articles being used are marked with the correct gender. Moreover, at the time English became the child's dominant language, errors remained very low. However, they remark that the overall low number of tokens observed provides challenges when making assertions about attrition and stagnation. Kupisch and Dressler ultimately conclude that grammatical gender can become target-like in heritage language learners of German with extensive exposure to the minority language at home, despite competing exposure to the majority language during schooling.

Section 3. Input and exposure in the classroom

Mougeon, Mougeon, and Rehner study the acquisition of third person plural (3PL) verb markings in two categories of French-speaking students in Canada, namely advanced speakers of French as a second language (FSL) and bilingual Francophones. Their chapter begins with a discussion of the complex landscape of French schooling in Canada and the proficiency levels of students corresponding to the various exposure scenarios in each of the educational contexts. Mougeon et al. analyze several corpora in order to better understand the impact of the discursive frequency of verbs, the students' exposure to French outside of the classroom, the students' frequency of use of French, properties of teacher speech, and the usage of 3PL verb markings in the varieties of French included in the study. As expected, the authors found that both FSL and Francophone students have a lower rate of acquisition of infrequent verbs compared to frequent verbs. Looking more closely at educational context, Mougeon et al.'s prediction that university students would exhibit higher rates of acquisition than immersion students for both frequent and infrequent verbs was confirmed. Moreover, frequency of use of French varied between educational contexts and across the different varieties investigated.

Regarding frequency of use, citing Mougeon and Beniak's (1991)[1] investigation of 3PL verb markings, Carroll (2017a: 11) points out that the students who come from homes where English is the primary language of communication and who use English regularly to communicate with their peers are not as practiced at speaking French. Carroll suggests that we might expect competition from representations of English and relevant English processing procedures in lower frequency of use scenarios. Mougeon et al. end their contribution by emphasizing Carroll's (2017b) call for research programs to include the type of descriptive work they have undertaken in order to better illustrate the complexity of the learning problems being studied.

The fifth contribution in the volume is from George, who examines the effects of explicit instruction on the ability of learners of Spanish as a second language to perceive prosodic differences between utterances with identical word order in the absence of any contextual cues. The chapter opens with a survey of previous work on the development of L2 Spanish intonation but points to a gap in the literature regarding the effects of instruction on the perception of intonational patterns by learners. This study attempts to fill that gap. George introduces Mennen's (2015) L2 Intonation Learning theory which claims that when phonetic, phonological, semantic, and frequency-based dimensions in the L1 and L2 intonation systems

---

1. Mougeon et al. use the 1978 corpus analyzed by Mougeon and Beniak (1991) to approximate the influence of caregiver speech exposure on the students in the current study.

are similar, the systems will merge, and when those dimensions are different, no merging will take place. The author predicts that learning should be straightforward when the final boundary tone of an utterance type in Spanish matches with the boundary tone of the utterance type in English.

With respect to the study at hand, George includes varieties of Spanish that vary in the realization of final boundary tones and predicts that explicit instruction will facilitate the identification of utterance type (i.e., wh-questions, yes-no questions, and declaratives) across those varieties. Eleven advanced learners of Spanish at an English-speaking university in the southeastern Unites States were measured on their ability to identify the three utterance types based on exposure from 7 regional macrodialects of Spanish. Measurements were taken before and after explicit instruction on the intonational contours of the utterances. Instruction touched on the regional differences found in the boundary tones across the macrodialects. Although there was a slight increase in scores from pretest to posttest on wh-questions and yes-no questions, results did not significantly increase after instruction, likely because participants were already performing well at the pretest. George argues, however, that advanced learners may still benefit from explicit instruction when the intonation patterns of the L1 and L2 do not match.

Section 4. Evidence in controlled first exposure language learning

Yilmaz, Lee, and Köylü compare the role of different types of evidence, i.e., models, corrective feedback, and a mix of the two, in the acquisition of the Turkish locative morpheme. Yilmaz et al. define models as "well-formed exemplars of the target language" produced by native speakers or proficient L2 speakers. Thus, models constitute positive evidence. Alternatively, they suggest that corrective feedback can be construed either as negative evidence, e.g., in the form of clarification requests with target-like exemplars not provided, or as negative evidence with concurrent positive evidence, e.g., in the form of recasts or explicit corrections. The authors cite Carroll's (2001) work suggesting that the more informative nature of explicit corrections is preferred over less informative types of corrective feedback since explicit corrections signal to the learner not only that an utterance contains an error, but where in the utterance the error is located and how to correct it.

Subsequently, Yilmaz et al. provide a survey of four studies (Herron and Tomasello 1988; Leeman 2003; Long et al. 1998 [Spanish]; Long et al. 1998 [Japanese]) comparing the effects of models and corrective feedback in L2 research. They identify a gap in the literature in that it is unclear if any of the findings can be extended to learners at the very early stages of learning given that the previous studies included learners who had familiarity with the target language. Furthermore, Yilmaz et al. posit that providing learners with models first followed by corrective feedback may be more conducive to learning at this stage than providing models or corrective feedback in isolation. To that end, the authors aimed to determine the extent to which models, corrective feedback, and a combination of both have on the development of the Turkish locative morpheme *-DA*, with its four allomorphs *-da*, *-de*, *-ta*, and *-te*, in true first exposure learners.

English-speaking university students with no prior knowledge of Turkish were randomly assigned to one of four study groups: models, corrective feedback, mixed (models + corrective feedback), or control (no exposure to modelled targets or corrective feedback). Participants from all four groups took part in two lab sessions each with a production task and a comprehension task and were tested at two different posttest sessions two weeks apart. Results from Yilmaz et al.'s study showed that the mixed group who were exposed to both models and corrective feedback consistently outperformed the control group who had no exposure to either type of evidence. In particular, they suggest that exposure to the target forms through models with subsequent corrective feedback is a more effective strategy than employing one or the other.

In another study of first exposure language learning, Pavlovskaya, Riches, and Young-Scholten explore how learners segment and store word forms at the initial stages of learning an L2. Pavlovskaya et al. begin their chapter with an overview of studies on segmentation in both L1 and L2, and then pivot the discussion to first exposure studies. In their literature review, they remark on different measures of exposure, i.e., exposure/trial counts (e.g., Carroll 2012, 2014) and exposure timed in minutes, hours, weeks, etc. (e.g., Gullberg et al. 2010; Gullberg et al. 2012; Rast 2008; Shoemaker & Rast 2013), and conclude that despite a learner's L1, segmentation is possible after minimal exposure to an L2. The authors also distinguish between controlled exposure to artificial languages and natural languages on the basis of ecological validity, citing Carroll (2014: 114–115). To maximize generalizability, the authors examine the ability of English-speaking adults to segment Russian on first exposure, specifically asking: (1) whether learners' abilities to detect target word forms increase over time; (2) whether learners are more accurate when Russian phonotactics align with English phonotactics; (3) whether learners are more accurate with strong-weak or weak-strong stress patterns; (4) whether learners show a preference for longer words; and (5) whether learners are able to generalize phonotactic properties to novel forms that they have not been exposed to.

The participants in Pavlovskaya et al.'s study completed an input phase and a test phase in a single session per day over four consecutive days. A word recognition task, a forced-choice task, and a shared word identification task were designed to test their abilities to segment Russian word forms. Cumulative exposure was measured across the four daily sessions. In alignment with findings from other first exposure studies, results showed that participants' accuracy scores increase as the amount of exposure increases, though results varied across the different tasks. Pavlovskaya et al. also found that participants' reliance on English phonotactics differed across tasks, and that in the forced-choice task in particular, there was a slight preference for words exhibiting Russian phonotactics only. Counter to their hypotheses, there was a trend toward an increase in accuracy detecting words with weak-strong stress patterns, and word length did not seem to affect accuracy scores. On the generalization task, Pavlovskaya et al. found that adults were readily able to apply phonological generalizations to novel forms after limited exposure. Ultimately, they argue that results from their generalization task suggest that participants are not simply storing word forms they have been exposed to but are instead demonstrating "creative linguistic behaviour".

Section 5. Input and evidence in the acquisition of syntactic structure

Håkansson explores the L1 and L2 development of word order in Swedish from the perspective of input. Swedish exhibits verb-second (V2) word order: The verb immediately follows the subject in the canonical word order (Håkansson's label = SVX), but when another element is in sentence-initial position, the verb immediately follows that element and the subject appears in postverbal position (Håkansson's label = XVS). As Håkansson remarks, the choice of SVX or XVS is constrained by information structure, but both word orders occur frequently. The puzzle for Håkansson is that while children produce both structures around the time multiword utterances begin to appear in their speech, L2 learners of Swedish show a strong preference for the SVX order.

Håkansson hypothesizes that the asymmetries between L1 and L2 learners in their acquisition of word order variations might have to do with differences in the linguistic properties of the stimuli they are exposed to. In particular, Håkansson explores the role of simplifications often seen in child-directed speech and teacher talk, and with respect to word order, suggests that both SVX and XVS patterns exist in child-directed speech (citing Josefsson 2003 and Waldmann 2008) but that XVS structures are not observed until later stages of Swedish teacher talk (citing Håkansson 1987: 35). I will note that Håkansson's use of the term *input* is akin to Carroll's use of the term *exposure*. Håkansson draws on Pienemann's (1998, 2015) Processability Theory, which predicts five stages in the L2 acquisition of morphosyntax corresponding to processing procedures that develop incrementally in an implicational fashion. This approach effectively couches the discussion in a theory of language processing while attempting to explain similar developmental trajectories for morphosyntactic production.

Håkansson's study aims to establish the extent to which word order varies between narratives directed at L1 speakers and L2 learners of Swedish and whether teachers' speech modifications are related to the learners' developmental stages as predicted by Processability Theory. Second language teachers of Swedish were asked to read and memorize a story, and then asked to retell the story to their students and to a group of L1 speakers of Swedish. The narratives produced by the teachers were recorded and transcribed, and the proportions of SVX and XVS word orders were calculated. Håkansson reports that all teachers in the study produced fewer instances of inversion when the narrative was directed to their L2 students, but argues that this particular speech modification might actually result in less textual cohesion. In addition, when paired with an analysis of student responses, it does not appear that there was a correspondence between teacher productions and the students' developmental stages. Essentially, Håkansson indicates that more research is still needed to better understand whether the strategies employed by teachers are having a facilitative or adverse effect on L2 learners' development of word order variations in Swedish.

The final contribution to the volume is by Pérez-Leroux, Roberge, Massam, Bejar, and Castilla-Earls who examine the development of DP recursion in English. In congruence with themes in Meisel's chapter and those recurrent in Carroll's research, Pérez-Leroux et al. make it a point to investigate DP recursion from the perspectives of both language development and linguistic theory, making explicit their assumptions regarding syntactic representations. Moreover, the authors point to Carroll's (2001: 236) discussion of the representational problem, and state that for them, studying grammatical development means studying how children come to have a mental system capable of encoding linguistic knowledge.

Pérez-Leroux et al. aim to better understand the role of grammatical complexity in language development by characterizing complexity on the basis of Merge (citing Chomsky's (2020: 9) definition) and posit that complexity is a result of the iterative application of Merge. Furthermore, they argue that semantic bootstrapping cannot facilitate solving the learning problem of DP recursion because it involves modification rather than complementation, drawing attention to literature which suggests that children do not use modification in early stages of development and that the recursive structures tend to appear much later. Their study was designed to examine the development of four recursive relations: comitatives (*with*), locatives (*in/on/next to*), possessives (*-s*), and relational nouns (*of*). They note that prior research has found asymmetries in the acquisition of the different recursive relations. Consequently, Pérez-Leroux et al. ask if development is comparable across all forms of recursive modification under investigation, and if not, whether the observed relative complexity is the same for children and adults.

Four participant groups broken down by age (i.e., four-year-olds, five-year-olds, six-year-olds, and adults) were included in the study, and an elicitation task with a picture and story context was used to encourage participants' production of the target recursive structures. Overall, Pérez-Leroux et al.'s results suggest that the four recursive structures display a similar developmental timeline, and that while children produce recursive structures less frequently than their adult counterparts, there does not appear to be a difference in complexity across the structures for children or adults. Accordingly, the authors suggest that the differences between the recursive modifications do not appear to be structural, and that the difficulty observed in the L1 development of these structures may be related (at least in part) to a requirement of sufficient evidence of the embedded structure before it can be used recursively.

Acknowledgements

A number of people have made the completion of this volume possible. I would first like to thank the LALD series editors Roumyana Slabakova and Lydia White and acquisition editor Kees Vaes for their patience and guidance during the process of compiling this volume. A special thank you also goes to Jürgen M. Meisel for the encouragement he provided. I also extend my gratitude to Dennis Storoshenko for facilitating the peer review process. And finally, thank you to those who served as reviewers and devoted their time to giving substantive feedback on the submissions, which has undoubtedly bolstered the quality of work in this volume.

References

Carroll, S. E. 1981. Notions fonctionnelles en grammaire transformationnelle: Dislocations et structures topicalisées en français contemporain. PhD dissertation, Université de Montréal.

Carroll, S. E. 1983. Remarks on FOR-TO infinitives. *Linguistic Analysis* 12(4): 415–451.

Carroll, S. E. 1986a. On non-anaphor reflexives. *Revue Québécoise de Linguistique* 15(2): 135–165.

Carroll, S. E. 1986b. Reflexives and the dependency relation "R". *Canadian Journal of Linguistics/Revue Canadienne de Linguistique* 31(1): 1–44.

Carroll, S. E. 1989a. Language acquisition studies and a feasible theory of grammar. *Canadian Journal of Linguistics/Revue Canadienne de Linguistique* 34(4): 399–418.

Carroll, S. E. 1989b. Second language acquisition and the computational paradigm. *Language Learning* 39(4): 535–594.

Carroll, S. E. 1995. The hidden danger in computer modelling: Remarks on Sokolik & Smith's connectionist learning model of French gender. *Second Language Research* 11(3): 193–205.

Carroll, S. E. 1996. Parameter-setting in SLA: Explanans and explanandum. *Behavioral and Brain Sciences* 19(4): 720–721.

Carroll, S. E. 2001. *Input and Evidence: The Raw Material of Second Language Acquisition*. Amsterdam: John Benjamins.

Carroll, S. E. 2005. Input and SLA: Adults' sensitivity to different sorts of cues to French gender. *Language Learning* 55(S1): 79–138.

Carroll, S. E. 2009. Re-assembling formal features in SLA: Beyond minimalism. *Second Language Research* 25(2): 245–253.

Carroll, S. E. 2012. First exposure learners make use of top-down lexical knowledge when learning words. In *Multilingual Individuals and Multilingual Societies*, K. Braunmüller, C. Gabriel & B. Hänel-Faulhaber (eds), 23–45. Amsterdam: John Benjamins.

Carroll, S. E. 2013. Introduction to the special issue: Aspects of word learning on first exposure to a second language. *Second Language Research* 29(2): 131–144.

Carroll, S. E. 2014. Processing 'words' in early-stage SLA: A comparison of first exposure and low proficiency learners. In *First Exposure to a Second Language: Learners' Initial Input Processing*, ZH. Han & R. Rast (eds), 107–138. Cambridge: CUP.

Carroll, S. E. 2017a. Exposure and input in bilingual development. *Bilingualism: Language and Cognition* 20(1): 3–16.

Carroll, S. E. 2017b. Explaining bilingual learning outcomes in terms of exposure and input. *Bilingualism: Language and Cognition* 20(1): 37–41.

Carroll, S. E. & Hracs, L. 2024a. Input processing in Conceptual Semantics. In *The Handbook of Second Language Acquisition and Input Processing*, J. Barcroft & W. Wong (eds), 87–102. New York NY: Routledge.

Carroll, S. E. & Hracs, L. 2024b. Learning functional categories in a second language on initial exposure: Classifiers. In *Proceedings of 50 ans de linguistique à l'UQAM*, R. Pinsonneault & Y. Léveillé (eds), 51–63. Montréal: l'Université du Québec à Montréal.

Carroll, S. E. & Hracs, L. In press. Constructed language and constructed languages in language acquisition studies: Similarities and differences between natural, lab, and artificial languages. To appear in *The Palgrave Handbook of Constructed Languages*, A. Long & J. W. Windsor (eds). London: Palgrave Macmillan.

Carroll, S. E. & Meisel, J. M. 1990. Universals and second language acquisition: Some comments on the state of current theory. *Second Language Acquisition* 12(2): 201–208.

Carroll, S. E. & Swain, M. 1993. Explicit and implicit negative feedback: An empirical study of the learning of linguistic generalizations. *Studies in Second Language Acquisition* 15(3): 357–386.

Carroll, S. E., Swain, M. & Roberge, Y. 1992. The role of feedback in adult second language acquisition: Error correction and morphological generalizations. *Applied Psycholinguistics* 13(2): 173–198.

Carroll, S. E., & Widjaja, E. 2013. Learning exponents of number on first exposure to an L2. *Second Language Research* 29(2): 201–229.

Carroll, S. E. & Windsor, J. W. 2015. Segmental targets versus lexical interference: Production of second-language targets on first exposure with minimal training. In *Transfer Effects in Multilingual Language Development*, H. Peukert (ed.), 53–85. Amsterdam: John Benjamins.

Chomsky, N. 2020. Fundamental operations of language: Reflections on optimal design. *Cadernos de Linguística* 1(1): 1–13.

Fodor, J. D. 1998a. Learning to parse? *Journal of Psycholinguistic Research* 27(2): 285–319.

Fodor, J. D. 1998b. Parsing to learn. *Journal of Psycholinguistic Research* 27(3): 339–374.

Gullberg, M., Roberts, L. & Dimroth, C. 2012. What word-level knowledge can adult learners acquire after minimal exposure to a new language? *International Review of Applied Linguistics* 50(4): 239–276.

Gullberg, M., Roberts, L., Dimroth, C., Veroude, K. & Indefrey, P. 2010. Adult language learning after minimal exposure to an unknown natural language. *Language Learning* 60(s2): 5–24.

Håkansson, G. 1987. Teacher Talk: How Teachers Modify Their Speech When Addressing Learners of Swedish as a Second Language [PhD dissertation]. Lund: Lund University Press.

Herron, C., & Tomasello, M. 1988. Learning grammatical structures in a foreign language: Modelling versus feedback. *French Review* 61(6): 910–923.

Hracs, L. 2021. Modelling exposure and input in language acquisition. PhD dissertation, University of Calgary.

Josefsson, G. 2003. Input and output: Sentence patterns in child and adult Swedish. In *The Acquisition of Swedish Grammar*, G. Josefsson, C. Platzack & G. Håkansson (eds), 95–133. Amsterdam: John Benjamins.

Kupisch, T. 2006. *The Acquisition of Determiners in Bilingual German-Italian and German-French Children*. Munich: Lincom.

Leeman, J. 2003. Recasts and second language development. *Studies in Second Language Acquisition* 25(1): 37–63.

Long, M. H., Inagaki, S. & Ortega, L. 1998. The role of implicit negative feedback in SLA: Models and recasts in Japanese and Spanish. *The Modern Language Journal* 82(3): 357–371.

Mennen, I. 2015. Beyond segments: Towards an L2 intonation learning theory (LILt). In *Prosody and Languages in Contact: L2 Acquisition, Attrition, Languages in Multilingual Situations*, E. Delais-Roussarie, M. Avanzie & S. Herment (eds), 171–188. Berlin: Springer.

Mougeon, R. & Beniak, É. 1991. *Linguistic Consequences of Language Contact and Restriction: The Case of French in Ontario*. Oxford: OUP.

Pienemann, M. 1998. *Language Processing and Language Development: Processability Theory*. Amsterdam: John Benjamins.

Pienemann, M. 2015. An outline of Processability Theory and its relationship to other approaches to SLA. *Language Learning* 65(1): 123–151.

Rast, R. 2008. *Foreign Language Input: Initial Processing*. Clevedon: Multilingual Matters.

Shoemaker, E. & Rast, R. 2013. Extracting words from the speech stream at first exposure. *Second Language Research* 29(2): 165–183.

Waldmann, C. 2008. Input och output. Ordföljd i svenska barns huvudsatser och bisatser [Input and Output. Word Order in Swedish Children's Main and Subordinate Clauses]. PhD dissertation, Lund University.

Theory in language acquisition research

CHAPTER 2

Linguistic approaches to language acquisition
Looking back at the formative years of a unified language acquisition theory

Jürgen M. Meisel
University of Hamburg

Acquisition research is an integral part of contemporary linguistic theorizing. 50 years ago, this was not the case. Change came about following a theoretical reorientation that established linguistics as a cognitive science, defining mental grammars as the prime object of study. Here I review an early proposal for developmental psycholinguistics and show how it shaped subsequent research, inspired by grammatical and acquisition theory. Summarizing analyses of German verb placement by L1 and L2 learners, I argue that this research of the 1970–80s achieved important insights into properties of learner grammars, discovered acquisition orders and established similarities as well as differences between L1 and L2 acquisition.

Keywords: L2 acquisition, L1 acquisition, mental grammars, developmental psycholinguistics, morphosyntax

Avant-propos

The study of language acquisition is an integral part of contemporary linguistic theorizing. Yet what may appear self-evident today is the result of fairly recent theoretical changes in the language sciences. It was only in the 1960s that psychologists and linguists engaged in comprehensive investigations of learners' linguistic knowledge at various points of acquisition. The question then is what led to this shift of research interests. The most plausible answer is that it is an immediate outcome of the cognitive turn in linguistic theorizing. The ensuing conceptualization of language as a mental faculty inevitably led to an interest in the question of how this faculty is acquired. This, in turn, triggered a steadily increasing number of studies of first language (L1) and subsequently also of second language (L2) acquisition. Importantly, these investigations laid the groundwork for a unified theory of language acquisition, designed to account for various acquisition types (monolingual and bilingual L1, child and adult L2, etc.), and calling for interdisciplinary cooperation to create a model integrating linguistic and psychological approaches. I propose to take a look at the formative years of this new research agenda in order to detect strengths and weaknesses, for such insights can provide guidance for current and future acquisition research.

1. Beginnings

Fifty years ago, developmental issues were not a major concern of linguistic research, and language acquisition played at best a marginal role in linguistic curricula. University courses on first language acquisition were scarce, and although second language learning was studied in applied linguistics and educational programs, the focus was entirely on foreign language learning in the classroom; classes dealing with L2 acquisition processes were virtually non-existent. This state of affairs only changed in the early 1970s, following the emergence of systematic research on language learning by individual learners, first in L1 and later on also in L2 acquisition.

Several textbooks appeared during the second half of the 1970s, offering comprehensive introductions to L1 acquisition, an indication that there now existed a potential readership of undergraduate and graduate students for such publications. But this target group was apparently not entirely ready for the insights that the new sub-discipline of the language sciences had to offer, as becomes apparent from the opening remarks by Peter de Villiers and Jill de Villiers (1979: 9), authors of one of the introductions to language acquisition:

> One of us teaches a course entitled 'Child Language', and it was one of the courses in the college catalogue, among other esoteric offerings such as 'Lichens of the Arctic' and 'The Polish Verb', that was ridiculed in a student publication: next to the course title the author had drawn a cartoon depicting a mindless-looking baby saying 'ba-ba'.

This is not to say that language acquisition had previously not been investigated at all. In fact, several studies of child language had appeared towards the end of the 19th century, mostly carried out by psychologists. I should at least mention the one by Clara Stern and William Stern (1907/1975),[1] an early but particularly

---

1. William Stern (1871–1938) taught at the University of Breslau (Wrocław) and as of 1916 in Hamburg, initially in the *Allgemeinen Vorlesungswesen* (university courses for the general pub-

insightful work, recommended reading still today. Yet for many years to come, children's language and its development played a marginal role in linguistics, and the study of language acquisition was not commonly part of linguistic curricula.

2. The cognitive turn

The absence of language development in linguistic theorizing is perhaps not surprising, given that linguists were primarily concerned with the description of constructions attested in language usage of linguistic communities, commonly relying on analyses of corpora comprising mostly literary samples. Grammars consisted of rules designed to capture the regularities characterizing these constructions, illustrated by lists of examples and of exceptions. Importantly, these descriptions were not intended to reflect the linguistic knowledge of individuals and could therefore shed no light on how it develops over time. Consequently, they were of limited interest for studies of mental activities, like learning. Only if language, as the object of linguistic studies, is conceptualized as a mental faculty, does the question of how this faculty is acquired become a central concern of linguistic theorizing.

It was the cognitive turn in linguistics that brought about such a shift of perspective and the ensuing redefinition of the object of research. This happened with the advent of the generative enterprise, which began to exert significant influence on the language sciences in the 1960s. It defined the mental grammar of the ideal speaker-hearer (or speaker-listener) as the object of linguistic research (Chomsky 1965: 3ff.). The notion of 'ideal speaker' has, of course, been the topic of an extensive and controversial debate that I will not engage in here in much detail. However, I should at least mention three points of particular relevance for the establishment of acquisition research as a genuine component of theoretical linguistics.

First and most importantly, identifying the ideal speaker as the model of linguistic theory entails a shift of interest from the language use of a speech community to the capacities that speakers must possess in order to be able to comprehend and produce speech. This does not merely amount to a quantitative change in that it increases the scope of tasks beyond the description of linguistic usage. It rather represents a qualitative change of the research paradigm by focusing on the underlying capacity to *generate* sentences rather than on utterances that occur

---

lic), and subsequently (1919) at the newly founded University of Hamburg. In 1933, the family left Nazi Germany, emigrating via the Netherlands to the United States, where William Stern taught at Duke University.

in speech corpora. In other words, the focus lies on the *knowledge* of competent speakers. This does not diminish the importance of empirical analyses, for the validity of hypotheses about properties of this knowledge must be checked against the occurrence of constructions in speech corpora. The resulting grammars are thus theories about speakers' knowledge based on their use. Yet these must not only account for empirically attested facts, but for potentially occurring ones as well, i.e., the database comprises both speech corpora and acceptability (or grammaticality) judgements.

Secondly, since the goal of linguistic theorizing now is to account for and hopefully explain the knowledge that enables speakers to generate sentence structures underlying the utterances that occur in speech and to distinguish between possible and impossible constructions, formal properties of linguistic objects are of particular interest. Linguistic research is, of course, not limited to the study of mental grammars, for speakers' linguistic knowledge comprises other factors that enable them to perform competently. Nor is the interest in formal properties a unique feature of cognitively oriented theories. What was different and new, however, is that these properties must be accounted for in terms of principles and mechanisms that can plausibly be argued to constitute mentally represented knowledge systems. Most importantly for our present purposes, this inevitably leads to the question of how mental grammars become part of the knowledge of individuals, in other words, how they are acquired. This is to say that, following the cognitive turn, acquisition theory became an integral and necessary part of linguistic theorizing.

The third point to be mentioned here concerns the terminological contrast between linguistic communities on the one hand and individual speakers, on the other. This, I contend, does not actually indicate a fundamental change of perspective. Rather, as Chomsky (1965:3) observed correctly, it has "been the position of the founders of modern general linguistics." Saussure (1916/1975), for example, distinguishes between *langage* (language faculty), *parole* (speech), and *langue* (language), the latter being designated as the object of linguistic research. Although he emphasizes that it is a *social* phenomenon, this refers primarily to the fact that no individual masters all varieties (dialects, registers, or sociolects) of a language. In fact, when he argues that 'language' is a grammatical system virtually present in every brain or rather in the brains of a set of individuals, Saussure (1916/1975:30) takes a position much closer to that of the concept of an ideal speaker than what critics of the this notion believe:

> C'est un trésor déposé par la pratique de la parole dans les sujets appartenant à une même communauté, un système grammatical existant virtuellement dans chaque cerveau, ou plus exactement dans les cerveaux d'un ensemble d'individus ; car la langue n'est complète dans aucun, elle n'existe parfaitement que dans la masse.[2]

The notion of 'ideal speaker' results from a similar line of reasoning: No particular individual possesses the knowledge attributed to the ideal speaker. We should therefore not be surprised to find that "nobody has met so far" (Abutalebi & Clahsen 2016: 855) an ideal speaker-hearer. It seems appropriate to emphasize that the term refers to a model representing the object of linguistic theorizing, and like all models of scientific activities, it specifies the constitutive properties of this object, the ones that must be accounted for, as opposed to those that may be disregarded, according to the theory. It is an idealization in that, outside laboratory conditions, no object of study actually possesses all constitutive properties. A critical discussion of the theory should, of course, include a review of the choice of features deemed to be relevant – or not. The elimination of variability as a constitutive property of the ideal speaker's linguistic knowledge, for example, has been the target of many critical comments, and rightly so, I believe. Objecting to specific hypotheses of a theory is what must be expected of a scientific debate, rejecting idealization as a procedure in theory building, however, amounts to a renunciation of scientific standards. It is reminiscent of the endeavour for exactitude in science described in a short story by Jorge Luis Borges (1960) in which he elaborates on an idea by Lewis Carroll (1893: 170), about a country where cartography has reached a state of such a perfection that it can make "a map of the country, on the scale of a *mile to the mile*."

> Have you used it much?" I enquired. "It has never been spread out, yet," said Mein Herr: "the farmers objected: they said it would cover the whole country, and shut out the sunlight! So we now use the country itself, as its own map, and I assure you it does nearly as well.

In sum, with the emergence of mentalistic theory, the study of language acquisition has been put on the agenda of linguistic theorizing. Crucially, it must explain how the knowledge that enables speakers to generate the sentence structures of their language becomes part of their mentally represented linguistic competence. Consequently, although this is certainly not the only task of acquisition research, one of its major goals is to explain the development of mental grammars.

---

2. It is a treasure amassed by the use of speech in the individuals belonging to the same community, a grammatical system virtually existing in every brain, or more exactly in the brains of a group of individuals; for the language is not complete in any of them, it only exists perfectly in the mass. (My translation, JMM)

3. Developmental psycholinguistics

Stimulated by the cognitive approach, a new generation of linguists and psychologists with an interest in linguistic theorizing engaged in studies of first language acquisition. This happened in the early 1960s, and the early 1970s witnessed a surge of such investigations. Earlier work had focused on those aspects of child language in which it differs from the adult norm, implicitly or explicitly assuming that children's speech was an incomplete version of adult language. Subsequently, it was recognized that "early speech is not an abbreviated and distorted form of adult language but the product of a unique first grammar" (Smith & Miller 1966:7). Thus, rather than limiting themselves to surveys of children's sounds and words, frequency counts, and case histories, the aim now was to uncover children's linguistic knowledge, the development of their grammars, and ultimately the nature of the human language capacity.

Initially, however, these researchers, too, apparently felt that the choice of their research topic required justification, as becomes obvious from the remark by the editors of the proceedings of one of the first conferences dealing with child language development from a cognitive perspective, held in 1965, Smith & Miller (1966:2).

> They [participants in the conference] were discussing the ungrammatical and often unintelligible, the sometimes cute but usually unimportant sounds that children make, a topic that might conceivably fascinate a devoted mother but that had been of little interest to scholars or scientists in any previous century.

Importantly, this new approach to child language research called for intensified cooperation across disciplines, especially joint efforts by psychologists and linguists. As pointed out by McNeill (1966:15), "Linguistic theory and studies of language acquisition have existed side by side, occasionally influencing each other, but in the main the two bodies of work have evolved separately." Ideally, theoretical and descriptive linguistics and psychology of language would merge into a new discipline, *developmental psycholinguistics*. "The aim is to develop a theory of language acquisition that will be consistent with linguistic theory and will cover the facts of acquisition as they are now known." (McNeill 1966:15)

This is undoubtedly a goal still worth pursuing in contemporary acquisition research. The question, however, is what counts as "facts of acquisition" determining a research agenda that can lead towards the objectives defined by this approach. As emphasized repeatedly, one crucial 'fact' is the learner's mental grammar. Yet for a theory of acquisition to qualify as an adequate treatment of linguistic development, it must achieve more than an account of *properties* of learners' underlying knowledge at a given point of development, even if this in itself is already a formidable task. Acquisition theory rather faces the threefold task of accounting for the properties of learners' grammars, of showing how these are *acquired*, i.e., implemented in child grammars, and of explaining the *development* from initial to final state grammars.

The facts to be covered by acquisition theory and to be addressed by acquisition research thus relate to at least these three tasks, i.e., to identify the properties of the mental grammars that can be attributed to very young children, to explain how they acquire this knowledge, and to explain how it can change in the further course of development. Since the three problems are closely related, the search for solutions indeed requires joint efforts by linguistic theory and acquisition studies, by linguists as well as psychologists. Reconsidering this cognitively oriented approach and its research agenda from today's perspective, there can be no doubt that it has been quite influential and successful. Although it did not actually lead to a unified discipline, developmental psycholinguistics, it did bring about closer cooperation between psychologists and linguists, already from early on.

Not surprisingly, however, proposals concerning formal properties of early grammars were largely dominated by linguistic theory. Yet answers to the *property problem* inevitably carry over into attempts to solve the *acquisition problem*. The theory of Universal Grammar (UG), for example, views UG as the core component of the Language Acquisition Device (LAD). UG principles define the initial state of L1 acquisition, the knowledge that children bring to the task of acquisition, and they constrain the properties of grammars at each point of L1 development. Children are therefore claimed to be able to access this grammatical knowledge previous to any experience with the target language. Consequently, acquisition requires the activation of this knowledge as well as inductive learning. In both cases, learners need to scan and parse the speech to which they are exposed, the primary linguistic data (PLD), assigning to them structural information, thus converting them into input useable for language learning (Carroll 2001). Note that although UG is frequently equated with the LAD, the latter also comprises discovery principles, bootstrapping learners into grammatical systems, and learning mechanisms, enabling them to acquire non-universal properties of grammars; see Meisel (2011: 18f.) for a more detailed discussion of these terms.

The contributions to the above-mentioned 1965 workshop on child language development, cf. Smith & Miller (eds) (1966), show that this concept of acquisition involving the interaction of innate and inductively attained knowledge was considered uncontroversial. What was and still is controversial is the proportional weight of the two knowledge sources as explanatory factors for language acquisition. There was broad consensus among the participants, mostly psychologists, that the fast rate and the general success of L1 learners strongly support the idea that children bring intrinsic knowledge to the task of language acquisition. In fact, Fodor (1966: 108f.) drew attention to a problem later termed Plato's problem

(Chomsky 1986), namely that early grammars contain information not overtly coded in the PLD and not inductively learnable. One point that led to some controversy, however, is the question of how much grammatical information should be attributed to the innate acquisition device. Whereas McNeill (1966) suggested that children have access to grammatical universals, Slobin (1966) argued that certain properties of child language are the result of learning or processing mechanisms, thus referring to a further explanatory factor of language acquisition research. This is to say that child grammars are not only shaped by structural information extracted from the PLD or provided by UG principles; rather, learning and processing mechanisms, too, play a role here and must therefore be taken into account in attempts to solve the property and the acquisition problem.

Not much has been said, so far, about the third problem that a cognitively oriented acquisition theory must tackle, the *developmental problem* (Felix 1984). The reason is that it is the least well studied one. Surprisingly so, for it can be argued to be the core issue of developmental psycholinguistics, since it follows inevitably from its founding hypothesis that a child's early linguistic knowledge, being a mental grammar, already exhibits systematic properties. Given that initial systems differ from their adult counterparts, they must change in the course of acquisition until they eventually develop into mature native grammars. Yet if initial as well as subsequent grammars are self-contained systems, the question arises as to what triggers the transition from one to the next. Should we assume that child grammars contain unstable or otherwise vulnerable domains? Or is their development caused by grammar-external forces? And which are the grammar-internal or external factors that can act as causes of change? These are under-researched issues to which I will return in Section 6.

4. Towards a unified language acquisition theory

At this point, I want to draw attention to a particularly important achievement of cognitively oriented linguistic theorizing on acquisition. Although it initially focused on first language acquisition, the shift of attention from products of language use by speech communities to the implicit knowledge of speakers opened a window of opportunities for the development of a unified acquisition theory. If children do come equipped with an intrinsic knowledge, a Language-Making Capacity (Slobin 1985), the null hypothesis should be that this LMC can also be activated in other acquisition types, e.g., when children acquire two languages from birth (2L1) or when another language is acquired later in life (L2). To the extent that the various types differ from L1 with respect to ultimate attainment or in how acquisition proceeds, one must determine whether the LMC changes over time and/or whether it becomes partially inaccessible. Its complete inactivation or total loss is *a priori* the least likely option.

The approach alluded to by these remarks may appear a rather obvious one, from today's perspective, but it actually took a few years for second language acquisition research to adopt this view and to undergo similar theoretical changes and set similar goals as research on L1 development. Only then could the question be addressed whether the two types of acquisition share essential properties. Previously, L2 studies had been concerned almost exclusively with foreign language learning in classrooms rather than with naturalistic L2 acquisition. The focus therefore was on the issue of how instruction can foster and guide the learning process, rather than on learners' language acquisition capacities. Moreover, applied linguistics, studying instructed learning, was based on behaviourist theories according to which learning crucially requires changing previously acquired *behaviour*. This is why L1 interference was regarded as the main factor determining L2 acquisition, the prediction being that "those elements that are similar to his [the learner's, JMM] native language will be simple for him, and those elements that are different will be difficult" (Lado 1957: 2), since "the grammatical structure of the native language tends to be transferred to the foreign language." (Lado 1957: 58).

Consequently, Contrastive Analysis (CA) was the dominant research paradigm of L2 studies. Ultimately, however, empirical research revealed that prognosticated errors do not necessarily occur in learners' speech, whereas learners encounter difficulties where CA does not foresee any. The problem with CA was that it compared systems resulting from linguistic analyses in order to predict difficulty or ease of learning. Yet these descriptive grammars did not even pretend to capture properties of mental grammars. Contrastive analyses therefore suffered from the outset from a logical inconsistency: transfer of knowledge can only happen in the minds of learners. Thus, linguistic phenomena that cannot reasonably be assumed to be part of learners' knowledge cannot be transferred from previously acquired systems to subsequently learned ones. It simply does not make sense to postulate transfer from L1 to L2 systems that are not mental representations of both the source and the target system. In other words, knowledge transfer cannot operate on linguistic systems that do not reflect the knowledge of speakers.

An explicitly cognitive orientation of second language acquisition research was initiated in the late 1960s, leading to a surge of empirical L2 studies in the 1970s. Corder (1967), in his seminal paper, for example, referred to children's innate predisposition to acquire language and an internal mechanism that makes the acquisition of grammar possible. He may also have been the first to explicitly raise the question whether the child's language-making capacity remains available to second language learners. He left no doubt that he himself believed that the same mechanism operated in both L1 and L2 acquisition, proposing:

> as a working hypothesis that some at least of the *strategies* adopted by the learner of a second language are substantially the same as those by which a first language is acquired. Such a proposal does not imply that the course or *sequence* of learning is the same in both cases. (Corder 1967:164)

In fact, he not only suggested the same underlying mechanism for L1 and L2 acquisition, he also introduced the notion of *transitional competence* and demanded that the focus of L2 research should be on the learner, rather than on learners' productions. Suggestions and reflections like these triggered a paradigm change in L2 research, leading to learner-oriented studies focusing on properties of approximative L2 systems and their development in the course of acquisition. This is to say that research in the 1970s and subsequently approached L2 acquisition in much the same way as cognitively oriented research on L1 development. These efforts resulted in a wealth of L2 investigations addressing the above-mentioned problems, concerning properties of learners' grammars, their acquisition and development, as is illustrated by edited volumes reporting on trends in L2 research during the 1970s, e.g., Felix (ed.) (1980).

Similar developments happened more or less simultaneously in other fields of acquisition research, e.g., child bilingualism, studying the simultaneous (2L1) or successive (cL2) acquisition of two or more languages in early childhood. This is not the occasion to summarize the history of this field, but it is worth remembering that research on simultaneous bilingualism was initiated more than 100 years ago by Jules Ronjat (1913).[3] In a case study of his son Louis acquiring French and German simultaneously, he already demonstrated that exposing children to two languages from birth allows them to develop two native languages. Few of the publications that appeared during the following 60 years enhanced significantly our understanding of the simultaneous acquisition of two or more languages from birth. Notable exceptions are the works by Milivoïe Pavlovitch (1920) and by Werner F. Leopold (1939–49/1970). Still, child bilingualism remained a marginal topic for years to come. In fact, Kenji Hakuta (1989:10) remarked in an interview conducted in 1983 with Werner Leopold "that bilingualism is still

---

3. Jules Ronjat (1864–1925), philologist and linguist, had also studied and practiced law. Born in Vienne (France), he worked on the history of Provençal, the regional variety of Occitan. In 1914, he moved to Geneva where he taught courses at the university and served as proofreader of Saussure (1916/1975). His posthumously published *Grammaire istorique des parlers provençaux modernes*, 4 vols. (Montpellier 1930–1941, 2 vols., Geneva/ Marseille 1980) still counts as one of the most important works on this language.

neglected within the field of psychology". Yet this period was actually the time when things changed. A number of influential publications had already appeared in the late 1970s, many more were published in the 1980s, and the "1990s saw an explosion of published work on BFLA [bilingual first language acquisition], and it continues to grow at a high rate", as De Houwer (2009: 13) observed.

These investigations demonstrated beyond any doubt that children exposed to more than one language from birth differentiate linguistic systems from very early on, they proceed through subsequent developmental phases just like the respective monolinguals, and they are able to attain native competences in the languages to which they are exposed; cf. Meisel (2004). Cross-linguistic interaction does not cause qualitative changes in the linguistic knowledge of simultaneous bilinguals; cf. Meisel (2007). To the extent that it does occur, it mostly affects language use, although there have been reports on quantitative effects, resulting in delayed or accelerated developments.

5. Linguistic approaches to language development

The cognitive turn in linguistic theorizing and subsequent research dealing with various types of acquisition opened up opportunities for fruitful cooperation between linguists and psychologists, and between acquisition researchers. Mental grammars are now the object of linguistic and of acquisition theory, and first and second language acquisition are both regarded as instantiations of the human Language-Making Capacity, sharing crucial properties in spite of substantial differences that distinguish them. Acquisition is now considered as an integral part of linguistic theory – an inevitable conclusion once it is acknowledged that an adequate linguistic theory must explain how properties attributed to mental grammars are acquired (and used). Importantly, this means that acquisition and grammatical theory are interdependent: on the one hand, one must not attribute to speakers knowledge that is not learnable by exposure to the primary linguistic data, unless it can be argued to be provided by the LAD. On the other hand, what is claimed to have been acquired and to be represented in learners' mental grammars must not violate principles and constraints of grammatical theory.

The development of a linguistically informed acquisition theory resulted in a rapidly growing number of empirical studies, first of L1 and soon later of L2 acquisition. This eventually had reverberations in university curricula. Departments of linguistics and linguistic programs in modern language departments began to offer undergraduate or graduate courses on acquisition or on psycholinguistics with a focus on developmental issues. It is also no coincidence that several journals specialising in L1 and/or L2 acquisition were first published in the 1970s and that textbooks for such courses began to appear at approximately the same time. These activities are further indications of the newly gained status of developmental research.

It is a fair assessment, I think, to conclude that this linguistic approach yielded results that led to new insights into first and second language acquisition, revealing properties of developing grammars, invariant acquisition orders and similarities as well as differences between these two acquisition types. We therefore know things today that we did not know 50 years ago.

5.1 Grammatical properties to be acquired: An illustrative example

A look at a specific example, the well-studied phenomenon of German verb placement, can substantiate and justify my admittedly quite positive view, but it can also help to detect some shortcomings. Note, however, that I can only present a summary of some crucial points of a debate that has been going on for years; see Meisel (2011) for a more detailed discussion.

(1) Verb placement in German
    a. Sie **füttert** den Hund (heute Abend)
        she feeds the dog (this evening)
        'She will be feeding the dog this evening'
    b. Sie **hat** (gestern) den Hund *gefüttert*
        she has (yesterday) the dog fed
        'She (has) fed the dog (yesterday)'
    c. Unseren Hund **will** sie *füttern*
        our dog wants she to feed
        'Our dog she wants to feed'
    d. Morgen **füttert** sie den Hund
        tomorrow feeds she the dog
        'Tomorrow she will feed the dog'
    e. ... dass sie den Hund **füttert**
        that she the dog feeds
        '...that she feeds the dog'
    f. ...dass sie den Hund *füttern* **will**
        that she the dog to feed wants
        '...that she wants to feed the dog'

Let us first look at the grammatical properties that need to be acquired. Details of morphosyntactic analyses vary, of course, depending on the theory on which they are based. Nevertheless, the crucial points to which I am referring here should not be controversial. In main clauses, German verbs can be placed in second position, following the subject (1a,b), clause-finally (1b,c), or clause-initially in yes/no interrogatives. A closer look reveals that only finite verbs (bold) appear in non-final position in main clauses. Moreover, second position does not necessarily mean that the verb follows the subject; rather, it is consistently placed in structural second position (V2 effect), no matter which element occupies the clause-initial position, subjects (1a,b), objects (1c), adverbs (1d) or subordinate clauses (no example). Non-finite verbal elements (italics), on the other hand, are always placed clause-finally. In subordinates (1e,f), however, they precede the finite verb in this clause-final position (1f).

According to the commonly accepted analysis that captures these observations, German is a V2 and an OV language; see the simplified structure in the tree diagram (2).

(2) Simplified sentence structure: German

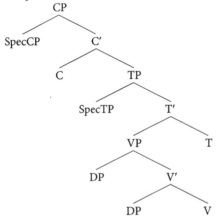

Non-finite verbs remain in their original position, whereas finite verbs are displaced. In main clauses, they end up in C, above the subject position. In subordinates, a complementizer occupies the head of C, obliging the verb to remain in a lower position (T).

Turning now to the acquisition problem, one might wonder how children cope with the task of discovering the properties of German grammar that account for this rather complex situation. Let me begin by stating explicitly what they need to know and what the possible sources of this knowledge are. Minimally, they must know what a syntactic category is and how it is structurally related to other constituents of a sentence, i.e., they must be able to assign to utterances hierarchical structures comprising syntactic categories, labelled V, N, etc. These are essential points, for they refer to constitutive features of human languages, not shared by animal communication systems. Importantly, their properties are not fully revealed by the PLD. Syntactic categories, for example, are abstract entities defined by their syntactic behaviour, including the fact that they project maximally to constituents like VP, NP. They constrain the domain of operation of syntactic processes, e.g., gender or number agreement within DP, and they are merged into hierarchical structures, as in (2). Moreover, although the fact that an element appears in different surface positions indicates that it can be displaced within the structure, the PLD reveal neither which item is moved nor what positions it can occupy. In (1), for example, it is always the finite verb that changes position, rather than another constituent being moved over the verb, e.g., the subject to the right in (1c) and (1d). Incidentally, this shows that what superficially presents itself as a linearization task actually requires placement of elements in different hierarchical positions. In sum, children must acquire abstract grammatical knowledge that is not fully encoded in the PLD. Since this type of knowledge is instantiated in all human languages, linguistic theory states that this information is provided by UG.

I am emphasizing these points because their importance tends to be underestimated by acquisition researchers who do not follow a mentalist approach. Usage-based approaches, for example, claim that children abstract syntactic categories gradually and in piecemeal fashion out of concrete pieces of language (e.g., words) that are learned inductively (Tomasello 2007). However, they have not provided a satisfactory explanation of how it is possible to discover and implement syntactic properties in an abstraction process that can only draw on functional (semantic) properties of the word on which they operate and on its distributional behaviour. Moreover, some approaches, especially in the field of psychology of language, reduce grammatical structure to linear sequences of sound to chunks of arbitrary stretches of the signal. The linear order of elements undoubtedly constitutes part of the logic determining formal properties of utterances. Yet although precedence, succession, adjacency, initialization, finalization, and so on, are essential notions, numerous syntactic phenomena, e.g., the above-mentioned V2 effect, can only be accounted for in terms of hierarchical relationships between the components of sentences, as they are represented in tree diagrams; see (2). In other words, *structure dependency* is an essential property of mental grammars, and since children acquire syntactic phenomena that reflect structure dependency, as I will show below, we may conclude that their grammars do not differ in this respect from mature ones.

Note that cross-linguistic comparisons show that there exist universal as well as language-particular features of acquisition. Consequently, an adequate acquisition theory must account for both types of phenomena. One way to do this is to assume that parts of grammatical knowledge are provided by the LAD, independently of the nature or amount of exposure to the PLD. Others are obviously learned inductively, and this requires sufficient exposure to the PLD. The latter case concerns lexical learning and all other features specific to particular languages, as for example the inventory of inflectional affixes of verbs. Of particular interest for acquisition research are instances where both knowledge sources, LAD and PLD, are involved, e.g., when learners draw on information contained in UG that needs to be triggered or specified by information obtained by analyses of the input data. Verb raising, for example, is an option offered by UG, yet the target position varies across languages and must therefore be inferred from input information. Similarly for verb-complement ordering where the child must choose between VO *versus* OV as the underlying order. This third acquisition type is captured by the notion of grammatical parameter, and Parameter Theory (Chomsky 1981) indeed gave a huge boost to acquisition research.

These well-studied phenomena should draw our attention to what actually happens in acquisition – a prerequisite for possible explanations of acquisition processes. Activation of knowledge provided by the LAD will require minimal exposure to the PLD. Its instantiation in early grammars should thus happen early, be fast and errorless, since universal principles are, by definition, never violated. In our example, this refers to the hierarchical organization of sentence structure, the nature of its constituents as grammatical categories and their properties. This includes the ±finite distinction for verbs and the fact that +finite elements can be displaced, as well as the option between head-initial or head-final ordering of categorial projections. The task of discovering the instantiations of this abstract grammatical knowledge in the target language, e.g., the items belonging to the class of finite verbs or the position to which they are raised, is guided and enhanced by the LAD, but it can nevertheless be expected to require some further exposure to the PLD. Learning particularities of the target language, finally, requires access to the input data over an extended period and possibly to particularly salient examples, e.g., in order to acquire the full set of verb markers (tense, person, number, etc.) encoding finiteness.

5.2 First language acquisition

Time to look at what actually happens in German L1 acquisition. Since acquisition of German word order is a well-researched phenomenon, especially due to longitudinal studies like those by Stern & Stern (1907/1975) and later on Miller (1976), Clahsen (1982) and others, we can base this discussion on solid empirical foundations. Analyses of spontaneous speech of children acquiring German as a first language reveal that once they use multi-word utterances, verbs are combined with subjects (SV) and with objects or adverbs, either preceding or following them (OV, VO). Importantly, however, already during this early phase of variable word order, typically before age 2;0 (years; months), they strongly prefer OV order; see (3). Shortly afterwards, still at around age 2;0, when most of their utterances consist of only two words (MLU 2.0, mean length of utterances), they distinguish between finite and non-finite verbs, placing the finite ones before objects or adverbs. What matters here is that, although they occasionally fail to move a finite element, they never raise a non-finite one. This is important, for it shows that they only deviate from the adult norm in that they do not always perform as required by the target grammar, but they never use options ruled out by UG – a first piece of evidence in favour of the claim that grammatical principles play a crucial role in guiding L1 development. Finally, once children use subordinate clauses, mostly sometime between age 2;6 and 3;0, verbs appear consistently in clause-final position, a case of virtually error-free acquisition.

(3) Verb placement in monolingual and bilingual German L1

I.	Variable word order; clause-final position preferred; no finiteness	OV
IIa.	Non-finite V in final position, finite V in second or clause-final position	±finite, V2
IIb.	Finite V categorically in second position	±finite, V2
III.	Subordinate clauses emerge; V consistently in final position	MC/SC

What I want to emphasize here is that this developmental sequence is in accordance with what has been said above about the knowledge sources on which children can rely when facing the task of discovering the properties of the target language. Properties constrained by UG-related information are acquired early and fast; these are instances where the decisive information is made available by the LAD. One observation supporting this claim is that already the earliest utterances consist of grammatical elements, i.e., they possess at least some properties of syntactic categories. There is ample evidence for errors of verb inflection during early acquisition phases, e.g., use of the wrong past participle ending, as in German *geschlagt (geschlagen) 'hit' or French *batté (battu) 'hit', or the English regular past tense affix attached to irregular verbs as in *wented. However, I know of no study reporting on children combining verbal affixes with nominal elements, or *vice versa*. The fact that such conceivable errors do not occur suggests strongly that the elements appearing in very early speech are indeed syntactic categories, contrary to what usage-based theories claim. Let me add that verbal elements used during phase (I), as seen in (3), exhibit different inflectional forms, but these are rote learned, not used productively. There is thus no evidence for the ±finite distinction at this stage. Remarkably, however, headedness does already play a role as is evidenced by the preference for OV over VO ordering.

Very soon afterwards, during phase (II) in (3), OV is used consistently, and two other properties, finiteness and verb raising to structural second position, emerge simultaneously – not surprisingly, for they are grammatically closely related. Nevertheless, it is quite remarkable that finite verbal elements – and only finite ones – are moved as soon as the notion of finiteness is instantiated in the developing grammar. Not only that, learners go straight for the target-conforming solution, rather than being distracted by ambiguous or even confusing information offered by the PLD. Remember that German verbs appear superficially before and after the object (VO, OV). Yet if VO were chosen as the underlying order, non-finite verbs in main clauses and both finite and non-finite verbs in subordinate clauses would have to be moved to the right. Rightward movement, however, amounts to lowering in hierarchical structures, an operation not tolerated by UG principles. Consequently, learners conforming to UG constraints have no choice but to analyze German as an OV language, raising finite verbs rather than lowering non-finite ones. Guidance by the LAD also explains why constructions like those in (1c) and (1d) unambiguously indicate that finite verbs move to C, i.e., the structural second position (V2).

Moreover, guidance by the LAD allows us to account for the otherwise puzzling fact that no word order errors occur in subordinates, once these structurally more complex constructions, that also require more processing capacity, emerge, typically between ages 2;6 and 3;0. Since a complementizer occupies the head of CP, the finite element cannot move further up than T. In other words, nothing needs to be learned, no further information has to be extracted from the PLD – the correct result is obtained by not doing what grammatical principles prevent one from doing. I should add that learning the full array of verb inflection forms requires approximately ten months, even for the present tense alone; see Meisel (1994).

To conclude, I think the discussion of this example does support the claim that the cognitive turn opened up opportunities for fruitful cooperation between theories of grammar and of acquisition. Based mainly on research from the 1970s and 1980s, it shows that linguistically informed acquisition research can not only account for properties of early grammars, it can also contribute significantly to an explanation of how these are acquired. In fact, given that a number of crucial acquisition problems are easily explained in this framework, e.g., the amazingly early choice of the head-final option for VP (OV), the connection between finiteness and raising of verbs, or the errorless acquisition of word order in subordinate clauses, the argument can be reversed. The fact that grammatical principles, motivated independently of any considerations referring to language acquisition, explain the acquisition of core properties of morphosyntax in a straightforward fashion, constitutes evidence supporting the assumption that these principles do capture properties of mental grammars.

5.3 Second language acquisition

This discussion would not be complete, however, if we did not consider the role cognitive approaches played in L2 research. After all, my claim has been that understanding first and second language acquisition as instantiations of the human Language-Making Capacity represents an important insight of cognitively oriented theorizing on language, its structure, and its acquisition. The question then is how L2 research or acquisition theory, more generally, have benefitted from the opportunities offered by the new approach.

Any answer to this question, referring several decades of research, can obviously only be a personally biased and rather superficial assessment, much like the discussion on L1 research. Nevertheless, there can be no doubt that the 1970s witnessed an impressive surge of published L2 research focusing on learners and their transitional competences, conceived as approximative grammatical systems. These studies produced significant insights into the nature of the linguistic knowledge of L2 learners. Based on analyses of a large number of grammatical, mostly syntactic phenomena, they showed that these approximative systems are indeed partial grammars of the target language. As expected, however, one also finds features of L2 speech that cannot be accounted for by native grammars, some of which have even been argued not to conform to UG principles. Not surprisingly, this claim as well as other explanations of the divergent forms or constructions are a matter of controversy. Whereas some scholars interpret them as effects of transfer from L1 grammars, others consider them as *creative constructions* (Dulay & Burt 1972), possibly resulting from operations particular to transitional grammars, or they attribute them to the workings of processing mechanisms, not as reflecting properties of the underlying knowledge systems. In spite of these controversies on how to explain certain findings, the empirical facts are widely agreed upon.

I will briefly discuss this situation, using verb placement in German as an example again. The empirical facts are summarised in (4), cf. Meisel et al. (1981). Interestingly, L2 learners follow an order of acquisition that is identical and invariant across individuals yet different from the L1 order presented in (3).

(4) Verb placement in German L2

I.	SVO/Adv	Fixed word order	SVO
II.	ADV-INI	Adverbials in initial position	*V3
III.	PART	Non-finite shift, V^{-fin} (incl. particles) in final position	*V lowering
IV.	INV	Subject-V inversion (=XVS)	~V2
V.	V-END	Clause-final V placement in subordinates (= $V^{-fin} V^{+fin}$)	*lowering

One crucial difference between L1 and L2 learners is that the latter treat German as an SVO language. Since the ones studied by Meisel et al. (1981) were all L1 speakers of Romance (SVO) languages, L1 transfer might be a possible explanation for this finding, one that is, however, not supported by the empirical data. Rather, initial SVO order also occurs in the speech of L2 learners whose L1 is not a VO language. Wode (1981), for example, analyzing the acquisition of English by L1 German children, found virtually no examples of OV order in L2 English. Similar results have been obtained in contexts where both the L1 and the L2 are OV languages, e.g., for L2 German or Dutch by L1 Turkish learners, all three OV languages. Thus, VO is generally the dominant order in L2 speech, and although OV order is attested in some studies, e.g., with Turkish learners of German or Dutch, it is not the dominant pattern. In fact, even authors arguing in favour of the transfer hypothesis found a preference only for OV, learners using both OV and VO, a behaviour not to be expected if L1 head-directionality were transferred to the L2 grammar. Moreover, when the L1 is a head-final but not a V2 language, like Turkish, both finite and non-finite verbs should appear in clause-final position. Yet even Schwartz and Sprouse (1996: 44) acknowledge that they did not find finite verbs in final position – in contradiction to the so-called Full Transfer hypothesis that they advocated. Their solution was to postulate a 'Stage 0', not attested in the data. Hardly a satisfactory way to proceed, for acquisition research cannot do without empirical accountability.

At any rate, no matter whether all, most, or many L2 learners initially treat German as a VO language, the crucial point is that those who do face rather different learning tasks than L1 children. To be able to produce surface strings conforming to the target norm, L2 learners starting from a basic SVO order have to rearrange the initial order according to the linguistic context. A number of generalizations or 'rules' can capture the necessary operations. The first effect attested in L2 speech is that of 'non-finite shift', phase III in (4). In utterances with discontinuous verbal constructions, non-finite parts of verbs, including separable particles, are now placed in clause-final position, as in *sie sieht ihn an* 'she is looking at him', for the verb *ansehen* 'to look at'. The next effect attested in L2 speech is that of 'subject-verb inversion', mimicking the V2 effect, phase IV in (4). When adverbs or objects are placed clause-initially, as happens frequently as of phase II in (4), subjects and finite verbs have to be inverted in order to avoid third position (*V3) of verbs. Interestingly, learners do not carry over these rules to subordinate clauses. Contrary to what one finds in children's language use, these appear from early on in L2 speech, almost exclusively exhibiting SVO order again. This means that learners have to discover that 'non-finite shift' is required in subordinates as well as in main clauses, plus another operation, 'verb-end placement', positioning finite verbs after non-finite ones clause-finally, and this only happens during phase V in (4).

The issue at stake now is to determine what the largely uncontroversial empirical facts in (4) can tell us about properties of L2 learners' mental grammars. At least the ones who initially analyze German as an OV language must rely on a grammar that differs from the L1 German one, because it must account for different kinds of displacement operations. Importantly, the generalized use of SVO in subordinates up to phase V provides strong evidence indicating that they continue to treat German as a VO language. Thus, placement of non-finite verbs in final position in phase III is *not* an indication of a change of head-directionality from VO to OV. In fact, another observation, not readily transparent from what is summarised in (4), points to another substantive difference between L2 and native grammars of German: verb movement during phase IV does not correlate with the acquisition of finiteness markers on verbs. Rather, even successful learners, the ones attaining phases IV or V, use target-deviant verbal inflection or none at all. L2 learners thus place non-finite verbs in grammatically finite positions, e.g., in structural second position, a phenomenon not attested in L1 speech. In other words, the tight connection between finiteness and verb raising, stated by native grammars and confirmed by L1 speech, does not seem to be part of the linguistic knowledge underlying L2 use of German; see Clahsen (1988).

Although approximative L2 grammars differ from native grammars, they generate target-like surface strings, typically not on all occasions, but at all acquisition levels. In phase I, for example, simple clauses of type (1a) are used correctly, as are utterances with particles or non-finite verbs at the end of the clause at phase III, or those at phase V where both verbal elements appear in final position in subordinates. Thus, in spite of the choice of VO as basic order and the lack of an operation raising finite verbs (and only these) to a position above subjects, learners are able to produce utterances not deviating from the target norm with respect to surface word order.

One way to explain this is to assume that they are sensitive to linear patterns and that the L2 grammar comprises the above-mentioned rules, non-finite shift, subject-verb inversion, and verb-end placement. The problem, however, is that it is not possible to formulate these operations as grammatical processes conforming to principles of UG, as demonstrated by Clahsen and Muysken (1986). To mention only the most serious problem, non-finite verbs in main clauses and both finite and non-finite verbs in subordinate clauses appear on the right. If we view this linearization as an operation connecting two stages, they are moved to the right, i.e., they are lowered in hierarchical structures. By hypothesis, this analysis ought not to be possible. This forces one to consider a different analysis: learners change VP headedness from head-initial to head-final in the course of L2 acquisition. In terms of Parameter Theory, this amounts to claiming that a parameter is reset to a different value. This is the approach taken by duPlessis et al. (1987) and others. In fact, to put their analysis through, they had to make a number of additional assumptions about grammatical theory and about the grammar of German, and they had to introduce additional parameters (Headedness parameter set differently for IP (= TP in (2)), Proper Government parameter, Adjunction parameter), some of which need to be reset.

This is obviously not the occasion to discuss these proposals in detail, and it may surprise some that I spend any time at all on a debate carried out over 25 years ago, couched in what might be considered an outdated theoretical framework. My reason for returning to it is that it can help to point out shortcomings that, in my opinion, have haunted L2 studies for many years, obstructing efforts to identify properties of learners' grammatical knowledge and to explain how these are acquired.

The first issue to be addressed concerns the question of how grammatical theory can constrain acquisition research. Since, according to the theory of Universal Grammar, UG is the core component of the LAD and UG principles constrain formal properties of grammars, we should expect to be able to decide between competing analyses by referring to UG principles and parameters, as illustrated above with the example of apparent rightward movement of verbs from second position of main clauses to final position of subordinate clauses. Unfortunately, however, a desirably broad consensus on what UG tolerates and what it excludes does not exist and has never existed. In fact, in view of more recent developments of grammatical theory, specifically the Minimalist Program, this question is more difficult to answer than ever. In the 1980s, a major problem was the proliferation of parameters. This was due to a tendency to account for every case of cross-linguistic variation in terms of UG parameters, without even considering the possibility of language-particular solutions. As a result, the theory of grammar offered acquisition research an almost unlimited choice of parameters, allowing for multiple alternative analyses of one and the same phenomenon.

There is of course no point in criticizing studies like the one by duPlessis et al. (1987) for drawing on this excessively rich source of supposedly explanatory mechanisms. What does need to be reviewed critically, however, is how different settings of parameters are stipulated, in an attempt to explain the developmental sequence in (4). The idea apparently is that every parameterized option attested in a grammar of the languages of the world is available to learners, LAD guidance meaning that they can pick any parameter from the full array offered by UG. Thus, the learners studied by du Plessis et al. (1987), French and English L1 speakers, are claimed to have drawn on options instantiated in Yiddish or Spanish. This idea has indeed become popular in generative acquisition research: acquiring English as Mandarin or Swahili. Although this cannot be ruled out *a priori*, it does not, I contend, qualify as a solution to either the property or the acquisition problem. In order to count as such, the choice of parameters and of the values to which they are set would have to be motivated independently, either by triggers encountered in the PLD or by system-internal factors. The unmotivated choice of a parameter, which may even be set to a value distinct from settings in both L1 and L2, is merely a stipulation. Since it reveals neither why an option is preferred over others, nor why L1 children do not choose it, it offers no insights into the properties of learners' grammars. As a solution to the acquisition problem, this approach fares even worse. Not only does it fail to explain why children go straight for the target option, without being confounded by information contained in the PLD, it also does not address the question of what triggered the observed development. Moreover, if learners could incorporate into a transitional grammar formal properties that are not part of the target grammar but offered by UG, they would have to be able to eliminate the non-target properties at a later developmental stage, in order to bring the approximative system closer to the target grammar. This is a serious problem for acquisition theory, for 'unlearning' seems to be impossible, unless learners can rely on negative evidence.

This objection to permitting a temporary activation of non-target properties in L2 grammars leads to a fundamental issue implicated in the question of how grammatical theory guides and constrains L2 acquisition research. As mentioned, it is generally acknowledged that L2 grammars differ from corresponding L1 systems. However, the question whether this indicates that learners resort to solutions not constrained by UG is an ongoing controversy. Note that all attempts at avoiding this conclusion rely on the possibility of parameter resetting. In other words, learners are claimed to make target-deviant choices, caused either by transfer from the L1 or by non-target UG offerings, and if these concern parametric choices, the initial settings are said to be changed during the further course of acquisition. Considering the fact that many or most generative L2 studies depend decidedly on the availability of this option, a comprehensive discussion of whether Parameter Theory indeed allows resetting of parameter values is an obvious necessity. Yet proponents of this hypothesis have never engaged in such a debate, not in the early years of the application of Parameter Theory to L2 acquisition (see Carroll 2001), nor subsequently.

In the present context, it is not possible to deal adequately with this issue. I will therefore only mention two basic points of criticism that cast doubt on the resetting hypothesis; see Meisel (2011:144f.) for an in-depth discussion. The first and in my opinion most important one is that there is no evidence for parameter resetting in *first* language development. Children never alternate between settings, e.g., V2 – non-V2, etc., and if they set a parameter to a non-target value, thus requiring a later reanalysis, this happens by inductive learning, not by changing parameter values. At any rate, such cases are extremely rare, according to what is reported in the published literature. One example is that of a bilingual French-German boy who seems to have set the V2 parameter to the wrong value in German, resulting in many word order errors, especially in subordinate clauses cf. Müller (1994). He eventually learns the correct ordering, but this takes almost two years, learning the target order for each complementizer separately. This is undoubtedly an instance of inductive learning, contrasting markedly with the rapid developmental changes in cases of parameter setting; cf. Carroll (1989). In sum, we find neither conceptual nor empirical support for the idea of parameter resetting in L1 development. If, however, child L1 learners cannot reset a parameter that has been set to a specific value after exposure to the PLD, the most plausible conclusion is that this is not an operation tolerated by UG. Consequently, it cannot be an option for L2 learners.

My second point concerns empirical accountability, an issue already raised in connection with the Full Transfer hypothesis. It should be self-evident that claims about properties of learner grammars or about the acquisition process must be empirically testable. Arguing in favour of the resetting hypothesis actually requires two types of evidence, one indicating that reanalysis has actually happened, the second one confirming that it is an instance of parameter (re)setting. Unfortunately, not even the former requirement is met consistently, although it is a rather obvious task. As an example, let me remind you that duPlessis et al. (1987) claim that learners change VP headedness from head-initial to head-final. One might therefore expect to find a significant increase in the number of verbs in final position. Yet this is not the case, and these authors try to account for the lack of empirical repercussions of their analysis by postulating that reanalysis to SOV is concurrent with the emergence of a rule moving finite verbs to (left-headed) IP. Acquiring two grammatical properties simultaneously is certainly a logical possibility. However, in the absence of a theoretically motivated explanation of the developmental simultaneity, it can only be qualified as an *ad hoc* solution. As it stands, it postulates concurrent instances of acquisitions, one effacing the empirical effects of the other.

Yet even if empirical evidence of reanalysis were available, one would still need to establish that it involves parameter resetting. Not to forget, the issue is not whether L2 acquisition is possible – who would doubt that? The question is which knowledge sources learners draw on when facing specific acquisition tasks. If they rely on inductive learning in instances where L1 development triggers parameterized knowledge, the different acquisition mechanisms are likely to generate different kinds of grammatical knowledge. Crucially, as already pointed out by Carroll (1989), learning and triggering can be distinguished empirically – a fact ignored by proponents of the resetting hypothesis; cf. Meisel (2011:144 ff.) for a detailed discussion.

The purpose of this section has been to substantiate the claim that research on L2 acquisition has benefited significantly from the cognitive turn. Focusing again on one example, German verb placement, my goal has been to emphasize that joint efforts of grammatical theorizing and empirically based acquisition research succeeded in uncovering some crucial properties of L2 learner's linguistic knowledge. It shares substantial properties with L1 grammars, and the acquisition process exhibits significant commonalities across individuals. These observations show that the LAD partially guides L2 acquisition. However, the fact that one also finds properties not attested in L1 speech suggests that other guiding factors too are at work here. They are arguably the cause of some fundamental differences between L2 and L1. This issue has been the object of a controversial debate extending well into the second half of the 50-year period under review. Unfortunately, it seems to have petered out without reaching a satisfactory conclusion. It may well be that this is due to what I have identified as shortcomings of some generative L2 studies, namely a predominance of grammatical considerations and an insufficient concern for aspects of acquisition. I will return to this topic in Section 7.

6. The developmental problem

The developmental problem has been grossly neglected in the preceding discussion, which focused entirely on the property and the acquisition problems. The reason is that it has been neglected by acquisition research over the past 50 years. Not only did a unified discipline, developmental psycholinguistics, never emerge, the explanation of the developmental logic has never been on the top of the research agenda of linguists or psychologists investigating language acquisition, jointly or separately. My suspicion is that its relevance is not generally recognized. Yet an account of learners' linguistic knowledge at various points in the course of acquisition does not qualify as a solution to the developmental problem, since it does not explain why mental grammars are altered at all or how the transition from one approximative system to the next happens.

The former issue is primarily a challenge for linguistic theory. Since at each point of development a learner's linguistic knowledge is a mental grammar, i.e., a self-contained stable system, it should, in principle, not be expected to change. The question thus is how to account for the changes that do happen, or, in other words, what is the source of instability. This is not an issue to be pursued here. I merely want to emphasize that studies investigating linguistic development, including acquisition as well as diachronic research, must rely on grammatical theory for information about which parts of linguistic systems are most likely to change. After all, we know that developmental changes are systematic, at least in that they proceed through strictly ordered phases, identical for all speakers. It will therefore not suffice to claim that learning happens by learners' noticing that their speech differs in certain respects from that of native speakers,[4] thus inciting them to revise their mental grammars. This cannot explain uniformity of change across learners; rather, one would expect only some of them to notice differences, and those who do should not all notice the same discrepancies. External causes are likely to play a role in triggering change, but they cannot explain why particular grammatical features are affected at the same time and in the same order across individuals. As for grammar-internal explanations, it should be useful to identify variable domains of grammars, for variation can be source as well as result of change. Linguistic theories that do not allow for optionality in grammar, thereby eliminating a theoretically founded account of variation, will obviously not fare well here.

The genuinely developmental issue implied by the developmental problem, however, is the need for a transition theory (Gregg 1996), explaining the course of acquisition, most importantly the logic underlying invariant patterns of development. The fact that some linguistic operations or forms are regularly acquired before others has long been known. Yet the theoretical significance of this observation only became evident when Roger Brown (1973) showed that some grammatical properties emerge in an order that is identical for all children acquiring a given language and perhaps even across languages. This discovery of possibly universal *developmental sequences* is arguably the most important insight gained by acquisition research over the past 50 years. It is therefore all the more disappointing that only limited progress has been made concerning the explanation of invariant acquisition orders.

Note that this concerns first as well as second language acquisition. As we have seen, L2 acquisition too proceeds through invariant developmental sequences. They are, however not identical to the ones observed in L1 development. This suggests that the logic determining the order of emergence of grammatical phenomena is different in L1 and L2 acquisition. Yet it is not clear what the nature of this logic is. Interestingly, the early morpheme order studies also failed to offer a plausible explanation for why just these phenomena emerge in a fixed order, let alone an explanation of the specific orders proposed by Brown (1973) or Dulay et al. (1982), among others. As for L1 morpheme order, Brown (1973) considered three possible explanatory factors: frequency of use of these forms in

---

4. This also leaves unanswered why they do *not* notice frequently occurring phenomena. See MacDonald & Carroll (2018) for a case of L2 learners apparently not noticing plural marking and an explanation of why they might not.

the parents' speech, semantic complexity, and grammatical complexity. He ruled out frequency as a determining factor, for he could not find a significant correlation between rank ordering of frequency averaged across parental pairs and mean order of acquisition by the children. As for semantic and grammatical complexity, he only alluded to tentative yet not satisfactory explanations.

The nature of the logic continues to be a matter of controversy. There is not even consensus whether it is primarily grammatical in nature (e.g., derivational complexity), rather than being input-driven (frequency of occurrence, frequency of exposure), or due to constraints on learning or processing (e.g., increasing processing complexity). In reality, the most likely solution is that all these factors are at play, though to a different degree, depending on acquisition type and developmental phase. I think there are good reasons to believe that grammatical principles and mechanisms play a decisive role in L1 development. This was already evident in the discussion of the acquisition of German word order; cf. Section 5.2. The Structure Building Hypothesis (Guilfoyle & Noonan 1992) offered further explanatory possibilities; they were not, however, pursued much further, probably due to revisions of Parameter Theory. Nevertheless, adopting a more recent version of Parameter Theory, Tsimpli (2014) demonstrated that it allows predicting the order of acquisition of core syntactic properties. More research along these lines is needed, but findings like these support the hypothesis that the underlying logic guiding L1 development is essentially grammatical in nature. In L2 acquisition, on the other hand, learning and processing mechanisms seem to play a more decisive role, as is argued by Pienemann (1998) or Dyson and Håkansson (2017), among others. Here too more research is required in order to make a convincing case for this hypothesis. Unraveling the developmental logic in first and second language acquisition remains a great desideratum.

7. Closure

In this look back, focusing on the first half of the 50 years of research that established acquisition theory as an essential component of linguistic theory, I have tried to highlight a number of features that characterize this enterprise and that contributed to its success. It got off to a good start with an appeal for cooperation between cognitively oriented linguistic theory and acquisition research, hitherto largely a concern of psychological studies. The principal goal of these joint efforts has been the study of learners' linguistic knowledge, conceptualized as mentally represented systems. Since these are regarded as instantiations of a universal language capacity that underlies all types of acquisition, this approach also called for a unified theory of L1 and L2 acquisition. Due to the focus on learners' mental grammars, acquisition research during the first half of the 50-year period was decidedly guided by grammatical theory, mostly syntax or morphology, even though it was carried out by psychologists as well as by linguists. Overall, this research paradigm has been successful in that it led to a wealth of information about properties of learner grammars and to valuable insights into acquisition processes.

I nevertheless want to add a few observations on what I view as past and current shortcomings, leading to some desiderata for the future. Throughout this paper, I have insisted on the view that the call for close cooperation between linguistics and psychology is a particularly important aspect of the research program initiated in the 1960s. Such joint efforts are required at all levels of scientific activity: theory building and the ensuing definition of research objects, choice of research questions and of appropriate methods of analysis, as well as of research methods, more generally. I would of course not have drawn an overall positive picture of the development of acquisition studies, if I thought that the call for cooperation had been ignored. I do believe, however, that there is room for improvement in this respect. Since the discussion in the preceding sections dealt mostly with generative investigation of learners' grammars, my critical remarks, too, will refer primarily to generative studies.

The main problem to which I want to draw attention concerns attempts at accounting for properties of learners' grammars in terms of grammatical principles alone. The pursuit of insights into the nature of learners' linguistic knowledge is undoubtedly one that promises to lead to a profound understanding of language acquisition and probably also of the human language capacity. Yet it is also an ambitious one, for we have only indirect access to this knowledge. Linguistic grammars can only be approximate models of mental grammars. They gain in plausibility if features and operations attributed to them can be shown to be processable and learnable. Remember that objections to contrastive analyses referred to precisely this point, that linguistic grammars were not psycholinguistically plausible. Generative grammars are, of course, subject to the same reservation. Although they explicitly aim at capturing knowledge as it is represented in speakers' mental systems, acquisition studies must be prepared to verify the validity of this claim, especially in instances where it supposedly reveals how grammatical properties are acquired. They cannot simply rely on linguistic theory to do their job.

As an illustration of the point I want to make, let me mention the Full Competence Hypothesis proposed by Poeppel and Wexler (1993), which gained some notoriety in 1990s. According to these authors, children have the full adult grammar, right from the onset of L1 acquisition. They do of course not dispute the fact that early utterances do not reflect such knowledge nor that they change over time until they resemble those generated by mature grammars. Nevertheless, Poeppel and Wexler (1993:18) insist that this hypothesis "has no developmental question associated with it." This is a remarkable statement, since it eliminates the developmental problem from the agenda of acquisition research. The only meaningful interpretation I can think of is that initially grammar-external factors are assumed to prevent children from using their 'full' grammar. Yet since acquisition proceeds through ordered phases, defined in terms of emerging grammatical properties, this interpretation too must explain the developmental logic, this time in reverse, following the order in which constraints are lifted. Unfortunately, proponents of this hypothesis offer no such explanation nor any other of developmental patterns.

Leaving aside the question whether approaches like this one actually provide insights into the nature of learners' linguistic knowledge at the initial state of acquisition, they certainly do not inform us about the course of acquisition. Relying exclusively on grammatical principles goes against the spirit of a research program calling for joint efforts of linguistic and acquisition theory. The question whether features detected in children's language stand in conflict with linguistic theorizing definitely requires an answer, but it is not the only one that matters. From an acquisition perspective, it is equally important to ask how and why features are incorporated into developing grammars, especially if they deviate from the target system. Pointing out that a target-deviant option is tolerated by UG is at best part of the answer. Observing that learners' grammars differ from those underlying the languages to which they are exposed should be a starting point, not a closure of acquisition research.

Nevertheless, this line of research, focusing entirely on how UG constrains learner grammars to the detriment of attempts to understand how acquisition is shaped by different learning mechanisms, is frequently pursued by generative studies of L2 acquisition. A prominent example is the Missing Surface Inflection Hypothesis (MSIH), as proposed by Prévost and White (2000). It attempts to account for discrepancies between L2 and L1 learners in their placement of finite and non-finite verbs. Recall that L1 children raise finite verbs – and only finite ones – as soon as evidence for the ±finite distinction is attested in their speech samples; see Section 5.2. On the other hand, even advanced L2 learners place non-finite verbs in finite positions and finite forms in non-finite positions, suggesting that the tight connection between finiteness and verb raising, postulated by grammatical theory and corroborated by L1 acquisition data, is not part of the linguistic knowledge of L2 learners; see Section 5.3. The MSIH contradicts this conclusion, claiming that non-finite forms in finite contexts are, in fact, finite elements, merely lacking inflectional markings.

This inevitably leads to the question: how do you know it is a finite verb when you see one? After all, finite elements are by definition the ones that carry information about TMA (tense, modality, aspect) and about person, number, and sometimes gender. In French and German, languages discussed by Prévost and White (2000),[5] these grammatical notions are encoded as verbal inflection for TMA and subject agreement. Placement higher than the base position (see (2) in Section 5.1) is also a defining property. But if applied when deciding whether raised elements are finite, this results in a circular argument. Prévost and White (2000: 103) present three arguments in defense of the MSIH, namely "that finite forms do not occur in non-finite contexts, that learners exhibit syntactic reflexes of finiteness and that inflected forms largely show accurate agreement." However, as I now argue, they are not convincing, neither conceptually nor empirically.

In fact, the first argument, as stated in this quote, is simply not correct. Not only do previous studies report that finite forms do occur in non-finite contexts, as is acknowledged by Prévost and White (2000: 109f.), they also encounter constructions of this sort in their own analyses. They nevertheless maintain their claim because (a) target-conforming placement of finite and non-finite verbs happens more frequently than target-deviant positioning, and (b) non-finite elements in finite contexts occur more frequently than finite forms in non-finite positions. Note that the MSIH predicts non-existence rather than lower frequency of occurrence of the latter error type. Moreover, the predominance of the former type is not equally strong in all learners. The reported ratio for the L2 German learners is 10.4%:8.4% for Ana (L1 Spanish) and 16.4%:5.8% for Zita (L1 Portuguese). Interestingly, rather than repeating the claim that *no* such constructions exist, Prévost and White (2000: 119) later state that "finite forms are *largely restricted* (my emphasis, JMM) to finite (raised) positions," concluding finally that "with a few exceptions, finite forms do not occur in non-finite contexts" (p. 125).

This is a rather cavalier treatment of empirical evidence. In fact, the third argument, referring to the use of agreement morphology, also suffers from a less than satisfying account of the empirical facts. Prévost and White (2000: 120f.) find that agreement is "largely correct" when it is provided by the two L2 French learners and that "accuracy is also very high" in L2 German, especially with the suppletive forms of *sein* 'be'. They take this as sufficient evidence in support of their

---

5. They analyze speech samples by four learners, two Arabic-speaking learners of French and two learners of German, one with L1 Portuguese, the other one with L1 Spanish. The data stem from two longitudinal studies, the European Science Foundation Project (Perdue 1993) and the longitudinal corpus of the ZISA (*Zweitspracherwerb italienischer und spanischer Arbeiter* – Second language acquisition by Italian and Spanish workers) project (Meisel 1991). There also exists a cross-sectional ZISA corpus; cf. Meisel et al. (1981).

assumption that agreement, involving features for agreement and finiteness, is in place in the learners' L2 grammars, notwithstanding the fact that error rates are high in some contexts, e.g., non-suppletive 1st person singular (Ana 25.5%, Zita 29.3%). What could have been interpreted as counterevidence, is never acknowledged, stipulating that "non-finite or bare forms ... are in fact finite defaults, rather than evidence of incorrect agreement." (Prévost & White 2000: 123).

A look at acquisition patterns could have led to a different conclusion, but curiously these authors decided not to take a developmental perspective. Rather, they report total numbers of occurrences across all interviews, although these stem from longitudinal corpora. In fact, Meisel (1991) discussed the development of agreement inflection by six of the twelve ZISA learners recorded longitudinally. Initially, they all use verbs that either lack inflection or end in -e or -en, the latter corresponding to the German infinitival, the former to the 1st person singular suffix. Since these forms refer to different grammatical persons, they cannot be interpreted as agreement markers. Remarkably, two learners continue to use only these forms during the following 67 and 84 weeks respectively, neither 2nd sg. -st, nor 3rd sg. -t. The other four learners do acquire markers for all three grammatical persons. However, they differ in when they first use these forms and in how consistently they use them. As for those discussed by Prévost and White (2000), Zita produces agreement inflection from early on, but error rates are high during the following two years. Ana, on the other hand, is slow in acquiring the various forms, but she makes steady progress towards the target norm. Similar developmental patterns are found with two other learners. Like Zita, Bruno uses agreement inflection from early on, but virtually without errors as of the 26th week of exposure to German; Giovanni exhibits a slow acquisition rate and a high frequency of uninflected or infinitival verbs.

In sum, even a cursory look at the course of acquisition of several individuals reveals that accuracy of subject-verb agreement is "very high" only in the most successful L2 learners and even there to various degrees at various points of time. How can these facts be reconciled with the assumption that all learners, at every point of acquisition, can rely on L2 grammars comprising finiteness, feature checking and displacement mechanisms, etc.? Are indeed all instances of missing or erroneous inflection finite defaults? The MSIH states that the problem concerns mere morphological mapping of abstract features. Alternatively, Prévost and White (2000: 129) speculate that a form may become "temporarily irretrievable" due to unspecified "processing reasons or to communication pressure" for which there is no independent evidence. However, proponents of the MSIH have yet to explain why realization of surface forms, a task easily performed by children acquiring an L1, should represent a particularly difficult challenge for adult L2 learners. After all, they use suppletive forms mostly correctly (Prévost & White

2000:121), although these are more diverse than the ones encoding the three grammatical persons in regular inflection. Moreover, infinitival forms are in fact not instances of *missing* surface inflection, since they do carry an inflectional marker, the infinitival suffix *-en*. Rather than lacking inflection, they are inflected erroneously. Consequently, the rate of erroneous agreement markings is considerably higher than what has been claimed, thus further weakening the argument that inflected forms largely show accurate agreement.

This brings me back to the main point of my objection to attempts at explaining acquisition solely in terms of grammatical principles, as is also the case here. Although Prévost and White (2000:103) phrase their second argument in defense of the MSIH carefully, claiming that L2 "learners exhibit syntactic reflexes of finiteness," they totally ignore other potential explanatory factors. Recall that they refused to adopt a developmental perspective, arguing that if L2 grammars were in some way impaired, "we should find evidence for variable placement of finite verbs, as well as agreement problems, throughout the data" (p.113). Now, as I have demonstrated, this is precisely what the data show. Yet Prévost and White (2000:126) expect to find unconstrained variation: "If features are lacking in IL grammars, feature-checking mechanisms cannot apply and finite forms should appear in any position." In other words, distributional learning or inductive learning are not expected to play any role at all. A theory of language acquisition without learning or perhaps even without acquisition?

In sum, there can be no doubt that investigations into the nature of mental grammars need to rely on grammatical theory, yet they will not obtain the desired results if they neglect factors that determine how properties are processed or learned. Importantly, this is not only an issue concerning acquisition and developmental problems, for these factors also shape the nature of the acquired knowledge. This has already become obvious in the discussion of the knowledge sources on which learners can draw; see Section 5.1. They not only determine developmental patterns (gradual vs. abrupt, early vs. late, etc.), they can also lead to different kinds of knowledge, e.g., generalized vs. item-by-item operations. Only where universal principles constrain acquisition do we not expect to find such effects, since, by definition, they constrain all grammars, at the initial as well as at the final state, and at every point of development. Whether this expectation is met, is, however, a question that acquisition research should address. Keeping in mind that learners can rely on innate as well as inductively learned knowledge, the issue is, more generally, which information source they access and to which degree when facing particular acquisition problems. The fact that linguistic theory offers solutions by means of universal or parameterized principles does not necessarily mean that learners always activate this knowledge, rather than scrutinizing input data for information.

This is where I see shortcomings in some generative acquisition studies, for this problem does not always seem to be recognized as such – possibly because it reflects the more general problem that acquisition research is typically assigned a consumer role, rather than being engaged in fruitful interaction with theoretical linguistics. Phenomena observed in children's speech call for theoretically motivated explanations, no matter whether the issue at stake is of interest for current linguistic theorizing. On the other hand, insights from acquisition can help to settle theoretical controversies, e.g., if only one of several competing hypotheses is compatible with developmental facts. Yet I cannot think of a single case where insights gained by acquisition research led to the change of a grammatical hypothesis of some significance.

In reality, cooperation resembles a one-way street: whereas studies on acquisition are often theoretically informed, linguistic theorizing pays little attention to insights from L1 studies and ignores L2 research almost altogether. However, acquisition research can do better than merely serving as a testing ground for linguistic theory. For example, a reliable answer to the question whether learners draw on innate or learned knowledge requires an understanding of processing and learning mechanisms. Only then is it possible to determine which parts of linguistic knowledge cannot be processed or learned and must thus be available prior to experience. Remarkably, Slobin (1966) already raised this issue when discussing McNeill (1966); see Section 4. The point is that the argument according to which mental grammars contain information not inductively learnable (poverty of stimulus, implied by Plato's problem) is only convincing if we can determine what kind of information learners can extract from the PLD and where this procedure fails.

This could have been an occasion for acquisition research to make a significant contribution to grammatical theorizing. However, generative L2 studies have notoriously neglected input analyses that might achieve this. Instead, the most common procedure is to invoke the poverty of the stimulus argument whenever a phenomenon is detected in the target language that is not in accordance with the L1 grammar, arguing that the knowledge required for its use can only have been made available by UG. Learning by analysis of the PLD is not even considered as an alternative explanation, although it has been shown that systematic analyses of learners' input, the "raw material" of acquisition (Carroll 2001), can explain how new properties get into the mental systems of learners. Note that 'input' consists of the constructs that are relevant to the solution to a particular learning problem, whereas 'exposure' is what is observable in particular learning contexts. Consequently, input to the language processor is distinct from input to the language acquisition mechanisms (Carroll 2017).

It should be obvious that inductive learning plays an important role in L1 as well as in L2 acquisition. However, if it is correct to assume that L2 learners have only partial access to UG (see Section 5.3.), they may be expected to resort to inductive learning in cases where L1 learners are guided by the LAD. Yet this can lead to fundamentally different solutions, as compared to corresponding ones in L1 grammars. L2 systems may therefore contain properties resulting from the application of non-domain-specific cognitive processes as well as of UG conforming ones. Consequently, 'UG or not UG?', is not really the question, although it has occupied L2 researchers for more than 25 years. Rather, L2 learners' linguistic knowledge can be characterized as a *hybrid system* – partially, not fully constrained by principles of UG; cf. Meisel (2011: 25ff.). Admittedly, this is not a view that most L2 researchers working within the generative framework would want to adopt, yet it is compatible with the one expressed by Chomsky (1997: 128):

> What about second language? That's harder. Like other kinds of growth, language acquisition happens easily at a certain age, but not later. There comes a time when the system doesn't work anymore. There are individual differences ... but for most people, after adolescence, it becomes very hard. The system is just not working for some reason, so, you have to teach the language as something strange.

Before closing this section and this paper, I want to add two short remarks on recent trends in acquisition research. The first one concerns methodological innovations. Most of the studies during the early part of the 50-year period analyzed spontaneous speech. This has changed dramatically, probably inspired by the rich methodological arsenal in psychology. Controlled and experimental data collection, brain imaging, eye-tracking, etc. are commonly used in current research, as are sophisticated statistical analyses. Investigations of language comprehension would not have been possible without these innovations. They also made it possible to study phenomena that do not occur in sufficient frequency or saliency in samples of speech production. Nevertheless, analyses of spontaneous production data are not a phenomenon of the past. In fact, longitudinal case studies are indispensable sources of information, especially for investigations of developmental problems. As Brown and Hanlon (1970: 51) commented 50 years ago, correctly, I believe:

> In closing, we would like to express the distaste experimentalists must feel for the assumptions, compromises, and qualifications involved in the use of naturalistic data. We find that naturalistic studies build an appetite for experiment – for controls, complete data, large samples, and statistical analysis. But we also find the reverse. The two kinds of research are complementary activities and complementary forms of evidence.

My second and last point is an appeal to pursue the research agenda discussed here. Focusing on the investigation of mental grammars of learners, it established the study of language acquisition as a genuine part of linguistics. Yet the interest in the development of sentence structures and in formal properties of learners' linguistic knowledge, more generally, seems to be dwindling in recent years. Such a change of the research agenda would be unfortunate, for the explanation of grammatical development is a genuine task of linguistic approaches to language acquisition.

References

Abutalebi, J. & Clahsen, H. 2016. Variability and its limits in bilingual language production. *Bilingualism: Language and Cognition* 19(5): 855–856.

Borges, J. L. 1960. Del rigor en la ciencia. *El Hacedor*. Buenos Aires: Emecé Editores.

Brown, R. 1973. *A First Language: The Early Stages*. Cambridge MA: Harvard University Press.

Brown, R. & Hanlon, C. 1970. Derivational complexity and order of acquisition in child speech. In *Cognition and the Development of Language*, J. R. Hayes (ed.), 11–53. New York NY: John Wiley.

Carroll, L. 1893. *Sylvie and Bruno Concluded*. London: Macmillan. Project Gutenberg, <https://www.gutenberg.org/ebooks/48795> (15 September 2021).

Carroll, S. E. 1989. Language acquisition studies and a feasible theory of grammar. *Canadian Journal of Linguistics* 34(4): 399–418.

Carroll, S. E. 2001. *Input and Evidence: The Raw Material of Second Language Acquisition*. Amsterdam: John Benjamins.

Carroll, S. E. 2017. Exposure and input in bilingual development. *Bilingualism: Language and Cognition* 20(1): 3–16.

Chomsky, N. 1965. *Aspects of the Theory of Syntax*. Cambridge MA: The MIT Press.

Chomsky, N. 1981. *Lectures on Government and Binding*. Dordrecht: Foris.

Chomsky, N. 1986. *Knowledge of Language: Its Nature, Origin, and Use*. New York NY: Praeger.

Chomsky, N. 1997. Questions – São Paulo. *DELTA* 13: 123–128.

Clahsen, H. 1982. *Spracherwerb in der Kindheit: Eine Untersuchung zur Entwicklung der Syntax bei Kleinkindern*. Tübingen: Narr.

Clahsen, H. 1988. Parameterized grammatical theory and language acquisition: A study of the acquisition of verb placement and inflection by children and adults. In *Linguistic Theory in Second Language Acquisition*, S. Flynn & W. O'Neil (eds), 47–75. Dordrecht: Reidel.

Clahsen, H. & Muysken, P. 1986. The availability of universal grammar to adult and child learners: A study of the acquisition of German word order. *Second Language Research* 2(2): 93–119.

Corder, S. P. 1967. The significance of learner's errors. *International Review of Applied Linguistics* 5(1–4): 161–170.

De Houwer, A. 2009. *Bilingual First Language Acquisition*. Bristol: Multilingual Matters.

de Villiers, P. A. & de Villiers, J. G. 1979. *Early Language*. London: Fontana/Open Books.

Dulay, H. C. & Burt, M. K. 1972. Goofing: An indicator of children's second language learning strategies. *Language Learning* 22(2): 235–252.

Dulay, H. C., Burt, M. K. & Krashen, S. 1982. *Language Two*. Oxford: OUP.

duPlessis, J., Solin, D., Travis, L. & White, L. 1987. UG or not UG, that is the question: A reply to Clahsen and Muysken. *Second Language Research* 3(1): 56–75.

Dyson, B. P. & Håkansson, G. 2017. *Understanding Second Language Processing: A Focus on Processability Theory*. Amsterdam: John Benjamins.

Felix, S. W. (ed.) 1980. *Second Language Development: Trends and Issues*. Tübingen: Narr.

Felix, S. W. 1984. Maturational aspects of Universal Grammar. In *Interlanguage*, A. Davies, C. Criper & A. Howatt (eds), 133–161. Edinburgh: EUP.

Fodor, J. A. 1966. How to learn to talk: Some simple ways. In *The Genesis of Language: A Psycholinguistic Approach*, F. Smith & G. A. Miller (eds), 105–122. Cambridge MA: The MIT Press.

Gregg, K. 1996. The logical and developmental problems of second language acquisition. In *Handbook of Second Language Acquisition*, W. C. Ritchie & T. K. Bhatia (eds), 49–81. San Diego CA: Academic Press.

Guilfoyle, E. & Noonan, M. 1992. Functional categories and language acquisition, *Canadian Journal of Linguistics* 37(2): 241–272.

Hakuta, K. 1989. An interview with Werner F. Leopold. *The Bilingual Research Group Working Papers*, 1–17. UC Santa Cruz.

Lado, R. 1957. *Linguistics across Cultures*. Ann Arbor MI: University of Michigan Press.

Leopold, W. F. 1939, 1947, 1949/1970. *Speech Development of a Bilingual Child: A Linguist's Record*. Evanston IL: Northwestern University Press. (Reprinted in 1970, New York NY: AMS Press)

MacDonald, D. & Carroll, S. E. 2018. Second language processing of English mass-count nouns by native speakers of Korean. *Glossa* 3(1): 1–27.

McNeill, D. 1966. Developmental psycholinguistics. In *The Genesis of Language: A Psycholinguistic Approach*, F. Smith & G. A. Miller (eds), 15–84. Cambridge MA: The MIT Press.

Meisel, J. M. 1991. Principles of Universal Grammar and strategies of language use. In *Point – Counterpoint: Universal Grammar in the Second Language*, L. Eubank (ed.), 231–276. Amsterdam: John Benjamins.

Meisel, J. M. 1994. Getting *FAT*: The role of Finiteness, Agreement and Tense in early grammars. In *Bilingual First Language Acquisition: French and German Grammatical Development*, J. M. Meisel (ed.), 89–129. Amsterdam: John Benjamins.

Meisel, J. M. 2004. The bilingual child. In *The Handbook of Bilingualism*, T. K. Bhatia & W. C. Ritchie (eds), 91–113. Oxford: Blackwell.

Meisel, J. M. 2007. On autonomous syntactic development in multiple first language acquisition. In *Proceedings of the 31st Annual Boston University Conference on Language Development*, H. Caunt-Nulton, S. Kulatilake & I.-H. Woo (eds), 26–45. Somerville MA: Cascadilla Press.

Meisel, J. M. 2011. *First and Second Language Acquisition: Parallels and Differences*. Cambridge: CUP.

Meisel, J. M., Clahsen, H. & Pienemann, M. 1981. On determining developmental stages in natural second language acquisition. *Studies in Second Language Acquisition* 3: 109–135.

Miller, M. 1976. *Zur Logik der frühkindlichen Sprachentwicklung: Empirische Untersuchungen und Theoriediskussion*. Stuttgart: Klett-Cotta.

Müller, N. 1994. Parameters cannot be reset: Evidence from the development of COMP. In *Bilingual First Language Acquisition: French and German Grammatical Development*, J. M. Meisel (ed.), 235–269. Amsterdam: John Benjamins.

Pavlovitch, M. 1920. *Le langage enfantin: Acquisition du serbe et du français par un enfant serbe*. Paris: Librairie Ancienne H. Champion.

Perdue, C. (ed.) 1993. *Adult Second Language Acquisition: Crosslinguistic Perspectives*. Cambridge: CUP.

Pienemann, M. 1998. *Language Processing and Second Language Development: Processability Theory*. Amsterdam: John Benjamins.

Poeppel, D. & Wexler, K. 1993. The full competence hypothesis of clause structure in early German. *Language* 69(1): 1–33.

Prévost, P. & White, L. 2000. Missing surface inflection or impairment in second language acquisition? Evidence from tense and agreement. *Second Language Research* 16(2): 103–133.

Ronjat, J. 1913. *Le développement du langage observé chez un enfant bilingue*. Paris: Librairie Ancienne H. Champion.

Saussure, F. de. 1916/1975. *Cours de linguistique générale*. Edited by C. Bally & A. Sechehaye/T. de Mauro. Paris: Payot.

Schwartz, B. D. & Sprouse, R. A. 1996. L2 cognitive states and the Full Transfer/Full Access model. *Second Language Research* 12(1): 40–77.

Slobin, D. I. 1966. Comments on 'Developmental psycholinguistics': A discussion of McNeill's presentation. In *The Genesis of Language: A Psycholinguistic Approach*, F. Smith & G. A. Miller (eds), 85–91. Cambridge MA: The MIT Press.

Slobin, D. I. 1985. Crosslinguistic evidence for the Language-Making Capacity. In *The Crosslinguistic Study of Language Acquisition, Vol. 2: Theoretical Issues*, D. I. Slobin (ed.), 1157–1256. Hillsdale NJ: Lawrence Erlbaum Associates.

Smith, F. & Miller, G. A. (eds) 1966. *The Genesis of Language: A Psycholinguistic Approach*. Cambridge MA: The MIT Press.

Smith, F. & Miller, G. A. 1966. Introduction. In *The Genesis of Language: A Psycholinguistic Approach*, F. Smith & G. A. Miller (eds), 1–13. Cambridge MA: The MIT Press.

Stern, C. & Stern, W. 1907/1975. *Die Kindersprache*. Leipzig: Barth. (Reprinted in 1975, Darmstadt: Wissenschaftliche Buchgesellschaft).

Tomasello, M. 2007. Acquiring linguistic constructions. In *Handbook of Child Psychology, Vol. II: Cognition, Perception, and Language*, W. Damon, R. M. Lerner, D. Kuhn, & R. Siegler (eds.), 255–298. New York NY: Wiley.

Tsimpli, I. 2014. Early, late or very late? Timing acquisition and bilingualism. *Linguistic Approaches to Bilingualism* 4(3): 283–313.

Wode, H. 1981. *Learning a Second Language*. Tübingen: Narr.

Gender in bilingual and heritage language acquisition

CHAPTER 3

Acquisition of morpho-syntactic features in a bilingual Italian child
An integrated approach to gender

Laura D'Aurizio, Johanna Stahnke & Natascha Müller
University of Wuppertal

> The present study investigates the interaction of gender with (declension) class in the acquisition data of one bilingual child (from two to five years old) who develops Italian as a weak language in combination with German in Germany. As reported in the literature, the Italian child acquires gender with ease, reflected in the nearly exceptionless target-like gender marking on determiners. Of the two possible errors, omission and commission, the Italian child vastly omits determiners. Nouns are inflected according to (declension) classes in adult Italian, most of which correspond to one gender. If the gender feature can be derived by class, as proposed by Lowenstamm (2007) for adult French, a different and integrated approach to gender acquisition is possible.
>
> **Keywords:** bilingual first language acquisition, Italian, gender feature, declension classes

1. Introduction

Gender is generally considered an inherent feature of the noun (Corbett 1991, 2006). Linguists distinguish between gender assignment (of the inherent feature of the noun) and gender agreement (the variable feature of adjectives and other categories that arguably agree in gender with the noun). A minority of researchers have contended against the plausibility of the view that gender is inherent to the noun from a cross-linguistic perspective. Carroll (1989) and Jakubowicz and Faussart (1998) in their psycholinguistic studies are the pioneers of the idea that the gender feature has different origins depending on the language in question. Boloh and Ibernon (2010: 3), in a review of the literature, conclude for French that it is possible that "determiners simply are the gender itself". We will discuss this view for child Italian.

The present chapter is organized as follows: in Section 2 we describe the inflectional system of Italian, focusing on class, gender, and number features. We present an overview of the relevant literature on the Italian gender system, while in Section 2.1 we focus on language acquisition and particularly on the acquisition of gender, number, and class features in the monolingual and bilingual literature. In Section 3, we present the parameter hierarchy from Biberauer et al. (2014), which lays the ground for our approach as introduced in Section 3.1, where we consider the taxonomy of parameters throughout the acquisition of the gender and class features. Section 4 comprises a short overview of the bilingual child who is the subject of this paper, determining his degree of language balance. In this section, we also introduce the data and the methods used to analyze the language acquisition process in Italian. Subsequently, we discuss the results of our analysis in light of the hereby applied methods. The results (Section 5) point to an instantaneous acquisition of the declension class feature. However, the bilingual data are characterized by frequent determiner omissions. Bare nouns are produced with pronouns and adjectives which exhibit target-deviant gender markings until the age of 2;11. We argue that these bare nouns are not marked for gender (but for declension class). This allows us to discuss the position of the gender feature within the syntactic structure of the Italian DP, as already suggested by Lowenstamm (2007). The paper ends with a summary and a discussion of the results as well as a review of different approaches concerning the analysis of the gender feature in Italian (Section 6).

2. Gender, number, and declension class in Italian

In this section, we present the Italian noun system focusing on the formal features gender, number, and declension class. First, we introduce the gender and the number features for Italian. Subsequently, since Italian inflects nouns in a well-studied declension class system, we will present the Italian declension classes following Acquaviva's (2009), Chini's (1995a), and Thornton's (2009) approaches.

Italian has two genders, masculine (M.) and feminine (F.), which are marked on articles in the singular and in the plural, as shown in Table 1. Evidently, the forms of determiners do not only vary with respect to gender and number, but their form also depends on phonological properties of the noun (resulting in elision or in a separate form of the article, *lo*).

Thornton et al. (1997: 39) estimate that the basic vocabulary of Italian consists of 49.8% masculine and 46.1% feminine nouns. Additionally, 2.8% of Italian nouns are either masculine or feminine and have the same form in the singular and plural for both genders (*il cantante* 'the singer' M.SG – *la cantante* 'the singer' F.SG)

Table 1. Article forms in adult Italian

	Singular		Plural	
	Definite	Indefinite	Definite	Indefinite
masculine	il *il libro* 'the book'	un, del *un libro* 'one book' *del pane* 'some bread'	i *i libri* 'the books'	dei *dei libri* 'some books'
feminine	la *la casa* 'the house'	una, della *una casa* 'one house' *della pasta* 'some pasta'	le *le case* 'the houses'	delle *delle case* 'some houses'
masculine noun beginning with s+C, x, y, z, ps, pt, pn,* gn, semi-vowel *i*, semi-vowel *j*	lo *lo squalo* 'the shark'	uno, dello *uno squalo* 'one shark' *dello spazio* 'some space'	gli *gli squali* 'the sharks'	degli *degli squali* 'some sharks'
masculine and feminine nouns elided (with vowel-initial nouns)	l' *l'acqua* 'the water'	un', un, dell' *un anello* 'one ring' *dell'acqua* 'some water'	gli, le *gli anelli* 'the rings'	degli, delle *degli anelli* 'some rings'

* Nouns starting in *pn* are generally considered as bearing the determiner *lo*. Therefore, words like *pneumatico* or *pneumologo* should be preceded by *lo*, although in many cases these words are found to be used with the determiner *il*. Concerning the determiner choice, Zanichelli, Treccani, and Accademia della Crusca answered the question about which one of both determiners should be used according to the Italian determiner system arguing that, although *lo* is generally considered as grammatically correct, both forms are nowadays found within Italian newspapers and are therefore accepted. <https://accademiadellacrusca.it/it/consulenza/il-pneumatico--lo-pneumatico/12>, <http://www.treccani.it/enciclopedia/pneumatico-il-o-lo_%28La-grammatica-italiana%29/>

and are therefore not considered in either gender group (Thornton et al. 1997: 40). The remaining 1.3% consist of *singularia* and *pluralia tantum*, nouns with different genders in the singular and plural (*il braccio* 'the arm' M.SG – *le braccia* 'the arms' F.PL) and nouns which can be masculine and feminine but have different plural forms (*il regista* 'the film director' M.SG – *i registi* 'the film directors' M.PL; *la regista* 'the film director' F.SG – *le registe* 'the film directors' F.PL) (Thornton et al. 1997: 26). The Italian gender system is generally described as morphologically and phonologically transparent (Bates et al. 1996: 993; Bianchi 2013: 540; Chini

1995a: 81; Kupisch et al. 2002: 114), since in 71.5% of all Italian nouns (Thornton et al. 1997: 38), the last occurring vowel is argued to act as a reliable cue for the gender of the noun: *-o* for masculine and *-a* for feminine singular nouns (Chini 1995a: 81). Moreover, gender agreement occurs in most cases where the gender of the noun is marked on determiners, adjectives (Benati 2004: 71), pronouns, and the past participle (Bianchi 2013: 540). Additionally, number is required in syntactic agreement, hence occurring in the agreement process with gender (Chini 1995a: 80).

However, Table 1 shows that the forms of the article depend on phonological properties of nouns, thus invalidating their function to express gender features. Furthermore, there are Italian adjectives which only inflect for number (like *gentile* 'nice' SG.; *amica gentile* 'nice friend' F.SG; *amico gentile* 'nice friend' M.SG; *amiche gentili* 'nice friends' F.PL; *amici gentili* 'nice friends' M.PL) or which do not inflect at all (like *rosa* 'rose') (see Rizzi 2013: 46ff.). Thornton et al. (1997) show that 31.7% of the adjectives included in *Vocabolario di Base della Lingua Italiana* only inflect for number, while only 1.9% have no agreement at all. Noticeably, the *-e* class adjectives are frequent in Italian, mostly because productive suffixes (e.g., *-ale* and *-ione*) occur within this declension class (Thornton et al. 1997: 38). In addition, past participle agreement is restricted to (direct) objects which do not appear in the canonical object position (VO).[1] Finally, in languages like Spanish and Italian, sound change has maintained the inherited declensions of Latin (unlike in French), and the "phonological segments on the right word edge coincide with inflections" (Loporcaro 2018: 57). It is therefore extremely difficult to distinguish between a system with phonological cues to gender, in which nouns ending in *-a* are feminine, for example, and a morphological system (Corbett 1991: 34ff.), in which nouns which belong to declension class II are feminine (cf. Thornton 2003: 469 who refutes this possibility).

Regarding the Italian declension system, Dressler and Thornton (1996) stress the fact that gender (and number) features are characterised through phonological and morphological properties within the declension class system (Thornton 2009: 18). As a matter of fact, class is a morphological diacritic (Aronoff 1994: 64) which equals lexical information and as such is also a relevant feature for nouns, adjectives, determiners, and pronouns in Italian. Chini (1995a: 81) distinguishes the seven classes in Table 2 which are based on traditional grammar:

---

1. For example, in unaccusative constructions if the auxiliary *essere* 'to be' has been chosen, in passive constructions which are formed with the auxiliary *stare* 'to be', or in constructions with a (direct) object clitic in which the clitic, via proclisis, attaches to the auxiliary verb.

Table 2. Declension classes in Italian (adapted from Chini 1995a: 81)

Declension class	Suffix SG	Suffix PL	Gender	Example
Class I	-o	-i	M.	*libro, libri* ('book', 'books')
Class II	-a	-e	F.	*casa, case* ('house', 'houses')
Class III	-e	-i	M.	*cane, cani* ('dog', 'dogs')
			F.	*ape, api* ('bee', 'bees')
Class IV	variable	like SG	M.	*re, re* ('king', 'kings')
			F.	*città, città* ('city', 'cities')
Class V	-a	-i	M.	*problema, problemi* ('problem', 'problems')
Class VI	-o (m.)	-i/-a	M.	*muro, muri/mura* ('wall'/'walls')
			F.	*uovo, uova* ('egg', 'eggs')
Class VII	-o	-i	F.	*mano, mani* ('hand', 'hands')

One or two genders as well as singular and plural morphology correspond to each of the seven classes. The first class comprises only masculine nouns. Nouns which belong to the first class are thus inflected for *-o* in the singular and *-i* in the plural. Class II comprises nouns which are inflected for *-a* in the singular and *-e* in the plural and which can only be feminine. The first and the second class constitute 71.5% of the Italian noun lexicon (Chini 1998: 42; Thornton et al. 1997: 38). Not only nouns are part of these two classes but adjectives, determiners, and pronouns are also inflected according to class I and II rules (*bello, bella – uno, una – questo, questa*) (Acquaviva 2009: 51). For these two noun classes, there is a one-to-one correspondence between gender and class.

The third inflection class comprises 20.9% of Italian noun types. In this class, nouns can be masculine as well as feminine (Dressler & Thornton 1996: 5). Overall, 44.4% are masculine and 43.4% are feminine; 12% of noun types belong to both genders (Thornton et al. 1997: 40). Nouns are inflected for *-e* in the singular and *-i* in the plural; nothing follows for gender from declension class and therefore its members are defined as opaque (Padovani & Cacciari 2003: 756). Acquaviva (2009: 52) argues that both nouns (*il cane* 'the dog' M.SG – *i cani* 'the dogs' M.PL; *la nave* 'the boat' F.SG – *le navi* 'the boats' F.PL) and adjectives (*la grande casa* 'the big house' F.SG – *le grandi case* 'the big houses' F.PL; *il grande libro* 'the big book' M.SG – *i grandi libri* 'the big books' M.PL) fall within this class. There are arguably no phonological cues which allow prediction of the gender of the noun from its root. Therefore, the noun's gender must be deduced from syntactic cues

(Thornton 2009:18).[2] Gender belongs to the lexical pieces of information of these nouns.[3]

The same is true of nouns belonging to class IV, the invariables, which cover 5.4% of the Italian vocabulary (Thornton et al. 1997:39). These are mostly monosyllabic (*il re* 'the king' M.SG – *i re* 'the kings' M.PL), nouns with a stressed final vowel (*la città* 'the city' F.SG – *le città* 'the cities' F.PL) or nouns that end in a consonant, mostly loanwords (*il computer* 'the computer' M.SG – *i computer* 'the computers' M.PL). Nouns ending in *-i* in the singular as well as in the plural form, which can be both masculine and feminine (*l(a)' analisi* 'the analysis' F.SG – *le analisi* 'the analyses' F.PL; *il brindisi* 'the toast' M.SG – *i brindisi* 'the toasts' M.PL), are also part of this category. Thornton (2003) observes that, as well as for the third class, gender is arbitrary for these nouns. Although Italian grammars often refer to this group of nouns as having feminine gender (Serianni 1988:110), Thornton (2003:11) argues that most speakers would assign masculine gender to a singular noun ending in *-i*. As with nouns of class III, syntactic cues will eventually enable the speaker to determine the gender and the number of the noun.

Finally, nouns belonging to classes V, VI, and VII, which represent 2% of all noun types (Chini 1998:42), are described as "incongruent" (Padovani & Cacciari 2003:756). "Gender incongruent nouns" are defined as nouns with vowel endings that do not conform to the inflectional rules of Italian, such as *il tema* 'the theme' (M.SG). Nouns belonging to class V are masculine (with few exceptions) and end in *-a* in the singular and in *-i* in the plural. Class V nouns thus have the same suffix as class II nouns in the singular, but trigger a different gender inflection on agreeing categories like adjectives. As Acquaviva observes, class V stems "may appear in a feminine noun, but then the noun cannot be class V" (Acquaviva

---

2. We carried out a small phonological analysis of the *-e* nouns in Italian. The data initially consisted of 1,341 types from the LIP Corpus. We firstly investigated the effect of suffixes on gender assignment as discussed in Gudmundson (2010). We then analyzed the 231 nouns which occur in the LIP Corpus without any affix, evaluating the occurrence of a relationship between different phonological features and the noun's gender. The penultimate vowels (i.e., the vowel before the final *-e*) as well as the stressed vowels were thus compared for phonological properties such as vowel height and frontedness. Moreover, we investigated the syllable weight and the quality of the consonants preceding the final *-e*. We were not able to find any correlation between phonological features and gender. However, it would be interesting to carry out a further phonological analysis of the *-e* nouns which considers different phonological features of the nouns in the adult language and their frequency in the child's input.

3. Teschner and Russell (1984:123ff.) discuss nouns ending in *-e* in Spanish and conclude that most of them are masculine (89.35%). With respect to the feminine nouns, they find that they are extremely frequent with first-syllable tonic /a/ (*carne* 'meat'). It would be interesting to pursue a phonological analysis of Italian *-e* nouns which arguably do not show a strong tendency towards masculine gender.

2009:57), marking the differences but also the similarities between class II and class V nouns. Concerning class VI, nouns belonging to this declension class are masculine in the singular, ending in -o, and feminine (-a ending), as in *l'uovo* 'the egg' M.SG – *le uova* 'the eggs' F.PL, or masculine (-i ending) in the plural. With respect to this last class, the noun's gender can be determined on the basis of number and the class it belongs to. Lastly, class VII contains nouns which, according to their declension behaviour, could be argued to be member of the first class, but in contrast to them, these are feminine (e.g., *la mano* 'the hand' F.SG – *le mani* 'the hands' F.PL).

The Italian declension system consists of seven classes and one or two genders correspond to each of them. Classes I, II, V, and VII are in a one-to-one correspondence with gender, since they consist of nouns of only one gender (masculine for classes I and V and feminine for classes II and VII). As for the classes III and IV, they consist of nouns which can have both genders, while nouns belonging to class VI are masculine in the singular and feminine in the plural forms. Hence, the noun's gender can be determined on the basis of number and the class it belongs to, although this does not apply to classes III and IV.

Concerning the structure of the DP in Italian, different approaches have been proposed, for example Lampitelli (2010:204) who assumes that the edge of lexicality (i.e., the hierarchically highest position where lexical features are located) is $\sqrt{P}$ (the root). The gender feature is located on n; as a consequence, D probes into nP for the value of the gender feature. Acquaviva (2009) adopts a different perspective and describes class but not gender as an inherent feature of the stem. If we take declension class as a feature of lexical words (at least in Italian, nouns among them, Acquaviva 2009:56), and if we follow Lowenstamm (2012:375), who claims that declension class (or profile) in Romance is a feature of n (the locus where categories are determined), then the edge of lexicality is nP. More importantly, Acquaviva (2009:55) stresses the fact that "the end vowels don't directly spell out such features but are there because Italian words must end in a vowel." In other words, the canonical shape of words is an unaccented end-vowel.

Two possibilities exist for the locus of the gender feature: the syntactic gender feature is merged either at the level of nP or outside the nP domain, in D for example (as suggested by Lowenstamm 2012). If merged on n, the gender feature acts as a probe on D or, put differently, it is an agreement feature; if merged on D, it does not act as a probe on D. It will sometimes be deducible from the class feature chosen in n, e.g., class I → masculine; with classes III and IV, gender is not in a one-to-one relation with declension class and must be deduced from syntactic cues. Further, gender is triggered by the class feature in 71.5% of Italian nouns. In this context, the determiner plays an essential role within the gender attribution process unless adjectives or pronouns occur. This becomes particularly clear in declension class III which contains nouns of both genders. As a matter of fact, nouns ending in -*e* are inflected identically for both genders. Invariable nouns, as well as plural nouns from class VI, show the same pattern.

2.1 Gender acquisition in Italian

Several studies have dealt with gender assignment and, although to a lesser extent, with gender agreement in Italian (Bates et al. 1996; Benati 2004; Bianchi 2013; Chini 1995a, 1995b, 1998; De Martino et al. 2011; Ferrari 2005; Gudmunson 2010). In most studies, phonological, morphological, and syntactic cues are central to the analysis of the origin of the gender feature since these are predictive cues to determine the gender of Italian nouns; these cues also exist in languages such as Russian (Bates et al. 1996: 993; Reeder et al. 2017: 18). However, gender is rarely defined on the basis of the interaction between class and number (Gudmunson 2010; Thornton 2009). In other words, it is possible that gender is epiphenomenal, derivable from another feature, or, to use Lampitelli's words (2010: 210), gender can belong to pieces of information which are predictable and not lexical.

Several works analysed the acquisition of Italian in monolingual, bilingual, and foreign language learners (Bates & Rankin 1979; Caselli et al. 2015; Chini 1995a, 1995b, 1998; Eichler, Hager & Müller 2012; Eichler, Jansen & Müller 2013). The Italian gender system is reported to be acquired with ease by monolingual Italian children. At the age of 3, children are able to mark the gender of the noun correctly (Chini 1995a: 130; Kupisch et al. 2002: 116; Pizzuto & Caselli 1992: 551). It must be added, though, that Italian children omit determiners extensively at an age before 3[4] (Antelmi 1997; Bottari et al. 1993/1994; Caprin & Guasti 2009: 38; Caselli et al. 1993; Chini 1995a; Kupisch et al. 2002), in other words, the assumption about the ease of gender acquisition is based on a relatively small number of DPs which contain a realized determiner. With regard to the target-like use of determiners, several studies showed that the occurrence of determiners for the masculine in Italian monolingual and bilingual children is delayed compared to the acquisition of the feminine determiners (Bottari et al. 1993/1994; Chini 1995a; Cipriani et al. 1993; Pizzuto & Caselli 1992).[5]

Gender agreement of Italian adjectives is understudied for early age groups. The rare studies which exist do not reveal much difficulty with gender agreement, but they are based on an extremely small number of tokens (Bianchi 2013: 542; Chini 1995a: 141ff.; Rizzi 2013: Chapter 3.2). According to these few studies, the

---

4. See Table 1 for details about the inflection of the determiner in Italian.
5. Pizzuto and Caselli (1992) and Caselli et al. (1993) report on *la* as the first realized form at ages 2;0/2;3, which in contrast to *il* is less affected by omission. The less frequent forms *lo/gli* are acquired latest (Caselli et al. 1993: 383–385).

child acquires adjective agreement at the age of 3;0 (Caselli et al. 1993; Chini 1995a) and is able to inflect adjectives following the gender and number agreement rules with nouns belonging to classes I, II and III. Caselli et al. (1993) and Chini (1995a) do not take into account other possible adjective endings, such as -*a* for masculine gender. These results are argued to show that gender is active at the syntactic level by the age of 3 in Italian monolingual children.

Considering bilingual first language acquisition, Hager (2014) is the largest study of different bilingual individuals. Hager finds that bilingual children also mark Italian gender with ease on determiners (see also Fey 2020 for a trilingual child), even if Italian is acquired as a weak language and together with a language with three genders, like German. Notwithstanding, Italian as a weak language gives rise to comparatively more gender errors than in balanced bilingual children (see also Eichler, Jansen & Müller 2013). However, the drawbacks of bilingual language acquisition are found if monolingual and bilingual children are compared according to their age. As illustrated in Hager (2014:196), an analysis carried out on the basis of the mean length of utterance (MLU) values does not show any substantial difference between both language groups. Since the MLU is generally considered a more reliable comparative criterion than age in bilingual children (Hager 2014:190), it appears that learning Italian as the weak language does not lead to considerable disadvantages for the acquisition of DP inflection. Kupisch (2006:114) studies a subset of these children and observes a bare-noun stage and a variation stage in which nouns occur with and without determiners.

Considering the number feature within the DP, Caselli et al. (1993) as well as Leonard et al. (2005) examine the use of singular and plural number in monolingual children at pre-school age and find that children are less accurate on plural than on singular noun inflection during the first stages of language acquisition (Caselli et al. 1993: 385–387; Leonard et al. 2005: 299). Caselli et al. (1993) consider *gli* an especially problematic case in the acquisition of Italian. Pizzuto and Caselli (1992:530) report that plural articles are used late in the acquisition process (after the age of 3;0). Bottari et al. (1993/1994: 361) analyze the employment of Monosyllabic Place Holders (MPHs) and definite articles in monolingual Italian children, concluding that number is generally acquired before gender. In other words, and contrasting with the studies on gender accuracy, acquisition of number is generally based on the (early or late) realization of determiners or MPHs. Results on the acquisition of number are contradictory, probably due to the fact that some studies take into account determiner omissions and presyntactic devices of determiner realizations while others only concentrate on whether a realized determiner appears in the target-like form together with the noun. Studies on number in Italian bilinguals are nonexistent.

The acquisition of the Italian declension system has not yet been investigated in any study on monolingual and bilingual children. Hager (2014: 270) categorizes the children's nouns on the basis of endings[6] and finds that 80% of all nouns are transparent for gender. It is possible that in the process of language acquisition the interaction of declension class and gender helps the child to acquire gender in Italian. Regarding previous studies about gender acquisition and gender agreement in Italian monolingual and bilingual children, many have followed a cue-based approach to gender acquisition and view determiners as expressions of gender attribution (see Ivanova-Sullivan & Sekerina 2019; MacWhinney 1978; Maratsos & Chalkley 1980; Mills 1986 for an overview). If we take a different route and define the Italian gender system (at least partly) as a morphological system in which class but not gender is an inherent feature of the stem (Acquaviva 2009), class defining the edge of lexicality (*n*P), the previous results about gender accuracy in Italian gender acquisition appear in a different light. They lead into defining gender accuracy by taking into account determiner omissions which are extremely frequent in the acquisition process before the age of 3.

We have argued in Section 2 that Italian gender is deducible from class, thus Italian can be argued to instantiate a morphological gender system. If merged on *n* (via a correspondence rule, e.g., class I = masculine), the gender feature acts as a probe on D or, put differently, it is an agreement feature; if merged on D, it does not act as a probe on D.

3. Parameter hierarchies in language acquisition

This section outlines class, gender, and number features of the Italian DP within the parametric approach, focusing on the epigenetic view from Biberauer et al. (2014).

Within the generative framework, language acquisition was initially related to a complex organized system, namely Universal Grammar (UG), whose capacity was assumed to narrow down the logical possibilities for language variation with the help of "a number of innate principles, with some of these having a number of parametrised options" (Bazalgette 2015: 9). The richly and highly structured Universal Grammar (Roberts 2019: 10) was then reassessed within the Minimalist Program (see Chomsky 1995), which proposes that parameters are not part of UG but rather result from the learning process. Accordingly, UG has turned into a minimally structured system, which is not the locus of linguistic variation and

---

[6]. Hager (2014) presupposed that adult Italian is a gender system which is based on phonological cues (noun endings).

thus of parameters anymore. Conforming to the current model, the three factors which enter in the acquisition of language in the individual – the innate endowment, the Primary Linguistic Data (PLD), and "principles not specific to the faculty of language" (Chomsky 2005: 6) – assume a fundamental role within the language acquisition process since they enable language acquisition through parameter setting.

Within the parametric approach, different views have been proposed concerning the way parameters should be considered in a language acquisition theory. Many approaches suggest that principles and, more importantly, parameters as proposed by Chomsky (1995, 2005, 2007) need to be rethought (Roberts 2019: 13). Among the different proposals which attempt to define principles and parameters anew (see Longobardi 2006; Newmeyer 2004; Smith & Law 2009), the epigenetic approach (also 'emergentist approach', see Holmberg & Roberts 2014: 61 as well as Newmeyer 2017: 550) from Biberauer et al. (2014) represents a reasonable model which considers the nature of parameters in the context of language acquisition. Based on the idea that micro- and macroparametric variation takes place within the language acquisition process, the parameter hierarchies represent a metaphor that is interpreted both as a "learning pathway" (Bazalgette 2015: 24) and as an organizational scheme for parameters at different levels. According to the epigenetic approach, parameters are defined as "emergent properties of the interaction of the three factors" (Roberts 2019: 7). UG provides the language acquirer with formal features. It interacts with the linguistic input and the processing principles in order to enable language acquisition. Within the 'emergentist' approach, the third factor is resumed in two fundamental principles, namely Feature Economy (FE) and Input Generalization (IG). On the one hand, FE states that the child is conservative with respect to the number of formal features needed in order to assign a structural representation to an input string (Biberauer et al. 2014: 110). IG expresses the fact that the child is liberal with respect to the extension of formal features beyond the input (Biberauer et al. 2014: 110). Both FE and IG are considered as "domain-general learning principles" (Bazalgette 2015: 20), whose function consists in solving the issues related to the language acquisition process through the implementation of cognitive mechanisms.

Furthermore, the epigenetic model considers the complexity and, related thereto, the markedness of grammatical systems. Since parameters are grouped according to the heads they affect, the complexity index of a determined language can be measured depending on the type of the parameter concerned (Biberauer et al. 2014). Thus, the differentiation in macro-, meso-, micro-, and nanoparameters, as proposed in Biberauer et al. (2014), relies on the idea that parameters can be distinguished according to the number of heads they involve.

(1) For a given value vi of a parametrically variant feature F:
   a. Macroparameters: all (functional) heads share vi;
   b. Mesoparameters: all functional heads of a given naturally definable class, e.g., [+V], share vi;
   c. Microparameters: a small subclass of functional heads (e.g., modal auxiliaries, pronouns) shows vi;
   d. Nanoparameters: one or more individual lexical items is/are specified for vi. (Biberauer et al. 2014: 109)

As shown in the taxonomy of parameters, the macroparameters affect all (functional) heads of the relevant type (Biberauer et al. 2014: 109). Here, FE and IG constitute "a minimax search/optimization algorithm" (Roberts 2019: 93) which leads the language acquirer through the parameter taxonomy following a NO>ALL>SOME procedure. As described in Picallo (2014: 7), "language learners start at the highest position of the hierarchy and keep testing down if the primary linguistic data is incompatible with a given option". Hence, the parameter hierarchy expresses markedness, since the language acquirer is supposed to go through every step of the hierarchy throughout the language acquisition process and to stop as soon as the relevant parameters for the acquired language are no longer contradicted by any input string. A language is therefore defined as unmarked if its features are shared by all (functional) heads of the relevant type, as expressed by macroparameters (for details see Biberauer et al. 2014; Roberts 2019).

The parameter taxonomy as proposed in Biberauer et al. (2014) can thus be considered as a learning path that serves as a basis for the acquisition of inflectional features. According to the epigenetic approach, the complexity of a grammatical system can be represented in a parameter hierarchy, since "moving down a hierarchy, ... systems become more marked, having a longer and more complex description than the higher options" (Biberauer et al. 2014: 115). Since FE and IG serve as a search algorithm, the acquirer is expected to look for the functional features which occur in the nominal inflection of the acquired language and, subsequently, to behave conforming to both FE and IG. Accordingly, if fewer features occur in the nominal inflection of one language system, then the language is assumed to have a low degree of grammatical complexity as well as to be unmarked and, along the same line of thought, languages with more features within the nominal inflection system are assumed to be marked and thus more complex to learn.

3.1 Parameter hierarchies in language acquisition: Declension classes in Italian

Gender and declension class constitute two features which can be found within determiner phrases of some languages, but not of others. Following Biberauer et al.'s (2014) approach to grammatical complexity, English is assumed to lack grammatical gender[7] and inflectional class altogether and thus to be unmarked. More complex are nominal inflection systems where at least one feature occurs within the nominal domain: an example is French, which is a grammatical gender system, but, arguably, lacks inflectional class (see Lowenstamm 2007 for discussion). Likewise, languages such as Svan inflect nouns according to a declension class system which includes information about number and case,[8] although they are reported to have no expression for grammatical gender (Tuite 1997: 15). Italian exhibits grammatical gender and class and is therefore assumed to be a relatively marked system.

Gender and declension class features are related in most languages, with exceptions of language systems in which only one feature occurs. According to Corbett (1991), a language system in which the gender value follows from the noun's inflectional class is called a morphological system (in contrast to phonological systems where phonological properties of the noun determine the noun's gender value). Morphological gender assignment is reported to be used target-like extremely early, in some languages as early as the age of 2 (Corbett 1991: 83). Due to early acquisition, morphological gender assignment systems are assumed to be unmarked. Otherwise, phonological systems are generally acquired later in life; the French gender system is reported to be used target-like at the age of 3[9] and thus represents a marked grammatical gender system (Corbett 1991: 87).

---

7. Considering grammatical gender, English represents the "default-language" since the gender distinction is restricted only to the third-person singular pronouns while nouns do not appear to be inflected according to gender or declension class. As reported in Corbett (1991: 83), the gender distinction in pronouns is only related to biological sex and it is thus not sufficient to establish the presence of a grammatical gender system in the English nominal inflection system.

8. We would like to thank Pilar Larrañaga for bringing such languages to our attention.

9. Most declension classes have not survived the massive sound changes in the modern French nominal system (for discussions about the presence of declension classes in the syntactic structure of the French nominal system see Lowenstamm 2012). Only one remaining declension class can be found in Modern French, namely nouns ending in -al in the singular and -aux in the plural (e.g., *cheval – chevaux, travail – travaux*). As a result, there is hardly evidence for inherited inflectional classes in modern French.

Following the present approach, we assume that class represents a parametrized feature in the Italian inflection system. The first and most general question concerning the acquisition of noun inflection within a parameter hierarchy is whether the language system has inflectional classes as a formal feature. When acquiring Italian, the child formulates a positive answer to this first question. The following assumption by the acquirer is that the class feature is shared by all (functional) heads in the Italian system. As already reported in Section 3, the higher the number of heads affected, the lower the markedness of a given grammatical system. The transparency of the Italian language system, as concerning the inflection of nouns as well as determiners, pronouns, adjectives (Acquaviva 2009: 51) and also verbs, leads the language acquirer to complete acquisition of the declension class system at an extremely early age. If class is concerned, the route to Italian is very short.

Concerning the gender feature, the Italian gender system can be described in Corbett's terms as a morphological system and is thus unmarked and acquired relatively early. In the following sections we will firstly formulate the research questions and subsequently describe the corpus investigated for the present research.

4. The study

The present study is concerned with the acquisition of the gender and class features in Italian by one Italian-German bilingual child who acquires the Romance language as his weak language. We define Italian as the child's weak language since, compared to the child's other language, the quality and quantity of input in Italian is substantially reduced (see Carroll 2017 for a detailed discussion of the quality and quantity of input and exposure in bilingual language acquisition). In contrast with German, the analyzed child speaks Italian only with some members of his family, while he grows up in Germany and attends a German kindergarten later in life. As we will show in the following section, the MLU values also show a preference towards German. Moreover, the concepts of weak and strong languages are related to the notion of balance in bilingualism (Meisel 2007: 496) and, accordingly, the subject of this study can be described as an unbalanced bilingual.

We chose to analyze the data from an unbalanced bilingual child in order to test whether language balance affects the acquisition of grammatical gender. According to the results from previous studies, gender is generally acquired by the age of 3 by monolingual and bilingual children. If grammatical gender is acquired by the same age even in the case of an unbalanced bilingual child, then we can confirm previous assumptions about the acquisition of grammatical gender in Italian and we can test whether the class feature is involved within the learning process. Concretely, the paper aims to answer two research questions, each concerning specific features of the DPs in Italian.

The first question involves the parameter taxonomy and the hereto related FE and IG principles. As shown in Section 2.1, the Italian nominal system is inflected according to gender and declension class, leading to the assumption that both features are present within the Italian DP. According to the FE principle, an increasing number of features in a certain domain leads to a greater markedness. Hence, the Italian system is assumed to be more marked than language systems which inflect the nominal domain according to either gender or declension class. This assumption contrasts with the fact that the Italian gender system is generally reported to be acquired early and with ease. Accordingly, the first research question addresses the effect of markedness on the Italian nominal system and its acquisition process by analyzing the relation between both features in the nominal domain.

Research question 1: Is the Italian nominal system marked?

We claim that both features are acquired following the acquisition pattern which is represented through the taxonomy of parameters. According to the assumption that declension class constitutes a parametrized feature and that it is thus acquired fast and with ease, we aim to analyze the nature of the relation between gender and class features. We anticipate the Italian nominal inflection system to be marked since it involves both gender and class features. Thus, the data should show that the acquisition of these features occurs later in the child's lifetime than generally claimed and that the production of target-like DPs is accordingly delayed.

The second research question, therefore, concerns the acquisition of grammatical gender in Italian, considering the possible interaction of gender with other grammatical features such as number and, most importantly, declension class.

Research question 2a: Does gender interact with other grammatical domains, particularly with declension class?
Research question 2b: If there is an interaction, does the gender feature follow from the class feature in Italian?

According to previous research as discussed in the preceding chapters, we expect to find an interaction between gender and class within the Italian nominal system. We assume that Italian has a morphological gender assignment system which inflects according to gender and class. Particularly, for some classes the gender feature follows from class, although this does not apply to every declension class in the Italian nominal inflection system. As a matter of fact, Italian exhibits declension classes such as classes III and IV where gender assignment is not morphological. We hence expect differences concerning the acquisition of classes such as class III and IV due to the different interaction of the gender and class features. However, the bilingual child of the current study produces only few nouns which belong to classes III and IV before the age of 3 and thus, we will not pursue this hypothesis any further. In order to confirm our predictions about the interaction between gender and class in Italian, we expect to find no (or very few) declension class errors. Nonetheless, determiner omissions are assumed to occur frequently with all classes until the gender system is definitely acquired.

The next section presents the longitudinal study of one bilingual child who acquires Italian as weak language. He was recorded in natural interactions every fortnight. Examining the acquisition of a weak language prevents the linguist from missing a developmental stage.

4.1 The Italian-German child Ja_di

Ja_di acquires German and Italian simultaneously from birth and is already subject of several works in the field of multilingualism (Cantone et al. 2008; Eichler 2011; Hager 2014; Kupisch 2006; Müller et al. 2011[10]). This child was chosen for this research since, developing Italian as a weak language, he shows low accuracy with noun phrases. Ja_di was recorded between the ages of 2;0.11 and 5;0.8. He was born in Germany and grew up in Hamburg. His mother is Italian and speaks almost only Italian with him, although the family lives in a German environment and German is the dominant language within the family (for an extensive description of Ja_di's bilingualism and language exposure see Cantone 2007: 90f.).

Ja_di's MLU development was already analyzed in several studies on language dominance (see Arencibia Guerra 2008; Cantone 2007; Cantone et al. 2008; Schmeißer et al. 2016). In the research field of multilingualism, the MLU is reported to be an effective and reliable method to measure language dominance

---

10. All language data were collected and transcribed in three projects funded by the DFG (German Research Foundation) under the direction of Prof. Dr. Natascha Müller from 1999 to 2013. The data originate from the following projects: (i) 'Frühkindliche Zweisprachigkeit: Italienisch-Deutsch und Französisch-Deutsch im Vergleich (1999–2005)' (project number 5483483); (ii) 'Die Architektur der frühkindlichen bilingualen Sprachfähigkeit: Italienisch-Deutsch und Französisch-Deutsch in Italien, Deutschland und Frankreich im Vergleich (2005–2008)' (project number 5452914); (iii) 'Code-Switching bei bilingual aufwachsenden Kindern in Deutschland, Italien, Frankreich und Spanien: Italienisch-Deutsch, Französisch-Deutsch, Spanisch-Deutsch, Italienisch-Französisch, Italienisch-Spanisch, Französisch-Spanisch (2009–2011)' (project number 107909018). The projects collected linguistic material from different bilingual children over a large period of time thus enabling the development of several longitudinal studies on multilingual language acquisition; see Hauser-Grüdl et al. 2010: 2638–2650 and Müller et al. 2011, 2015.

even in parental questionnaires based on a calculation of the child's three longest utterances (Arencibia Guerra 2008; Ezeizabarrena & Garcia: 2018; Hager 2014; Schmeißer et al. 2016; Yip & Matthews 2006). With respect to Ja_di's language development, his MLU values calculated on a word basis show that he develops German faster than Italian. The information about the MLU-development of Ja_di are taken from Hager (2014: 196). Figure 1 presents the MLU-difference and the MLU values in both languages, Italian and German, on the y-axis. In order to show all data in one figure, German is represented as positive values and Italian as negative values. Ja_di's age is plotted on the x-axis. Figure 1 illustrates that the MLU values in Italian are lower than in German, especially from 2;0 to 3;5. The line tends towards zero in the first recording sessions and increases from 2;4 progressively.

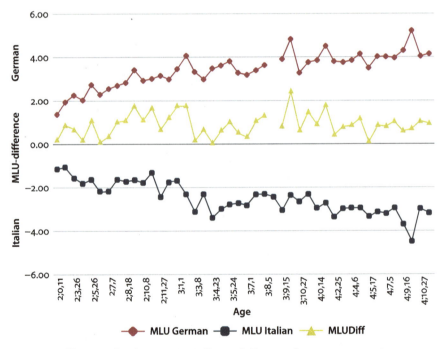

Figure 1. Ja_di's MLU-development in Italian and German from 2;0.11 to 5;0.8

The noun type (N-type) difference is another important measure if grammatical features of noun phrases are considered. Figure 2 shows Ja_di's noun type difference and the noun type lexicon in both languages on the y-axis. As for the MLU values, both Italian and German noun type values are illustrated by two different lines in one figure. The figure illustrates that by the age of 4;0 Ja_di's vocabulary contains no more than 287 noun types in Italian and as many as 421 in German.

Ja_di's noun lexicon is smaller in Italian than in German through all recording sessions. The development of the noun type lexicon is similar to the acquisition process of other bilingual children with an unbalanced language development, as reported in Pillunat (2007).

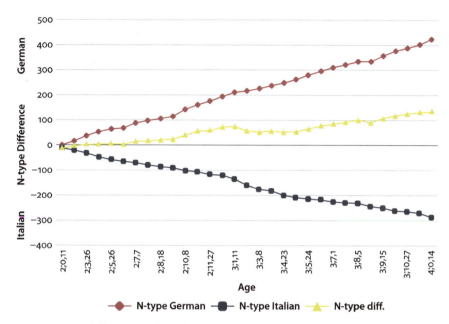

Figure 2. N-type difference in the Italian-German bilingual child Ja_di

For this study, we coded all of Ja_di's nouns in declension classes according to the form used for the reference to one and to more than one object. We coded them from the age of 2;0.11 until 5;0.8. We looked at the referent (singular / plural) of every form used by the bilingual child in order to establish the declension class of every noun. The suffix -*e*, for instance, represents the plural suffix of class II and the singular suffix of class III. In such a case, the number of referents allows us to determine the declension class involved. Moreover, we coded the gender and the number marking as marked on the determiner. Regarding the gender feature, we looked at the gender used by Ja_di and at the grammatical gender of the noun in the Italian language system (see also Hager 2014). Within this approach, we coded all Ja_di's DPs in conformity with the child's declension class system, resulting in a system with nine declension classes. Moreover, since Italian children often omit articles especially in the first stages of language acquisition, we coded every article omission (see Kupisch 2006: 238).

5. Results

The Italian declension classes and their frequency in Ja_di's lexicon are represented in Figure 3. Most nouns belong to the first and second declension classes with 307 and 392 tokens, respectively, while the third and the fourth classes occur less frequently in Ja_di's vocabulary with 187 and 76 tokens, respectively. The fifth, sixth and seventh classes appear in less than 5% of all cases, with only 24, 6, and 10 tokens, respectively. The percentage values are calculated on the overall produced nouns. The values on the bars represent the absolute number of nouns for each declension class.

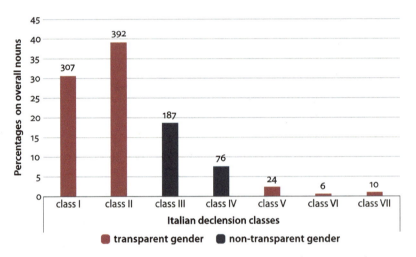

Figure 3. Frequency of declension classes in Ja_di's vocabulary from 2;0 until 5;0

In previous studies on Ja_di's gender acquisition, Hager (2014: 264) reports that he has an overall gender accuracy of 93.7% as a result of a cue-based categorization. A similar result can also be achieved using declension classes: since most nouns used by the bilingual child belong to classes I and II, where class and gender are in a one-to-one-relationship, the child is able to deduce the gender of the noun relying on the declension class information.

The frequency of nouns within declension classes changes with age. As shown in Figure 4, in the first three intervals, i.e., from 2;0 to 3;5, Ja_di uses mostly nouns which are part of the first two declension classes. From 3;5 to 4;0, most tokens still belong to classes I and II, although the production of invariable nouns as well as of nouns belonging to classes III, V, VI, and VII increases. As can be deduced from Figure 4, there is a trend: class II, which contains feminine nouns ending in *-a* in the singular and *-e* in the plural, is the most used from age 2 to 4 years. Within the last two intervals, nouns belonging to the first declension class increase in number

Chapter 3. Acquisition of morpho-syntactic features 73

of tokens compared to nouns belonging to class II, becoming the most frequent class.

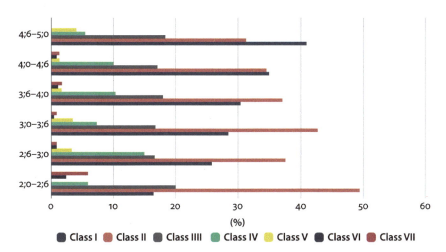

Figure 4. Frequency of declension class in Ja_di by age (absolute numbers)

It must be added, though, that both figures do not represent the total amount of tokens produced by Ja_di. In fact, all tokens were categorized within declension classes according to the adult language system, omitting the tokens which did not fit in any class (available per hyperlink).[11] Hence, there were tokens following different inflectional rules than in the adult system of Italian. The classification of tokens in declension classes was carried out according to the noun's inflection in the singular and in the plural. Table 3 shows the declension classes used by Ja_di.

Concerning the gender feature and target-like uses, Figure 5 reports feminine and masculine gender forms in classes I, II, and III since they are the most frequent in Ja_di's vocabulary. In order to reveal the peculiarity of Ja_di's vocabulary especially for class III, we reported the data as resumed in Figure 5. Target-like nouns of class I and class II largely prevail and both classes are used in a target-deviant way in only a few cases, as for example in *un* 'one' M.SG *bottiglia* 'bottle' F.SG Particularly interesting are the results for class III; as is clearly depicted, this class is used mostly with masculine gender. In fact, of 87 nouns belonging to class III produced from 2;0 to 3;6, 75 are masculine nouns and only 12 are feminine. In only three cases, target-deviant uses of nouns from class III are found in Ja_di's vocabulary.

---

11. <https://www.mehrsprachigkeit.uni-wuppertal.de/de/publikationen/codings-of-child-data/>

Table 3. Ja_di's declension classes – the asterisks symbolize that the examples from Ja_di's DPs are target-deviant

Declension class	Suffix SG	Suffix PL	Examples
Class I	-o	-i	*ospito – ospiti ('guest' – 'guests')
Class II	-a	-e	*ala – ale ('wing' – 'wings')
Class III	-e	-i	*valigie – valigi ('suitcase' – 'suitcases')
Class IV	invariables	= SG	*pinna – pinna ('fin' – 'fins')
Class V	-a	-i	*gamba – gambi ('leg' – 'legs')
Class VI	-o	-a	*domenico – domenica ('Sunday' – 'Sundays')
Class VII	-o	-i	*gioco – giochi ('toy' – 'toys')
Class VIII	-a	-i	*signora – signori ('lady' – 'ladies')
Class IX	-i	-i	*denti – denti ('tooth' – 'teeth')

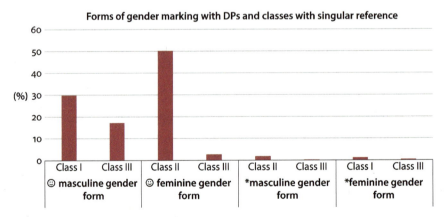

Figure 5. Target-like and target-deviant DPs in Ja_di's lexicon from 2;0 to 3;6 – ☺ = target-like, * = target-deviant

Target-deviant uses of nouns belonging to classes I, II, and III need to be related to another important aspect of Ja_di's vocabulary, the production and the omission of determiners.[12]

This aspect of language acquisition in bilingual children was already considered by Kupisch (2006:70), who reports the rate of determiner omissions in Ja_di. Figure 6 relates to Kupisch's results and sums up the realisations and omissions of D in the three most frequent classes I, II, and III. In Figure 6, the realisations and the omissions for each class are represented in percentages on the overall number of nouns per age span on the y-axis. In the first phases, i.e., from 2;0 to 2;11, there are numerous omissions and only few realisations compared to the amount of omissions. By 3;0, the realisations increase in number, exceeding the omissions and leading to an inversed pattern. We carried out a t-test to determine whether there were significant differences in determiner omissions among the three classes, considering the omissions with nouns from classes I, II, and III as our variables. Even though determiner omissions in classes I and II are frequent in early acquisitional stages, there are significantly more errors with class III nouns, with a difference both between classes I and III ($t(5) = 7.952$, $p < .001$) as well as between classes II and III ($t(5) = 10.679$, $p < .001$). Finally, when classes I and II are grouped together, the difference becomes even more marked ($t(5) = 11.767$, $p < .001$).

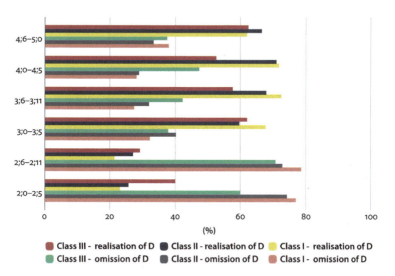

Figure 6. Realisation and omission of determiners with nouns of classes I, II, and III in Ja_di

---

12. All instances of determiner omissions were counted, regardless of whether they were grammatical or not (see Stahnke 2022 for a study on determiner acquisition as such). For a discussion of this issue see Section 6.

Concerning DPs with an overt determiner, Figure 7 shows that from the very beginning the determiner production is mostly target-like.

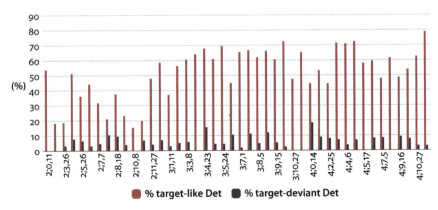

Figure 7. Target-like and target-deviant determiners in Ja_di's DPs

However, before the age of 2;11.27, errors occur due to an overgeneralization of either the masculine or the feminine determiner forms. Let us consider the following examples from Ja_di's language production data.

(2) a. *questo bimba (Ja_di 2;3.26)
       'this$_{F.SG}$ child$_{F.SG}$'
    b. questo tavolo (Ja_di 2;4.15)
       'this$_{M.SG}$ table$_{M.SG}$'
    c. *questo aiutano (Ja_di 2;7.7)
       'this$_{M.SG}$ help$_{PL}$' (they help)

In (2a), (2b), and (2c)[13] the masculine singular form of the Italian demonstrative pronoun *questo* 'this$_M$' is used in an utterance with a feminine (2a) and a masculine (2b) noun as well as the subject in contexts where the plural form should be used (2c). The feminine form *questa* 'this$_F$' appears first at the age of 2;8.18 and, once it emerges, it is mostly used target-like. However, as also reported within different studies (Caprin & Guasti 2009: 25; Pizzuto & Caselli 1992: 521; among others), we consider the example in (2a) as the result of the copula verb omission and thus not as a target-deviant inflected determiner.

The study of adjectives may provide more insights with respect to the two options: (i) if gender was a feature of *n*P, then adjectives should agree in gender

---

13. Before the age of 2;11, *questo* is also used in the subject position and combined with verbs which are inflected for the plural form. This could indicate that *questo* does not have the feature "singular" yet.

with bare nouns, and (ii) if gender was a feature of D, then adjectives should not be marked for gender if the noun phrase only contains a bare noun. We also considered the occurrence and the inflection of adjectives in the bilingual child data and found that almost 90% of the overall occurrences of adjectives are marked with masculine gender, even though they occur with nouns exhibiting a final -*a* in the singular form. However, adjectives are too infrequent to consider this point more thoroughly.

As for determiner omissions, Figure 8 reveals that Ja_di's data are affected by a high rate of target-deviant bare nouns until the age of 2;11.27 (> 20%). Moreover, Ja_di's DPs consist mostly of bare nouns, confirming the high rate of determiner omissions as illustrated in Figure 6. Ja_di's declension system consists of nine different classes which are reported in the next sections.

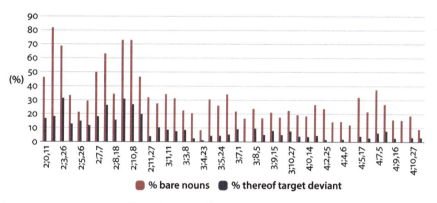

Figure 8. Percentage overall production of bare nouns and target-deviant bare nouns on overall noun production in Ja_di

5.1 Classes I and II

Class I and class II are the most commonly occurring classes in Ja_di's declension system. As reported in Figure 3 and in Hager (2014: 270), these classes constitute around 70% of the total tokens in the bilingual child's lexicon. Both classes correspond to one gender: class I to the masculine and class II to the feminine. Gender is deducible in all cases from class, constituting a one-to-one-relationship between gender and class.

In class I are classified all nouns which, as in the adult Italian declension system (Table 2), end in -*o* in the singular and in -*i* in the plural and were used as masculine nouns according to the adult gender system: *aereo* 'airplane' – *aerei* 'airplanes'; *bambino* 'child' – *bambini* 'children'; and *regalo* 'gift' – *regali* 'gifts'. Dealing with tokens, it also occurred that one noun was first used as being part of class I and then as a member of another class, for example *aereo* 'airplane' – *aerei* 'airplanes', which is used as a feminine noun (**è una grossa aereo* 'is a big airplane' F.SG) at 4;9.16 on a par with adult *mano* 'hand' (see Table 2), and as a masculine noun (*siamo partiti con uno* piccolo aereo* 'we left with a small airplane' M.SG) at 3;2.19.

In class II exist all nouns which, as in the adult Italian declension system (see Table 2), end in *-a* in the singular and in *-e* in the plural and were used as feminine nouns according to the adult gender system. It occurred that one noun was first used as being part of class II and then as a member of another class. An example is the word form *ala* 'wing' F.SG – *ali* 'wings' M.PL; Ja_di inflects the plural form as feminine (**le ale* 'the wings' F.PL) at 3;8.24 but as masculine (*le ali* 'the wings' M.PL) at 3;4.1 and 4;4.27.

Note that class I and II nouns are inflected almost always in a target-like way, thus excluding possible Italian words like **aerea* instead of *aereo* 'airplane' and **bocco* instead of *bocca* 'mouth'. Ja_di thus manages to use the proper inflection with nouns of these classes with only a very few exceptions as reported in Table 3. The very few target-deviant uses in classes I and II are also shown in Figure 5.

5.2 Class III

Class III is the third class which occurs most frequently in Ja_di's lexicon with around 20% of tokens, as reported in Figure 3. This class consists of nouns ending in *-e* in the singular and in *-i* in the plural and has arbitrary gender. Surprisingly, Ja_di does not commit many gender errors with nouns belonging to class III; the determiner is mostly chosen correctly. Although not many nouns of this class occur with determiners, the bilingual child is able to use the appropriate one.

5.3 Classes IV, V, VI, and VII

These classes are the least frequent in Ja_di's lexicon. Class IV appears with a frequency of 7%, while classes V, VI, and VII occur in only 3% of all cases. Nouns of class IV have arbitrary gender, class V entails masculine gender, class VI is a class with non-fixed gender but nouns are marked as masculine in the singular and as feminine in the plural, and lastly, class VII nouns have feminine gender. Ja_di is able to mark the correct gender in almost all cases of nouns of classes IV, V, VI, and VII on determiners. Ja_di rarely classifies nouns of these classes as belonging to classes I or II. An example is *il braccio* 'the arm' M.SG – *le braccia* 'the arms' F.PL, which is marked as being part of class I in *il braccio* 'the arm' M.SG – **i bracci* 'the arms' M.PL

5.4 Classes VIII and IX

The previously considered classes are also reported in Table 2 and are hence present in both the adult and child nominal inflection system. However, Ja_di's language production data consists of two additional classes: class VIII contains feminine nouns which are inflected as in class V (*-a* SG., *-i* PL., as in *l(a)'arma* 'the weapon' – *le armi* 'the weapons', which are generally considered exceptions of class V); class IX consists of invariable nouns ending in *-i* that can be both masculine and feminine (*l(a)'analisi* 'the analysis' – *le analisi* 'the analyses' F.; *il brindisi* 'the toast' – *i brindisi* 'the toasts' M.), although in Ja_di's lexicon they normally occur with masculine gender except for one noun (*la ali* 'the wing' F.SG). Both classes are in a direct relationship with gender: if the noun is part of class VIII it is feminine, if it belongs to class IX it is masculine. Both classes occur rarely: class VIII has 13 tokens while class IX has only 6 tokens. Determiners are realized in almost all of these cases.

5.5 Summary of the Italian data

The analysis of Ja_di's data has shown that he acquires the Italian declension classes in a (mostly) target-like way from the beginning: nouns are mostly inflected in accordance with the target-system. Moreover, he uses nouns belonging to different declension classes, though preferring classes I, II, and III which are also the most common ones in Italian adult language. For the vast majority of nouns used by the child, class and gender are in a one-to-one correspondence. Gender errors are extremely rare, however, determiner omissions are very frequent until the age of 3;0. Determiner omission is found in all classes, although class III is mostly affected. If determiners are realized, their form mostly corresponds to adult Italian. However, until the age of 2;11.27, bare nouns can occur with pronouns or adjectives which are not marked for gender.

6. Discussion and conclusion

The present paper has focused on bilingual language acquisition and in particular, on the acquisition of the gender and class features in the bilingual child's weak language. The results provide useful hints about the language acquisition process in Italian and interesting suggestions for further research which will be discussed in what follows. Moreover, the generally accepted theory that gender is a feature on *n* (or the root) and that D is a probe is examined and confronted with a different view.

Data analysis shows that Ja_di inflects nouns in 99% of the cases target-like. In fact, out of a total of 1,744 DPs, only 19 contain nouns which are inflected in a target-deviant way and can thus be considered as declension class errors. Comparing our study with results from previous studies about the acquisition of the nominal inflection system in Italian, we can thus assert that Italian children acquire the nominal inflection system from early on and instantaneously. Moreover, we analyzed Ja_di's DPs focusing on the acquisition of class and gender features and we were able to classify all of Ja_di's DPs, either as target-like or as target-deviant, the result being that class I and class II occur most frequently: they are connected to one gender and most nouns in Italian belong to these two classes (71.5% as in Thornton et al. 1997: 38). The language acquisition data show that the bilingual Italian child tries to establish a correspondence between declension class and gender. The child acquires the different declension classes of nouns and considers them as the solution to determine the gender of the noun. Moreover, target-deviant gender marking on determiners is extremely rare in Ja_di. Both genders are acquired in a target-like way from early on. At the time when target-like gender marking occurs on determiners, Ja_di omits them most of the time, leading to a frequent production of bare nouns almost until the age of 2;11. As shown in Section 5, bare nouns are not marked for gender, since pronouns or adjectives used in an utterance with a bare noun do not agree in gender (and number) with that noun. This result leads to the conclusion that the bilingual child marks gender in a target-like way once he has realized determiners. Starting from the age of 2;11, the production of determiners increases together with, again, target-like use of gender and number marking on determiners. To summarize, bare nouns which are unmarked for gender co-exist with DPs which contain a determiner with the adult-like expression of gender (and number).

The present results allow us to consider the acquisition of the gender and class features in a different light. Importantly, an approach such as the one proposed here, which assumes that the class feature is an inherent feature of the noun in Italian and that gender follows from the class features for some classes, can explain 99% of the overall occurring DPs. Considering different analysis methods as applied in the literature and focusing in particular on the cue-based approach, the advantages of a declension class approach become clear. Our approach leads to a descriptively adequate analysis in comparison to a cue-based categorization, since, by focusing on the occurrence of phonological cues, gender accuracy is about 94% in bilingual children's DPs (Hager 2014: 206). However, if we take into consideration the language-specific differences with respect to declension classes (and their frequencies), we can account for these results as suggested from the cue-based categorization and suggest an analysis that allows us to explain almost all the DPs within the bilingual child's data. This leads to the conclusion that focusing on the class feature leads to a more comprehensive data analysis compared to a cue-based approach.

For the sake of clarity, the research questions as formulated in Section 4 are restated here:

> Research question 1: Is the Italian nominal system marked?
> Research question 2a: Does gender interact with other grammatical domains, particularly with declension class?
> Research question 2b: If there is an interaction, does the gender feature follow from the class feature in Italian?

Based on our analysis, research question 1 may be partially confirmed. While the class feature is acquired instantaneously and without learning in Italian and, accordingly, gender and class are in a one-to-one relationship for five of the seven Italian nominal classes, different features, such as class, gender, number, and (if we also consider the pronominal system) case, are involved in the Italian DPs. On the one hand, we can clearly state that the Italian child largely omits determiners, especially in class III, until the age of 2;11. However, when determiners are produced, Ja_di commits extremely few target-deviant gender markings on determiners. On the other hand, bare nouns are not marked for gender in Ja_di's data, as shown in Section 5, and these are extremely frequent until the age of 3. As a matter of fact, the markedness of the Italian system is reflected by extremely frequent determiner omissions. Nevertheless, Italian also constitutes a morphological gender system (see Sections 2.1 and 3.1). As reported in Corbett (1991: 83), morphological gender systems are generally acquired well before the age of 3. The Polish gender system, for instance, is reported to be acquired by the age of 2 (Corbett 1991: 83; Schwartz et al. 2014: 7 for an overview of monolingual Russian children). Comparing these results with Ja_di's data, the bilingual child's DPs clearly point to the conclusion that the Italian gender system can be considered as acquired from very early on. This leads to the conclusion that, although the Italian system is marked as concerning the number of features involved within the nominal inflection, the Italian morphological gender system is, instead, unmarked and thus generally acquired very early.

Our second research question addresses the possibility of gender interacting with other grammatical features like class. Clearly, the bilingual child tries to establish a relation between class and gender while acquiring Italian, a language where gender and class interact in a one-to-one relationship in the majority of its declension classes. As a matter of fact, the gender of more than 70% of all noun-types is in perfect correspondence to class, i.e., all nouns belonging to classes I and II. According to this line of argumentation, gender is in many cases derivable by the class feature and thus interacts with declension class. In the remaining cases, gender is not derivable by class. However, determiner omissions occur both with nouns where gender can be derived from the class feature as well with nouns where class and gender do not interact. This leads us to investigate the position of the gender feature within the nominal domain.

Is gender a feature of the domain of lexicality ($\sqrt{P}$ or nP) or is it located outside this domain? Even though we are unable to provide a definite answer to this question on the basis of our data, we will discuss the theoretical implications for both scenarios in Italian in what follows. First, let us assume that gender is a feature of n. In this case, D and other syntactic categories agree with gender, and the many NPs without determiners observed in Italian would have a gender feature despite the lack of D. Importantly, this approach cannot explain the missing gender markings on pronouns and adjectives if used with bare nouns in an utterance. On the other hand, if we hypothesize that D is the locus of gender in Italian, then nouns without determiners should be analyzed as genderless (under the assumption that D is not projected in early grammar) and consequently, omission of the determiner does not result in a gender error since the gender feature is absent. Under this analysis, there is no agreement between nP and D, only a correspondence: nouns belonging to all classes, except for classes III and IV, are thus in a one-to-one relationship with gender. This is in line with our predictions about the gender location within the syntactic structure of the Italian DP, since Ja_di produces determiners that are nearly always marked for gender in a target-like way, while determiner omissions and, hence, bare nouns are combined with categories which lack a gender marking.

We have reported that determiner omissions in Italian primarily occur with nouns of class III, where the correspondence between class and gender is imperfect. Thus, we may conclude that the child is not able to derive gender by class in such cases. In order to mark gender with nouns belonging to class III, i.e., a class where the gender and class features do not interact, the child must take into account syntactic cues. Thus, determiner omissions with this declension class may simply express the fact that the necessary syntactic cues for gender marking are not available to the child yet. The observation that determiners are omitted in these contexts invites the analysis that gender is to be located on D. However, this conclusion is not completely satisfactory because early D omissions also pertain to classes I and II.

Even though the focus of our study was not number, the data analysis reveals some interesting implications for further research in Italian, where number and gender are expressed by one suffix only. It would also be worthwhile to further investigate the interaction between number, class, and gender. Considering our results, we could not find any interaction between number and either the gender or the class feature in Ja_di's data.

Moreover, it would be interesting to carry out an analysis of gender markings in bilingual children through the use of pseudowords in Italian DPs, as in the study of Pérez-Tattam et al. (2019) for Spanish and Basque. The declension class approach would then be supported by the data if, on the one hand, the bilingual Italian children could inflect the determiners target-like with nouns belonging to classes to which only one gender corresponds, i.e., classes I, II, V, VI, and VI. On the other hand, target-deviant DPs would occur with pseudowords from classes III and IV, where the children rely on syntactic cues to derive gender and, in absence of syntactic cues, gender markings on determiners would thus be target-deviant.

Finally, the limitations of this study need to be mentioned. The data derive from only one bilingual child, thus we cannot describe a tendency for the whole language system but rather report the results obtained from the data observation. This might influence the results of our analysis. However, it should also be considered that, although Ja_di acquires Italian as a weak language, he marks the gender feature (almost) always in a target-like way when determiners are realized. Therefore, more research needs to be done in this field in order to confirm or deny the approach followed in this study.

Concluding, we want to stress the importance of studies about the language acquisition process, a topic which has currently received too little attention. The task of theoretical linguists is to study language systems and to develop hypotheses from their observations. However, hypotheses need to be tested and, in the face of evidence against them, need to be re-evaluated. Within the linguistic framework, researchers in language acquisition assume a fundamental role by carrying out studies to test the theoretical hypotheses on the best possible research subject: the language learner. Boeckx (2014: 159) mentions a "gap between theoretical work and language acquisition studies" which, as it seems, still needs to be filled.

References

Acquaviva, P. 2009. The structure of the Italian declension system. In *Selected Proceedings of the 6th Décembrettes*, F. Montermini, G. Boyé & J. Tseng (eds), 50–62. Somerville MA: Cascadilla Proceedings Project.

Antelmi, D. 1997. *La prima grammatica italiana*. Bologna: il Mulino.

Arencibia Guerra, L. 2008. Sprachdominanz bei bilingualen Kindern mit Deutsch und Französisch, Italienisch oder Spanisch als Erstsprachen. PhD dissertation, Bergische Universität Wuppertal.

Aronoff, M. 1994. *Morphology by Itself: Stems and Inflectional Classes*. Cambridge MA: The MIT Press.

Bates, E. & Rankin, J. 1979. Morphological development in Italian: Connotation and denotation. *Journal of Child Language* 6(1): 29–52.

Bates, E., Devescovi, A., Hernandez, A. & Pizzamiglio, L. 1996. Gender priming in Italian. *Perception & Psychophysics* 58(7): 992–1004.

Bazalgette, T. O. 2015. *Algorithmic Acquisition of Focus Parameters*. PhD dissertation, University of Cambridge.

Benati, A. 2004. The effects of processing instruction and its components on the acquisition of gender agreement in Italian. *Language Awareness* 13(2): 67–80.

Bianchi, G. 2013. Gender in Italian-German bilinguals: A comparison with German L2 learners of Italian. *Bilingualism: Language and Cognition* 16(3): 538–557.

Biberauer, T., Holmberg, A., Roberts, I. & Sheehan, M. 2014. Complexity in comparative syntax: The view from modern parametric theory. In *Measuring Grammatical Complexity*, F. J. Newmeyer & L. B. Preston (eds), 103–127. Oxford: OUP.

Boeckx, C. 2014. What principles and parameters got wrong. In *Linguistic Variation in the Minimalist Framework*, M. C. Picallo (ed.), 155–178. Oxford: OUP.

Boloh, Y. & Ibernon, L. 2010. Gender attribution and gender agreement in 4- to 10-year-old French children. *Cognitive Development* 25(1): 1–25.

Bottari, P., Cipriani, P. & Chilosi, A.-M. 1993/1994. Protosyntactic devices in the acquisition of Italian free morphology. *Language Acquisition* 3(4): 327–369.

Cantone, K. F. 2007. *Code-switching in Bilingual Children*. Dordrecht: Springer.

Cantone, K. F., Kupisch, T., Müller, N. & Schmitz, K. 2008. Rethinking language dominance in bilingual children. *Linguistische Berichte* 215: 307–343.

Caprin, C. & Guasti, M. T. 2009. The acquisition of morphosyntax in Italian: A cross-sectional study. *Applied Psycholinguistics* 30(1): 23–52.

Carroll, S. E. 1989. Second language acquisition and the computational paradigm. *Language Learning* 39(4): 535–594.

Carroll, S. E. 2017. Exposure and input in bilingual development. *Bilingualism: Language and Cognition* 20(1): 3–16.

Caselli, M. C., Bello, A., Rinaldi, P., Stefanini, S. & Pasqualetti, P. 2015. *Il primo vocabolario del bambino: Gesti, parole e frasi. Valori di riferimento fra 8 e 36 mesi delle Forme complete e delle Forme brevi del questionario MacArthur-Bates CDI*. Milano: Franco Angeli.

Caselli, M. C., Leonard, L. B., Volterra, V. & Campagnoli, M. G. 1993. Toward mastery of Italian morphology: A cross-sectional study. *Journal of Child Language* 20(2): 377–393.

Chini, M. 1995a. *Genere grammaticale e acquisizione. Aspetti della morfologia nominale in italiano L2*. Milano: Francoangeli.

Chini, M. 1995b. Grammatiche a confronto: La categoria grammaticale del genere nella competenza di nativi italofoni e nelle interlingue di apprendenti dell'italiano come L2. In *L'universo delle lingue. Confrontare lingue e grammatiche nella scuola, Quaderni del Giscel*, P. Desideri (ed.), 277–294. Firenze: La Nuova Italia.

Chini, M. 1998. Genuserwerb des Italienischen durch deutsche Lerner. In *Eine zweite Sprache lernen*, H. Wegener (ed.), 39–60. Tübingen: Narr.

Chomsky, N. 1995. *The Minimalist Program*. Cambridge MA: The MIT Press.

Chomsky, N. 2005. Three factors in language design. *Linguistic Inquiry* 36(1): 1–22.

Chomsky, N. 2007. Approaching UG from below. In *Interfaces + Recursion = Language?: Chomsky's Minimalism and the View from Syntax-Semantics*, U. Sauerland & H.-M. Gärtner (eds), 1–29. Berlin: Mouton de Gruyter.

Cipriani, P., Chilosi, A. M., Bottari, P. & Pfanner, L. 1993. *L'acquisizione della morfosintassi in ita-liano: Fasi e processi*. Padua: Unipress.

Corbett, G. G. 1991. *Gender*. Cambridge: CUP.

Corbett, G. G. 2006. Gender, grammatical. In *Encyclopedia of Language & Linguistics*, K. Brown (ed.), 749–756. Oxford: Elsevier.

De Martino, M., Bracco, G. & Laudanna, A. 2011. The activation of grammatical gender information in processing Italian nouns. *Language and Cognitive Processes* 26(4–6): 745–776.

Dressler, W. U. & Thornton, A. M. 1996. Italian nominal inflection. *Wiener Linguistische Gazette*, 55–57, 1–24.

Eichler, N. 2011. *Code-Switching bei bilingualen Kindern. Eine Analyse der gemischtsprachlichen Nominalphrasen unter besonderer Berücksichtigung des Genus*. Tübingen: Narr.

Eichler, N., Hager, M. & Müller, N. 2012. Code-switching within the DP and gender assignment in bilingual children: French, Italian, Spanish and German. *Zeitschrift für französische Sprache und Literatur* 122(3): 227–258.

Eichler, N., Jansen, V. & Müller, N. 2013. Gender in French-German, Italian-German, Spanish-German and Italian-French children. *International Journal of Bilingualism* 17(5): 550–572.

Ezeizabarrena, M-J. & Garcia, F. I. 2018. Length of utterance, in morphemes or in Words? MLU3-w, a reliable measure of language development in early Basque. *Frontiers in Psychology* 8: 2265.

Ferrari, F. 2005. A Syntactic Analysis of the Nominal Systems of Italian and Luganda: How Nouns Can Be Formed in the Syntax. PhD dissertation, New York University.

Fey, S. 2020. Der Genuserwerb am Beispiel eines trilingualen Kindes: Spanisch, Italienisch und Französisch im Vergleich. Bachelor's thesis, University of Hamburg.

Gudmundson, A. 2010. *L'acquisizione del genere grammaticale in italiano L2*. Stockholm: US-AB.

Hager, M. 2014. Der Genuserwerb bei mehrsprachig aufwachsenden Kindern – Eine longitudinale Untersuchung bilingualer und trilingualer Kinder der Sprachkombinationen deutsch-französisch/italienisch/spanisch, französisch-italienisch/spanisch und deutsch-spanisch-katalanisch. PhD dissertation, Bergische Universität Wuppertal.

Hauser-Grüdl, N., Arencibia Guerra, L., Witzmann, F., Leray, E. & Müller, N. 2010. Cross-linguistic influence in bilingual children: Can input frequency account for it? *Lingua* 120(11): 2638–2650.

Holmberg, A. & Roberts, I. 2014. Parameters and the three factors of language design. In *Linguistic Variation in the Minimalist Framework*, C. M. Picallo (ed.), 61–81. Oxford: OUP.

Ivanova-Sullivan, T. & Sekerina, I. A. 2019. Distributional regularity of cues facilitates gender acquisition: A contrastive study of two closely related languages. In *Proceedings of the 43rd Annual Boston University Conference on Language Development*, M. M. Brown & B. Dailey (eds), 311–323. Somerville MA: Cascadilla Press.

Jakubowicz, C. & Faussart, C. 1998. Gender agreement in the processing of spoken French. *Journal of Psycholinguistic Research* 27(6): 597–617.

Kramer, R. 2009. Definite Markers, Phi Features and Agreement: A Morphosyntactic Investigation of the Amharic DP. PhD dissertation, University of California, Santa Cruz.

Kupisch, T. 2006. *The Acquisition of Determiners in Bilingual German-Italian and German-French Children*. Munich: Lincom.

Kupisch, T., Müller, N. & Cantone, K. F. 2002. Gender in monolingual and bilingual first language acquisition: Comparing Italian and French. *Lingue e Linguaggio* 1(1): 107–149.

Lampitelli, N. 2010. Nounness, gender, class and syntactic structures in Italian nouns. In *Romance Languages and Linguistic Theory: Selected Papers from 'Going Romance' Groningen 2008*, B. Bok-Bennema, B. Kampers-Mahne & B. Hollebrandse (eds), 195–214. Amsterdam: John Benjamins.

Leonard, L. B., Caselli, M. C. & Devescovi, A. 2005. Italian children's use of verb and noun morphology during the preschool years. *First Language* 22(3): 287–304.

Longobardi, G. 2006. A minimalist program for parametric linguistics? In *Organizing Grammar: Linguistic Studies in Honor of Henk van Riemsdijk*, H. Broekhuis, N. Corver, R. Huybregts, U. Kleinhenz & J. Koster (eds), 407–414. Berlin: De Gruyter Mouton.

Loporcaro, M. 2018. *Gender from Latin to Romance*. Oxford: OUP.

Lowenstamm, J. 2007. On little n, ROOT, and types of nouns. In *The Sounds of Silence: Empty Elements in Syntax and Phonology*, J. Hartmann, V. Hegedus & H. V. Riemsdijk (eds), 105–143. Oxford: Elsevier.

Lowenstamm, J. 2012. Feminine and gender, or why the feminine profile of French nouns has nothing to do with gender. In *Linguistic Inspirations. Edmund Gussmann In Memoriam*, E. Cyran, H. Kardela & B. Szymanek (eds), 371–406. Lublin: Wydawnictwo Katolicki Uniwersytet Lubelski.

MacWhinney, B. 1978. The acquisition of morphophonology. *Monographs of the Society for Research in Child Development* 43(1/2): 1–123.

Maratsos, M. P. & Chalkley, M. A. 1980. The internal language of children's syntax: The nature and ontogenesis of syntactic categories. In *Children's Language*, Vol. II, K. E. Nelson (ed.), 127–214. New York NY: Gardner Press.

Meisel, J. M. 2007. The weaker language in early child bilingualism: Acquiring a first language as a second language? *Applied Psycholinguistics* 28(3): 495–514.

Mills, A. E. 1986. *The Acquisition of Gender: A Study of English and German*. Berlin: Springer.

Müller, N., Arnaus Gil, L., Eichler, N., Geveler, J., Hager, M., Jansen, V., Patuto, M., Repetto, V. & Schmeißer, A. 2015. *Code-Switching: Spanisch, Italienisch, Französisch. Eine Einführung*. Tübingen: Narr.

Müller, N., Kupisch, T., Schmitz, K. & Cantone, K. F. 2011. *Einführung in die Mehrsprachigkeitsforschung: Deutsch, Französisch, Italienisch*. Tübingen: Narr.

Newmeyer, F. J. 2004. Against a parameter-setting approach to typological variation. In *Linguistic Variation Yearbook*, P. Pica (ed.), 181–234. Amsterdam: John Benjamins.

Newmeyer, F. J. 2017. Where, if anywhere, are parameters? A critical historical overview of parametric theory. In *On Looking into Words (and Beyond)*, C. Bowern, L. Horn & R. Zanuttini (eds), 547–569. Berlin: Language Science Press.

Padovani, R. & Cacciari, C. 2003. Il ruolo della trasparenza morfologica delle parole in Italiano. *Giornale Italiano di Psicologia* 4: 749–771.

Pérez-Tattam, R., Ezeizabarrena, M. J., Stadthagen-González, H. & Mueller Gathercole, V. C. 2019. Gender assignment to Spanish pseudowords by monolingual and Basque-Spanish bilingual children. *Languages*, 4(3), 58, 1–18.

Picallo, C. M. 2014. *Linguistic Variation in the Minimalist Framework*. Oxford: OUP.

Pillunat, A. 2007. Der Erwerb des Lexikons durch mehrsprachige Kinder: Französisch, Italienisch und Deutsch im Vergleich. Master's thesis, Bergische Universität Wuppertal.

Pizzuto, E. & Caselli, M. C. 1992. The acquisition of Italian morphology: Implications for models of language development. *Journal of Child Language* 19(3): 491–557.

Reeder, P. A., Newport, E. L. & Aslin, R. N. 2017. Distributional learning of subcategories in an artificial grammar: Category generalization and subcategory restrictions. *Journal of Memory and Language* 97: 17–29.

Rizzi, S. 2013. *Der Erwerb des Adjektivs bei bilingual deutsch-italienischen Kindern*. Tübingen: Narr.

Roberts, I. 2019. *Parameter Hierarchies & Universal Grammar*. Oxford: OUP.

Schmeißer, A., Hager, M., Arnaus Gil, L., Jansen, V., Geveler, J., Eichler, N., Patuto, M. & Müller, N. 2016. Related but different: The two concepts of language dominance and language proficiency. In *Language Dominance in Bilinguals: Issues of Operationalization and Measurement*, C. Silva-Corvalán & J. Treffers-Daller (eds), 36–65. Cambridge: CUP.

Schwartz, M., Minkov, M., Dieser, E., Protassova, E., Moin, V. & Polinsky, M. 2014. Acquisition of Russian gender agreement by monolingual and bilingual children. *International Journal of Bilingualism* 19(6): 726–752.

Serianni, L. 1988. *Grammatica italiana. Suoni forme costrutti*. Torino: UTET.

Smith, N. & Law, A. 2009. On parametric (and non-parametric) variation. *Biolinguistics* 3(4): 332–343.

Stahnke, J. 2022. The Acquisition of French Determiners by Bilingual Children: A Prosodic Account. *Languages* 7: 200.

Teschner, R. & Russell, W. 1984. The gender patterns of Spanish nouns: An inversed dictionary-based analysis. *Hispanic Linguistics* 1(1): 115–132.

Thornton, A. M. 2003. L'assegnazione del genere in italiano. In *Actas del XXIII Congreso Internacional de Lingüística y Filología Románica*, Vol. I, F. Sánchez Miret (ed.), 467–481. Tübingen: Niemeyer.

Thornton, A. M. 2009. Constraining gender assignment rules. *Language Sciences* 31(1): 14–32.

Thornton, A. M., Iacobini, C. & Burani, C. 1997. *BDVDB. Una base di dati sul Vocabolario di Base della lingua italiana*. Roma: Bulzoni.

Tuite, K. 1997. *Svan. Languages of the World / Materials*. Munich: Lincom.

Yip, V. & Matthews, S. 2006. Assessing language dominance in bilingual acquisition: A case for mean length utterance differentials. *Language Assessment Quarterly* 3(2): 97–116.

CHAPTER 4

Gender assignment in German as a heritage language in an English-speaking context
A case study of acquisition and maintenance

Tanja Kupisch[1,2] & Roswita Dressler[3]
[1] University of Konstanz [2] UiT The Arctic University of Norway
[3] University of Calgary

We present a case study of a heritage speaker of German, Luisa, who is growing up in an English-speaking part of Canada, focussing on the acquisition of grammatical gender in German. While German has cues to gender assignment, the acquisition of gender in this setting is compromised by the magnitude of gender cues and form syncretism, and the absence of gender in English. We present longitudinal, naturalistic data from three periods: age 1–2, age 4–5, and age 7. We ask whether Luisa develops grammatical gender akin to monolingual children or whether there are indications of delay, stagnation, or attrition, as observed for heritage speakers of other languages. The results show monolingual-like development despite a shift in dominance from German to English.

Keywords: gender assignment, German, heritage speaker, language dominance, cross-linguistic influence

1. Introduction

Cross-linguistic influence (CLI) in the languages of heritage speakers (HSs) is often said to be *unidirectional*, affecting the heritage language but not the dominant societal language in which HSs tend to be more proficient. With respect to grammatical gender, for example, studies with adult heritage speakers have shown divergent acquisition outcomes from monolingual speakers, including a two-way instead of a three-way gender system (Polinsky 2008), similarities with late bilingual speakers (Montrul et al. 2008), or the occasional assignment of non-target gender (e.g., Bianchi 2013; Stoehr et al. 2012; Kupisch et al. 2013). Moreover, Bianchi (2013), Stoehr et al. (2012), and Kupisch et al. (2013) have compared adult early bilinguals when speaking a majority language and when speaking a heritage language (HL), confirming indeed that only the HL was affected.

A close look at the literature on bilingual development during *childhood* shows that, at least during the age prior to 4 years, CLI can be *bidirectional*, depending not only on language dominance but also on factors such as structural overlap, involvement of an interface,[1] and markedness (see, e.g., Hulk & Müller 2000; Kehoe et al. 2004).[2] This means that during early development, the language in which a bilingual child is more proficient may also be subject to CLI. However, there is a lack of research on what happens between early childhood and adulthood, i.e., when heritage speakers become substantially more exposed to the societal language and (in many cases) shift to that language. In this paper, we will take a closer look at this gap in the literature, which Montrul (2018) has identified as "the missing link". We will do so based on a case study of grammatical gender in a bilingual child who grows up with German as her HL.

Grammatical gender is a well-studied phenomenon in monolingual and bilingual language acquisition, including in early and late bilinguals. The acquisition of gender marking differs across languages depending on the transparency of the gender marking systems being acquired. Transparent systems, such as those in Spanish and Italian, are acquired early (e.g., Kupisch et al. 2002; Pérez-Pereira 1991), while more opaque systems, like those found in Dutch and Norwegian, are late acquired (e.g., Rodina & Westergaard 2015; Unsworth 2013). German appears to be an intermediate case. While there are formal cues to gender assignment on the nouns, these represent merely regularities, and the transparency of structural cues (e.g., articles) is further compromised by interactions between case and gender as well as syncretism. In early bilingual language acquisition, gender marking is subject to CLI and there can positive or negative effects based on the language combinations. English has generally been reported to have a delaying effect on the acquisition of gender systems in other languages (e.g., Unsworth et al. 2014; Kaltsa et al. 2017).

In this paper, we report on a case study of a HS of German, Luisa, who grows up in Calgary (Alberta, Canada), presenting data from three phases that may be considered crucial for the development of the heritage language: the emergence of grammar (1;7–2;7), first schooling in the majority language (4;9–5;5), and primary school (7;1–7;5). We ask whether (1) Luisa shows the same development

---

1. Most authors refer to the syntax-pragmatics interface, but other interfaces have been discussed as well (see Kupisch & Rothman 2016; Lleó 2016)
2. Such bidirectional influence does not necessarily imply that it is bidirectional with respect to one specific phenomenon (although this is a possibility), but rather that depending on the phenomenon (its frequency, markedness, etc.) it can affect either one or the other language.

of the German gender system as monolingual children do, or whether there are differences due to exposure to English (resulting from CLI or simply relatively less exposure to German), and (2) whether there are indications that the development of the gender system stagnates or attrites as exposure to and use of English increases. In doing so, we will focus on gender assignment. We show that gender marking is successfully acquired and maintained despite the aforementioned challenges.

In what follows, we introduce gender marking in German (Section 2) and summarize relevant research on the acquisition of gender (Section 3), before we present the Study (Sections 4 and 5) and discuss the results (Section 6). Before we proceed, however, a note on terminology: We will use the term 'simultaneous bilingual first language learner' (2L1) for children with exposure to two languages between birth and 3 years, while 'early sequential bilingual' (eL2) means first exposure to the second language after the age of 3 years. Heritage speakers (HSs) can be 2L1 or eL2 learners of the majority language. If relevant, this distinction will be made. The abbreviation 'L2' will be used for adult second language learners.

2. Gender marking in German

German has a three-way gender system with masculine, feminine, and neuter gender. Gender is marked on determiners (definite and indefinite articles, demonstratives, possessives) and attributive adjectives, as well as on relative pronouns. Masculine gender is often considered to be the default for assignment because it has the highest frequency, although the distribution of the three genders may vary depending on the type of corpus; in some cases masculine and feminine gender reach equal frequencies (see Corteen 2018 for an overview). Another argument for considering masculine the default gender for assignment is its use with loanwords (Steinmetz 2006). On the other hand, Opitz and Pechmann (2016) have provided evidence that masculine gender requires increased processing load, which would speak against masculine as the default in German. An alternative suggestion has been to consider neuter as the default, because neuter is assigned when verbs and adjectives are converted into nouns (e.g., *rot* 'red' > *das Rot* 'the Red', *lesen* 'read' > *das Lesen* 'the reading'). In short, the question of the default gender in German is still being debated.

The most frequent elements on which gender marking is visible are articles, which are obligatory in most cases with singular count nouns. While gender is a lexical property of the noun, articles receive gender by agreement. Nevertheless, in studies on gender marking, the article has often been taken as an indicator of assignment, the idea being that a speaker who produces der_M $Sonne_F$ 'the sun' does so not because she has problems with agreement but because she takes the noun to be masculine. Strictly speaking, it is unclear whether the problem is due to wrong assignment or wrong agreement. If a speaker produces *der_M $Sonne_F$, they might have (erroneously) assigned masculine gender to the noun and – via "correct" agreement – used the article der_M. Alternatively, the speaker might have correctly assigned feminine gender to the noun but had problems with agreement. If a speaker produces die_F $Sonne_F$, the most obvious interpretation is that both assignment and agreement are correct. However, it is theoretically possible that the speaker has assigned masculine gender by mistake (*$Sonne_M$), but since they also failed to realize correct agreement, ended up producing a correct DP. There would be no way of finding out what the problem is except for asking speakers to justify their choices. Since this is not a possibility when working with small children, we follow previous research, taking the article to be an indicator of assignment, but we acknowledge, for the reasons just mentioned, that this is not entirely unproblematic.

German has two numbers, three genders, and four cases. Gender interacts with number, definiteness, and case, and there is a lot of syncretism, which makes structural cues to nominal gender somewhat opaque. The paradigms of indefinite and definite marked DPs are illustrated in Tables 1 and 2, respectively, with relevant examples in bold. As Table 1 shows, the definite singular article is syncretic with feminine and neuter nouns marked with nominative (NOM) and accusative (ACC) case. Further, although gender is unambiguously marked on definite singular articles in the NOM case, the adjective is underspecified with respect to gender here. By contrast, DPs containing indefinite articles show syncretism between masculine and neuter articles in the NOM case (in spoken German also in the ACC case), but the adjective is unambiguously marked for gender (Table 2). Plural DPs are not marked for gender and there is no indefinite plural article.

Table 1. Examples of gender marking in German (DPs with definite articles)

	Masculine	Feminine	Neuter
NOM, SG	**der schwarze** Hund	**die schwarze** Katze	**das schwarze** Auto
GEN, SG	des schwarzen Hundes	der schwarzen Katze	des schwarzen Autos
DAT, SG	dem schwarzen Hund	der schwarzen Katze	dem schwarzen Auto
ACC, SG	den schwarzen Hund	**die schwarze** Katze	**das schwarze** Auto
NOM, PL		die schwarzen Hunde/Katzen/Autos	
GEN, PL		der schwarzen Hunde/Katzen/Autos	

Table 1. (continued)

	Masculine	Feminine	Neuter
DAT, PL		den schwarzen Hunden/Katzen/Autos	
ACC, PL		die schwarzen Hunde/Katzen/Autos	
	'the black dog/s'	'the black cat/s'	'the black car/s'

Table 2. Examples of gender marking in German (DPs with indefinite articles)

	Masculine	Feminine	Neuter
NOM, SG	ein **schwarzer** Hund	eine **schwarze** Katze	ein **schwarzes** Auto
GEN, SG	eines schwarzen Hundes	einer schwarzen Katze	eines schwarzen Autos
DAT, SG	einem schwarzen Hund	einer schwarzen Katze	einem schwarzen Auto
ACC, SG	einen schwarzen Hund	eine schwarze Katze	ein **schwarzes** Auto
	'a black dog'	'a black cat'	'a black car'

Besides structural cues to nominal gender (i.e., elements in syntactic agreement with the noun), there are also morphological, phonological, and semantic cues. German generally follows the natural gender rule in that nouns referring to male persons are masculine, and nouns referring to female persons are feminine (e.g., $Mann_M$ 'man', $Lehrer_M$ 'teacher' vs. $Frau_F$ 'woman', $Lehrerin_F$ 'teacher'), but there are some exceptions. Moreover, gender is sometimes also assigned according to semantic fields, e.g., nouns referring to chemicals tend to have neuter gender ($Blei_N$ 'lead', $Kadmium_N$ 'cadmium'), nouns denoting alcoholic beverages tend to have masculine gender ($Wein_M$ 'wine', Gin_M 'gin'), and nouns denoting sciences are feminine ($Linguistik_F$ 'linguistics', $Psychologie_F$ 'psychology') (Köpcke & Zubin 1996). These rules have psycholinguistic validity, although they apply to relatively small noun classes (Schwichtenberg & Schiller 2004).

German also has a number of morphological rules, as specific suffixes are associated with specific genders. For example, the derivational suffixes *-heit, -keit, -ung, -schaft,* and *-ei*, all forming abstract nouns, are associated with feminine gender. Other suffixes are associated with neuter gender, such as the diminutive suffixes *-chen* and *-lein* and the prefix *ge-*, which adds the meaning 'collective' to a noun (Heidolph et al. 1984; Mills 1986; MacWhinney et al. 1989). Another morphological rule is the 'Last-Member Principle' (Köpcke & Zubin 1984), which states that compound nouns are assigned the gender of the final segment, e.g., $Wein_M$ 'wine', $Glas_N$ 'glass' → $Weinglas_N$ 'wine glass'. There are also non-suffixal endings ("pseudo-suffixes") based on which gender can be reliably predicated, e.g., nouns in -*el*, -*en*, and -*er* are associated with masculine gender (Heidolph et al. 1984; MacWhinney et al. 1989).

Finally, there are numerous phonological cues to gender assignment, but they reflect probabilistic tendencies rather than rules. The most frequently mentioned regularity is the schwa-rule, according to which dysyllabic nouns ending in [ə] are associated with feminine gender (e.g., *Katze$_F$* 'cat'). Moreover, monosyllabic nouns beginning or ending in consonants tend to be associated with masculine gender. In a detailed analysis of adult language, Köpcke (1982) and Köpcke and Zubin (1983, 1984) showed associations of the endings of monosyllabic nouns and their initial sounds with (mostly masculine) gender. For example, monosyllabic words beginning with [kn], [dr], [tr], and [s]+consonant, nouns ending in nasal+consonant, and nouns with two initial and two final consonants tend to be masculine. Some monosyllabic nouns, however, are associated with feminine gender, e.g., nouns ending in [ft], [xt], [uːr], or [yːr] (Köpcke & Zubin 1983:169).

3. The acquisition of gender (with a focus on German)

3.1 Monolingual German children

The acquisition of gender is closely related to the acquisition of articles, because articles are the most frequent gender-marked elements. Based on naturalistic, longitudinal data, Mills (1986:63) reports first uses of definite articles around age 1;10–2;2, and Stern and Stern (1928:44, 86) around 1;2–1;10. However, children's earliest articles are often not gender-marked but constitute reduced or underspecified forms like *ei* or *de*. Such forms can be considered proto-articles, which have the function of marking a syntactic position while the acquisition of morphology lags behind (e.g., Bottari et al. 1993/1994). Sporadic use of gender-marked articles is reported from age 2;0–2;4 in Mills' data and from 1;9 in Bittner (2006), although Bittner argues that children's early articles do not mark gender but case. In a larger dataset with six children aged 1;4–3;8, Szagun et al. (2007) report article use from age 1;5 onwards, though with substantial individual variation. Article omission is frequent until the age of 2;6, and it is possible that children omit articles to avoid using forms they are not certain about (Kupisch 2006; Mills 1986; Lindauer in prep.).

First use has to be distinguished from "acquisition", defined here as the point when children cease to make mistakes in gender marking (90% accuracy). In both Mills' (1986) and Szagun et al.'s (2007) studies, error rates drop to a very low level by age 3;0. However, error rates can vary across children and seem to be mildly correlated with the frequencies of individual nouns in adult child-directed speech.

Finally, children vary in terms of whether they use definite or indefinite articles first (Szagun et al. 2007).

There is some evidence for children's early awareness of phonological regularities and the natural gender rule, but it is difficult to exclude competing factors. As mentioned above, it is not clear whether German children's earliest articles show morphological markings, including gender agreement. Based on longitudinal data, Mills (1986: 64) observed that the feminine indefinite article *eine* was the most common early form, used also with nouns of masculine or neuter gender. When indefinite articles became more frequent, there was fluctuation between *ein* and *eine*, sometimes in combination with the same noun. Mills speculated that the incorrect use of the indefinite article may be due to "the high frequency of the ending *-e* in the article and adjective paradigms [...] leading to an overgeneralization of the *-e* ending on all prenominal units."[3] Definite articles appeared later than indefinite articles. When errors with definites occurred, *die* was the most frequently overused form, and the children produced far more definite articles with feminine nouns than with nouns of the other two genders. On the other hand, *die* also occurred with nouns containing masculine cues, e.g., *Hund* (monosyllabic nouns tend to be masculine) and *Bagger* (*-er* is a cue for masculine), suggesting that the early use of *die* cannot be due to the acquisition of the feminine cue alone (i.e., the high frequency of the schwa-ending). Mills' account is largely in line with Stern and Stern (1928), who reported a distinction between masculine and feminine forms by 2;6 as well as gender errors resulting from overuse of *die*. In terms of specific phonological cues, masculine articles have been reported to be combined with monosyllabic nouns (Mills 1986: 83; Müller 1990: 227; Wegener 1995: 16) and nouns ending in *-el, -en*, and *-er* (Szagun et al. 2007). There is massive evidence that children combine *die* with nouns ending in schwa: see Mills (1986: 85) for L1 German, Müller (1994: 214) and Eichler et al. (2013) for 2L1 German-Romance, Dieser (2009) for 2L1 German-Russian, and Wegener (1995: 16) and Ruberg (2013) for eL2 German. It is also typical that when there are errors with feminine nouns, children tend to use masculine gender instead, when errors occur with neuter nouns, masculine is used instead, and when errors are made with masculine nouns, feminine is used instead. Feminine and neuter are rarely substituted for one another (Mills 1986).

The study that has attempted the most fine-grained quantification of phonological cues and gender marking in German child speech is Szagun et al. (2007). They classified children's nouns in terms of five classes (in the following referred to as "assignment classes"):

---

3. The use of the orthographic ending *-e* in this quote might be a bit misleading. The author refers to the aforementioned schwa-ending.

I.   Polysyllabic nouns ending in -*e*;
II. Monosyllabic nouns with final and/or initial consonants;
III. Polysyllabic nouns ending in -*el, -en,* and *er*;
IV. Polysyllabic nouns with specific endings and deterministic gender assignment (e.g., masculine words ending in -*or, -ig, -ling, -ist*);
V.   nouns not following any pattern.

In classes I–III, they further distinguished between nouns following the general assignment patterns (i.e., F in class I; M in classes II and III) and nouns not following these patterns. They found errors to be more frequent when nouns did *not* follow the general assignment pattern, which points to children's sensitivity to these cues.

Overall, despite individual variation, the following tendencies have been observed for the acquisition of gender by monolingual German children: (i) although the German gender marking system poses challenges, children's development of gender in German happens comparatively fast, (ii) it is possible that children's first determiner-like forms (in German) are not marked for gender, (iii) the omission of articles or the use of underspecified forms may be strategies to avoid gender marking, (iv) children seem to be sensitive to some phonological and/or semantic cues, and (v) feminine definite articles emerge early and neuter articles late.

3.2   The acquisition of gender by bilingual children

There is some evidence that the development of gender systems in bilingual children largely resembles monolingual development. In Müller's (1999) study of three German French children, gender was marked from around 1;10–2;4. Initially, the children mostly omitted determiners, except for French *un* and German *ein*, which seemed to be used as numerals and irrespectively of the gender of the noun they preceded. Subsequently, the children started using determiners productively and assigned gender based on phonological and semantic criteria. The children (over)used feminine definite articles with nouns ending in schwa, even if these nouns were masculine. For instance, they produced *die*$_F$ *Hase*$_M$ 'rabbit' or *die*$_F$ *Affe*$_M$ 'monkey', or they used the correct gender but adjusted the noun ending, as in *der *Aff* 'the monkey' (monosyllabic nouns being associated with masculine). One of the children also overused *der* with monosyllabic nouns (*der*$_M$ *Haus*$_N$ 'house', *der*$_M$ *Geld*$_N$ 'money', *der*$_M$ *Bett*$_N$ 'bed'), indicating sensitivity to the tendency for monosyllabic nouns to be masculine. The definite neuter article occurred comparatively late (ages 2;4–2;8) and remained a problem until the age of 5; neuter nouns were initially classified as masculine (Müller 1999: 393).

Eichler et al. (2013) also investigated gender marking in 2L1 children (ages 2;0–3.5 years) acquiring a Romance language along with German. Knowledge of cues was not explicitly addressed, but they mention the that children were aware of the schwa-rule, as was evident from overgeneralizations such as *die_F Junge_M* 'the boy' (p. 565), and that neuter gender posed more problems than the other two genders. Although many of the children grew up in Germany, the bilingual children made more assignment errors in German than in their Romance languages, suggesting that the transparency of the assignment system can be more important than language dominance. In a study of several children acquiring German along with a Romance language, Hager (2014) found that the children showed gender agreement with the definite article, while indefinite articles showed inconsistent agreement with the same nouns (e.g., *die_F Maus_F, eine_F Maus_F, ein_N Maus_F* 'ART mouse'). This indicates that (at least some) children do not overuse particular genders but particular article forms (see also Granfeldt 2018: 685).

While the aforementioned studies indicate that 2L1 children show similar acquisition paths and similar types of errors as monolinguals, considering bilingual studies more widely conveys a rather heterogeneous picture. One intervening factor is CLI, which can affect *gender discovery*, i.e., the moment when children start marking gender on gender targets (e.g., articles or adjectives) and the *rate of correct gender marking*. The idea behind studies focusing on CLI in the acquisition of grammatical gender is that a language with a more transparent gender marking system can influence a language with a less transparent gender marking system positively (resulting in acceleration) or, conversely, that a language with a less transparent gender marking system can affect a language with a more transparent system negatively (resulting in deceleration) (see Cornips & Hulk 2008; Eichler et al. 2013; Hulk & van der Linden 2010; Kupisch et al. 2002 for various cases of acceleration and deceleration).

Hager (2014) addressed the question whether the language combination plays a role by comparing bilingual children who all have German as one of their languages, but who differ in terms of their Romance language. She found that the acquisition of German was affected more when German was acquired along with French as compared to German being acquired along with Catalan, Italian, or Spanish. This indicates that the transparency of the gender marking system of the contact language plays a role (French having the least transparent system of the aforementioned Romance languages). Having a second L1 without any gender marking system may be seen as an even greater disadvantage. Unsworth et al. (2014: 793) have found disadvantages for Greek-English bilinguals compared to Greek-Dutch bilinguals. Similarly, Kaltsa et al. (2017) have shown that Albanian-Greek bilinguals were more aware of gender values in Greek compared to English-

Greek bilinguals, arguably because Albanian has gender while English does not.[4] Schwartz et al. (2015) reported that Russian-German and Russian-Hebrew bilinguals had an advantage over Russian-English and Russian-Finnish bilinguals in terms of error rates, although all bilinguals were found to make the same types of errors.

Other studies have focused on German as an eL2. Wegener (1995) investigated children with Polish, Russian, and Turkish as their L1s. The children started out using bare nominals; amongst their first articles *ein* was the most frequent indefinite and *die* the most frequent definite article, arguably due to the high token frequency of these forms in the input. Subsequently, children used articles for case-marking or argument-marking functions: *r*-forms (e.g., *der*) for subjects, *s*-forms (e.g., *das*) for direct objects, and *e*-forms (e.g., *die*) for plurals (see also Bittner 2006). The children eventually used articles successfully, according to Wegener (1995: 15) primarily due to lexical learning, but they also showed sensitivity to formal rules. For example, after only 13–15 months of exposure, the L1-Polish and L1-Russian children assigned masculine gender to monosyllabic nouns and nouns in *-er*, and feminine gender to nouns ending in schwa. The L1 Turkish children in grade 4 performed at chance, possibly due to the absence of gender in Turkish. Ruberg (2013) also studied sequential bilingual children (ages 4;0–6;3) with the same HLs as Wegener. Despite some quantitative differences, there were qualitative similarities between the groups: All children, except for the L1-Turkish children, made use of morpho-phonological cues, assigning gender more often correctly if the nouns ended in schwa (associated with feminine) or were monosyllabic (associated with masculine). When a noun did not exhibit a prominent gender cue, children mainly defaulted to masculine. Generally speaking, these studies show that at least some eL2 children are sensitive to assignment rules, but, as observed before, children whose L1 has a gender system have an advantage over children whose L1 has no grammatical gender.

One factor that potentially contributes to mixed results in eL2 studies is the role of age of onset (AoO). According to Carroll (1999), after age 4–5, children whose L1 does not have grammatical gender, are unable to acquire this feature in an L2 and need to resort to item-based learning (Carroll 1989: 581). They also seem to be especially sensitive to natural gender cues (Carroll 1999), unlike L1 learners. Meisel (2018) further claims that the gender-marking on determiners produced by children with first exposure after 3;7 is inconsistent with the generalisations made by (2)L1 children with exposure from birth, even if their other language has gender. He has identified the following criteria that differentiate the acquisition of

---

4. However, the authors mention that an alternative explanation could have been that the Albanian-Greek children were simply more proficient.

gender in 2L1 acquisition as opposed to L2 acquisition (Meisel 2018: 8). These criteria can help us identify qualitatively different acquisition patterns:

(1) a. 2L1 children go through a developmental stage of article omission, while this is not the case for adult L2 learners.
b. 2L1 children often start with one article type, while L2 learners tend to use definite and indefinite articles from the start.[5]
c. L2 learners show higher rates of gender assignment errors at the initial stage and their gender assignment errors persist for a longer period of time.
d. L2 learners show more fluctuation in the rate of errors (sometimes over periods of 24 months).
e. In 2L1 acquisition, gender assignment errors are often due to rule-based overgeneralizations of formal properties of nouns, while L2ers tends to overuse only one gender form (which may differ between definites and indefinites).

Lemmerth and Hopp's (2018) study on lexical and syntactic CLI in German-Russian bilinguals (2L1 and eL2) speaks to the role of AoO in gender marking. In production, the children assigned gender correctly independently of whether the respective nouns had congruent or different genders in the children's two languages. However, when eye-tracking data was used to investigate whether the children use articles and adjectives to anticipate the noun (and its gender), differences between simultaneous and sequential learners emerged. The 2L1 bilinguals behaved like monolingual controls, while the eL2 bilinguals made use of gender marking only with nouns that had equivalent genders in the two languages. This may imply that sequential bilinguals assign gender in the L2 by first accessing the lexicon of their L1, while there is no such influence in 2L1 bilinguals.

In contrast to studies highlighting the role of AoO, Montrul et al. (2008) presented data from HSs of Spanish showing that despite exposure to the language from birth, these learners made similar errors to late bilinguals, suggesting that variable and insufficient input played a role. Their ideas resonate with earlier claims by Schlyter (1993), who submitted that most studies supporting parallel developments in bilinguals and monolinguals were based on bilinguals with two equally strong languages. In cases of unbalanced simultaneous bilinguals, however, the weaker language may share some feature with an L2 (Schlyter 1993). This is why the criteria in (1a)–(1e) above are also relevant to 2L1 acquisition. Indeed,

---

5. This criterion may be considered problematic, because Szagun et al. (2007) have shown that some L1 German children start using definites and indefinites simultaneously. Also, there may be differences in L2 acquisition depending on whether the learner's L1 has no articles, both definites and indefinites, or just one of the two articles.

even very transparent gender marking systems, such as Russian, may be affected in minority language settings, as shown by Polinsky's (2008) example of Russian HSs in the US, who developed a two-way gender system instead of a three-way system.

3.3 Research questions

As shown in the literature overview, 2L1 bilinguals acquiring two languages with articles have been shown to pattern with monolinguals with respect to qualitative aspects of gender development (trajectory and error type), but there may be delays, especially if the children's other language has no gender. Furthermore, the claim has been made that some HSs might show L2-like properties despite exposure from birth. Meisel's criteria, summarized in (1a) through (1e) above, provide an excellent basis to investigate the latter claim. With these observations in mind, we pose the following questions:

RQ1. Does the development of German as a HL resemble that of monolingual and bilingual German children with other language combinations in a quantitative way (delays compared to monolinguals) and/or qualitative way (L2-like or qualitatively different errors from monolinguals)?

RQ2. Are there any signs of stagnation or attrition after a substantial increase in majority language exposure?

We investigated these questions based on corpus data from a bilingual German-English child with German as her heritage language. As to RQ1, it is possible that similar acquisition patterns as in monolingual German children are found because the child has comparatively little exposure to English during the early stages of acquisition. Another possibility is that the acquisition of gender marking is slowed down compared to monolinguals and/or shows qualitative differences from monolinguals, since previous studies with 2L1 and eL2 children have shown that exposure to another L1 without a gender-marking system (e.g., English) can slow down acquisition or even lead to L2-like patterns, as reported by Schlyter (1993) for simultaneous bilinguals for properties other than gender marking.

Previous research is rather inconclusive concerning the relative importance of AoO and frequency of exposure. Following Carroll (1989), qualitative differences from monolingual development are expected with an AoO after 5 years. This would also follow from Meisel (2018), who provided evidence for a sensitive phase around the age of three and a half years. Since Luisa has been exposed to German from birth, neither Carroll (1989) nor Meisel (2018) would predict such qualitative differences. On the other hand, since Montrul et al. (2008) have shown

L2-like acquisition outcomes for adult HSs, insufficient exposure during childhood might also play a role. Therefore, concerning RQ2, one possible outcome for the present study is stagnation or attrition during periods when exposure to English becomes more massive (Luisa's Phases 2 and 3). This might even be the case if no differences from monolinguals are observed during Phase 1. Alternatively, it is possible that Luisa's gender marking system is monolingual-like because it has stabilized and is invulnerable to reduced use and exposure to German and/or increasing use and exposure to English.

4. Study

4.1 Participant

This study follows Luisa, a child growing up with German and English in the urban centre of Calgary in western Canada. She was born in Canada, has two German-speaking parents and an older brother. Luisa's mother and primary caregiver is a native speaker of German, born in Germany, who immigrated to Canada as an adult nine years before Luisa's birth. At the time of the study, she and the brother (less than 2 years older) spoke German 100% of the time with Luisa. Luisa's father was born to German-speaking parents in Canada. He used mostly German with Luisa and English only 10% of the time. German was the family home language.

Luisa has grandparents in Canada, who live in a nearby town. They mostly spoke German to her and served as her caregivers on occasion. The mother reported that the German-speaking grandparents used English only 20% of the time with Luisa. Luisa's other set of grandparents live in Hamburg, Germany and the family visits them for two weeks on an annual basis. The mother also reported daily reading of German books. Luisa did not attend English daycare because the grandparents or other German-speaking friends or relatives watched her. She had a German playgroup with other German-English bilinguals that she met once a week. As a result, Luisa was growing up in Canada, surrounded by English, but until age 3;9 she heard primarily German. However, she lived in an English-dominant neighbourhood and was exposed to English outside of the home. She was also exposed to English whenever non-German-speaking family members or friends of the family came to visit.

Three time periods in childhood are important to this investigation of bilingual language development. **Phase 1**, from ages 1;10–2;7, represents Luisa's early childhood years, during which her primary contact with English was interactions with her English-speaking cousins. **Phase 2** (4;9–5;5) corresponds with the year in which Luisa began formal schooling. Between Phases 1 and 2, at age 3;9, Luisa began preschool in English, which she attended for two half days a week (2×2.5 h/wk) for the school year (September to June). At age 4;9, when Phase 2 began, she started to attend half-day Kindergarten[6] (5×2.5 h/wk). During that school year, she also continued to attend half-day preschool two mornings a week (2×2.5 h/wk) and scheduled sports lessons (1.5 h/wk), resulting in regular contact with English speakers. This contact added up to approximately 19 hours a week in an English-only environment during Phase 2. **Phase 3** of the study occurred during the second half of Luisa's grade two school year. She was 7;1–7;5 years of age. By this time, she had been in full day schooling in English (5×6 h/wk) for 1.5 years. She also continued to take part in extracurricular activities conducted in English. The family maintained German as the primary home language. We observed during all three phases that Luisa responded to her parents in German. Table 3 summarizes an estimated percentage of relative exposure during the three phases.[7]

Table 3. Estimated percentage of exposure based on parental questionnaire

	English	German
Phase 1	minimal	100%
Phase 2	20%	80%
Phase 3	50%	50%

4.2 Data collection

The free speech data collected over the course of this study consists of video and audio recordings in both German and English. Video recordings were used in Phase 1 when Luisa was very young, oblivious to the camera and videographer, and the use of video assisted the transcription. One researcher, the first author and a native speaker of German, played with Luisa, interacting in German, while a research assistant recorded the session. After 30 minutes the adults switched places and the interaction continued in an English mode with the research assistant, a native speaker of English who did not know German. This order was alternated in subsequent sessions such that the sessions did not always begin

---

6. Since Luisa's birthday falls in December, she was eligible to begin Kindergarten in September of the year she turned five. In other words, she began Kindergarten at age 4;9.

7. We assume that Luisa is awake 13 h/day and 7 days/wk (=91 h), then 19 h/wk of English exposure (=17%), rounded up in case she read English books at home or visited English speaking family. The mother listed German movies/TV and audiobooks as "often" (1.5 h/day) and English movies/TV and audiobooks as "less often" (1.5 h/wk).

with the same language. In Phases 2 and 3, the researcher used an MP3 audio recorder, which was less conspicuous and did not require an additional researcher in the room. In these phases, the second author interacted with Luisa in English, recorded the session and then left the recorder for Luisa's mother to use. Luisa's mother then recorded a session of her interacting in German with Luisa.

While many of the sessions were free play sessions, some contained targeted interactions in which Luisa was asked to tell a story from a picture book. All of the recordings were approximately 30 minutes each and were transcribed for analysis. During Phase 1 there were fewer recordings in English than in German because the interaction was difficult when Luisa was smaller, especially during the English part of the recording, which had to be interrupted twice. Luisa, realizing the research assistant's inability to understand German, sometimes refused to play with her interlocutor. The total number of recordings amounts to (German/English) 13/10.5 hours in Phase 1, 3.5/3 hours in Phase 2, and 2.5/3 hours in Phase 3.

For a first impression of Luisa's development in the two languages, we calculated the word-based MLU (mean length of utterances). It shows that the two-word stage was reached earlier in German, and that German developed faster during Phase 1. By the time Phase 2 started, Luisa's proficiency in English had increased substantially, as reflected by the higher MLU in this language.

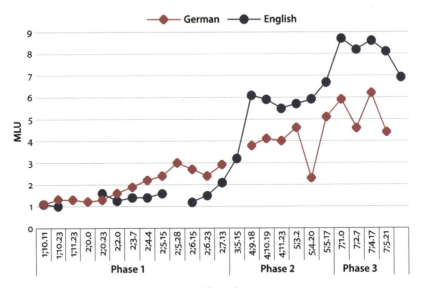

Figure 1. Overview of recordings and word-based MLU

4.3 Coding

All instances of DPs (excluding proper nouns) were extracted from the transcriptions. Cases in which either the article or the noun was not clearly comprehensible and mixed DPs containing German and English elements (e.g., *die cat, a Katze*) were excluded, which led to exclusion of 1.0% of the data (see Table 2). The remaining DPs were coded in terms of (i) whether a determiner was used or not, (ii) number (singular and plural), and (iii) occurrence within a prepositional phrase. The coding was done by two research assistants (native speakers of German) and double-checked by the first author.

Since plural DPs are not marked for gender, they were excluded, which led to the exclusion of 8.4% of the data. Licit determiner omissions without any gender marker (bare plural and mass nouns, exclamations, nouns following certain prepositions) were also excluded (25.9%). Articles following prepositions (as separate words and as contractions) were excluded due to ambiguity (9.4%). For example, the PP *in Haus* could the spoken contracted form of *in ein$_N$ Haus$_N$* 'into a house' (sometimes spelled as *in' Haus*), which would be correctly gender-marked or an instance of incorrect gender assignment *in ein(en)$_M$ Haus$_N$* 'into a house'.[8] All other DPs, i.e., those with indefinite and definite articles as well as other gender-marked determiners (possessive pronouns and demonstratives) were coded for gender marking. Table 4 provides an overview.

Table 4. Overview of coded NPs/DPs

	Phase 1	Phase 2	Phase 3	Total
DPs coded for gender marking (*die/meine Katze* 'the/my cat')	373 (41.9%)	124 (35.1%)	220 (38.7%)	717 (39.6%)
Licit bare Ns (*Katzenfutter* 'cat food', *Katzen* 'cats')	157 (17.6%)	108 (30.6%)	205 (36.1%)	470 (25.9%)
Bare Singular Ns (*Katze* 'cat', *Auto* 'car')	255 (28.6%)	–	–	255 (14.1%)
Proto-determiner + N (*ei Katze, a Katze* 'D cat')	21 (2.4%)	–	–	21 (1.2%)
PPs (*mitn Auto* 'with the car', *im Netz* 'in the net', *aufm Blatt* 'on the leaf')	37 (4.2%)	81 (22.9%)	52 (9.2%)	170 (9.4%)
Plural DPs (*die/ alle/viele Katzen* 'the/all/many cats')	37 (4.2%)	38 (10.8%)	77 (13.6%)	152 (8.4%)

---

8. In addition, DPs embedded in PPs frequently involve dative case, which is more error prone than nominative and accusative case; in many such cases it is impossible to tease apart case marking errors and gender-marking errors.

Table 4. (continued)

	Phase 1	Phase 2	Phase 3	Total
DPs w/ unclear reference (*ei Klötze* 'a cubes', *den rechten* 'the right')	4 (0.4%)	–	5 (0.9%)	9 (0.5%)
Mixed DPs (*ein Truck* 'a truck')	3 (0.3%)	2 (0.6%)	9 (1.6%)	14 (0.8%)
Partially incomprehensible DPs (*ein xxx, xxx Katze*)	4 (0.4%)	–	–	4 (0.2%)
	891	353	568	1812

5. Results

In this section we report quantitative and qualitative data on gender marking for the three Phases. For RQ1, which concerns development, Phase 1 is particularly relevant. For RQ2, which concerns stagnation or attrition, Phases 2 and 3 are more relevant.

For a first overview, Table 5 summarizes the number of noun types and tokens with error rates across Phases. Phase 1 has been divided into two phases. In Phase 1a (until 2;3.7) omission dominates and only indefinite articles are used. In Phase 1b (after 2;3.7) omissions have ceased and both definite and indefinite articles are used (see also Figure 2 below). Error rates decrease over time but are already low from the beginning. All the three genders are used from the start.

Table 5. Overview of gender assignment

	Gender marking (Incorrect/Total)		Distribution of genders		
	Types*	Tokens	Masculine	Feminine	Neuter
Phase 1a	3/50 (6%)	5/91 (5.5%)	27 (54%)	7 (14%)	16 (32%)
Phase 1b	4/107 (3.7%)	4/282 (1.4%)	31 (29%)	42 (39.2%)	34 (31.8%)
Phase 2	4/100 (4%)	4/124 (3.2%)	49 (49%)	30 (30%)	21 (21%)
Phase 3	3/175 (1.7%)	3/220 (1.4%)	70 (40%)	60 (34.3%)	45 (25.7%)

* If an item occurred both correctly and incorrectly gender-marked, they were counted as separate types.

5.1 Phase 1 (Early development)

Figure 2 shows absolute numbers of determiner use and article omission in obligatory contexts during Phase 1. Articles are found from the first recording at 1;10.11, but omissions predominate until 2;3.7. At 2;5.15, article omission drops below 10%.

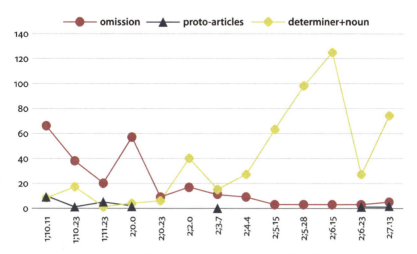

Figure 2. Article omission and determiner use (absolute numbers)

In the early Phase 1, DPs with non-target-like gender marking amounts to 6% (Types) and 5.5% (Tokens); in the late Phase 1 to 3.7% (Types) and 1.4% (Tokens) (see Table 5).

The period before 2;0.23, characterized by article omissions, shows a very small number of proto-articles (*ei*) and some instances of the masculine/neuter indefinite *ein* and its reduced variant *'n* (triangles in Figure 2). Omission and (proto-)article use are in free variation, i.e., occurring with the same nouns (e.g., Ø/*'n*/*ei Schaf*$_N$ 'sheep'; Ø/*'n*/*ei Pferd*$_N$ 'horse'). *Ein*$_{M/N}$ is used independently of nominal gender, i.e., including with nouns of feminine gender (*ein Katze*$_F$ 'cat', *ein Tür*$_F$ 'door').

At 2;2.0, the feminine indefinite *eine*$_F$ starts to be used along with *ein*, *'n*, and *einen*. Articles mostly agree in gender, except in three cases: *eine$_F$ *Schrank*$_M$ 'a closet', *einen$_M$ *Tür*$_F$ 'a door', and *eine$_F$ *Bauwagen*$_M$ 'a construction trailer', but the latter two nouns are used with agreement as well (*ein*$_M$ *Bauwagen*$_M$, *eine*$_F$ *Tür*$_F$). At 2;3.7 Luisa uses her first definite article, *die*$_F$ (*die*$_F$ *Katze*$_F$); at 2;4.4 *das*$_N$ is used for the first time (*das*$_N$ *Schaf*$_N$). Correct gender marking predominates, but there are three exceptions (*eine*$_F$ *Honigtopf*$_M$ 'a honey pot', *ein Tür*$_F$ 'a door', *ein*$_{M/N}$ *Schokolade*$_F$ 'a chocolate'). Again, *Tür* is also found with the feminine article *eine*.

At 2;5.15 Luisa uses most articles (der_M, die_F, $das_{N/M}$, den_M, $ein_{N/M}$, $eine_F$), article omission has ceased, and articles are correctly gender-marked.

5.1.1 Nouns by assignment categories

Table 6 presents all nouns types with gender-marked determiners from the perspective of assignment classes and potential cues. Incorrectly marked types were excluded (see below). For this analysis, which is inspired by Szagun et al. (2007), noun types were categorized as belonging to one of the following gender assignment categories: I. disyllabic feminine nouns in -e, II. monosyllabic masculine nouns beginning and/or ending in a consonant, III. masculine nouns in -el, -en, -er, IV. disyllabic nouns with other gender cues (e.g., -chen, -lein), and V. nouns whose gender cannot be assigned based on any of the rules in (I–IV). To the original list, we added VI. compounds and VII. nouns denoting male or female persons, i.e., nouns with natural gender cues. For classes I–III, we distinguished nouns that do vs. do not follow the general assignment pattern (for the other classes, this distinction is irrelevant).[9] For example, Row 1 shows that Luisa has used 29 nouns that are disyllabic and end in schwa. Of these 29 types, 26 (90%) follow the general assignment pattern (being feminine) while three do not follow this pattern (being masculine). Those nouns that do not follow the general assignment pattern are particularly interesting, because they should be especially error-prone if the child followed particular assignment regularities.

Table 6 shows that Luisa uses nouns from various assignment classes with correct gender marking; especially for classes II and III, this includes both nouns that follow the general assignment patterns and nouns contradicting them. The exhaustive list of DPs with non-target-like gender in Phase 1 is given in (2). The examples indicate that no particular gender assignment rule is being (over)used. On the contrary, especially Examples (2a) and (2d) seem to suggest the opposite, because the nouns provide clear gender cues to feminine and masculine, respectively. As mentioned before, some of the nouns (2a, b, c, g) also appear with the target gender. It is further noticeable that the list included relatively many compounds, but the child also uses compounds frequently (see Table 3). All in all, no particular error pattern is evident. On the contrary, gender marking is largely correct regardless of whether the nouns follow particular assignment patterns or not. Neuter gender does not appear to pose particular problems either.

---

9. As mentioned above, for class II (monosyllabic nouns with final/initial consonant) we followed Szagun et al.'s (2007) categorization and the assumption that masculine is the default gender, but it should be noted that especially this category combines nouns with various cues, cueing *mostly* masculine but also neuter and feminine gender (cf. Köpcke & Zubin 1996).

Table 6. Correctly gender-marked DPs in Phase 1 according to assignment class (in class I–III the regularly assigned gender is marked in bold)

	Total types	Masc.	Fem.	Neuter
I. Polysyllabic Ns in -e	29	3	**26** (90%)	–
II. Monosyllabic Ns with final/initial consonant	45	**25** (56%)	3	17
III. Polysyllabic Ns in -el, -en, -er	19	**9** (47%)	4	6
IV. Polysyllabic Ns with specific endings and deterministic assignment	14	2	1	11
V. Compounds	18	8	5	5
VI. Ns denoting man/woman	4	2	2	–
VII. Ns with no common regularities	8	2	–	6
	137*	51	41	45

* Total Number here is lower than those in Table 2 because incorrectly gender-marked cases were deducted and Phases 1 and 2 were taken together.

(2) a. ein$_M$ Katze$_F$ 'a cat' (1;10.24)
 b. ein/einen$_M$ Tür$_F$ 'a door' (1:10.24/ 2;2.0/ 2;4.4)
 c. eine$_F$ Bauwagen$_M$ 'a construction trailer' (2;2.0)
 d. eine$_F$ Schrank$_M$ 'a closet' (2;2.0)
 e. eine$_F$ Honigtopf$_M$ 'a honey pot' (2;4.4)
 f. ein$_M$ Schokolade$_F$ 'a chocolate' (2;4.4)
 g. 'ne$_F$ Spinnennetz$_M$ 'a spider web' (2;6.15)

A final question is whether in those cases where articles have been omitted, certain assignment categories or genders are overrepresented as a result of avoidance strategies. Recall that determiner omission had been argued to be a potential strategy to avoid gender markings (e.g., Mills 1986; Ruberg 2013; Lindauer in prep.). If this were the case, we would expect different numbers of bare nouns vs. nouns with determiners in specific classes, and we would expect that determiners are used more in classes where cues are known to be more reliable, e.g., with nouns ending in schwa.

To explore this possibility, bare singular nouns (excluded when coding gender assignment; cf. Table 4) were also coded for gender following the same procedure as for the analysis presented in Table 6.[10] Figure 3 illustrates the number of nouns by genders in each assignment category, comparing nouns with and without preceding determiners. The distribution of the three genders looks similar if we compare bare nominals and nouns with gender-marked determiners (less so in classes IV–VII, arguably due to the low number of types here).

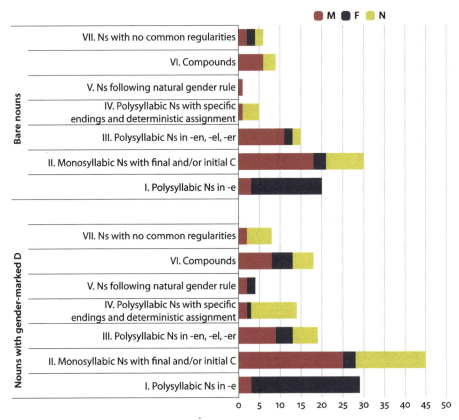

Figure 3. Distribution of noun (tokens) in Luisa's data by assignment class: Comparison of bare nouns and nouns with gender-marked determiners

We finally investigated whether one of the three genders was overrepresented amongst bare nominals (which could also point to an avoidance strategy): Omissions were about twice as frequent with masculine ($n=99$) and feminine nouns ($n=95$) than with neuter nouns ($n=54$), thus roughly corresponding to the dis-

---

10. This analysis was only done for Phase 1 because in Phases 2 and 3, determiner omissions are restricted to contexts where they are licit (plural and mass nouns, proper names, vocatives, and exclamative contexts).

tribution of these genders in German, where neuter nouns are comparatively less frequent.

5.2 Phase 2 (Kindergarten and primary school)

The data of the four recordings in Phase 2 and the five recordings in Phase 3 were analysed in the same manner as for Phase 1. Again, few gender-marking errors could be found (see Table 5). The exhaustive list is summarized in (3) for Phase 2, and in (4) for Phase 3. Note that *Wiese* 'meadow' and *Küche* 'kitchen' appear with correct gender marking elsewhere, and that (3b) is only identifiable as non-target-like because of the adjectival agreement.[11]

(3) a. den$_M$ Trampolin$_N$ 'a trampoline' (7;5.21)
    b. ein$_{M/N}$ blöder$_M$ Zeug$_N$ 'a stupid stuff' (7;4.17)
    c. ein$_{M/N}$ kleine$_F$ Wiese$_F$ 'a small meadow' (7;4.17)
    d. sein$_{M/N}$ Wohnung$_F$ 'his apartment' (7;2.7)

(4) a. ein$_{M/N}$ Küche$_F$ 'a kitchen' (4;9.18)
    b. eine$_F$ Kittel$_M$ 'a gown' (4;11.24)
    c. ein$_{M/N}$ Barbiepuppe$_F$ 'a barbie doll' (5;3.2)

As in Phase 1, the errors do not point to the overuse of particular gender regularities. On the contrary, the nouns *Wiese* 'meadow' and *Küche* 'kitchen' (due to the schwa-ending) and *Wohnung* (due to the suffix) should cue feminine gender, and *-el* in *Kittel* 'gown' should cue masculine gender.

6. Discussion and conclusions

Based on the case study of Luisa, a child who grew up in Canada with German as her heritage language, this paper addressed the questions of (i) whether the development of German as a HL resembles that of monolingual German children and (ii) whether there any signs of stagnation or attrition after a substantial increase in majority language exposure.

---

11. An anonymous reviewer has correctly pointed out that since we have based our analysis on determiners elsewhere, it would be justified to exclude this example. We included such examples to be able to show that even under the strictest possible coding procedure the error rate is still very low.

6.1 Early development: Emergence and quantity

Part of our first question was whether in the case of Luisa the development of German as a HL resembles that of monolingual German in a quantitative way. This would be plausible since previous studies have pointed out possible delays if a gender-marking language is acquired along with a language that has a less transparent gender system (e.g., Rodina & Westergaard 2015; Unsworth 2013) or no gender at all (e.g., Unsworth et al. 2014; Schwartz et al. 2015; Kaltsa et al. 2017).

Hager (2014) found that such delays are especially common in German as the weaker language, but in her study the children acquired German mostly as their majority language and along with Romance languages, i.e., languages with comparatively more transparent gender-marking systems. The situation might look different if German has a minority language status and is acquired along with English.

During the earlier stages, Luisa's development of gender marking resembles that of monolingual German children: First articles and a small number of proto-articles appear before age 2;0 but they do not seem to have a gender-marking function, as reported by Mills (1986) and Stern and Stern (1928) for monolinguals. During this period, a small number of proto-articles (*ei*) and some instances of the masculine/neuter indefinite *ein* are used independently of nominal gender, i.e., including with nouns of feminine gender (*ein Katze$_F$* 'cat', *ein Tür$_F$* 'door'). In this period, there is also one similarity with the data reported by Müller (1999), indicating that children initially (1;10–2;4) used indefinite articles irrespectively of nominal gender, although relevant instances in our corpus are very low.

In terms of quantity, similar to the L1 German children studied by Mills (1986), Luisa ceases to drop articles before 2;6, and by the same time error rates in gender marking drop below 10%. If anything, her development can be considered fast compared to monolinguals. In Szagun et al. (2007: 459), most children reach this point around 3;0 years.[12] It is also interesting to compare the data to that presented by Hager (2014), who has quantified target-like gender agreement in 19 German-Romance bilingual children. Like Szagun for monolingual German, Hager found that the German-Romance children varied a lot in terms of accuracy in gender marking, and that generally error rates dropped below 90% after age 3;0. For the period between 2;0 and 3;5 accuracy rates range between 65–100%, but the majority shows between 80% and 90% accuracy (Hager 2014: 224). Comparing these findings to Luisa's case, it seems safe to conclude that Luisa's development in gender marking is not delayed, but – if anything – rather advanced.

---

12. The exact ages are not provided.

6.2 Early development: Quality of errors

Another possibility we have explored is whether Luisa's development differs from that of monolingual children in terms of qualitative aspects. We have introduced Meisel's (2018) criteria for the identification of L1-like and L2-like features in gender-marking, according to which L1 children (i) show an early stage of article omission, (ii) typically start with one article type, (iii) show low error rates which do not persist for a long period of time, and (iv) make overgeneralization errors. Based on these criteria, Luisa's development resembles that of an L1 learner, because unlike L2 learners, Luisa does not default to one gender (or article type) and non-target-like gender assignment is infrequent. Discussion of the last criterion is less straightforward, because overgeneralization of gender assignment regularities is typical for L1 children, but absent in our corpus.

The few gender marking errors in our corpus indicate that Luisa does not overgeneralize particular assignment rules, unlike monolingual and bilingual German children in most previous studies. On the contrary, at least some of the errors occur with nouns that provide reliable cues. For example, $Tür_F$ 'door' ends in the cue [y:r], which is associated with feminine gender; $Schrank_M$ 'closet' is a monosyllabic noun beginning and ending in consonant clusters, thus providing cues for masculine gender. The remaining cases concern compound nouns, which require combined cue knowledge, i.e., how to assign gender to the individual nouns and the Last-Member Principle. The head nouns in some of the compounds in (2) have reliable cues, e.g., -*en* in $Wagen_M$ 'coach' and consonant clusters in *Topf* 'pot'. We suspect that the absence of overgeneralization errors is due to the low number of errors overall.[13] We have further classified bare nouns and noun with correctly marked determiners to see whether it is plausible that certain noun classes were avoided to avoid wrong gender marking. However, omissions occur with all three genders, and with a similar distribution as the distribution of genders in the target language (i.e., with a lower proportion of neuter). Additionally, nouns from various classes and with different genders appear as bare nouns and nouns with determiners (Figure 3).

Finally, there is an interesting difference with respect to previous studies on German-Romance children, according to which neuter gender seems to pose particular problems (Müller 1990; Eichler et al. 2013). We see two possible explanations: One is that Luisa's development is extremely fast so that the phase in which neuter gender posed problems has been missed. The other possible explanation is

---

13. Note also that many previous studies do not provide an exhaustive list of non-target-like assignments. This means that we do not know the number of instances that did *not* result from the overgeneralization of rules and makes direct comparisons impossible.

that neuter gender is particularly problematic for children whose other language has feminine and masculine gender while lacking neuter gender, and that bilingual children whose other language has no gender at all do not have this problem. To tease these two possible explanations apart, more data would be needed from children who acquire a three-way gender system together with a genderless language.

6.3 Later development

Our second research question was whether there are signs of stagnation or attrition after a substantial increase in majority language exposure. To answer this question, data from Phase 2 and 3 are relevant, where English has become Luisa's dominant language. These data show that the number of non-target-like gender marking is extremely low. Like in Phase 1, non-target-like assignment in Phases 2 and 3 do not seem to be indicative of rule-based overgeneralizations either, as most of the nouns contain reliable gender cues: The schwa ending in *Wiese$_F$* 'meadow', *(Barbie)puppe$_F$* '(Barbie)doll', and *Küche$_F$* 'kitchen', the *-ung* suffix in *Wohnung$_F$* 'apartment', and the *-el* ending in *Kittel$_M$* 'gown'. However, the number of instances is so low that it would not justify any claim about stagnation or attrition during the pre- and primary school years. Of course, we cannot exclude the possibility of attrition at a later age. We assume that the likelihood decreases with growing age and continuous German use.

7. Conclusions

We have shown the problem-free acquisition of German gender in a minority language context, and there were no indications that this system was becoming unstable during the primary school years. Our study adds to those reporting positive effects of extensive use of the minority language at home (e.g., De Houwer 2007; La Morgia 2011). More generally, the study shows, based on the acquisition of grammatical gender, that it is possible to acquire and maintain a heritage language in a minority language setting even if schooling is in the majority language. It contradicts the idea that non-transparent or semi-transparent systems are generally late-acquired.

Funding

This study was made possible through a fellowship to the first author for a post-doctorate position as part of the Province of Alberta's ACCESS grant in SLA (2006–2007).

Acknowledgements

We wish to thank the participant and her family for their availability and for welcoming us at all times. Special thanks to Jacqueline Clydesdale, who supported the first part of the data collection, and to Anne-Sophie Hufer and Simone Waitz who assisted in coding the data.

References

Bianchi, G. 2013. Gender in Italian–German bilinguals: A comparison with German L2 learners of Italian. *Bilingualism: Language and Cognition* 16(3): 538–557.

Bittner, D. 2006. Case before gender in the acquisition of German. *Folia Linguistica* 40(1–2): 115–134.

Bottari, P., Cipriano, P. & Chilosi, A. M. 1993/1994. Protosyntactic devices in the acquisition of Italian free morphology. *Language Acquisition* 3(4): 327–369.

Carroll, S. E. 1989. Second language acquisition and the computational paradigm. *Language Learning* 39(4): 535–594.

Carroll, S. E. 1999. Input and SLA: Adults' sensitivity to different sorts of cues to French gender. *Language Learning* 49(1): 37–92.

Cornips, L. & Hulk, A. 2008. Factors of success and failure in the acquisition of grammatical gender in Dutch. *Second Language Research* 24(3): 267–295.

Corteen, E. M. 2018. The Assignment of Grammatical Gender in German: Testing Optimal Gender Assignment Theory. PhD dissertation, University of Cambridge.

De Houwer, A. 2007. Parental language input patterns and children's bilingual use. *Applied Psycholinguistics* 28(3): 411–424.

Dieser, E. 2009. *Genuserwerb im Russischen und Deutschen: Korpusgestützte Studie zu ein- und zweisprachigen Kindern und Erwachsenen*. München: Sagner.

Eichler, N., Jansen, V. & Müller, N. 2013. Gender acquisition in bilingual children: French-German, Italian-German, Spanish-German and Italian-French. *International Journal of Bilingualism* 17(5): 550–572.

Granfeldt, J. 2018. The development of gender in simultaneous and successive bilingual acquisition of French: Evidence for AoO and input effects. *Bilingualism: Language and Cognition* 21(4): 674–693.

Hager, M. 2014. Der Genuserwerb bei mehrsprachig aufwachsenden Kindern –Eine longitudinale Untersuchung bilingualer und trilingualer Kinder der Sprachenkombinationen deutsch-französisch/italienisch/spanisch, französisch-italienisch/spanisch und deutsch-spanisch-katalanisch. PhD dissertation, Bergische Universität Wuppertal.

Heidolph, K. E., Flämig, W. & Motsch, W. 1984. *Grundzüge einer deutschen Grammatik* (2nd ed.). Berlin: Akademie-Verlag.

Hulk, A. & Müller, N. 2000. Bilingual first language acquisition at the interface between syntax and pragmatics. *Bilingualism: Language and Cognition* 3(3): 227–244.

Hulk, A. & van der Linden, E. 2010. How vulnerable is gender? In *New Directions in Language Acquisition: Romance Languages in the Generative Perspective*, P. Guijarro-Fuentes & L. Domínguez (eds), 107–134. Newcastle upon Tyne: Cambridge Scholars.

Kaltsa, M., Prentza, A., Papadopoulou, D. & Tsimpli, I. M. 2017. Language external and language internal factors in the acquisition of gender: The case of Albanian-Greek and English-Greek bilingual children. *International Journal of Bilingual Education and Bilingualism* 20: 1–22.

Kehoe, M., Lleó, C. & Rakow, M. 2004. Voice onset time in bilingual German-Spanish children. *Bilingualism: Language and Cognition* 7(1): 71–88.

Köpcke, K.-M. 1982. *Untersuchungen zum Genussystem der deutschen Gegenwartssprache*. Tübingen: Niemeyer.

Köpcke, K.-M. & Zubin, D. 1983. Die kognitive Organisation der Genuszuweisung zu den einsilbigen Nomen der deutschen Gegenwartssprache. *Zeitschrift für germanistische Linguistik* 11: 166–82.

Köpcke, K.-M. & Zubin, D. 1984. Sechs Prinzipien für die Genuszuweisung im Deutschen: Ein Beitrag zur natürlichen Klassifikation. *Linguistische Berichte* 93: 26–50.

Köpcke, K.-M. & Zubin, D. 1996. Prinzipien für die Genuszuweisung im Deutschen. In *Deutsch-typologisch. Institut für deutsche Sprache Jahrbuch 1995*, E. Lang & G. Zifonun (eds), 473–491. Berlin: Walter de Gruyter.

Kupisch, T. 2006. *The acquisition of determiners in German-French and German-Italian children*. Munich: Lincom.

Kupisch, T., Akpinar, D. & Stöhr, A. 2013. Gender assignment and gender agreement in adult bilinguals and second language learners of French. *Linguistic Approaches to Bilingualism* 3(2): 150–179.

Kupisch, T. & J. Rothman. 2016. Interfaces with syntax in language acquisition. In *Manual of Grammatical Interfaces in Romance*, S. Fischer & C. Gabriel (eds), 551–586. Berlin: De Gruyter.

Kupisch, T., Müller, N. & Cantone, K. F. 2002. Gender in monolingual and bilingual first language acquisition: Comparing Italian and French. *Lingue e Linguaggio* 1: 107–150.

La Morgia, F. 2011. Bilingual First Language Acquisition: The Nature of the Weak Language and the Role of the Input. PhD dissertation, Dublin City University.

Lemmerth, N. & Hopp, H. 2018. Gender processing in simultaneous and successive bilingual children: Cross-linguistic lexical and syntactic influences. *Language Acquisition* 26(1): 21–45.

Lindauer, M. In preparation. The Acquisition of German by Italian and Turkish Heritage Language Speaking Children: Sociolinguistic Aspects and Production Experiments on Proficiency in German Verb Placement, Morphosyntax and Prosody. PhD Dissertation, University of Konstanz.

Lleó, C. 2016. Acquiring phonology and its interfaces: 2L1, L2, L3. In *Manual of Grammatical Interfaces in Romance*, S. Fischer & C. Gabriel (eds), 519–550. Berlin: De Gruyter.

MacWhinney, B., Leinbach, J., Taraban, R. & McDonald, J. 1989. Language learning: Cues or rules? *Journal of Memory and Language* 28(3): 255–277.

Meisel, J. M. 2018. Early child second language acquisition: French gender in German children. *Bilingualism: Language and Cognition* 21(4): 656–673.

Mills, A. E. 1986. *The Acquisition of Gender: A Study of English and German*. Berlin: Springer.

Montrul, S. 2018. Heritage language development: Connecting the dots. *International Journal of Bilingualism* 22(5): 530–546.

Montrul, S., Foote, R. & Perpiñán, S. 2008. Gender agreement in adult second language learners and Spanish heritage speakers: The effects of age and context of acquisition. *Language Learning* 58(3): 504–553.

Müller, N. 1990. Developing two gender-assignment systems simultaneously. In *Two First Languages: Early Grammatical Development in Bilingual Children*, J.M. Meisel (ed.), 193–234. Dordrecht: Foris.

Müller, N. 1994. Gender and number agreement within DP. In *Bilingual First Language Acquisition. French and German Grammatical Development*, J.M. Meisel (ed.), 53–88. Amsterdam: John Benjamins.

Müller, N. 1999. Gender and number in acquisition. In *Gender in Grammar and Cognition: Approaches to Gender*, B. Unterbeck & M. Rissanen (eds), 351–399. The Hague: Mouton de Gruyter.

Opitz, A. & Pechmann, T. 2016. Gender features in German. Evidence for underspecification. *The Mental Lexicon* 11(2): 216–241.

Pérez-Pereira, M. 1991. The acquisition of gender: What Spanish children tell us. *Journal of Child Language* 18(3): 571–590.

Polinsky, M. 2008. Gender under incomplete acquisition: Heritage speakers' knowledge of noun categorization. *Heritage Language Journal* 6: 40–71.

Rodina, Y. & Westergaard, M. 2015. Grammatical gender in Norwegian: Language acquisition and language change. *Journal of Germanic Linguistics* 27(2): 145–187.

Ruberg, T. 2013. *Der Genuserwerb ein- und mehrsprachiger Kinder*. Hamburg: Dr. Kovac.

Schlyter, S. 1993. The weaker language in bilingual Swedish-French children. In *Progression and Regression in Language: Sociocultural, Neuropsychological and Linguistic Perspectives*, K. Hyltenstam & A. Viberg (eds), 289–308. Cambridge: CUP.

Schwartz, M., Minkov, M., Dieser, E., Protassova, E., Moin, V. & Polinsky, M. 2015. Acquisition of Russian gender agreement by monolingual and bilingual children. *International Journal of Bilingualism* 19(6): 726–752.

Schwichtenberg, B. & Schiller, N.O. 2004. Semantic gender assignment regularities in German. *Brain and Language* 90(1–3): 326–337.

Steinmetz, D. 2006. Gender shifts in Germanic and Slavic: Semantic motivation for neuter? *Lingua* 116(9): 1418–1440.

Stern, C. & Stern, W. 1928. *Die Kindersprache: Eine psychologische und sprachtheoretische Untersuchung*. Leipzig: Barth.

Stoehr, A., Akpinar, D., Bianchi, G. & Kupisch, T. 2012. Gender marking in L2 learners and Italian-German bilinguals with German as the weaker language. In *Multilingual Individuals and Multilingual Societies*, K. Braunmüller & C. Gabriel (eds), 153–170. Amsterdam: John Benjamins.

Szagun, G., Stumper, B., Sondag, N. & Franik, M. 2007. The acquisition of gender marking by young German-speaking children: Evidence for learning guided by phonological regularities. *Journal of Child Language* 34(3): 445–471.

Unsworth, S. 2013. Assessing the role of current and cumulative exposure in simultaneous bilingual acquisition: The case of Dutch gender. *Bilingualism: Language and Cognition* 16(1): 86–110.

Unsworth, S., Argyri, F., Cornips, L., Hulk, A., Sorace, A. & Tsimpli, I. 2014. On the role of age of onset and input in early child bilingualism in Greek and Dutch. *Applied Psycholinguistics* 35(4): 765–805.

Wegener, H. 1995. *Die Nominalflexion des Deutschen – verstanden als Lerngegenstand.* Tübingen: Niemeyer.

Input and exposure in the classroom

CHAPTER 5

Acquisition of 3PL verb markings by (very) advanced FSL learners and bilingual Francophone students

Raymond Mougeon,[1] Françoise Mougeon[1]
& Katherine Rehner[2]
[1] York University [2] University of Toronto

This study examines acquisition of distinctive 3PL markings of French verbs by bilingual Francophone students attending French-medium high schools in four Ontario Francophone communities of varying demographic strength and by learners enrolled in high school immersion or university FSL programs in Toronto. It documents the impact of the following factors: (i) the discursive frequency of the verbs; (ii) the students' exposure to French in and outside of school, (iii) their individual frequency of use of French, (iv) teachers' in class speech, and (v) invariant vs. variable use of the 3PL verb markings in the local varieties of French. The impact of these factors is manifested by different patterns of intergroup hierarchies in rates of acquisition.

Keywords: French verbal morphology, French immersion, Ontario Francophones, language dominance

1. Introduction

The present study examines acquisition of the distinctive third person plural (3PL) verb markings of French by Canadian students who are (relatively) advanced speakers of French as a Second Language (FSL) and by bilingual Francophone students. The presence of these two categories of French-speaking students in Canada can be ascribed to changes in Canada's linguistic policies during the latter part of the past century. There are Francophone communities in each of Canada's ten provinces. However, apart from Quebec (where French is a majority language) and New Brunswick (where French is spoken by about one third of the population), in each of the remaining eight provinces, Francophones represent only a small proportion of the total population. Over the last century the number of Francophones has dwindled considerably in these provinces, notably because of provincial assimilationist policies, which up to the late 1960s or 1970s had banned French-language schooling. However, in 1982, Canada's new constitution opened the door to a reversal of such policies by guaranteeing the right to French-medium schooling for Francophones living outside Quebec and New Brunswick.[1]

While such schooling has been an important tool in the struggle of Canada's Francophone minorities to maintain their linguistic and cultural heritage, its impact has been mitigated by several factors. First, outside Quebec and New Brunswick, Francophones tend to reside in localities where they are clearly outnumbered by Anglophones. Therefore, in such localities, outside the French-medium schools, Francophone children receive considerable amounts of exposure to English and communicate extensively in that language in daily life. Further, these children are oftentimes raised in homes where English rather than French is the primary medium of communication (e.g., homes where only one parent is of French mother-tongue).

That said, outside Quebec and New Brunswick, there are some localities where the demographic strength of Francophones is strong – including a few where Francophones are clearly in the majority and where children use French more often than English outside the French-medium schools. As such, outside Quebec and New Brunswick, Francophone students enrolled in French-medium schools can be placed on a continuum which reflects the respective strength of French and English in their communicative repertoire. At one end of the continuum are students who live in strong Francophone communities and whose main language of communication outside of the school is French, and at the other end are students who reside in weak Francophone minority communities, whose primary source of exposure to French is through their French-medium education and who communicate mostly in English outside of school. Research on the acquisition of French by students on this continuum (e.g., Mougeon & Beniak 1991 and Nadasdi 2000) has documented substantial differences in the students' rates of acquisition of French reflecting the demographic strength of Francophones in the students' communities and the frequency with which the students use French in daily life.

During roughly the same period that French-medium schooling for Francophone children expanded outside Quebec and New Brunswick, FSL education benefited from the support of the federal government through special funding to the provinces. Such funding was used to develop improved FSL education such

---

[1]. The new Canadian constitution also guaranteed the right to be educated in English to Quebec's English-speaking minority.

as French immersion or Intensive French programs, in which students develop their FSL proficiency by studying French as well as other subjects taught in the language. While these students' proficiency in French has been found to be clearly higher than that of students attending traditional FSL programs, where French is taught only as a subject (Swain & Lapkin 1982), it is still below that of same-age unilingual Francophone students (e.g., Harley 1986). This finding is not surprising since unilingual Francophone students have had numerous opportunities to use French in the different domains of society compared to the immersion students' limited opportunities to use French outside the confines of the immersion classrooms.

That said, other studies have compared French immersion students with bilingual Francophone students and thus have provided a nuanced perspective, not only on the French language proficiency of the French immersion students but also on that of the Francophone students (e.g., Mougeon et al. 2010). Specifically, such comparisons have revealed that, on the one hand, French immersion students have acquisition rates of certain aspects of French that are comparable to those of English-dominant Francophone students and, on the other hand, for other aspects of French, immersion students have acquisition rates that are lower than those of English-dominant Francophone students (e.g., Canale et al. 1978; Harley 1979; Harley & Swain 1978; Mougeon et al. 2010).

At the postsecondary level, in Canada, FSL students can continue learning French. In bilingual-English/French or unilingual-French universities, students can not only take courses taught in French, but they can engage in interactions with Francophones outside of the classroom to further develop their proficiency. For example, Rehner et al. (2022) found that FSL students attending a bilingual-English/French university reach a level of mastery of prepositional use with place names which is higher than that achieved by French immersion students but also which is comparable to that achieved by Francophone students in minority communities.

The present study of the acquisition of the distinctive 3PL markings of French verbs arrives at findings which are generally in keeping with those of Rehner et al. (2022) by comparing six groups of students: (i) FSL immersion students; (ii) FSL university students; (iii) and four groups of bilingual Francophone students – those who live in a strong majority community and those who live in communities where Francophones are, to varying extents, outnumbered by Anglophones. The comparison reveals a ternary intergroup hierarchy in rates of acquisition of the 3PL verb markings, with the Francophone students from the majority community outperforming the Francophone students from the two strongest minority communities, whose rates are about on par with those of the FSL university students, who in turn outperform the Francophone students from the weakest minority community and the FSL immersion students, whose rates are comparable.

Further, an analysis of the data, taking into account the discursive frequency of the verbs and the students' individual frequency of extra-curricular use of French, uncovers intergroup acquisition hierarchies which are more nuanced than this basic ternary pattern. Lastly, we show how the use of verbs without their 3PL markings by immersion teachers and by Francophone teachers in their in-class speech and by Francophones in the community helps to explain why the Francophone students from the weakest minority community have an acquisition rate which is not higher than that of the French immersion students. In sum, our study underscores the theoretical relevance and the potential usefulness for Canada's educational-linguistic policies of conducting research on the impact of extra-linguistic and linguistic factors on the acquisition of French on the Francophone – FSL language proficiency continuum.

2. Prior research

2.1 Acquisition of the 3PL verb forms

Studies which examined acquisition of the 3PL verb markings by FSL learners in Europe have found that native-like automatization of these markings occurs only in the final stage of target language learning (e.g., Ågren & van de Weijer 2013; Bartning 2016). Typically, before that stage, the 3PL verb forms are variably replaced with singular (i.e., morphologically unmarked) forms. Several explanations have been proposed for this finding: (i) there are only a few French verbs which have a distinctive morphophonology in the 3PL; (ii) plurality is recoverable via means other than verbal morphology (e.g., plural markings on the subject, situational cues); and (iii) the morphophonology of the distinctive verb forms is heterogeneous and largely unpredictable.

Several Canadian studies have also investigated acquisition of the 3PL verb markings. Mougeon and Beniak's (1991) study is based on a speech corpus collected in 1978 among Francophone students in the same four Ontario localities where the Francophone student corpus for the present was collected in 2005. In these localities, Francophones represented different proportions of the local population, ranging from very high to very low. The students were aged 15 or 18 and had been schooled entirely in French. However, outside school, they used French in daily life with varying levels of frequency. These authors found that the students' mastery of the distinctive verb markings varied according to their community of residence, ranging from a 99% rate for students in the very strong

Francophone community to 73% for those in the weakest minority community. They also found that the more frequently the students used French outside school, the higher their rate of mastery of the distinctive verb markings. Lastly, they found that verb frequency had a strong influence on the rate of mastery of such markings. With the four most frequent verbs, the rates were almost 100%, but with the remaining verbs, they were substantially lower.

Harley (1992a, b) examined the acquisition of the 3PL verb markings by 16-year-old students in three types of immersion programs. While Harley's results pointed to a slight advantage for the students attending an early-immersion program (whose acquisition rate of 73% was somewhat more native-like than that of the mid- and late-immersion students), the results failed to show any meaningful statistical differences across the three learner groups, whose performance all fell significantly below that of same-age unilingual Francophone students from Quebec City.

Nadasdi (2001) and Mougeon et al. (2010) examined acquisition of the distinctive verb markings by 14- to 18-year-old mid-immersion students. These students were compared with the 14- to 18-year-old Francophone students examined by Mougeon and Beniak (1991). The comparison revealed that the immersion students had a rate of mastery of 81%, which almost matched that of the Francophone students who communicated primarily in English outside of their French-medium schools. This finding was unexpected, since the immersion students' level of curricular and extra-curricular exposure to French was lower than that of these Francophone students. In the present study, we propose an explanation for this finding, which hinges on the community input of the Francophone students. Lastly, Nadasdi (2001) also found that verb frequency had a sizable impact on the rates of mastery, a finding in line with that of Mougeon and Beniak (1991).

2.2 Acquisition of other aspects of French morphosyntax

Lapkin and Swain (1977) compared 10-year-old early immersion students with unilingual and bilingual Francophone students in a study of French language proficiency based on cloze test data. Two main patterns of intergroup rates of accuracy in responding to the test items can be inferred from their study. On the one hand, with items such as determiners, the unilingual students had higher accuracy rates than did the bilingual Francophone students, who, in turn, had higher rates than the immersion students. On the other hand, with other items such as prepositions and verbs, the unilingual students had the highest rates of accuracy, while the bilingual Francophone students and the French immersion students' lower rates were comparable.

In their research on the mastery of aspects of the French verb system by 10-year-old students attending an early total French Immersion program in Toronto, Harley and Swain (1978) compared the immersion students with bilingual Francophone students attending French-medium schools in Toronto and with unilingual Francophone students. These authors found that the immersion students' rates of mastery of French verb usage were always lower than those of the Francophone students and that in most cases (e.g., use of the conditional and the subjunctive) the immersion students' rates were lower than those of the bilingual Francophone students, which in turn were lower than those of the unilingual students.

Canale et al. (1978) examined the acquisition of sociolinguistic variants by 7-year-old French immersion students and by control groups of Francophone students attending French-medium schools who were either predominant users of French at home, predominant users of English at home, or unilingual Francophones. Their study focused on two alternations: (i) standard *être allé* 'have gone/ went' vs. vernacular *avoir été* 'have been' and (ii) standard auxiliary *être* vs. vernacular auxiliary *avoir* used with several verbs of motion and with reflexive verbs. These authors found that the immersion students had an almost nil rate of use of vernacular *avoir été*, which stood in contrast with the higher rates of this variant found for the bilingual and unilingual Francophone students. The fact that the immersion students had learned French almost entirely in the classroom while the Francophone students had learned this language in both the schools and the community is a likely explanation for this finding. However, with the alternation between auxiliaries *être* vs. *avoir*, Canale et al. found that the immersion students and the English-dominant Francophone students were using almost exclusively *avoir*, while the French-dominant and unilingual students had a head start in acquiring *être*. According to these authors, these findings were ascribable to the markedness of auxiliary *être* in the French verb system (it is used with only a limited number of verbs). Despite their having learned French exclusively or primarily in the classroom and hence, having been intensively exposed to standard auxiliary *être*, these young students were still at a developmental stage where they were overgeneralizing unmarked auxiliary *avoir*.

Harley (1979) examined acquisition of grammatical gender by 7-year-old and 10-year-old immersion students and same age Francophone students residing in the minority community of Sudbury, Ontario and in the majority communities of Rayside, Ontario and Quebec City. All the students from Quebec City and Rayside were from unilingual or predominantly French-speaking homes, while the students from Sudbury included both children raised in homes where French was the dominant language of communication and children raised in homes where the dominant language was English.[2] Harley focused on six different rules 'governing' gender choice. She documented different intergroup hierarchies in rates of contraventions across the different rules. For instance, with the rule which aligns grammatical gender with the sex of higher animate beings (e.g., *le* [masc.] *papa* [masc.] 'the dad' vs. *la* [fem.] *maman* [fem.] 'the mom'), the English-dominant students from Sudbury and the French immersion students had comparable rates of errors and stood apart from the French-dominant students from Sudbury, Rayside and Quebec City who had nil or almost nil error rates. However, with the rule that the names of sciences are always feminine, only the immersion students made errors.

Mougeon et al. (2010) examined acquisition of standard/formal vs. vernacular/informal variants by 15- to 18-year-old French immersion students residing in Toronto. To assess the impact of classroom input on the students' learning of variants, these authors analysed a corpus of French immersion teachers' in-class speech. They also compared the immersion students with Francophone students who, outside of the French-medium schools, communicated primarily in French and with Francophone students who communicated primarily in English.

Mougeon et al. found that, in general, the immersion students had rates of use of the vernacular/informal variants which were lower than those of the English-dominant Francophone students, who, in turn, had lower rates than those of the French-dominant Francophone students. This pattern was found, for instance, with the use of non-clitic pronouns *nous autres* (vernacular) vs. *nous* (standard) both meaning 'us'. As pointed out by Mougeon and Rehner (2017), this hierarchy of intergroup differences reflected the influence of the community input and educational input of the immersion and Francophone students. Specifically, the immersion students had received no or only minimal exposure to French in the community, the English-dominant Francophone students had received somewhat more exposure to French in that context, and the French-dominant Francophone students had received even more exposure to French. Further, analysis of the immersion teachers' speech revealed their strong disinclination to use informal/vernacular variants. In this respect, Mougeon and Rehner (2017, 2019) showed that the teachers of the Francophone students use informal/vernacular variants to a varying extent in the classroom and thus further expose their students to such forms. Mougeon et al. (2010), however, documented exceptions to this general pattern of intergroup differences when the vernacular variants were strongly marked socially and thus avoided by both the immersion and Francophone teachers. In such cases, both the immersion students and the English-dominant Francophone students used these marked variants marginally or not at

---

2. See Canale et al. (1978) for further information on these Francophone student corpora.

all and stood apart from the French-dominant students who used them significantly more often.

Pirvulescu et al. (2014) examined the acquisition of object clitic pronouns by monolingual Francophone children aged respectively three, four, and five, all living in Montreal, and by same-age bilingual Francophone children living in Toronto. All of the bilingual children had been categorized as balanced in both languages on the basis of parental assessment of their frequency of use French and English and their fluency in both languages. Their study featured a further comparison in which the 4-year-old balanced bilinguals were contrasted with two groups of same age bilinguals, but who were either dominant in French or dominant in English.

Pirvulescu et al. found that from age three to age five, the bilingual learners remained consistently behind the monolingual learners and exhibited higher rates of null object. In relation to the impact of language dominance, they found that the French-dominant children exhibited rates of acquisition higher than those of the balanced bilingual children and of the English-dominant ones. However, they also found that the acquisition rates of the English-dominant children were almost the same as those of the balanced bilinguals. In discussing their results, the authors remarked that the intergroup differences in rates of acquisition revealed by both comparisons could be ascribed in part to the variable level of French input received as well as to the special status of the object clitics in the grammar of French.

Finally, Rehner et al. (2022) examined acquisition of the use of prepositions *à* vs. *en*, to express motion to or location in localities and countries, by all of the student groups focused upon in the present study. These groups include 15- to 18-year-old immersion students, university FSL students, and control groups of bilingual Ontario Francophone students attending French-medium schools in Hawkesbury, Cornwall, North Bay, and Pembroke where Francophones represent respectively 80%, 27%, 14%, and 6% of the local population.

This aspect of prepositional usage was selected because Alexandre (2004) had found that its acquisition by bilingual Ontario Francophone students is especially challenging. In their own study, Rehner et al. found that *à* was easier to learn than *en*, reflecting a difference in the rules governing the choice of these prepositions.

With *à*, these authors found rates of acquisition ranging from 70% to 100% and with *en* of 29% to 96%. Further, with *à*, they found a ternary intergroup hierarchy: the Hawkesbury students outperformed the Cornwall, North Bay, and FSL university students, whose similar rates of mastery surpassed those of the immersion and Pembroke students (whose rates were on a par). However, with *en*, the intergroup hierarchy was more complex: the Hawkesbury students outperformed the Cornwall and North Bay students, whose similar rates were higher than those of the FSL university students, which were in turn higher than those of the Pembroke students, with the immersion students at the lowest end. In other words, with *en*, the intergroup hierarchy provided clearer evidence of the impact of differential exposure to French on acquisition. Lastly, Rehner et al. were able to nuance these hierarchies by examining the additional influence of students' individual frequency of use of French outside of the school context.

3. Method

3.1 Corpora

This study draws on three student speech corpora collected in 2005 among: (i) high school Francophone students in majority and minority Ontario Francophone communities; and (ii) FSL undergraduate students at a bilingual university in Toronto, Ontario; and, in 1996, among (iii) high school French immersion students from the greater Toronto area. To capture the impact of the students' educational input, the study uses two corpora of teacher in-class speech recorded: (i) in 2005, in the same high schools where the Francophone student corpus was collected and (ii) in 1987 in immersion programs in the greater Toronto and Ottawa areas. To assess the influence of the Francophone students' community-based input, the study uses Raymond Mougeon and Édouard Beniak's corpus collected in 1978 in the same four Francophone communities examined in the present study. This corpus provides an indication of the variety of French the Francophone students heard as children.

3.1.1 *Francophone student corpus*

The Francophone student corpus was collected in 2005 by Raymond Mougeon, Terry Nadasdi, and Katherine Rehner using hour-long recorded face-to-face semi-directed interviews which broached a variety of topics. The students were aged 15 and 18 years and attended French-medium high schools in Hawkesbury, Cornwall, North Bay, and Pembroke, Ontario. These students had also attended French-medium elementary schools and, thus, have been schooled entirely in French.[3] All students in the corpus are from homes with at least one Francophone parent. In Hawkesbury, Cornwall, North Bay, and Pembroke, Francophones represented respectively 81%, 27%, 14%, and 6% of the local population (Census of Canada 2001).

---

3. In the French-medium schools, the only subject not taught in French is English Language Arts, which is typically introduced in Grade 3 (i.e., around age eight).

This representation determines the communities' ability to develop a network of autonomous economic and cultural institutions in which French can be used and their ability to resist linguistic exogamy, a factor that brings about a penetration of English into the home domain, resulting in less than full intergenerational transmission of French (e.g., Castonguay 1979 and Mougeon 2014). In this way, the students' community of residence provides a general indication of their levels of exposure to French and English. Further, the students also exhibited variation in their individual frequency of active use of French in daily life (e.g., with their parents, siblings, colleagues or customers in their part-time jobs or while shopping). Along with Mougeon and Beniak (1991), we distinguish three categories of frequency of use of French (FUF): (1) 80% of the time or more – high FUF; (2) 79% to 40% of the time – mid FUF and (3) 39% of the time or less – low FUF. The distribution of students according to FUF and community of residence is presented in Table 1. As can be seen, there is a preponderance of high FUF students in the Hawkesbury sample, somewhat over 25% of mid FUF students and no students with low FUF, reflecting the strong majority status of the local community. In contrast, in the minority communities' samples, the high FUF students are clearly outnumbered, or absent (in Pembroke), and the distribution of students across the FUF categories fluctuates according to the proportional representation of Francophones in the three localities.

Table 1. Distribution of Francophone students by frequency of use of French and community

Community (% Francophones locally)	High FUF N	Mid FUF N	Low FUF N
Hawkesbury (81%)	37	13	0
Cornwall (27%)	8	22	21
North Bay (14%)	2	20	28
Pembroke (6%)	0	1	30

3.1.2 *FSL university student corpus*

The FSL university student corpus was collected by Françoise Mougeon via individual semi-directed interviews with 61 undergraduate FSL students in their 1st or 4th year of study on the bilingual (French-English) campus of a university in Toronto. These interviews lasted about one hour and focused on topics which, for the most part, were the same as those broached in the high school Francophone students' interviews.

All these students came from homes where English or a language other than English and French was spoken. In addition to the undergraduate FSL courses that they were each taking, the students could also enroll in French-medium courses and interact in French across the campus. The students provided information on their engagement in extra-curricular interactions involving an active commitment to using French (e.g., part-time work in a local Francophone business, friendship ties with Francophones, additional studies in French). On the basis of this information, Mougeon and Rehner (2015) distinguished three categories of students: (1) highly-engaged ($N=12$), (2) moderately-engaged ($N=22$), and (3) minimally-engaged ($N=27$), which we will use in the present study as high, mid, and low FUF.

3.1.3 *FSL high school immersion student corpus*

The FSL immersion student corpus was collected by Raymond Mougeon and Terry Nadasdi among 41 students (age 15 or 18) enrolled in a mid-immersion program housed in English-language high schools in the greater Toronto area, featuring 50% French-medium instruction in Grades 5 to 8, followed by 20% from Grades 9 to 12. None of these students came from a home where French was spoken. Further, since the greater Toronto area has only a marginal Francophone population, the French-medium classrooms were about the only places in which the students had local opportunities to use and be exposed to French. Still, nine students reported having had opportunities to interact with Francophones by staying with a Francophone family for one week or longer, for the most part in Quebec. We have designated these nine students as mid FUF and the remaining 32 students as low FUF.

3.1.4 *Francophone teacher speech corpus*

A corpus of 59 teachers' in-class speech was collected by Raymond Mougeon, Terry Nadasdi, and Katherine Rehner in the same French-medium high schools where the Francophone student corpus was collected. Many of these 59 teachers were the instructors of the Francophone students mentioned above. Table 2 shows that the teachers are roughly evenly distributed across the four communities, with most of the teachers being born either locally or elsewhere in Ontario, ten born in Quebec, two in New Brunswick, and one in France.

Table 2. Distribution (*n*) of teachers by community of residence and birthplace

Communities	Local	Birthplace Other Ontario	Quebec	New Brunswick	France	Total
Hawkesbury	5	7	2	0	0	14
Cornwall	6	5	4	1	0	16
North Bay	6	10	0	0	0	16
Pembroke	0	7	4	1	1	13
Total	17	29	10	2	1	59

3.1.5 *French immersion teacher speech corpus*

The corpus of French immersion teachers' in-class speech was gathered by Allen et al. (1987) from a sample of seven Grade 3 and 6 immersion teachers from the greater Toronto and Ottawa areas. While these teachers are not the actual instructors of the immersion students focused upon in the present study, this is the only corpus available to us. However, as shown by previous research (e.g., Mougeon et al. 2010), despite this shortcoming, this corpus provides useful comparative data revealing a high degree of alignment between immersion teachers' and students' variant choices and suggesting that teachers' in-class speech can have a great deal of influence on students' acquisition of sociolinguistic variation. While it would have been nice to have a corpus of in-class university teacher speech, none is available.

3.2 Data on the Francophone community speech norms

Since Mougeon et al.'s (2010) study was part of a research project which focused on high school immersion and Francophone students, collection of adult speech corpora was not undertaken. However, Raymond Mougeon and Édouard Beniak had collected in 1978 a corpus of semi-directed interviews among 118 15- and 18-year-old Francophone students in the same four Francophone communities that are examined in the present study (see Mougeon & Beniak 1991). These students would have been roughly 35–45 years of age by 2005. Therefore, their 1978 speech provides some indication of the parental norm that the students interviewed in 2005 would have heard as children. In fact, several of the students interviewed in 2005 provided support to this assumption when they revealed during the interview that their parents had taken part in the 1978 interviews.

4. Data analysis

As pointed out by Mougeon and Beniak (1991), only about 600 verbs (5%) out of a total of 12,000 or so French verbs show a morphophonologically marked form in the 3PL of the present indicative, while the phonological realization of the 3rd person singular and plural forms for the remaining 95% are indistinguishable. Further, the distinctive plural markings of these 600 verbs are largely heterogenous and unpredictable. Two verbs mark plurality with an entirely different form (e.g., *ils sont* 'they are' vs. *il est* 'it/he is'); others do so with a form which is minimally related to the singular (e.g., *ils savent* 'they know' vs. *il sait* 'it/he knows); still others involve only an additional final consonant in the 3PL, but for the verbs which belong to this category (*dire* 'say', *connaître* 'know', *vivre* 'live', *devoir* 'must', and *mettre* 'put'), there are no fewer than four different final consonants.

In our student speech corpora, we found 10,124 tokens of the distinctive verb forms used in a 3PL context. Of these, 8,590 were used with the expected plural markings (see Examples (1) and (3)) and 1,534 were used without such markings, most of them being used with a 3rd person singular morphology (see Examples (2) and (4)), and a few being used in the infinitive (see Example (5)).

(1) *du bord de ma mère ils **viennent** de Rivière-du-Loup*
 'on my mother's side they come from *Rivière-du-Loup*'
 (Francophone North Bay student)

(2) *mon oncle et ma mère **vient** pour déjeuner*
 'my uncle and my mother come for breakfast'
 (Francophone North Bay student)

(3) *t'sais eux sont anglophones t'sais ils **peuvent** pas apprendre le français*
 'you know they are Anglophones you know they cannot learn French'
 (Francophone Hawkesbury student)

(4) *pis eux-autres ils **peut** parler en français*
 'And them they can speak French' (Francophone Cornwall student)

(5) *les gens français ils ne **prendre** pas le temps d'écouter*
 'French people don't take the time to listen' (FSL university student)

The main purpose of our study is to document intergroup hierarchies in acquisition of the distinctive 3PL verb forms. To this end, we will first examine the acquisition rates of the six groups of students included in the study, namely the Francophone students from Hawkesbury vs. Cornwall vs. North Bay vs. Pembroke, vs. the FSL university students vs. the high school immersion students in relation to *être, avoir, aller,* and *faire* (i.e., the frequent verbs with distinctive forms that are easier to automatize) and with respect to the less frequent verbs (i.e., those that are harder to automatize). This analysis will be followed by a more-fine grained examination of the rates of acquisition of the distinctive verb markings according verb frequency and the students' frequency of use of French outside of the classroom. This will enable us to arrive at a more nuanced documentation of the intergroup differences in rates of acquisition of the distinctive verb forms. Lastly, we will analyze the data on the immersion teachers' and Francophone teachers' in-class speech and on the community input of the Francophone students. This will shed some light on the finding that the Pembroke and French immersion students have comparable rates of acquisition of the distinctive markings of 3PL verbs.

The GoldVarb X statistical analysis program (Tagliamonte 2006), which runs a stepwise logistic regression analysis to identify predictors of variation, was used to calculate the rates of acquisition and to assess the influence of the factors mentioned above. GoldVarb produces factor weights that measure the influence that each factor has on the use of the 3PL verb markings. The closer the factor weight value is to 1.00, the stronger the influence, and, conversely, the closer it is to 0 the weaker the influence. The neutral factor weight value is 0.50. The size of the range between the highest and lowest weight values provides an indication of the magnitude of intergroup variation captured by the analysis. GoldVarb also calculates a measure of the level of the statistical significance of the intergroup frequency differences. This measure is indicated by a χ^2 value whose upper threshold of significance is .05. When the program has found that the frequency differences are not statistically significant, we do not report the factor weights calculated by GoldVarb. The reader will find more detailed information on the use of GoldVarb in second language acquisition research in Young and Bayley (1996).

5. Research issues

As mentioned above, previous Canadian studies on acquisition of the 3PL verb forms by bilingual students focused on only a few of the six categories of students included in the present study. Further, in assessing the impact of verb frequency or of exposure to and use of French, these studies considered them as independent factors. Therefore, it is not possible to use the findings of these studies to formulate expectations regarding the influence of verb frequency and FUF on the hierarchies of intergroup differences in rates of acquisition of the 3PL verb forms. Still, it is possible to formulate several expectations based on the study of prepositional use with place names by Rehner et al. (2022), which distinguished the 'easier' preposition *à* from the more difficult preposition *en*, a distinction similar to the degree of difficulty based on verb frequency used in the present study:

- concerning verb frequency, with the frequent distinctive verbs, all six student groups will have high acquisition rates and there will not be much difference between the student groups, in keeping with the fact that such verbs are easy to automatize; however, with the infrequent distinctive verbs, which are harder to automatize, we expect that there will be lower acquisition rates and a sharper intergroup hierarchy;
- with both categories of verbs, the FSL university students will have higher acquisition rates than will the immersion students, reflecting the positive impact of their having continued to learn French past the high school level and on a bilingual university campus;
- with both categories of verbs, the FSL university students will have acquisition rates approximating those of the students from the minority communities – this expectation is based on the findings of Rehner et al. (2022); if this expectation is confirmed, possible reasons for it will have to be explored;
- with the frequent verbs, the immersion and Pembroke students will have comparable rates of acquisition, but with the infrequent verbs, the Pembroke students will have a clearly higher rate of acquisition, reflecting the fact that they have been schooled entirely in French and have been somewhat exposed to French in the community;
- with both categories of verbs, the students from Hawkesbury will have the highest rates of acquisition reflecting intensive exposure to French in the community;
- concerning FUF, with both categories of verbs, FUF will have no or only limited impact on acquisition by the Hawkesbury, Cornwall, and North Bay students.[4] This reflects that the frequency of use of French of even the low FUF students from these three communities is high enough to ensure a high rate of acquisition;
- with both categories of verbs, FUF will have a limited impact or no impact on the immersion students' acquisition, in line with the suggestion that limited exposure to French in a Francophone family of the mid FUF students is not high enough to increase their mastery of the distinctive verbs;
- lastly, with both categories of verbs, the university students who are the most highly engaged in interactions with Francophones will have significantly higher acquisition rates than the mid and low FUF university students.

---

4. We remind the reader that there is only one mid FUF student and no high FUF students in the Pembroke corpus, thus the Pembroke students were excluded from the analysis of the impact of FUF.

6. Results

Let us start with the analysis of the rates of acquisition of the six groups of students found for the frequent and infrequent distinctive verbs. The results of this analysis are displayed in Table 3. As can be seen, in keeping with our expectations, each of the student groups displays a lower rate of acquisition with the infrequent verbs than with the frequent ones. Further, with the frequent verbs, the percentages are all quite high and do not vary much (89%–98.4%). In contrast, with the infrequent verbs, the percentages fluctuate to a much larger extent (28.6%–93.4%). The factor weights express a similar contrast (47 points with the frequent verbs vs. 70 points with the infrequent verbs). Further, the percentages and factor weights reveal the following intergroup hierarchy with respect to the frequent verbs: the Hawkesbury students' rate of acquisition is higher than that of the North Bay and Cornwall students, whose similar rates are higher than those of the university, Pembroke, and immersion students (whose rates are all on a par). With the infrequent verbs, the percentages and factor weights reveal an intergroup hierarchy that is somewhat different: the Hawkesbury students are outperforming the Cornwall, North Bay, and university students, whose similar rates are higher than those of the Pembroke and immersion students (whose rates are on par).

Our expectation that the university students would have higher rates of acquisition than the immersion students for both categories of verbs is strongly confirmed with the infrequent verbs (.43 vs. .19) and to a lesser degree with the frequent verbs (.38 vs. .29). Our expectation that the rates of the university students would approximate those of the students from the minority communities is confirmed. In fact, our findings show that the university students' rates of acquisition are comparable to those of the Cornwall and North Bay students, and higher than those of the Pembroke students with the infrequent verbs (Cornwall .49; North Bay .44; university .43; vs. Pembroke .23) but, surprisingly, less so with the frequent ones (North Bay .54; Cornwall .47; university .38; Pembroke .33).

Our expectation that the immersion and the Pembroke students would have comparable rates of acquisition with the frequent verbs has been met (Pembroke .33; Immersion students .29). However, the expectation that the Pembroke students would have a rate of acquisition clearly higher than that of the immersion students with the infrequent verbs is not confirmed (Pembroke .23; Immersion students .19).

Lastly our expectation that with both categories of verbs the students from Hawkesbury would have the highest acquisition rates has been met (see their rates expressed in percentages and factor weight in Table 3).

Table 3. Rates of acquisition of the frequent and infrequent 3PL verbs by six groups of students

Groups	Number of verb used with 3PL markings	%	Weights
Frequent verbs			
Hawkesbury	1620	98.4	.76
Cornwall	1417	94.7	.47
North Bay	1392	95.8	.54
FSL University	847	92.3	.38
Pembroke	1016	90.5	.33
FSL High School Immersion	665	89	.29
Significance	0.000		
Total, %, and range	6957	94.2	47
Groups	Number of verb used with 3PL markings	%	Weights
Infrequent verbs			
Hawkesbury	511	93.4	.89
Cornwall	392	62.3	.49
North Bay	355	58.1	.44
FSL University	156	56.7	.43
Pembroke	145	34.3	.23
FSL High School Immersion	72	28.6	.19
Significance	0.000		
Total, %, and range	1631	59.5	70

Table 4 reveals that our expectation of no or limited impact of FUF on acquisition among the Francophone students is confirmed for the Hawkesbury students. They have almost identical rates of acquisition at both the high and mid FUF levels. However, among the Cornwall and North Bay students, at the high and mid FUF levels, the factor weight values are higher than .50 and at the low FUF level they are clearly below .50. This pattern disconfirms our expectation. Turning to the FSL students, we see that the expected impact of FUF on the acquisition rates of the university students is confirmed. The factor weights and the percentages show a positive linear effect on acquisition (i.e., the higher the level of FUF, the higher the acquisition rates). Lastly, contrary to our expectation, FUF has an influence on acquisition among immersion students revealed by marked intergroup differences in terms of factor weight and percentage at the mid and low FUF levels. That said, our analysis of the impact of FUF on acquisition of the frequent verbs has revealed that even the low FUF students have high rates of acquisition, a finding which confirms that the plural markings of these verbs are easy to automatize.

Table 4. Rates of acquisition for the frequent 3PL verbs by six student groups according to FUF

FUF	Frequent verbs									
	Hawksbury		Cornwall		North Bay		FSL university		FSL immersion	
	*(N) %	Weight	*(N) %	Weight	*(N) %	Weight	*(N) %	Weight	*(N) %	Weight
High	(1161) 98.6	NS	(240) 98.4	.72	(69) 97.2	.58	(303) 96.8	.68	–	–
Mid	(460) 97.9	NS	(717) 94.5	.53	(618) 97.6	.62	(309) 93.4	.50	(198) 97.1	.77
Low	–	–	(459) 93.1	.35	(705) 94.1	.39	(235) 85.8	.30	(468) 85.9	.39
Signif.	NA		0.006		0.005		0.000		0.000	
%, Range	98.4	NA	94.7	37	95.8	23	92.3	38	89	38

* (N) = Number of verbs used with plural markings

Turning now to the infrequent verbs, Table 5 shows that among both the Cornwall and North Bay students, the percentages and factor weights found for the three FUF levels pattern sharply and linearly, a finding which disconfirms our expectation of no impact on acquisition. We see that among the Hawkesbury students, FUF also influences acquisition and thus disconfirms our expectation; however, the factor weights and percentages of the mid FUF are, surprisingly, higher than those of the high FUF students. Among the FSL university students, the high FUF students have, as expected, higher acquisition rates than the mid and low FUF students both in terms of percentage and factor weights, but the difference is not marked. Lastly, among the immersion students, as expected, FUF does not have an influence on acquisition, since both the mid and low FUF students have comparable low rates of acquisition.

One interesting outcome of having documented the impact of FUF on the acquisition of the infrequent verbs is that a comparison between the different student groups at the same or different FUF levels provides a more nuanced intergroup hierarchy in the rates of acquisition. Recall that when FUF is not considered, the intergroup hierarchy for the infrequent verbs is as follows (see Table 3): Hawkesbury students outperforming the Cornwall, North Bay, and university students, whose similar rates outpace those of the Pembroke and immersion students (whose rates are on a par). However, when the impact of FUF is taken into account, as in Table 5, the hierarchy becomes more fine-grained and is no longer ternary: the Hawkesbury students are outpacing the high FUF Cornwall and North Bay students, who are outperforming the mid FUF Cornwall and North Bay students and the high FUF university students, whose performance is higher than the low FUF Cornwall and North Bay students and the mid and low FUF university students, who in turn are outpacing the mid and low FUF immersion students. Thus, if we focus, for instance, on the university students, we see that when FUF is not factored in, their overall rate of acquisition is in second position on the hierarchy scale, on a par with that of the students from the minority communities of Cornwall and North Bay. However, when FUF is taken into account, the rate of acquisition of the high FUF university students falls to third position, and the rates of the mid and low FUF university learners are in fourth position along with those of the low FUF Cornwall and North Bay students.

Table 5. Rates of acquisition of the infrequent 3PL verbs by six student groups according to FUF

FUF	Infrequent verbs								
	Hawksbury		Cornwall		North Bay		FSL university		FSL immersion	
	*(N) %	Weight	*(N) %	Weight	*(N) %	Weight	*(N) %	Weight	*(N) %	Weight
High	(351) 91.9	.42	(110) 85.9	.77	(37) 86	.81	(59) 69.4	.63	–	–
Mid	(160) 97	.67	(187) 68	.54	(171) 71.5	.63	(54) 47.4	.40	(15) 36.6	NS
Low	–	–	(95) 42	.29	(147) 44.7	.36	(43) 27.6	.50	(57) 27.1	NS
Signif.	0.019		0.000		0.000		0.009		NA	
%, Range	93.4	25	62.3	48	58.1	45	56.7	23	28.6	NA

* (N) = Number of verbs used with plural markings

7. Discussion

The discussion of our findings focuses on two main issues: (i) the intergroup differences in rates of acquisition of French morphosyntax found among the Francophone students and (ii) the respective position of the FSL university students and the FSL immersion students vis-à-vis each other and vis-à-vis the Francophone student groups in their acquisition of French morphosyntax. These issues are discussed in light of the findings of the present study and of our study of the acquisition of prepositional use with place names (see Table 6), and of the findings of research on acquisition of other aspects of French morphosyntax by bilingual Francophone students.

Concerning the first issue, Table 6 shows that, overall, among the Francophone students, we have found the following intergroup hierarchy in rates of acquisition. The rates of the students from the strong majority community of Hawkesbury are higher than those of the students from the minority communities of Cornwall and North Bay, which in turn are higher than those of the students from Pembroke, the weakest of the three minority communities. This overall intergroup hierarchy is in line with the findings of Mougeon and Beniak's (1991) study of the acquisition of the 3PL verb markings and of the reflexive pronouns by Francophone students based on data collected in 1978 in these same localities. This hierarchy is also in keeping with Harley (1979), who found that Francophone students from the majority community of Rayside, Ontario had a better mastery of the rules governing gender than did Francophone students from the minority community of Sudbury.

These convergent results underscore the impact of the proportional representation of Francophones at a local level on the acquisition of French morphosyntax by Francophone students. That said, Table 6 also shows that with the frequent verbs, whose 3PL markings are easy to automatize, all four groups have very high acquisition rates, and the intergroup hierarchy is tenuous. In contrast, with the infrequent verbs, whose markings are harder to automatize, there are sizable intergroup differences in rates of acquisition, and the intergroup hierarchy is clear. A similar contrast is also observable with prepositions *à* and *en* (Rehner et al. 2022). The intergroup differences are less sizeable, and the intergroup hierarchy is less sharp with easy preposition *à* than with the more difficult *en*. Harley (1979) arrived at similar results. She found that all of the Francophone student groups in her study had a (near) perfect mastery of the rule assigning the feminine to the names of sciences and disciplines, but with the more complex rule assigning the feminine to inanimate nouns (and lesser exotic animals) ending in a consonant, the students from the minority community had a markedly lower rate of mastery than did those from the majority community.

We have seen above that intergroup differences in acquisition rates of the 3PL markings are also influenced by FUF. The influence of this factor on acquisition of other aspects of French morphosyntax has been documented by previous research on the acquisition of object clitic pronouns (e.g., Harley 1979; Nadasdi 2000; and Pirvulescu et al. 2014). In the present study, we have refined the assessment of the impact of FUF by cross-tabulating it with exposure at the community level. This more fine-grained analysis revealed that the impact of FUF is more or less evident across the different groups of Francophone students. This finding echoes that of Mougeon and Beniak's (1991) study of the acquisition of the reflexive pronouns by Francophone students from the 1978 corpus. For instance, these authors found that among the Cornwall students, those who communicated mostly in French at home had a 90% rate of acquisition of the reflexive pronouns as early as age seven and that the students who communicated mostly in English in this setting reached this acquisition level only at age 15. Further, among the Pembroke students, neither those who communicated mostly in French nor those who communicated mostly in English reached the 90% level at the end of secondary school. Measuring the cumulative effect of exposure to French in the community and of FUF among bilingual students from different age groups, like Mougeon and Beniak did, is a potentially fruitful line of research to sharpen our understanding of the impact of extra-linguistic factors on acquisition.

Turning now to the second issue, Table 6 shows that the FSL university students have rates of acquisition of the four aspects of French morphosyntax which are always higher than those of the FSL immersion students. This pattern likely reflects that the university students have spent more years learning French than the immersion students, they have access to Francophones on the campus of their bilingual college, and they are of an age where they can more readily search out opportunities to engage in potentially useful interactions with Francophones in the wider community.

Concerning the FSL students' positions vis-à-vis the Francophone students, and starting with the immersion students, Table 6 shows that with the 3PL markings of the frequent verbs and preposition *à* (i.e., the two easiest aspects of French morphosyntax), the immersion students' rates are comparable to those of the Pembroke students. However, with the infrequent verbs and *en*, their rates of acquisition are below those of the Pembroke students.[5] Thus, it appears that the mostly classroom-based exposure to French of the immersion students is high enough for them to reach levels of mastery of the easy elements comparable to or not too remote from those of students from a weak minority Francophone com-

---

5. The rates of acquisition of prepositions *à* and *en* are from Rehner et al. (2022).

munity, but too low to bring them to the level of mastery of the more difficult aspects reached by these same Francophone students.

This finding is understandable since the immersion students have been schooled only partially in French and have had no or only marginal exposure to French outside the classroom, while the Pembroke students have been schooled entirely in French and have had some opportunities to use French outside the French-medium schools. We saw above that when FUF is taken into account in the analysis, a similar pattern is observable. With the frequent verbs, the immersion students have rates of acquisition which are as high as those of the Francophone students from the minority communities in the three FUF categories, but with the infrequent verbs, the immersion students have rates which are consistently below those of these same groups of Francophone students. Previous research comparing French immersion students with bilingual Francophone students arrived at similar results. There are some aspects of French morphosyntax where immersion students have rates of mastery which are not too remote from those of bilingual Francophone students considered as a whole or from those of English dominant Francophone students, but for most aspects of French morphosyntax, the rates of mastery of the immersion students are lower than those of the bilingual Francophone students, including those who are dominant in English (Canale et al. 1978; Harley 1979; Harley & Swain 1978; Lapkin & Swain 1977; Mougeon et al. 2010).

Table 6. Patterns of acquisition of prepositions *à* and *en* with place names and frequent vs. infrequent 3PL verbs by the six student groups

Groups	Easy		Challenging	
	à (%)	Frequent verbs (%)	en (%)	Infrequent verbs (%)
Hawkesbury students	97	98	96	93
Cornwall students	93	95	78	62
North Bay students	90	96	83	58
FSL university students	90	92	64	57
Pembroke students	68	90	54	34
FSL immersion students	73	89	29	29

Returning to the findings of the present study, Table 6 shows that while the immersion students' rate of acquisition of the infrequent verbs is lower than that of the Pembroke students, the intergroup difference is modest. Mougeon et al. (2010) arrived at similar results when they compared the immersion students examined in the present study with Francophone students from the 1978 corpus;

however, these authors did not delve into possible reasons for this finding. The data in Tables 7 and 8 shed some light on this unresolved issue.

Table 7 presents data on the frequency of use of 3PL markings with the infrequent verbs in the 1978 Francophone student corpus. These data reveal that variable absence of 3PL marking was already a feature of the speech of the parental generation in the three minority communities (and most notably in Pembroke), whereas in Hawkesbury such absence was marginal. Table 8 provides data on the educational input of the students. These data show that both the Francophone and the immersion students are exposed to near categorical use of the 3PL markings of infrequent verbs in the classroom.

Taken together, these data show that, unlike the immersion students who are exposed almost exclusively to the nearly invariant use of such plural markings by their teachers, the Pembroke students are also exposed to the variable norm of the community, and this likely mitigates, to some extent, the effect of exposure to invariant use of the 3PL markings in their educational input. These findings highlight the importance of considering both educational and community input in order to better understand the extra-linguistic factors that condition language acquisition.

Table 7. Rates of use of infrequent 3PL verbs without the distinctive markings in the 1978 data according to community of residence[*]

Hawkesbury	Cornwall	North Bay	Pembroke
3%	21%	24%	51%

[*] Adapted from Mougeon and Beniak (1995)

Table 8. Rates of use of 3PL markings with infrequent verbs in the classroom speech of teachers in the Francophone communities and of immersion teachers

Teacher groups	Total N of infrequent 3PL verbs	Distinctive markings on infrequent 3PL verbs	
		N	%
Hawkesbury teachers	73	72	98.6
Cornwall teachers	115	114	99.1
North Bay teachers	152	147	96.7
Pembroke teachers	109	109	100
Immersion teachers	23	22	95.6

8. Conclusion

As Carroll (2017: 40) points out, "[t]here is a great need for more descriptive research that will tell us how language use varies in different kinds of bilingual families and classroom contexts. However, to know what to observe and count, we also need to unpack the complexity of specific learning problems." Our study has made some significant headway in this regard by refining our understanding of the extra-linguistic and linguistic factors that impact on the acquisition of French morphosyntax by bilingual Francophone and FSL high school and university students. There are, at the same time, opportunities to further expand the continuum of advanced French language proficiency that has guided the present study by adding the speech of both younger and older learners such as Mougeon and Beniak's (1991) study of the acquisition of reflexive pronouns by 7- to 18-year-old Francophone students. Future research on the acquisition of French as a second language would also benefit by including learners residing in majority communities. Research by Sankoff et al. (1997) on the use of sociolinguistic variants by older FSL speakers suggests that in such settings these learners can use variants that are emblematic of Canadian spoken French at levels which can approximate those found in corpora of Quebec French. Research focusing on the acquisition of French morphosyntax by FSL learners in such settings could provide a useful complement to these findings and, along with the present study, would help in responding to Carroll's timely call.

References

Ågren, M. & van de Weijer, J. 2013. Input frequency and the acquisition of subject-verb agreement in number in spoken and written French. *Journal of French Language Studies* 23(3): 311–333.

Alexandre, N. 2004. Variation in the Spoken French of Franco-Ontarians: Preposition *de* Followed by the Deictic Pro-forms ˛*ca* and *la, aller* in Compound Past Tenses and Prepositions *a`, au* and *en* Preceding Geographical Place Names. MA thesis, York University.

Allen, P., Cummins, J., Harley, B. & Swain, M. 1987. *Development of Bilingual Proficiency Project*. Toronto ON: OISE, University of Toronto.

Bartning, I. 2016. Morphosyntax and discourse in high level second language use. In *Advanced Proficiency and Exceptional Abilities in Second Languages*, K. Hyltenstam (ed.), 43–70. Berlin: Walter de Gruyter.

Canale, M., Mougeon, R. & Beniak, E. 1978. Acquisition of some grammatical elements in English and French by monolingual and bilingual Canadian students. *Canadian Modern Language Review* 34(3): 505–524.

Carroll, S. E. 2017. Explaining bilingual learning outcomes in terms of exposure and input. *Bilingualism: Language and Cognition* 20(1): 37–41.

Castonguay, C. 1979. Exogamie et anglicisation chez les minorités canadiennes françaises. *Canadian Journal of Sociology* 16(1): 39–52.

Census of Canada. 2001. *Detailed Mother Tongue, for Canada, Provinces, Territories, Census Metropolitan Areas and Census Agglomerations, 2001 Censuses – 20% Sample Data – Cat. No. 97F0007XCB2001002*. Ottawa ON: Statistics Canada.

Harley, B. 1979. French gender 'rules' in the speech of English-dominant, French-dominant and monolingual French-speaking children, *Working Papers in Bilingualism* 19: 129–156.

Harley, B. 1986. *Age in Second Language Acquisition*. Bristol: Multilingual Matters.

Harley, B. 1992a. Patterns of second language development in French immersion, *Journal of French Language Studies* 2(2): 159–183.

Harley, B. 1992b. Aspects of the oral second language proficiency of early immersion, late immersion, and extended French students at grade 10. In *Comprehension-based Second Language Teaching*, R. Courchêne, J. Glidden, J. St. John & C. Thérien (eds), 371–388. Ottawa ON: Ottawa University Press.

Harley, B. & Swain, M. 1978. An analysis of the French verb system by young learners of French. *Interlanguage Studies Bulletin* 3: 35–79.

Lapkin, S. & Swain, M. 1977. The use of English and French cloze tests in a bilingual education program evaluation: Validity and error analysis. *Language Learning* 27(2): 279–310.

Mougeon, F. & Rehner, K. 2015. Engagement portraits and (socio)linguistic performance: A transversal and longitudinal study of advanced L2 learners. *Studies in Second Language Acquisition* 37(3): 425–456.

Mougeon, R. 2014. Maintien et évolution du français dans les provinces du Canada anglophone. In *Colonisation, globalisation et vitalité du français*, S. Mufwene & C. Vigouroux (eds), 211–276. Paris: Odile Jacob.

Mougeon, R. & Beniak, É. 1991. *Linguistic Consequences of Language Contact and Restriction: The Case of French in Ontario*. Oxford: OUP.

Mougeon, R. & Beniak, É. 1995. Le non-accord en nombre entre sujet et verbe en français ontarien: Un cas de simplification? *Présence Francophone* 46: 53–65.

Mougeon, R., Nadasdi, T. & Rehner, K. 2010. *The Sociolinguistic Competence of Immersion Students*. Bristol: Multilingual Matters.

Mougeon, R. & Rehner, K. 2017. The influence of classroom input and community exposure on the learning of variable grammar. *Bilingualism: Language and Cognition* 20(1): 21–22.

Mougeon, R. & Rehner, K. 2019. Patterns of sociolinguistic variation in teacher classroom speech. *Journal of Sociolinguistics* 23(2): 163–185.

Nadasdi, T. 2000. *Variation grammaticale et langue minoritaire: Le cas des pronoms clitiques en français ontarien*. Munich: Lincom.

Nadasdi, T. 2001. Agreeing to disagree: Variable subject-verb agreement in immersion French. *Canadian Journal of Applied Linguistics* 4(1): 87–101.

Pirvulescu, M., Pérez-Leroux, A. T., Roberge, Y., Strik, N. & Thomas, D. 2014. Bilingual effects: Exploring object omission in pronominal languages. *Bilingualism: Language and Cognition* 17(3): 495–510.

Rehner, K., Mougeon, R. & Mougeon, F. 2022. Variation in choice of prepositions with place names on the French L1–L2 continuum in Ontario, Canada. In *Variation in Second and Heritage Languages: Crosslinguistic Perspectives*, R. Bayley, D. Preston & X. Li (eds), 223–252. Amsterdam: John Benjamins.

Sankoff, G., Thibault, P., Nagy, N., Blondeau, H., Fonollosa, M.-O., & Gagnon, L. 1997. Variation in the use of discourse markers in a language contact situation. *Language Variation and Change* 9(2): 191–218.

Swain, M. & Lapkin, S. 1982. *Evaluating Bilingual Education: A Canadian Case Study*. Clevedon: Multilingual Matters.

Tagliamonte, S. 2006. *Analyzing Sociolinguistic Variation*. Cambridge: CUP.

Young, R. & Bayley, R. 1996. VARBRUL analysis for second language acquisition research. In *Second Language Acquisition and Linguistic Variation*, R. Bayley & D. Preston (eds), 253–306. Amsterdam: John Benjamins.

CHAPTER 6

L2 intonation perception in learners of Spanish

Angela George
University of Calgary

> While the field of L2 variation, particularly with L2 Spanish, is expanding, to date little is known about the acquisition of variable intonation that occurs in final boundary tones of yes-no questions. The present study investigates the effects of explicit instruction on the accurate identification of utterance type (yes-no questions, broad-focused declarative statements, and wh-questions). Eleven L1 English learners of Spanish in an advanced university level Spanish class listened to 21 Spanish utterances to identify the utterance type before and after receiving explicit in-class instruction. Two L1 Spanish listeners served as a control. Learner gains in identification of utterance type were not significant, and there was no statistically significant effect of explicit instruction on the identification of the utterances.

> **Keywords:** L2 Spanish intonation, variation, yes-no questions, L2 Spanish learners

1. Introduction

Second language (L2) learners often find it difficult to master first language (L1) pronunciation, particularly when learning the target language (TL) as an adult. One area that has caused difficulty in terms of both production and perception is L2 prosody and more specifically L2 intonation (Henriksen 2013). For example, an utterance such as *There is a mosquito* can sound like a statement or a question and can also be stated with irony or sarcasm, all by changing the intonational contours. Saito (2018: 286) claims that the development of L2 intonation is "'gradual' and 'slow' in nature". Problems with suprasegmental features of the language can result in unpleasant exchanges of communication for L2 speakers and their interlocutors (Mennen 2006). Research on the area of L2 intonation in general and also on Spanish has received little attention (Henriksen 2013). However, some recent studies with L2 learners abroad, and cross-sectional studies of learners at different proficiency levels, shed light on the developmental patterns of L2 Spanish intonation. Familiarity and exposure to target dialect(s) has been shown to benefit the perception of regional varieties by L2 classroom learners (Matsuura et al. 1999; Nibert 2005; Sullivan & Karst 1996; Tauroza & Luk 1997) and by study abroad learners (Schmidt 2009; Trimble 2013).

Previous phonological research has focused on segmental phonology more so than suprasegmental phonology (Henriksen 2013; Flege 2002). Intonational phonology, however, has been explored, quite extensively with L1 Spanish speakers and less so with L2 Spanish speakers (Henriksen 2013). This could be due to the high degree of variation found in L1 speakers (e.g., Prieto & Roseano 2010). The field is growing, and a handful of studies have begun to explore the development of L2 intonation by learners of Spanish.

A particularly interesting case of L2 Spanish intonation to study are statements and questions. In English, a yes-no question is distinct from a statement not only due to intonation (high (H%) vs. low boundary tone (L%), respectively), but also due to word order (Table 1). This is not the case in Spanish, where intonation may be the only cue to distinguish a question from a statement when the word order remains the same (Hualde & Prieto 2015). As a result, L2 learners of Spanish who are English L1 speakers cannot use the same information as in their L1 to distinguish statements from yes-no questions. That is, they cannot solely rely on word order, but they need to primarily use intonational cues. On the other hand, wh-questions follow similar syntactic and intonational patterns in English and Spanish, so the L2 learners do not have to rely on intonation. Statements such as the one shown in Table 1 in both Spanish and English have boundary tones with similar underlying characteristics (Beckman & Pierrehumbert 1986; Estebas-Vilaplana & Prieto 2008).

Table 1. Examples of sentences in English and Spanish with their boundary tones

	English	Spanish
Statement	There is a meeting. (L%)	Hay una reunion. (L%)
Yes-no question	Is there a meeting? (H%)	¿Hay una reunion? (H%)
Wh-question	When is the meeting? (L%)	¿Cuándo es la reunion? (L%)

Complicating matters even further for English-speaking learners of Spanish, is the variation found in final boundary tones of L1 Spanish intonation of absolute interrogatives (e.g., Prieto & Roseano 2010). For example, Castilian and Mexican varieties end in a high boundary tone (Face 2008; Willis 2005), while Puerto Rican Spanish ends in a low boundary tone (Quilis 1987). This may also pose issues for learners of Spanish who may perceive a yes-no question made by a Puerto Rican speaker as a statement.

Provided the similarities between English and Spanish questions in terms of their boundary tones, the intonation of both types of sentences should be easy for L2 learners to perceive. Given, however, the difference in the significance of the intonational information between the two question types in Spanish, it is not clear whether one is easier to learn than the other for L2 learners. The current study seeks to determine if L2 learners of Spanish can perceive the difference between statements and questions with identical word order when they are not given any context clues about the utterance by examining the effects of implicit instruction.

2. Background

Research on the development of L2 Spanish intonation is in its infancy. A handful of studies on production and perception offer valuable insights into the field. This section will highlight some of those contributions by examining studies that focus on the perception of intonation by learners of Spanish as well as the effects of explicit instruction on the development of L2 Spanish intonation.

Research on L2 Spanish intonation perception has shown some differences in the ability to perceive different intonational contours based on proficiency level and also the type of utterance under study (Brandl et al. 2020; Nibert 2005, 2006; Trimble 2013; Zárate-Sández 2018). Brandl et al. (2020), Trimble (2013), and Zárate-Sández (2018) will be discussed in further detail next, since their investigations pertain directly to the current study. In all three studies, L2 Spanish learners were tasked with distinguishing between yes-no questions and declarative statements; Brandl et al. (2020) also examined wh-questions and Trimble (2013) also examined regional differences in yes-no question final boundary tones and how that affected perception.

Zárate-Sández (2018) investigated perception of final boundary tones in 17 intermediate, 20 advanced, and 18 very advanced L2 Spanish learners. The control groups in the study consisted of 17 L1 American English speakers, 17 L1 Spanish speakers (representing 5 macro dialects of Spanish), and 16 English-Spanish bilinguals (heritage speakers of Spanish). To measure perception, participants were asked to listen to an utterance and repeat it, since it was posited that accurate repetition would indicate accurate perception. The original utterance was a declarative sentence uttered by an Argentine Spanish speaker. This sentence was manipulated to create 10 stimuli with increasingly higher final boundary tones in each stimulus. Two L1 Spanish speakers judged each stimulus (the 10 utterances) as sounding native-like, indicating they were unaware they had been manipulated.

By manipulating the location of the final boundary tone on a scale from low to high, the excepted type of utterance was also being manipulated, with declaratives having lower boundary tones and yes-no questions having higher boundary tones. Contrary to the prediction made by the researcher that yes-no questions in Spanish would be more difficult for L2 Spanish-speakers to distinguish from declaratives (since they must rely on intonation and not word-order like in English), the results indicated that all participants were able to perceive higher boundary tones as yes-no questions and lower boundary tones as declarative statements. This was regardless of the proficiency level of the participant.

Brandl et al. (2020) investigated the development of broad and narrow-focused statements, yes-no questions, and wh-questions in a cross section of L1 English learners of L2 Spanish with varying proficiency levels, including 38 low-beginner, 35 high-beginner, 41 low-intermediate, 22 high-intermediate, and 53 advanced, in addition to a control group of 10 L1 Spanish speakers. The proficiency level of the L2 Spanish learners was based on the level of the university Spanish course in which they were enrolled. In this study, upon hearing an utterance, participants also saw an utterance on the screen. Participants were asked to determine if the two utterances matched. For example, if they heard *Daniel iba a Bolivia* 'Daniel went to Bolivia' and saw *¿Daniel iba a Bolivia?* 'Did Daniel went to Bolivia?', that would be a mismatch. If they heard *Daniel iba a Bolivia* 'Daniel went to Bolivia' and saw *Daniel iba a Bolivia* 'Daniel went to Bolivia', that would be a match. The utterances came from 8 speakers of 8 macro-dialects of Spanish. When tasked with identifying utterances that matched, all participants, both L1 Spanish speakers and all learner groups, were above 90% accurate for all utterance types. However, when the utterance's visual appearance did not match its aural form, accuracy in identifying these mismatches decreased and differences among L1 and L2 Spanish speakers were found. L1 Spanish speakers correctly identified mismatches with broad focus declaratives 76% of the time and 81% of the time for narrow focus declaratives. The learner groups ranged from 7% to 34% accuracy, with the advanced learners identifying mismatches significantly more than the other beginner learner groups. For yes-no questions, the L1 Spanish speakers correctly identified mismatches 61% of the time, while the learner groups accuracy was between 6% and 14%, again with advanced learners being more accurate than beginning learners. In terms of wh-questions, L1 Spanish speakers were 98% accurate in identifying mismatches, a level similar to advanced and high-intermediate L2 learners. Low-intermediate learners followed with 83% accuracy, followed by high-beginner learners at 74% and low beginner learners at 66%. In summary, learners more accurately identified mismatches if the mismatch contained a wh-question than if it contained a yes-no question or either type of declarative statement. This study demonstrates that, as predicted, wh-questions are the easiest to perceive and yes-no questions are the most difficult. In addition, the developmental pattern shows that only learners at the high-intermediate and advanced levels pay attention to intonational cues when listening to questions. Statements are much easier to identify even for beginning learners who demonstrated a high level of accuracy.

Trimble (2013) took macro-dialect under consideration for advanced learners in his perception study. Of the 24 advanced learners in the study, 9 had never studied abroad, 9 recently studied abroad for one semester in North-Central Spain and 6 in Mérida, Venezuela. The control groups consisted of L1 Spanish speakers from Mérida, Venezuela and 19 late-beginning learners. The task was to identify if the utterance was a yes-no question or a declarative statement. The listeners heard three different Spanish speakers, one from Mérida Venezuela, one from the USA and one from North-Central Spain. It should be noted that in Mérida, Venezuela, yes-no questions end in a low final boundary tone unlike in North-Central Spain where they end in a high boundary tone. The utterances were split into parts and the listeners heard either all or part of each utterance. In total, there were 24 utterances by each of the three speakers recorded. When the participants listened, they were tasked with identifying the type of utterance, declarative statement or yes-no question. The results indicated that learners were 58% accurate in identifying the utterance type when they heard part of the utterance and 89% accurate when they heard all of the utterance, indicating that they were relying on final boundary tones to identify the utterance. Participants were more accurate at identifying declaratives (78%) than yes-no questions (63%). The researcher found that L2 advanced learners who had previously studied in Mérida, Venezuela were more accurate at identifying yes-no questions and declaratives than L2 late-beginning learners. However, the same did not hold true for the advanced learners who had previously studied in North-Central Spain in that they did not differ statistically from late-beginning learners due to overall high levels of accuracy in the identification of yes-no questions and statements. Trimble (2013) also found a heavy influence of L1, with learners still associating a final fall in a question to their L1 of English and not the L2 questions in Mérida Venezuelan Spanish.

The aforementioned studies did not examine the teaching and training of L2 Spanish intonation. Exposure to training on variable input has increased perceptive abilities (Bradlow et al. 1997; Nishi & Kewley-Port 2007; Palmeri et al. 1993; Rasmussen & Zampini 2010). Dialectal variations are often not taught in the Spanish classroom (Gallego & Conley 2014), which could be why there are few studies on explicit instruction of this type of variation on L2 development. Two studies that involved training learners to perceive or produce regional dialectal variation will be discussed next.

Regarding training on Spanish phonology for L2 learners, Rasmussen and Zampini (2010) found that explicit instruction aids in the perception of some regional features in L2 learners studying abroad in Andalucía, Spain, but they did not investigate any intonational features or patterns. Addressing this gap, Craft (2015) found no effect of instruction in a group of learners who spent 6 weeks abroad in Valencia, Spain. While the number of participants was limited to 5 in the experimental group (received instruction while abroad) and 3 in the control group (received no instruction while abroad), all participants differed significantly from locals in their production of boundary tones in statements and yes-no questions. Participants in both groups increased their production of low boundary tones in statements from 62% to 81% for the experimental group and from 68% to 91% in the control group. On the contrary, participants in both groups remained steady in their production of high boundary tones for yes-no questions which remained between 96%–100% in the pretest and posttest. While this study did not test perception, it did use perception activities to train learners to produce certain intonational patterns for statements and yes-no questions. No studies, to my knowledge, have examined the effects of instruction on the perception of intonational patterns.

3. Theoretical background

Mennen's (2015:173) L2 Intonation Learning theory (LILt) attempts to account for the learning of suprasegmentals by offering the following four dimensions where differences between L1 and L2 intonation may reside:

i. the systemic dimension, which refers to the inventory and distribution of structural phonological elements;
ii. the realisational dimension, which refers to the way the systemic elements are phonetically implemented;
iii. the semantic dimension, which refers to how systemic elements are used to signal intonation function; and
iv. the frequency dimension, which refers to the frequency of use of the structural elements.

According to this theory, categories within L1 and L2 intonation systems that are similar will result in the merging into one category and categories that are different will result in two sounds. Along the way, transfer from L1 to L2 may occur. Within this theory, the systemic and semantic dimensions for final boundary tones of statements, yes-no questions, and wh-questions are similar for Spanish and English, apart from dialects of Spanish whose yes-no questions end in a low boundary tone. These similarities should be encouraging to L2 learners of Spanish and should result in no difficulties in terms of perceiving the different types of utterances. Dialect identification should also be easy when the final boundary tone of the utterance in the L1 dialect matches that of the L2. When it does not match, learners may have a more difficult time identifying the utterance type. Sociolinguistic variation can play a role in this theory, particularly to the frequency dimension, with some learners being more exposed to the dialects with a low boundary tone for yes-no questions. According to Clopper and Bradlow (2009), L2 learners will attend to phonologically or sociolinguistically relevant cues if they also occur in their L1.

The current study adds to the limited number of studies on the teaching and learning of variable intonation by investigating how L2 learners perceive variable intonational patterns, particularly since L2 Spanish learners in the U.S. are often exposed to different varieties of Spanish through their instructors, contact with Spanish-speakers, and media. Previous studies did not address the role of technology, or the role instruction may play on the perception of intonational phrasing, especially when that phrasing differs from what is found in the L1. To add to the previous studies on the perception of intonation, the current study explores the development of the perception of absolute interrogatives and declaratives in a variety of Spanish dialects, some of which do not mimic American English in terms of intonational phrasing. The following research questions are posed:

- Do L2 Spanish listeners transfer L1 intonational information, specifically final boundary tone, to L2 intonation?
- What, if any, is the role of explicit instruction on the ability to accurately identify utterance types (absolute interrogatives, broad focus declaratives, and wh-questions)?

Based on the previous studies reviewed, it is hypothesized that participants will transfer their knowledge of their L1 to their L2 when distinguishing between wh-questions, yes-no questions, and declaratives. This would mean that they should have few issues in accurately identifying wh-questions. Listeners can rely on both the final falling boundary tone and the interrogative word in the question, similar to English. Listeners may have more difficulty identifying final falling yes-no questions, as is commonly heard in some macro-dialects of Spanish, including Puerto Rican Spanish. This low boundary tone is not heard in English and therefore may not transfer to Spanish. In other words, if participants can transfer L1 prosodic perception to L2, they will be more accurate in identifying the types of utterances; if not, they will be less accurate. It is also hypothesized that instruction will result in increased accuracy of the identification of the three types of utterances and in particular will aid in the identification of yes-no questions with low boundary tones, which are less common than yes-no questions with high boundary tones.

4. Methodology

4.1 Participants

The 11 participants were third- and fourth-year students enrolled in advanced Spanish courses at a large regional university in the Southeastern USA. They were L1 speakers of English ranging in age from 21–42, with an average age of 25.5. On average, they spent 6.77 years learning Spanish. The participants reported varying degrees of contact with primarily L1 Latin American Spanish speakers. Their average proficiency score on a grammar-based 25-point multiple choice test created by Geeslin and Gudmestad (2010) was 75.27%. Two additional adult male L1 speakers of Spanish were also included in the study to serve as a control group. One was from Colombia and the other from Puerto Rico. Two adult female heritage speakers of Spanish were also included in the study. These speakers grew up speaking Spanish at home and attended school in English, with the exception of the Spanish classes they were enrolled in at the university. It is a limitation of the study that more L1 Spanish speakers were not included, and it is suggested to rectify this in the future.

4.2 Instruments

4.2.1 *Pretest*

The participants completed a background questionnaire in which they provided information about their previous experiences learning Spanish. This included the number of years they spent learning Spanish, how and where they learned Spanish, and the geographic variety of Spanish they currently speak or wish to speak. They also completed a 25-question multiple choice Spanish proficiency test based on Geeslin and Gudmestad (2010) which tested both grammar and vocabulary.

4.2.2 *Dialect and utterance identification task*

Prior to receiving any instruction about intonation, the participants completed a pretest where they listened to 21 utterances presented in random order. These utterances were taken from the Interactive Atlas of Spanish Intonation (found here: http://prosodia.upf.edu/atlasentonacion). Then after listening to each utterance, on a sheet of paper, the participants selected the type of utterance (question or statement) and the macrodialect of the speaker based on the country (Mexico, España (Madrid), Argentina, Perú, Colombia, España (Andalucía), Venezuela, Puerto Rico, Ninguno (None)). Of the 21 utterances, there were 7 declaratives, 7 yes-no questions, and 7 wh-questions, each from 7 regional macrodialects

(Colombia, Puerto Rico, Argentina, Mexico, Peru, North-Central Spain, and Southern Spain). While it is possible participants could identify dialects based on other information in the utterances outside of intonation, this was controlled for as much as possible. For example, word-order was not an issue in the yes-no questions and declaratives, and neither were major distinguishing regional phonological features, such as consonant lenition, the interdental fricative instead of the alveolar fricative in North-Central Spain, and the palatal fricative in parts of Argentina. The contours of each dialect for declaratives were similar with either one or two high peaks and ending in a final low boundary tone. For yes-no questions, each utterance ended in a high boundary tone except for the one pronounced by the Puerto Rican speaker. That utterance ended in a low boundary tone. For wh-questions, the intonational contours were also very similar, with one or two high peaks and then a low final boundary tone. Wh-questions could be easily identified due to the interrogative word included in the utterance.

4.2.3 Input during explicit instruction

A few days after the pretest, participants received explicit whole-class face-to-face instruction on the intonational contours of the three types of utterances from the instructor for approximately 20 minutes. This involved viewing spectrograms and listening to recordings from the Interactive Atlas of Spanish Intonation. The instructor, who was also the researcher, indicated the various macrodialects by presenting audio recordings from the Atlas of neutral broad-focused declarative statements, information-seeking yes-no questions, and wh-questions, and then highlighting the overall contours and differences in pitch accents and boundary tones for each sentence type along with the origin of each speaker, pointing out regional differences found in the boundary tones of the utterances. The recordings were the same ones used in the pretest and posttest. Prior to this instruction, participants did not appear to know anything about intonation.

4.2.4 Posttest

One week after this instruction, participants listened to the 21 utterances again and provided the same information as before, the utterance type and the macrodialect of the speaker of each utterance.

5. Analysis

The researcher recorded the answers from the pretest and the posttest. A correct answer for utterance type received a score of 1 and an incorrect answer received a 0. The scores for each utterance type for each participant were added together with the highest possible being 7. Given that the data were not normally distributed, the non-parametric Related-Samples Wilcoxon Signed Rank test was performed instead of parametric paired *t*-tests in order to compare increases in the accurate identification of utterance type from the pretest to the posttest.

6. Results

Table 2 displays the average out of a total possible of 7 for each utterance type. The average for identifying declaratives remained the same both before and after explicit instruction. This average increased slightly for yes-no questions and wh-questions, but the increase was not significant.

Table 2. Identification of utterance type by 11 L2 Spanish listeners

Sentence type	Pretest average (SD)	Posttest average (SD)	Related-samples Wilcoxon signed rank test *p*-value
Declaratives (*N*=7)	6.91 (0.31)	6.91 (0.31)	*p*=.64
Yes-no questions (*N*=7)	6.45 (0.69)	6.64 (0.67)	*p*=.09
Wh-questions (*N*=7)	6.45 (0.69)	6.91 (0.30)	*p*=.09

When dividing the utterances into types, significant improvement was not found since the *p*-values for the Related-Samples Wilcoxon Signed Rank tests were all above .05.

Table 3 displays the individual variation evident in the identification of utterance type by the 11 participants in the study. The total possible number of utterances for each type is 7. The macro-dialect of the speaker of the misidentified utterances is shown in parenthesis.

Table 3. Individual identification by utterance type (and in parenthesis the dialects they misidentified)

Participant	Declaratives Pre / Post	Yes-no questions Pre / Post	Wh-questions Pre / Post	Total Pre / Post
1	7 / 7	7 / 7	7 / 7	21 / 21
2	7 / 7	6 / 7 (Puerto Rico)	5 / 7 (Peru, Mexico)	18 / 21

Table 3. *(continued)*

Participant	Declaratives Pre / Post	Yes-no questions Pre / Post	Wh-questions Pre / Post	Total Pre / Post
3	7 / 7	5 / 7 (Colombia, Puerto Rico)	6 / 6 (Mexico / Mexico)	18 / 20
4	7 / 7	6 / 7 (Puerto Rico)	6 / 7 (Puerto Rico)	19 / 21
5	6 / 7 (Puerto Rico)	6 / 7 (Puerto Rico)	6 / 7 (Colombia)	18 / 21
6	7 / 7	7 / 7	7 / 7	21 / 21
7	7 / 7	5 / 6 (Puerto Rico)	6 / 7 (Southern Spain)	18 / 20
8	7 / 7	7 / 7	7 / 7	21 / 21
9	7 / 7	6 / 7 (Puerto Rico)	7 / 7	20 / 21
10	6 / 7 (Argentina)	6 / 7 (Puerto Rico)	7 / 7	19 / 21
11	7 / 7	7 / 7	7 / 7	21 / 21
L1 Spanish listener from Colombia	7 / 7	7 / 7	6 / 7 (Peru)	20 / 21
L1 Spanish listener from Puerto Rico	7 / 7	7 / 7	6 / 7 (Peru)	20 / 21
Heritage listener of Colombian descent	7 / N/A	7 / N/A	7 / N/A	21 / N/A
Heritage listener of Mexican descent	6 / 7 (Southern Spain)	7 / 7	7 / 7	20 / 21

Four of the participants (1, 6, 8, and 11) accurately identified all utterance types on both the pretest and the posttest. The most any participant misidentified for any given utterance type was 2 out of 7 utterances. Three participants became less accurate in their identification of utterance type from pretest to posttest. However, this inaccurate identification was limited to yes-no questions only, where participants misidentified these as declarative statements. Only two participants misidentified a declarative utterance. Both times, these participants identified the utterance as a yes-no question. As suspected, the participants had issues identifying the Puerto Rican yes-no questions, misidentifying them as declarative statements. Two participants identified the Colombian yes-no question as a declarative. Five participants identified wh-questions as declarative utterances, which is quite surprising given the interrogative word present in the question.

The last five rows of Table 2 include four additional listeners, two who are L1 Spanish speakers and two who are heritage speakers of Spanish. Both L1 Spanish speakers accurately identified the utterance type for all but one utterance, a wh-question produced by a Peruvian speaker misidentified as a declarative. It is a bit unclear why this would have happened. The heritage speaker whose family is from Colombia did not complete the posttest, but accurately identified each utterance type on the pretest. The heritage speaker whose family is from Mexico also exhibited a high degree of accuracy, misidentifying a declarative spoken by a speaker from Southern Spain as a yes-no question. This dialect was most likely unfamiliar to the participant.

7. Discussion

As expected, identification of utterances with similar intonational contours in Spanish and English was high. Seven participants misidentified the Puerto Rican yes-no question as a declarative statement. The L1 Spanish speakers did not, and it is interesting to note that one was from Puerto Rico and one was not. Likewise, the heritage speakers also correctly identified the Puerto Rican yes-no question and neither listener was of Puerto Rican descent or spoke Caribbean Spanish. On the pretest, six L2 Spanish listeners misidentified one or two wh-questions, which is surprising given the interrogative word present in the utterance, making it unnecessary to rely on intonation alone. Identification of all types was highly accurate by all participants. The slight increase by the L2 listeners from the pretest to the posttest was not significant. These findings of fairly high accuracy of the perception of utterance types is in line with previous studies that also found similar results with advanced L2 learners of Spanish who are L1 speakers of English (Brandl et al. 2020; Nibert 2005, 2006; Trimble 2013; Zárate-Sández 2018).

It was hypothesized that the absolute interrogatives from Puerto Rico would result in misidentification since the final boundary tone differs from that found in the other Spanish macrodialects presented to the participants and from English. This hypothesis is partially supported as seven of the eleven L2 Spanish listeners identified the yes-no question by the Puerto Rican speaker as a statement. The only other macrodialect that resulted in misidentifying a yes-no question was the Colombian dialect, which occurred for two participants. Both L1 Spanish participants correctly identified the yes-no question by the Puerto Rican speaker.

The results of this study partially align with those of Brandl et al. (2020), Trimble (2013), and Zárate-Sández (2018) in that most L2 Spanish listeners associate a final fall with declaratives and a final rise with yes-no questions. Some participants in Trimble (2013) who had more experience with a Spanish macrodialect consisting of absolute questions with final falls also more frequently distinguished these utterances from declaratives. According to Henriksen et al. (2010), individual variation is in line with what is generally known about second language acquisition: when new elements are added to the interlanguage, variability increases until the more native-like element replaces the element that previously had been in use. The new element in this case for some participants was the final fall on the yes-no question uttered by the Puerto Rican speaker.

In terms of the role of explicit teaching, since there were no significant differences from pretest to posttest on the identification of utterance types, there is no clear link between explicit instruction on different types of utterances and their intonational patterns and the ability to identify these utterances. These non-significant differences could also be explained by the fact that several participants were at or near ceiling, so there was no room for improvement. A few participants increased their accuracy in distinguishing the utterances, but only by a little. Therefore, more research would be needed to determine if indeed explicit instruction could be useful. Craft (2015) also found no effect of intonational instruction on the production of statements and yes-no questions since both the control and experimental group produced more target-like productions while studying abroad.

The results also align with Mennen's (2015) LILt. This theory posits that if the two intonational patterns are similar in both languages, they will merge into one system. It seems most participants' ability to distinguish utterance types falls under this category. The high level of accuracy of identifying utterances as declaratives and wh-questions could be a result of similarities between the L1 and L2, aligning with both the systemic dimension and semantic dimension of the theory. For the participants that could accurately distinguish between the yes-no question final fall and the declarative statement final fall, they may not be transferring L1 intonational information to their L2 but instead creating a new category. The role of frequency could also be at play, certainly in terms of how often participants hear yes-no statements as final falls and also in terms of how often they hear declarative statements versus questions.

8. Implications, limitations, and future directions

This research contributes to the scarce research on the teaching of L2 intonation to L2 learners of Spanish. More specifically this included the teaching of variable intonation, which has been known to cause problems even to L1 Spanish speakers who cannot distinguish a yes-no question from a statement when both end in a low boundary tone which occurs in some regional dialects. Even though advanced learners have a high level of accuracy of identifying sentence-types, they also may benefit from explicit instruction particularly when intonational patterns do not match those of their L1. More research would be needed to determine this.

The limitations of this study include the low number of participants. In the future, including more L1 Spanish speakers as well as heritage speakers of Spanish could provide further evidence to support the LILt. This study did not include a baseline of English utterances, so it is unclear if the participants can distinguish these utterances in English. Furthermore, the participants were considered advanced learners solely due to their previous history taking Spanish courses and the level of the class in which they were enrolled at the time of the study. They also completed a proficiency test, but it assessed grammar and vocabulary as opposed to aural proficiency levels. A more global level of proficiency or an oral measure might provide a clearer picture. Additionally, there may have been a memory effect since the same utterances were used in the pretest and the posttest, although the order was changed. The utterances were also slightly different, and the participants could have detected this and used that to help with identification on the posttest. Finally, participants could be hearing other cues and really should be in some cases. This could be why the scores are so high for wh-questions. Although, in the pretest, the participants also exhibited a similar high average for identifying yes-no questions.

A future study would benefit from not only more participants, but participants with varying levels of proficiency ranging from beginner to very proficient. Additionally, a future study should use a control group of more L1 speakers of each macrodialect as well as heritage speakers of various macrodialects. Perhaps their identification would match that of the participants, although background variables, such as exposure and familiarity with other L1 Spanish dialects, would most likely play a role.

Instruction on the features under study only took place during part of one class period. It could be beneficial to provide more in-depth instruction where learners are able to practice more with the structures under study to increase their accuracy and understanding of variable intonation in Spanish. If this practice includes feedback, Carroll (2001) suggests it could facilitate the learning of the variable structure under study as long as the learners interpret the corrections as feedback, the feedback is relevant to the information being exchanged, and the feedback is used by the learner. If the feedback is in the form of modeling, comprehension may occur more quickly due to the "repeated exposure" that can "strengthen the parsing procedures needed to analyse it" (Carroll 2001: 350). Asking the participants to reflect on their learning experience could also provide more clarification on how they completed the pretest and posttest.

Finally, examining the production of the utterances in a future study will allow for the investigation of the relationship of production and perception. Only one previous study to date on L2 Spanish intonation has done this, Craft (2015), so adding further studies allows for a clearer picture of L2 intonation to emerge.

9. Conclusions

Of the few studies conducted on L2 Spanish intonation, most focus on production or perception of utterance types, often not considering regional differences in intonational patterns and also leaving out the effects of explicit instruction. The current study reports on the effects of explicit instruction, noting high accuracy of sentence type identification on the pretest and no significant effect of instruction. Difficulty in identifying utterances whose final boundary tone in the L2 differ from that expected in the L1 occurred with more than half of the participants, showing that these participants may be mapping information about intonation from their L1 onto their L2.

References

Beckman, M. E. & Pierrehumbert, J. B. 1986. Intonational structure in Japanese and English. *Phonology* 3: 255–309.

Bradlow, A. R., Pisoni, D. B., Akahane-Yamada, R. & Tohkura, Y. I. 1997. Training Japanese listeners to identify English /r/ and /l/, IV: Some effects of perceptual learning on speech production. *The Journal of the Acoustical Society of America* 101(4): 2299–2310.

Brandl, A., González, C., & Bustin, A. 2020. The development of intonation in L2 Spanish. In *Hispanic Linguistics: Current Issues and New Directions*, A. Morales-Front, M. J. Ferreira, R. P. Leow & C. Sanz (eds), 12–31. Amsterdam: John Benjamins.

Carroll, S. E. 2001. *Input and Evidence: The Raw Material of Second Language Acquisition*. Amsterdam: John Benjamins.

Clopper, C. G. & Bradlow, A. R. 2009. Free classification of American English dialects by native and non-native listeners. *Journal of Phonetics* 37(4): 436–451.

Craft, J. 2015. The Acquisition of Intonation by L2 Spanish Speakers While on a Six Week Study Abroad Program in Valencia, Spain. Master's thesis, Florida State University.

Estebas-Vilaplana, E. & Prieto, P. 2008. La notación prosódica del español: Una revision del SP-ToBI. *Estudios de Fonética Experimental* 17: 265–283.

Face, T. L. 2008. *The Intonation of Castilian Spanish Declaratives and Absolute Interrogatives*. Munich: Lincom.

Flege, J. E. 2002. Interactions between the native and second-language phonetic systems. In *An Integrated View of Language Development: Papers in Honor of Henning Wode*, P. Burmeister, T. Piske, & A. Rohde (eds), 217–244. Trier: Wissenschaftlicher Verlag Trier.

Gallego, M. & Conley, R. 2014. Raising dialectal awareness in Spanish as a Foreign Language courses. *Cauce* 36–37: 135–158.

Geeslin, K., & Gudmestad, A. 2010. An exploration of the range and frequency of occurrence of forms in potentially-variable structures in second language Spanish. *Studies in Second Language Acquisition* 32(3): 433–463.

Henriksen, N. 2013. Suprasegmental phonology in second language speech. In *The Handbook of Spanish Second Language Acquisition*, K. Geeslin (ed.), 166–182. Malden MA: Wiley-Blackwell.

Henriksen, N., Geeslin, K. & Willis, E. 2010. The development of L2 Spanish intonation during a study abroad immersion program in Leon, Spain: Global contours and final boundary movements. *Studies in Hispanic and Lusophone Linguistics* 3(1): 113–162.

Hualde, J. I. & Prieto, P. 2015. Intonational variation in Spanish. European and American variarion. In *Intonation in Romance*, S. Frota & P. Prieto (eds), 350–391. Oxford: OUP.

Matsuura, H., Chiba, R. & Fujieda, M. 1999. Intelligibility and comprehensibility of American and Irish Englishes in Japan. *World Englishes* 18(1): 49–62.

Mennen, I. 2006. Phonetic and phonological influences in non-native intonation: An overview for language teachers. *QMUC Speech Research Center Working Papers* WP-9: 1–18.

Mennen, I. 2015. Beyond segments: Towards an L2 intonation learning theory (LILt). In *Prosody and Languages in Contact: L2 Acquisition, Attrition, Languages in Multilingual Situations*, E. Delais-Roussarie, M. Avanzie & S. Herment (eds), 171–188. Berlin: Springer.

Nibert, H. J. 2005. The acquisition of the phrase accent by intermediate and advanced adult learners of Spanish as a second language. In *Selected Proceedings of the 6th Conference on the Acquisition of Spanish and Portuguese as First and Second Languages*, D. Eddington (ed.), 108–122. Somerville MA: Cascadilla Proceedings Project.

Nibert, H. J. 2006. The acquisition of the phrase accent by beginning adult learners of Spanish as a second language. In *Selected Proceedings of the 2nd Laboratory Approaches to Spanish Phonetics and Phonology*, M. Díaz-Campos (ed.), 131–148. Somerville MA: Cascadilla Proceedings Project.

Nishi, K. & Kewley-Port, D. 2007. Training Japanese listeners to perceive American English vowels: Influence of training sets. *Journal of Speech, Language, and Hearing Research* 50(6): 1496–1509.

Palmeri, T. J., Goldinger, S. D. & Pisoni, D. B. 1993. Episodic encoding of voice attributes and recognition memory for spoken words. *Journal of Experimental Psychology: Learning, Memory, and Cognition* 19(2): 309–328.

Prieto, P. & Roseano, P. (eds) 2010. *Transcription of the Intonation of Spanish*. Munich: Lincom.

Quilis, A. 1987. Entonación dialectal hispánica. In *Actas del I Congreso Internacional sobre el Español de América*, H. L. Morales (ed.), 117–164. San Juan: Academia Puertorriqueña de la Lengua Española.

Rasmussen, J. & Zampini, M. 2010. The effects of phonetics training on the intelligibility and comprehensibility of native Spanish speech by second language learners. In *Proceedings of the 1st Pronunciation in Second Language Learning and Teaching Conference*, J. Levis & K. LeVelle (eds), 38–52. Ames IA: Iowa State University.

Saito, K. 2018. Advanced second language segmental and suprasegmental acquisition. In *The Handbook of Advanced Proficiency in Second Language Acquisition*, P. A. Malovrh & A. G. Benati (eds), 282–303. Hoboken NJ: John Wiley & Sons.

Schmidt, L. 2009. The effect of dialect familiarity via a study abroad experience on L2 comprehension of Spanish. In *Selected Proceedings of the 11th Hispanic Linguistics Symposium*, J. Collentine, M. García, B. Lafford & F. Marcos Marín (eds), 143–154. MA: Cascadilla Proceedings Project.

Sullivan, K. P. & Karst, Y. N. 1996. Perception of English accent by native British English speakers and Swedish learners of English. In *Proceedings of the Sixth Australian International Conference on Speech Science and Technology*, P. MacCormack (ed.), 509–514. Canberra.

Tauroza, S. & Luk, J. 1997. Accent and second language listening comprehension. *RELC Journal* 28(1): 54–71.

Trimble, J. 2013. Perceiving intonational cues in a foreign language: Perception of sentence type in two dialects of Spanish. In *Selected Proceedings of the 15th Hispanic Linguistics Symposium*, C. Howe, S. Blackwell & M. L. Quesada (eds), 78–92. Somerville MA: Cascadilla Proceedings Project.

Willis, E. W. 2005. Tonal levels in Puebla Mexico Spanish declaratives and absolute interrogatives. In *Theoretical and Experimental Approaches to Romance Linguistics: Selected Papers from the 34th Linguistic Symposium on Romance Languages*, R. S. Gess & E. J. Rubin (eds), 351–363. Amsterdam: John Benjamins.

Zárate-Sández, G. 2018. "Was that a question?" Perception of utterance-final intonation among L2 learners of Spanish. In *Proceedings of the 9th Pronunciation in Second Language Learning and Teaching Conference*, J. Levis (ed.), 76–86. Ames IA: Iowa State University.

Evidence in controlled first exposure language learning

CHAPTER 7

Isolated and combined effects of models and corrective feedback in the acquisition of the Turkish locative morpheme

Yucel Yilmaz, Senyung Lee & Yılmaz Köylü
Indiana University | Chonnam National University | The Hong Kong University of Science and Technology

This study investigated the relative effects of models, corrective feedback, and a mixed treatment including both models and corrective feedback in the development of the Turkish locative morpheme. Native speakers of English were assigned to one of four conditions: models, corrective feedback, mixed, or control. Participants performed one input-based and one output-based task with a native Turkish speaker and received treatment according to their group assignments. Learners' performance was measured through a multiple-choice task and an oral picture description test once immediately after the treatment and once two weeks after the treatment. Results showed that the mixed treatment in which learners received models first and then corrective feedback was the most effective treatment.

Keywords: corrective feedback, negative evidence, positive evidence, explicit correction, models

1. Introduction

Negative evidence refers to information indicating what is impossible in the target language and can be obtained either through instruction informing learners about the incorrect uses of second language (L2) forms or through corrective feedback (i.e., reactions a learner receives from the interlocutor indicating that the learner's language production is not target-like). There are two competing positions regarding the role of negative evidence in L2 acquisition. Researchers operating within the cognitive-interactionist framework (e.g., Ellis 1991; Gass & Mackey 2006; Long 1996; Pica 1988) advocate that negative evidence has, at least, a facilitative role in L2 acquisition. Another group of researchers (e.g., Krashen 1981; Schwartz 1993; Truscott 1999; VanPatten 2013), in contrast, hold that negative evidence can only produce a superficial form of L2 knowledge and that it cannot have a beneficial impact on learners' competence. For the second group, the driving force of L2 acquisition is positive evidence, or information that indicates what is possible in the target language. Conclusive evidence about the long-term effect of negative evidence on ultimate L2 attainment is elusive because it is hard to determine how the presence versus complete absence of negative evidence impacts L2 acquisition in the long run. Most adult language learners, while being mainly exposed to positive evidence, are also exposed to some amount of negative evidence either through instruction or through naturalistic conversations containing implicit corrective feedback (Long 1980). However, it is still possible to investigate the role of negative evidence in the rate of L2 acquisition in the short term by manipulating the availability of negative evidence in controlled experiments.

Previous research comparing the performance of groups that received corrective feedback to the performance of control groups that received neither negative nor positive evidence has provided ample evidence for the facilitative role of negative evidence (Goo et al. 2015; Li 2010; Lyster & Saito 2010). However, relatively less is known as to how well corrective feedback groups can perform in comparison to groups that receive positive evidence through models or in comparison to groups that receive both models and corrective feedback. The current study examines the extent to which native speakers of English who have not been exposed to the target language (i.e., Turkish) before the experiment benefit from positive evidence through models, corrective feedback, and a mix of models and corrective feedback in the development of the Turkish locative morpheme.

In the current study, any improvement made by learners on one or both of two knowledge types (i.e., implicit and explicit knowledge) was considered L2 development. Most second language acquisition (SLA) researchers (e.g., Ellis 2005; Hulstijn 2005; Long 2015) draw a distinction between explicit knowledge, the knowledge that can be easily articulated and brought into conscious awareness, and implicit knowledge, the knowledge that cannot be easily verbalized or brought into conscious awareness. Ellis (2005) stated there is no disagreement in the field about the positive role of implicit knowledge in L2 acquisition because researchers with different theoretical orientations agree that implicit knowledge underlies fluent, spontaneous language use. Some researchers see value in explicit knowledge as well. For example, Long's (2015) cognitive-interactionist theory of SLA considers explicit knowledge helpful in speeding up the acquisition of implicit knowledge in instructed settings. According to Long (2015), explicit knowledge can facilitate noticing non-salient linguistic features and discrepancies between input and output. In addition, it can help make learners sensitive to the cues they need to focus on during language processing. Because of the theoretical importance of both knowledge types, Ellis (2015) suggested that both types of knowledge should be measured in instructed L2 acquisition studies. Following Ellis's (2015) suggestion, in this study, learners' improvement on both knowledge types were considered when comparing the relative effects of models, corrective feedback, and a mix of models and corrective feedback.

2. Models versus corrective feedback in the context of L2 interaction

Models refer to the provision of well-formed exemplars of the target language by native speakers or more proficient L2 speakers to L2 learners. One of the researchers that has assigned a central role to positive evidence, and therefore models, is Krashen (1981), who has viewed understanding input carrying positive evidence as a necessary and sufficient condition for L2 development. According to the Natural Approach that Krashen and Terrell (1983) developed based on Krashen's (1981) ideas, learners should not be asked to produce output at the initial stage of their language development. Krashen and Terrell (1983) believed that output production is not necessary for developing productive skills because production emerges from listening to a lot of comprehensible input. In addition, pushing learners to produce output can increase anxiety and block the linguistic information contained in the input from reaching learners' developing linguistic system. Naturally, not pushing learners to speak will lead to decreased opportunities to make oral errors and receive feedback correcting these errors. Krashen (1981), however, is not concerned with the lack of opportunities for corrective feedback because the role of feedback is limited according to him. It can help develop learners' conscious but not subconscious knowledge, which is the basis for fluency in the target language. Long (1996) agrees with Krashen (1981) in that positive evidence plays an essential role in L2 acquisition but disagrees about the role of negative evidence. Long's (1981, 1996) Interaction Hypothesis states that negative evidence obtained through corrective feedback during conversational interaction may be facilitative of L2 development because these instances can draw learners' attention to the mismatches between their production and the target-like form in the L2. The role of attention in L2 learning is theoretically supported by Schmidt and Frota's (1986: 311) claim that "a second language learner will begin to acquire the target-like form if and only if it is present in comprehended input and 'noticed' in the normal sense of the word, that is consciously" (see also Schmidt 1990, 2001).

Corrective feedback can be provided in many different ways. Some feedback types only include negative evidence and withhold the target-like form that could serve as positive evidence (e.g., clarification requests), whereas some others provide negative evidence along with positive evidence as in the case of recasts (i.e., target-like reformulations of learners' non-target-like productions) or explicit corrections (i.e., explicit rejection of the learner's non-target-like form). The former group has been referred to as prompts, whereas the latter as reformulations (Ranta & Lyster 2007). We selected a type of reformulation, explicit corrections, as our corrective feedback strategy in this study because the participants in this study had not been exposed to the target language (i.e., Turkish) before the experiment and, therefore, could not be expected to learn from feedback types not including positive evidence. Explicit corrections have been considered explicit relative to other forms of reformulations, such as recasts, that include only the reformulation of the learner's error. Explicitness in this sense refers to (i) whether the feedback includes metalinguistic terminology, clues, or rules, or (ii) whether it is direct about the corrective intent of the interlocutor. According to Carroll (2001), feedback types such as explicit corrections are preferable to less explicit types of feedback because they are sufficiently informative. They indicate not only whether the learner's utterance includes an error but also the location of the error and how the error should be corrected. Carroll (2001) predicts that feedback types that are this informative would not occur frequently in real life. This prediction has received empirical support in that explicit feedback types such as explicit corrections have been found to be one of the least frequent feedback types in instructed foreign and second language contexts (Sheen 2004). Despite their low frequency, explicit correction has been found to be an effective form of feedback. It has been shown (Yilmaz 2012, 2013, 2016) that receiving explicit correction is more beneficial than having opportunities to produce the target structure without receiving any feedback. In addition, explicit corrections have been shown to lead to higher linguistic gains than more implicit feedback types, such as recasts (Yilmaz 2012, 2013).

To the best of our knowledge, no study so far compared the relative effectiveness of models and explicit corrections. However, several previous studies investigated the relative effectiveness of models and other types of corrective feedback (see Table 1 for a summary of previous studies). The evidence gleaned from this research is mixed. Herron and Tomasello (1988) compared the effects of models and prompts using two beginner-level French classes. The participants were familiar with one of the target forms of the study, negation, but not with the other, direct object pronouns. Each participant was exposed to models for one structure and to corrective feedback for the other. There were two treatment phases for direct object pronouns. In the first phase, all learners received explicit instruction in their L1 (i.e., English) on direct object pronouns as well as models including direct object pronouns. In the second phase, the feedback group received prompts, whereas the model group was exposed to further models. For the other target structure, negation, the groups went through only the second phase because they were familiar with the target structure. Learners' performance on the posttests showed that the feedback group made fewer errors on both structures than the model group.

Long et al. (1998) reported two studies investigating the relative effectiveness of models and corrective feedback (recasts): one with learners of Japanese and another with learners of Spanish. The model and recast treatments involved learners performing communication games with one of the researchers. During the model treatment, learners heard pre-recorded models describing pictures, whereas, during the recast treatment, learners described the pictures themselves and received recasts. The control group received placebo treatments. The Japanese study revealed no significant differences between the model and recast groups, and neither group significantly outperformed the control group. The Spanish study targeted topicalization and adverb placement in Spanish. As in the Japanese study, no learning took place for the object topicalization. However, in adverb placement, both groups outperformed the control group, and the recast group outperformed the model group.

Leeman's (2003) study included four treatment groups: recasts, negative evidence (repetition), enhanced positive evidence, or unenhanced positive evidence. The recast group received negative evidence including the reformulation of learners' gender and number agreement errors, whereas the negative evidence group received the repetition of the learner's error. The enhanced positive evidence group heard models of the target structures that were enhanced with stress, whereas the control group received positive evidence that was not enhanced. The results of the study showed no differences between the experimental groups when they were compared to each other directly. However, the groups displayed differences with respect to whether they outperformed the unenhanced positive evidence (control) group. Of interest to the current study is the performance of the two negative evidence groups in comparison to the unenhanced positive evidence group. In none of the comparisons did the negative evidence (repetition) group outperform the unenhanced positive evidence group. However, the recast group outperformed the unenhanced group in three of the four comparisons. To summarize, Leeman's (2003) results showed that only the recasts, not the corrective feedback type with no positive evidence, outperformed the model group.

Overall, as shown in Table 1, previous research showed mixed results about the relative effectiveness of models versus corrective feedback. On the one hand, three feedback groups failed to outperform model groups: the recasts on two structures in Long et al.'s (1998) Japanese study, the recasts on object topicalization in Long et al.'s (1998) Spanish study, and the repetitions on two structures in Leeman (2003). On the other hand, three feedback groups outperformed model groups: the recasts on adverb placement in Long et al.'s (1998) Spanish study, the

Table 1. Studies comparing the effects of models and corrective feedback

Study	Design	Tests	Target feature	Results
Herron & Tomasello (1988)	Classroom-based post-test only Groups: Prompts and models	Controlled oral and written production tests	French negation and direct object pronouns	CF advantage
Long et al. (1998) Japanese Study	Lab-based, pretest/post-test/control group Groups: Recasts and models	Oral picture description task	Japanese adjective ordering and locative construction	No difference
Long et al. (1998) Spanish Study		Oral picture description and grammaticality judgment	Spanish topicalization / Spanish adverb placement	No difference / CF advantage
Leeman (2003)	Lab-based, pretest/immediate post-test/delayed posttest Groups: Recasts, repetitions, unenhanced models, enhanced models	Oral picture description	Spanish gender and number agreement	Partial CF advantage (only recasts outperformed models)

recasts on two structures in Leeman (2003), and the prompts on two different structures in Herron and Tomasello (1988). This inconsistency in findings, along with methodological differences across studies (e.g., feedback type used, target languages), makes reaching a conclusion about the relative effectiveness of feedback versus models difficult. In addition, since the previous studies focused on learners who had some familiarity with the target language, it is not clear whether the findings of these studies can be extended to the relative utility of models versus corrective feedback for true beginners who have just started to learn the target language. Finally, since none of the previous studies included a condition combining models and corrective feedback, to what extent such a combination can be effective for true beginners is not known. Providing learners with models first and then corrective feedback may be more compatible with the cognitive demands of L2 learning than providing them with either models or corrective feedback alone.

Housen and Pierrard (2005) have proposed that L2 learning goes through three macro-processes: knowledge internalization, knowledge modification, and knowledge consolidation. Of these, the first two may be related to the benefits of providing models and corrective feedback together. Knowledge internalization is the first stage in L2 acquisition and concerns establishing form-meaning connections through noticing and input processing. In knowledge modification, learners restructure non-target-like aspects of their knowledge by refining the form-meaning links through additional input or negative feedback. It could be that the first process in acquisition, knowledge internalization, may be better supported by a treatment which provides positive evidence through models but does not require output production. In such a treatment, the task conditions may be favorable for learners to allocate their full attention to process models and detect the link between form and meaning, since output production cannot be a factor competing for attentional resources. In addition, it is possible that corrective feedback can better serve the cognitive needs of learners who are at the stage of modifying their knowledge. Learners may be more ready to refine their initial hypotheses after having established a form-meaning connection and generated an initial hypothesis as to how the target linguistic feature works. Therefore, they may be more receptive to benefitting from the information that corrective feedback can convey about the grammaticality of their utterances.

In the present study, we examined the isolated and combined effects of models and corrective feedback on the learning of a grammatical structure by true beginners and asked the following research question: Is there any difference in the effects of models, corrective feedback, and models plus corrective feedback on the development of the Turkish locative morpheme?

3. Method

3.1 Design

The design of the present study included two posttests (Posttest I, Posttest II) and a control group. The independent variable was type of interaction (models, corrective feedback, mixed, or control), and the dependent variable was participants' development in the Turkish locative morpheme as measured by an oral picture description test and a multiple-choice test. A pretest was not administered because we only recruited participants who had never been exposed to Turkish prior to the study and it was possible to assume that they had no knowledge of the target structure.

3.2 Participants

Forty participants (26 females, 14 males) volunteered to participate in this study. All participants were students enrolled in an undergraduate or graduate program at a large Midwestern university in the United States (M_{age}=22.1 years, SD=4.06, range=18–40), and they were native speakers of English. In order to include true beginner-level learners of Turkish, participants had to meet the following recruitment criteria: (i) they had never been exposed to Turkish, (ii) they had never been formally trained in linguistics. Thirty-two participants reported having a beginner to intermediate-level knowledge of another language (e.g., Spanish, French, Italian, German, Japanese, and Arabic).

3.3 Target structure

It was important in this study to select a linguistic structure that was developmentally appropriate for true beginners (Spada & Lightbown 1999). Since we recruited participants who had zero knowledge of Turkish, we wanted to make sure that the target structure is not a feature that can be learned only in advanced stages of Turkish grammar. Targeting a structure that is normally learned in advanced stages of grammatical development might have obscured the effects of different instructional treatments because learning such a target structure might have been too challenging for true beginners. In this regard, we selected the Turkish locative morpheme -DA as the target structure because it was appropriate for the learners' developmental stage. This rationale is in line with Pienemann's Processability Theory (1998), according to which the production of L2 forms can only take place if the linguistic processor can handle them.

The locative morpheme in Turkish is -DA, with four allomorphs: -da, -de, -ta, and -te.[1] The distinction between -d and -t depends on whether the final segment of the stem is voiced or voiceless. When a word ends with a vowel or a voiced consonant, the locative morpheme starts with a -d. When the final segment of the stem is a voiceless consonant, the locative morpheme starts with a -t. Vowel harmony also plays a role in the formation of different allomorphs of the Turkish locative marker as the vowel in the locative marker is conditioned by the backness of the vowel in the final syllable of the word it attaches to. When the last syllable of

---

[1] A reviewer argues that the multiple functions of the Turkish locative morpheme that can be expressed using various prepositions in English (i.e., *in, on, over*) might have facilitated the acquisition of the Turkish locative morpheme, presumably because the participants may have received more input. However, since the participants were only exposed to Turkish in a lab setting and as the number of the locative morphemes they were exposed to was controlled for, such a facilitation might not have been the case.

the word has a back vowel (a/ı/o/u), the back vowel -*a* is used in the locative morpheme. When the last syllable of the word has a front vowel (e/i/ö/ü), -*e* is used (Göksel & Kerslake 2005; Kornfilt 1997). The following examples demonstrate the distribution of the four allomorphs of the locative morpheme in Turkish.

(1) Turkish locative morpheme
    a. armut kama-da
       pear   knife-LOC
       'The pear is on the knife.'
    b. armut tepsi-de
       pear   tray-LOC
       'The pear is on the tray.'
    c. armut tabak-ta
       pear   plate-LOC
       'The pear is on the plate.'
    d. armut etek-te
       pear   skirt-LOC
       'The pear is on the skirt.'

3.4 Procedure

The study was conducted in a research lab over three sessions. Figure 1 represents the study procedure. Before the first session, participants were asked to complete an online vocabulary self-study session. Each participant was instructed to study 32 Turkish nouns using <www.quia.com>. On the website, participants could see flashcards showing a picture and written form of the noun both in Turkish and English (e.g., *elma* 'apple'), and could listen to an audio recording of the word. Participants had to score 95 out of 100 in an untimed 32-item multiple-choice vocabulary test in order to qualify to schedule the first treatment session. Each scheduled participant was randomly assigned to one of four groups.

The scheduled participants met with the experimenter at a lab for the first treatment session within three to four days after taking an online multiple-choice vocabulary test. At the beginning of the first treatment session, to ensure that the participants still remembered the Turkish words that they had studied using the web study module <www.quia.com>, a timed vocabulary test was administered in the experimenter's presence. Each participant saw one picture in a PowerPoint slide at a time, and they had to verbally name all of the 32 pictures correctly. At the end of this vocabulary test, participants were introduced to the plural marker -*lAr* in Turkish, as well as three expressions required to interact with the experimenter during the treatment tasks. These expressions were *büyük mü küçük mü?* 'Big or small?', *ne renk?* 'What color?', and *ve* 'and'. When the participants answered every

Chapter 7. Isolated and combined effects of models and feedback   171

item in the vocabulary test correctly and were confident with the newly introduced expressions, the experimenter administered two treatment tasks based on the participant's group (see the section on Treatment Tasks for detailed information). The vocabulary test took about 10 minutes, and two treatment tasks took between 30 and 45 minutes.

The second session was administered three to four days later, and the participants completed the two treatment tasks according to their group (see the section on Treatment Tasks for detailed information). Immediately after the treatment tasks in the second session, Posttest I was administered. Two weeks after the second session, each participant came to the lab one more time and took Posttest II in the experimenter's presence. Posttest I and Posttest II each took about 25 minutes. In all posttests, an oral picture description test was administered first, followed by a multiple-choice test. All participants' oral production during the treatment tasks and posttests were audio-recorded by the experimenter.

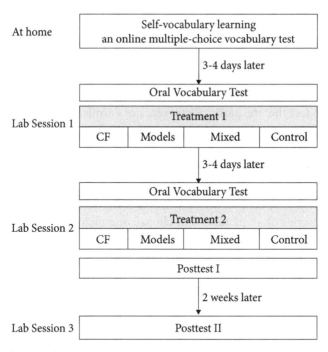

Figure 1. Study procedure

3.5 Treatment tasks

In each of the two treatment sessions, one participant and one of the researchers, who is a native speaker of Turkish (the experimenter), performed two oral, meaning-based tasks in Turkish. Although the nature of the interaction differed across groups, all treatment tasks were similar in that one interlocutor described a picture, and the other interlocutor selected a picture among three options. The participant and the experimenter met at a research lab and sat at different computers facing away from each other. Both interlocutors had a set of 48 slides on their screens in each task. One of the interlocutors saw one picture in each slide and was asked to describe the picture in Turkish. The other interlocutor saw three pictures in each slide and was asked to select the picture that matched the description. The three pictures only differed in the size, color, or number of the objects. The participants naturally asked one or two follow-up questions about the size, color, or number of the object to be able to choose the correct picture, rendering each task a two-way meaning-based task.

Participants were randomly assigned to one of four groups: models, corrective feedback, mixed, or control. Although all the participants completed two oral tasks in each treatment session, their interaction with the experimenter differed depending on their group. Across the four groups, the amount of exposure to the correct target forms, the amount of exposure to the key nouns (i.e., the nouns that the locative morpheme was attached to), and the amount of production of the key nouns were experimentally controlled for. We did not strictly control for possible exposure to the target forms in Turkish outside of the context of the experiment. However, the fact that the participants were not enrolled in Turkish classes at the time of the study might have minimized the possibility for them to be exposed to Turkish outside the experiment.

3.5.1 *Models group*

In the models group, the participants' first task was to listen to the experimenter describing a series of 48 pictures and choose one picture among three pictures. The purpose of this task was to give the participant an opportunity to hear the correct target forms in Turkish. Choosing the correct picture was not the focus. This task was designed in such a way to direct the learners' attention to meaning rather than form. Of the 48 pictures, 32 displayed a scene where one object was placed on another object (i.e., experimental items). These 32 items required the locative morpheme -*DA*. The rest of the 12 items were pictures of a single object or multiple objects placed next to each other (i.e., filler items). Thus, the locative morpheme -*DA* was not necessary to describe those twelve items. Example (2) illustrates an episode during the first task in the models group.

(2) The first task in the models group (comprehension task with the locative morpheme)

Experimenter: *armut tabakta*
'The pear is on the plate.'

Participant: *Büyük mü küçük mü?*
'Big or small?'

Experimenter: *Büyük*
'Big'

The participants' second task in the models group was to describe a series of 48 pictures to the experimenter so that the experimenter could choose one picture among three options in each slide. Everything including the picture stimuli was the same as in the first task, except that the two interlocutors' roles were switched. When the participant made an error with the locative morpheme, the experimenter did not give any feedback. The purpose of this task was to control for the amount of output opportunities for the key nouns across the groups.

Example (3) illustrates such an instance where the locative morpheme -*DA* was necessary since the picture showed a pear on a plate.

(3) The second task in the models group (production task without corrective feedback)

Participant: *armut *tabak*
'pear   plate'
(Intended utterance: The pear is on the plate.)

Experimenter: *Büyük mü küçük mü?*
'Big or small?'

Participant: *Büyük*
'Big'

3.5.2 *Corrective feedback group*

The corrective feedback (CF) group started with the task in which the participant described a series of 48 pictures one at a time, and the experimenter selected one picture among three options. Of the 48 items, 32 were experimental items and 12 were filler items. In this task, when the participant made an error with the locative morpheme, the experimenter explicitly pointed out the error and provided a reformulation of the erroneous part. The experimenter immediately asked a follow-up question to prevent participants from repeating the correct form. The purpose of the experimenter's follow-up question was to experimentally control opportunities to produce the correct form across the groups. Example (4) shows how corrective feedback was given in this task.

(4) The first task in the CF group (production task with corrective feedback)
    Participant: *tabak kutu*
                    'plate box'

    Experimenter: That's wrong, you should say *kutuda*.
                    'on the box'
                    Büyük mü küçük mü?
                    'Big or small?'

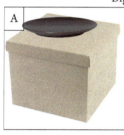 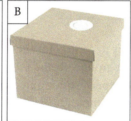 

    Participant: *Büyük*
                    'Big'

The second task in the CF group involved different picture stimuli. The experimenter had 48 slides, all of which presented a single object or multiple objects next to each other. The experimenter described the object(s), and the participant selected one picture among three options, which differed in the color, size, or number of the object. No locative morpheme was used because the pictures did not present any scenes where an object was placed on another object. The purpose of the second task was to control for the amount of exposure to the key nouns across the groups. Example (5) shows the interaction in this task.

(5) The second task in the CF group (comprehension task without the locative morpheme)

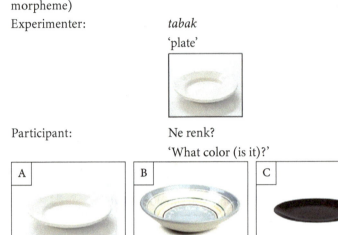

Experimenter: *tabak*
'plate'

Participant: Ne renk?
'What color (is it)?'

Experimenter: Beyaz
'White'

In addition, it was necessary to control for the number of encounters with the correct target forms across the groups. In the CF group, participants heard the correct target forms from the experimenter only when they made an error with the locative morpheme, as in Example (2), while the participants in the models group heard the correct target forms for all 32 experimental items. In order to match the number of encounters of the correct target forms between the models group and the CF group, the experimenter asked more questions to the participants. After the second task was over, the experimenter revisited the items for which the participant produced the correct target form. The experimenter said, "Let's go back to Item 22. You said, *elma tabakta*, right?" When the participant responded with yes or no, the experimenter then said, "Okay, let's go to Item 24. You said, *tabak kutuda*, right?" These extra questions ensured that the participants in the CF group heard the correct target forms as many times as in the models group.

3.5.3 *Mixed group*

The mixed group received the treatment of both the models group and the CF group. In the first treatment session, all the participants in the mixed group performed the two tasks used in the models condition. In the second treatment session, they performed the two tasks used in the CF condition. The decision to administer the tasks of the models group in the first session was made to approximate the common second language learning process where learners encounter L2 input before producing language.

3.5.4 *Control group*

The control group received neither modeling nor corrective feedback. The purpose of the control group was to have a group of participants who were exposed to neither the model target forms nor corrective feedback but who only produced the key nouns as many times as the participants in the three experimental groups did. We wanted to make sure that all four groups had the same output opportunities for the key Turkish nouns used in this study. The treatment for the control condition was designed to see if the Turkish locative marker is something that can be guessed by beginner-level learners of Turkish without any instructional treatment, when analyzed by two outcome measures described below. In both treatment sessions, the participants in the control group performed two tasks in the same order. The first task of the control group was the same as the second task of the models group, as in Example (3). The participants described each picture where one object was placed on another object, and the experimenter selected one picture among three options. When the participant made an error with the locative morpheme, the experimenter did not provide any feedback and asked a follow-up question. The second task of the control group was the same as the second task of the CF group, as in Example (5). Thus, in the control group, the interactions between the experimenter and the participant did not involve any use of the locative marker. Table 2 summarizes the treatment tasks used in the four groups.

Table 2. Treatment tasks in the four groups

		Experimental groups		Control group
	Models	Corrective feedback	Mixed	
Session 1	1. comprehension task with the locative morpheme	1. production task with corrective feedback	1. comprehension task with the locative morpheme	1. production task without feedback
	2. production task without feedback	2. comprehension task without the locative morpheme	2. production task without feedback	2. comprehension task without the locative morpheme
Session 2	1. comprehension task with the locative morpheme	1. production task with corrective feedback	1. production task with corrective feedback	1. production task without feedback
	2. production task without feedback	2. comprehension task without the locative morpheme	2. comprehension task without the locative morpheme	2. comprehension task without the locative morpheme

3.6 Outcome measures

An oral picture description test and a multiple-choice test were used as outcome measures in Posttest I and Posttest II. The multiple-choice test was designed to gauge learners' knowledge about the allomorphic variation for the target linguistic structure under conditions considered to be favorable for the use of explicit knowledge (Ellis 2005). One of these conditions was that learners had enough time to plan their responses, and the other was that giving a correct response was possible just by attending to the form (Ellis 2005). The oral picture-description was used to gauge learners' ability to produce the target linguistic structure spontaneously while their focus is primarily on message creation and meaning. The task involved a time limit, and its primary focus was on message creation, which are two features that make the use of implicit knowledge more likely (Ellis 2005). Both tests started with instructions and two practice items, and the order of the items was randomized. In both tests, half of the experimental items ($n = 8$) were taken from the treatment tasks (i.e., repeated items), and the other half ($n = 8$) were used only in the posttests (i.e., novel items). The number of appearances of the repeated and novel items were counterbalanced across the two posttests.

The oral picture description test presented participants with one picture at a time and asked them to describe the picture verbally, focusing on the location of the object(s). Each item automatically moved to the next item after eight seconds. The test consisted of 16 experimental items and 16 fillers. The experimental items presented pictures of one object placed on another object, and the fillers presented pictures of a single object or multiple objects next to each other. The 16 experimental items consisted of four sets, with each set targeting one of the four allomorphs of the Turkish locative morpheme. The test was computer-delivered using SuperLab (Cedrus 2003).

In the multiple-choice test, each item presented one word as a cue as well as a picture. Participants were asked to choose one option that correctly described the picture among four options. This test was untimed. It consisted of 16 experimental items and 16 fillers. For example, the experimental item targeting the form *tarak kutuda* 'comb on a box' presented the cue "*tarak* _____" below a picture, and provided four options: *kutuda, kutude, kututa,* and *kutute*. The four options each included both orthographic and aural forms. Participants could hear the aural forms multiple times by clicking a button. This test was computer-delivered using <www.quia.com>, an online learning platform.

One might argue that some familiarity with the vowel harmony may help participants rule out options such as *kutude* and *kutute* as the allomorphs in those words violate the vowel harmony in Turkish. That is because in a word like *kutu*, the final vowel *-u* is a back vowel, which requires that the additional vowels in the suffixes attached to the noun stem also be back vowels such as *a*. It is, however, highly unlikely that such was the case in our study because the participants neither had formal linguistic training before, nor exposure to Turkish or another language in which vowel harmony functions like it does in Turkish.

3.7 Scoring

Learners' responses to the multiple-choice test were scored dichotomously as each item had one correct answer. A reliability coefficient was computed for the multiple-choice items using Cronbach's alpha, and the coefficient was found to be acceptable ($\alpha = .628$).[2] Learners' responses to the oral picture description test were coded by the experimenter for obligatory contexts, correct suppliance in obligatory contexts, suppliance in nonobligatory contexts, and misformations in obligatory contexts. Responses that included both the noun in the subject and the noun in the predicate position were considered as obligatory context (*masa kitap*), the provision of the correct allomorph was coded as correct suppliance (*kitap masada*), the suppliance of an incorrect allomorph as misformation (*kitap masade*), and the provision of a morpheme in the wrong context as suppliance in nonobligatory contexts (*kitapta masa*). A second rater coded 100% of the data for these categories. Interrater reliability was acceptable as indexed by Cohen's kappa ($\kappa = .86$ for the locative morpheme). The percentage agreement between the two coders was 93.7% for obligatory contexts, 99.2% ($\kappa = .96$) for correct suppliance, 99.2% ($\kappa = .95$) for misformations, and 100% for suppliance in non-obligatory contexts. Next, an adjusted target language use (ATLU) score was computed using the formula proposed by Ono and Witzel (2002):

$$(6) \quad ATLU = \frac{(n\ correct\ suppliance\ in\ obligatory\ contexts)\ (2) + (n\ misformations\ in\ obligatory\ contexts)\ (1)}{(n\ obligatory\ context)\ (2) + (n\ suppliance\ in\ nonobligatory\ contexts)\ (2)}$$

ATLU is a combination of two morpheme quantification measures, Suppliance in Obligatory Contexts (SOC) and Target Language Use (TLU) (Pica 1983), "as it takes into account (a) obligatory contexts, and (b) correct suppliance in obligatory contexts (both characteristic of SOC and TLU), as well as (c) misformations in obligatory contexts (characteristic of SOC), and (d) suppliance in non-obligatory contexts (characteristic of TLU)" (Ono & Witzel 2002: 55).

---

[2] Hair et al. (2006) argue that reliability values of .60 may be acceptable in exploratory studies and research in the social sciences.

3.8 Analysis

Before we carried out any statistical analyses, we checked the data from each outcome measure and time point (Posttest I and Posttest II) for normality using the recommended ±1 range for skewness and kurtosis (Phakiti 2014). The skewness values ranged from 0.341 to 1.054, and the kurtosis values ranged from −1.634 to 0.733, and no severe or consistent departure from normality was detected. To determine the relative effectiveness of models, corrective feedback, and models plus CF groups, we first carried out a mixed-design Analysis of Variance (ANOVA) model, where test type (multiple-choice, oral picture description) and time (Posttest I, Posttest II) were within-subjects factors and group (models, corrective feedback, mixed, control) was a between-subjects factor. We followed up on interaction effects with less complex ANOVA models and post hoc multiple comparison tests. We also computed Cohen's d to estimate the magnitude of the difference between the scores of different experimental groups as well as of the difference between two posttest scores of the same experimental group.

4. Results

4.1 Descriptive statistics for the multiple-choice test

Table 3 displays the means and standard deviations for the multiple-choice tests at Posttest I and Posttest II. At both time points, the highest-scoring group was the mixed group, whereas the lowest scoring group was the control group. Note that participants in this study had no knowledge of Turkish prior to this study. The CF and models groups followed the mixed group at both times. The control group's scores ranged from 0.26 to 0.31 (maximum score = 1.00) even though they had no prior knowledge of the target structure, suggesting that the availability of options might have allowed the control group to guess some of the answers correctly.

Table 3. Descriptive statistics for the multiple-choice test

Group	Posttest I M	Posttest I SD	Posttest II M	Posttest II SD
Control ($n=10$)	0.31	0.10	0.26	0.06
Models ($n=10$)	0.48	0.15	0.49	0.13
CF ($n=10$)	0.48	0.21	0.48	0.27
Mixed ($n=10$)	0.58	0.21	0.55	0.16

4.2 Descriptive statistics for the oral picture description test

As shown in Table 4, the mixed group at Posttest I and the CF group at Posttest II were the highest-scoring groups. At Posttest I, the CF and models groups were the second and third highest-scoring groups respectively. At Posttest II, however, the mixed and models groups followed the CF group with identical scores. The control group was the lowest scoring group at both times, with an average score of 0. This was an expected finding because the control group had received neither positive nor negative evidence, and the oral picture description test, unlike the multiple-choice test, did not lend itself to guessing.

Table 4. Descriptive statistics for the oral picture description test

Group	Posttest I M	Posttest I SD	Posttest II M	Posttest II SD
Control ($n=10$)	0.00	0.00	0.00	0.00
Models ($n=10$)	0.13	0.25	0.22	0.30
CF ($n=10$)	0.48	0.39	0.33	0.36
Mixed ($n=10$)	0.63	0.24	0.22	0.31

4.3 Inferential statistics

A mixed-design ANOVA, where test type and time were within-subjects factors and group was a between-subjects factor, revealed a statistically significant test type ($F(3,36)=6.65$, $p=.004$), time ($F(1,36)=39.79$, $p<.001$), and group ($F(3,36)=7.50, p=.001$) main effects. In addition, time by test type ($F(1,36)=6.08$, $p=.019$), test type by group ($F(3,36)=6.23$, $p=.002$), and time by test type by group ($F(3,36)=7.06$, $p=.001$) interaction effects were statistically significant. These results showed that the interaction between test type and group was modified by time. We followed up on this three-way interaction (time by test type by group) by running two mixed-design ANOVAs for each level of time, Posttest I and Posttest II. In these models, test type was a within-subjects factor and group was a between-subjects factor. The model for Posttest I showed significant effects for test type by group interaction, $F(3,36)=8.88, p<.001$, test type, $F(1,36)=18.53$, $p<.001$, and group, $F(3,36)=10.31, p<.001$. Two follow-up univariate ANOVAs, one for the multiple-choice test and one for the oral picture description test, were conducted to follow up on the significant test type by group interaction effect. Group was a between-subjects factor in these models. In both models, the group effect was significant (multiple-choice, $F(3,36)=3.80, p=.018$; oral picture description, $F(3,36)=12.78, p<.001$), but the Tukey post hoc multiple comparisons revealed different patterns in terms of the differences between the experimental groups.

In the univariate ANOVA for the multiple-choice test, the mixed group performed statistically better than the control group ($MD=0.26$, $p=.011$, $d=1.50$), but not better than the models (mixed vs. models, $MD=0.10$ $p=.644$) or CF (mixed vs. CF, $MD=0.10$, $p=.644$) group. Neither the models group ($MD=0.17$, $p=.164$) nor the CF group ($MD=0.17$, $p=.164$) performed statistically better than the control group, and there was no statistical difference between the models and CF groups ($MD=0.00$, $p=1.000$). In the univariate ANOVA for the oral picture description test, the mixed and CF groups outperformed both the control (mixed vs. control, $MD=0.63$, $p<.001$; CF vs. control, $MD=0.49$, $p=.001$) and models groups (mixed vs. models, $MD=0.50$, $p=.001$; CF vs. models, $MD=0.36$, $p=.021$). There was no statistical difference between the mixed and CF group ($MD=0.14$, $p=.611$) and between the models and control group ($MD=0.13$, $p=.693$).

The mixed-design model for Posttest II showed a non-significant test by group interaction effect, $F(3,36)=0.81$, $p=.493$, a non-significant task effect, $F(1,36)=0.91$, $p=.346$, and a significant group effect, $F(3,36)=4.377$, $p=.010$, which means that there was a group effect on both tasks at Posttest II. Tukey post hoc multiple comparisons revealed that the mixed and CF groups outperformed the control group (mixed vs. control, $MD=0.26$, $p=.026$; CF vs. control, $MD=0.28$, $p=.015$). No other comparison was statistically significant (models vs. control group, $MD=0.22$, $p=.065$; mixed vs. models, $MD=0.03$, $p=.978$; CF vs. models, $MD=0.05$, $p=.927$; CF vs. mixed, $MD=0.02$, $p=.996$).

We also conducted two additional mixed design ANOVAs, one for each outcome measure to follow up on the significant three-way (time by task by group) interaction which was shown by our main statistical model. In these additional follow-up models, time was a within-subjects factor and group was a between-subjects factor. The first model, which was run for the multiple-choice test, revealed a significant main effect for group, $F(3,36)=5.26$, $p=.004$, a non-significant main effect for time, $F(1,36)=0.35$, $p=.911$, and a non-significant interaction effect between time and group, $F(3,36)=0.52$, $p=.669$. This means that there was no change in learners' scores on the multiple-choice test from Posttest I to Posttest II. The second mixed-design ANOVA, which was run for the oral picture description task, showed significant main effects for group, $F(3,36)=8.26$, $p<.001$, and time, $F(1,36)=9.95$, $p=.003$, and a significant interaction effect between time and group, $F(3,36)=8.26$, $p<.001$. Follow-up paired-samples t-tests carried out with a Bonferroni correction for multiple comparisons (.05/4=.0125) showed that the models group's ($t(9)=1.39$, $p=.020$, $d=0.32$) and the CF group's scores ($t(9)=2.95$, $p=.016$, $d=-0.39$) did not significantly change from Posttest I and Posttest II, whereas the mixed group's scores ($t(9)=3.11$, $p=.011$, $d=-1.40$)

significantly dropped from Posttest I to Posttest II. A *t*-value could not be calculated for the control group since the standard error of the difference between their Posttest I and Posttest II scores was zero, which means that their scores remained the same.

4.4 Summary of results

To summarize, in the multiple-choice test, the mixed group's scores were statistically higher than the control group's scores at both times, whereas the CF group's scores were statistically higher than the control group's scores only at Posttest II. The models group's scores were not higher than the control group's scores at either time. There were no statistical differences between the experimental groups in the multiple-choice test at either time point. As the effect sizes in Table 5 show, when the multiple-choice test scores at both times were combined, the group that outperformed the control group with the largest margin was the mixed group.

Table 5. Effect sizes (Cohen's *d*) and summary of effects

	Multiple-choice			Picture description			Tests combined
	Post-test I	Post-test II	Total	Post-test I	Post-test II	Total	Total
Models vs. Control	1.33	2.27	1.80	0.74	1.04	0.89	1.34
CF vs. Control	1.03	1.12*	1.08	1.74*	1.30*	1.52	1.30
Mixed vs. Control	1.94*	2.40*	2.17	3.71*	1.00*	2.36	2.26
Models vs. CF	0.00	0.05	0.02	−1.07*	−0.33	−0.70	−0.34
Models vs. Mixed	−0.55	−0.32	−0.43	−2.04*	0.00	−1.02	−0.73
CF vs. Mixed	−0.48	−0.41	−0.44	−0.46	0.33	−0.07	−0.26

* $p<.05$

In the oral picture description test, the mixed and CF groups statistically outperformed the control and models groups at Posttest I, but there were no differences between the models and control group or between the CF and mixed group. The mixed and CF groups statistically outperformed the control group at Posttest II. There were no other statistically significant differences between the groups at the Posttest II. Finally, the mixed group's scores significantly dropped from Posttest I to Posttest II, but there were no other significant changes in groups' scores from Posttest I to Posttest II in general. The effect sizes shown in Table 5 indicate that, when Posttest I and Posttest II oral picture description test scores were combined, the group that outperformed the control group with the largest margin was the mixed group again. This time, the mixed group was followed by the CF group.

5. Discussion

Our research question asked whether there was any difference in the effect of models, corrective feedback, and a mix of models and corrective feedback on the acquisition of the Turkish locative morpheme. Our results showed that the group that most frequently outperformed the control group was the mixed group. In addition, in terms of effect sizes (i.e., the magnitude of the difference between each group's scores and the control group's scores) combined for the two time points (Posttest I and Posttest II), the mixed group had the largest effect (multiple-choice, $d=2.17$; oral picture description, $d=2.36$; combined, $d=2.26$). Based on these results, it is possible to conclude that the mixed treatment including the provision of models in the first task and corrective feedback in the second, was the most effective.

The finding that the mixed group was the most effective treatment indicates that initially allowing learners to process language receptively through models without expecting them to produce language or to be accurate pays off if corrective feedback is provided consistently after this initial stage. It could be that the provision of models and corrective feedback in this configuration was more effective because the resulting treatment was more closely aligned with the cognitive demands of knowledge internalization and knowledge modification, two of the macro-processes of L2 learning proposed by Housen and Pierrard (2005). As discussed previously, knowledge internalization concerns establishing form-meaning connections. The first stage in the mixed treatment involving the exposure to models might have effectively led the learners to discover the meaning of the locative morpheme because the form-meaning link was made clear by the task through the use of pictures and simplified language. In addition, the task gave learners the opportunity to allocate their full attention to the form-meaning link since it did not involve communicative pressure, which could have distracted learners from the main task of linking form and meaning. As discussed previously, knowledge modification involves learners eliminating non-target-like aspects of their knowledge with the help of additional input or negative evidence. Corrective feedback together with production opportunities provided in the second stage of the mixed treatment might have contributed to the elaboration of learners' knowledge about how the target form works. While production opportunities might have allowed learners to test their hypotheses about the rule behind the allomorphic variation, the negative evidence provided through explicit corrections might have allowed them to confirm or disconfirm these hypotheses.

Although the mixed group is clearly the most effective treatment, it is not easy to determine which group performed the second best. One performance indicator (e.g., the magnitude of the difference between the experimental groups and the control group when tests and time points were combined) showed that the CF and models groups performed similarly. Other indicators, however, showed an advantage for the CF group: (i) The CF group statistically outperformed the control group more often than the model group did; (ii) The CF group also statistically outperformed the models group in one of the four comparisons; (iii) When the groups' combined effect sizes were compared directly, the CF group led to higher effect sizes than the model groups. Overall, then, it seems that the CF group performed better than the models group. This result is consistent with the results of three previous studies. Herron and Tomasello's (1988) results in general, Leeman's (2003) results regarding recasts, and Long et al.'s (1998) results on adverb placement in the Spanish study also showed an advantage for corrective feedback over models. By contrast, the result of the current study concerning the better performance of corrective feedback is not in line with the results of Leeman's (2003) study regarding the performance of repetitions, the Japanese study reported in Long et al. (1998), and the Spanish study reported in Long et al. (1998) regarding object topicalization. As discussed in the literature review, given the fact that these studies were different in many methodological features, it is almost impossible to single out a factor that can explain why these studies produced different results. However, one can tentatively suggest that the relative ease with which learners interpret the feedback might have played a role in these different results. Carroll (2001: 390) has stated that "the best feedback and correction is probably the most explicit – which is the least likely to occur" because it does not require learners to infer whether there is an error, the location of the error, and how it should be corrected. The feedback provided in the current study and Herron and Tomasello (1988) might have been more effective than models because they did not leave much room for inference. The feedback provided in this study might have achieved this by being direct in conveying the message that there was an error in the learner's utterance (*"that's wrong"*) and how the learner should correct the error by providing the correct form (*"you should say..."*). The feedback provided in Herron and Tomasello (1988) was also unambiguous, but in a different way; the feedback procedure included many feedback moves and an instance of implicit feedback was followed by gradually more explicit metalinguistic cues ("*pay attention to the position of the pronoun*", "*place the pronoun before the infinitive*"). In contrast to the feedback types used in the current study and Herron and Tomasello (1988), the repetitions in Leeman (2003) ("*but, you said...*") might have been less effective because they were relatively ambiguous regarding both whether the learner has made an error and how the error should be corrected.

As mentioned in the introduction, many SLA researchers (e.g., Ellis 2005; Hulstijn 2005) distinguish between explicit knowledge and implicit knowledge. According to Ellis (2005), factors such as degree of awareness, time available, focus of attention, and utility of knowledge of metalanguage can help researchers separate tests of implicit knowledge from tests of explicit knowledge. Based on Ellis's (2005) claims, we argue that the multiple-choice test in the current study was more likely to tap into explicit knowledge because learners had enough time to plan their responses and the task instructions explicitly drew learners' attention to the form. In the oral picture description test, however, the conditions were relatively more favorable for the use of implicit knowledge, again based on Ellis's (2005) work; there was a time limit, and the primary focus was on meaning and message creation. Therefore, given our findings that the mixed and CF groups outperformed the control group on both of these tests, it could be that a combination of models and CF and CF alone have value for the development of both conscious and unconscious knowledge. However, it is necessary to keep two important caveats in mind. As pointed out in the previous literature (e.g., Ellis 2005), there are no pure measures of either knowledge type. A test that is designed to tap into one type of knowledge can tap into the other knowledge type as well. In addition, it is not possible to make any definitive claims about the nature of knowledge a task can measure without evidence of whether learners were aware of the knowledge they had during the tests.

One final caveat that merits consideration is the difference between the feedback (mixed and CF) and models groups in their developmental trend. As Table 4 shows, both the mixed and CF groups scored lower on the oral picture description test at Posttest II than at Posttest I. In fact, the mixed group's scores significantly dropped from Posttest I to Posttest II. By contrast, the models group scored higher at Posttest II than at Posttest I. These differences in trends did not lead to a statistically better performance for the models group at Posttest II. However, future research using posttests with longer delays is needed to determine whether the models group's increase in score can reach a level where the models group performs statistically better than feedback groups.

Although the target structure in the current study was the locative morpheme, it is possible, as a reviewer argued, that the results may be extended to the acquisition of the ablative marker -*DAn* in Turkish as participants would have an almost identical learning task of identifying the correct vowel harmony as well as the appropriate choice of either *d-* or *t-* as the initial consonant in the ablative morpheme. However, without empirical data substantiating such a claim, we cannot make generalizations.

Limitations of the study should be noted. One major limitation is that we cannot completely rule out the possibility that differences in knowledge of Turkish among participants existed prior to the treatment since no pretest was administered. We acknowledge that the participants' status as true beginners is based on their self-reported lack of knowledge of Turkish, not on external measures. In addition, a majority of the participants, 32 out of 40, reported having some knowledge of an additional language (e.g., Spanish, French, Italian, German, Japanese, and Arabic) to varying degrees, which might have influenced their learning of the Turkish locative morpheme. However, in this set of languages, the only language in which the locative marker is expressed as a postposition attached to the end of the noun as in Turkish is Japanese. Since the participants' knowledge of those additional languages was only at a beginner-to-intermediate level, it is not plausible to assume that cross-linguistic interferences gave L2 Japanese participants (where L3 is Turkish) an advantage compared to participants with other L2s. Still, future studies should more tightly control the additional language backgrounds of the participants.

Another limitation of the study is the highly controlled nature of the interactions between the learner and the experimenter. Even though such an experimental design helped eliminate potentially confounding variables, it may have also led to unnatural language exchanges between the experimenter and the participants. It would be useful for future research to investigate the effects of models, corrective feedback, and the combination of both in a classroom setting. In addition, the experimenter in this study was one of the researchers. Although the experimenter had had extensive experience in giving instructional treatment in an unbiased way in other instructional effects studies, this could be a confounding factor. Finally, Posttest II in the current study took place two weeks after the last treatment session. A posttest with a longer delay could not be used because of the limitations in scheduling meetings with the participants. A 14-day delay, which was categorized as a short-term delay in Li's (2010) meta-analysis, is within the range of posttest timings adopted in previous corrective feedback studies. Future research can adopt posttests with longer delays to determine the extent to which learners can retain the knowledge they gain from the treatment conditions of the current study.

6. Conclusion

This study investigated the effect of models, corrective feedback, and models plus corrective feedback on the acquisition of the Turkish locative morpheme -*DA*. We targeted beginner-level learners of L2 Turkish and followed a design with two posttests and a control group. The main findings were twofold. First, when compared to the control group, the mixed group showed the highest learning gains with the largest effect size, regardless of the task. This finding suggests that initial exposure to the target form followed by corrective feedback is more effective in learning a new L2 feature than using CF or models alone. Our study has expanded the current understanding of the effects of models and corrective feedback in L2 acquisition and produced a novel finding that the provision of models and corrective feedback together is the most effective treatment for learners who have just begun to learn an L2. Given the theoretical and pedagogical relevance of this line of research, future research into the role of models, corrective feedback, and models plus corrective in L2 acquisition is warranted.

References

Carroll, S. E. 2001. *Input and Evidence: The Raw Material of Second Language Acquisition*. Amsterdam: John Benjamins.

Cedrus. 2003. *SuperLab [Computer software]*. Cedrus Corporation. <https://cedrus.com>

Ellis, R. 1991. Grammar teaching practice or consciousness-raising? In *Second Language Acquisition and Second Language Pedagogy*, R. Ellis (ed.), 232–241. Clevedon: Multilingual Matters.

Ellis, R. 2005. Measuring implicit and explicit knowledge of a second language: A psychometric study. *Studies in Second Language Acquisition* 27(2): 141–172.

Ellis, R. 2015. Form-focused instruction and the measurement of implicit and explicit L2 knowledge. In *Implicit and Explicit Learning of Languages*, P. Rebuschat (ed.), 417–441. Amsterdam: John Benjamins.

Gass, S. M. & Mackey, A. 2006. Input, interaction and output: An overview. *AILA Review* 19: 3–17.

Göksel, A. & Kerslake, C. 2005. *Turkish: A Comprehensive Grammar*. New York NY: Routledge.

Goo, J., Granena, G., Yilmaz, Y. & Novella, M. 2015. Implicit and explicit instruction in L2 learning. In *Implicit and Explicit Learning of Languages*, P. Rebuschat (ed.), 443–482. Amsterdam: John Benjamins.

Hair, J. F., Black, W. C., Babin, B. J., Anderson, R. E. & Tatham, R. L. 2006. *Multivariate Data Analysis* [6th edn]. New York NY: Pearson.

Herron, C., & Tomasello, M. 1988. Learning grammatical structures in a foreign language: Modelling versus feedback. *French Review* 61(6): 910–923.

Housen, A. & Pierrard, M. 2005. *Investigations in Instructed Second Language Acquisition*. Berlin: De Gruyter.

Hulstijn, J. H. 2005. Theoretical and empirical issues in the study of implicit and explicit second-language learning. *Studies in Second Language Acquisition* 27(2): 129–140.

Kornfilt, J. 1997. *Turkish*. New York NY: Routledge.

Krashen, S. D. 1981. *Second Language Acquisition and Second Language Learning*. New York NY: Pergamon Press.

Krashen, S. D. & Terrell, T. D. 1983. *The Natural Approach: Language Acquisition in the Classroom*. New York NY: Pergamon Press.

Leeman, J. 2003. Recasts and second language development. *Studies in Second Language Acquisition* 25(1): 37–63.

Li, S. 2010. The effectiveness of corrective feedback in SLA: A meta-analysis. *Language Learning* 60(2): 309–365.

Long, M. H. 1980. Input, Interaction and Second Language Acquisition. PhD dissertation, University of California, Los Angeles.

Long, M. H. 1981. Input, interaction and second language acquisition. *Annals of the New York Academy Sciences* 379(1): 259–278.

Long, M. H. 1996. The role of the linguistic environment in second language acquisition. In *Handbook of Second Language Acquisition*, W. Ritchie & T. K. Bhatia (eds), 413–468. Cambridge MA: Academic Press.

Long, M. H. 2015. *Second Language Acquisition and Task-based Language Teaching*. Oxford: Wiley-Blackwell.

Long, M. H., Inagaki, S. & Ortega, L. 1998. The role of implicit negative feedback in SLA: Models and recasts in Japanese and Spanish. *The Modern Language Journal* 82(3): 357–371.

Lyster, R. & Saito, K. 2010. Oral feedback in classroom SLA: A meta-analysis. *Studies in Second Language Acquisition* 32(2): 265–302.

Ono, L. & Witzel, J. 2002. Recasts, Salience, and Morpheme Acquisition. Unpublished manuscript, Department of Second Language Studies, University of Hawaii.

Phakiti, A. 2014. *Experimental Research Methods in Language Learning*. London: Bloomsbury.

Pica, T. 1983. Methods of morpheme quantification: Their effect on the interpretation of second language data. *Studies in Second Language Acquisition* 6(1): 69–78.

Pica, T. 1988. Interlanguage adjustments as outcome of NS-NNS negotiated interaction. *Language Learning* 38(1): 45–73.

Pienemann, M. 1998. *Language Processing and Second Language Development: Processability Theory*. Amsterdam: John Benjamins.

Ranta, L. & Lyster, R. 2007. A cognitive approach to improving immersion students' oral language abilities: The awareness-practice-feedback sequence. In *Practice in a Second language: Perspectives From Applied Linguistics and Cognitive Psychology*, R. DeKeyser (ed.), 141–160. Cambridge: CUP.

Schmidt, R. 1990. The role of consciousness in second language learning. *Applied Linguistics* 11(2): 129–158.

Schmidt, R. 2001. Attention. In *Cognition and Second Language Instruction*, P. Robinson (ed.), 3–32. Cambridge: CUP.

Schmidt, R. & Frota, S. 1986. Developing basic conversation ability in a second language: A case study of an adult learner. In *Talking to Learn: Conversation in Second Language Acquisition*, R. Day (ed.), 237–326. New York NY: Newbury House.

Schwartz, B. D. 1993. On explicit and negative evidence effecting and affecting competence and linguistic behavior. *Studies in Second Language Acquisition* 15(2): 147–163.

Sheen, Y. 2004. Corrective feedback and learner uptake in communicative classrooms across instructional settings. *Language Teaching Research* 8(3): 263–300.

Spada, N. & Lightbown, P. M. 1999. Instruction, first language influence, and developmental readiness in second language acquisition. *The Modern Language Journal* 83(1): 1–22.

Truscott, J. 1999. What's wrong with oral grammar correction. *Canadian Modern Language Review* 55(4): 437–456.

VanPatten, B. 2013. Mental representation and skill in instructed SLA. In *Innovations in SLA, Bilingualism and Cognition: Research and Practice*, J. Schwieter (ed.), 3–22. Amsterdam: John Benjamins.

Yilmaz, Y. 2012. The relative effects of explicit correction and recasts on two target structures via two communication modes. *Language Learning* 62(4): 1134–1169.

Yilmaz, Y. 2013. Relative effects of explicit and implicit feedback: The role of working memory capacity and language analytic ability. *Applied Linguistics* 34(3): 344–368.

Yilmaz, Y. 2016. The effectiveness of explicit correction under two different feedback exposure conditions. *Studies in Second Language Acquisition* 38(1): 65–96.

CHAPTER 8

First exposure to Russian word forms by adult English speakers
Disentangling language-specific and language-universal factors

Natalia Pavlovskaya, Nick Riches & Martha Young-Scholten
Newcastle University

> How language learners *segment* (recognise and store words) in the speech stream has typically been explored with children (Jusczyk 1997). Researchers have only recently begun to examine how adults segment an unfamiliar natural language after first exposure without instruction (Gullberg et al. 2010; Gullberg et al. 2012; Carroll 2012, 2013, 2014; Shoemaker & Rast 2013). We report on a study of how 28 English-speaking adults begin to segment words after hearing them in fluent Russian during four sessions. The results showed that segmentation improved significantly over time. Segmentation patterns reflected the influence of English phonotactics and sensitivity to weak-strong stress. We conclude that beyond native language bias, adults deploy the segmentation mechanisms similar to those children use.
>
> **Keywords:** segmentation, first exposure, phonotactics, prosody, implicit learning

1. Introduction

The continuous speech stream does not provide discrete meaningful units to the listener yet proficient speakers of a given language perceive and process this continuous stream as units including those known as words (Carroll 2012: 25). The language learner's first task is to convert this stream into words. Research dating back to the late eighties has employed novel stimuli to investigate how first language (L1)-acquiring babies segment the speech stream via analysis of phonetic, phonotactic, and prosodic cues to word boundaries (see summary in Jusczyk 1997). While Vainikka and Young-Scholten (1994, 1998), Schwartz and

Eubank (1996), and Pienemann (1999, 2007) stressed the need to look at the 'initial state' in second language (L2) syntax, models of L2 development did not until the mid-1990s also include how learners process the speech stream (Carroll 1999, 2001). This has depended on designing appropriate methodology such as the first exposure paradigm which controls exposure to an unfamiliar language from the moment of the learner's first encounter with it. We are beginning to discover how adult learners segment speech from studies, for example, by Rast (2008, 2010); Gullberg et al. (2010); Gullberg et al. (2012); Carroll (2012, 2013, 2014); and Shoemaker and Rast (2013).

In the following, we report on a first exposure study using existing and new techniques of a new language pairing, English and Russian. We start with background information on what research shows babies, L2 learners, and adult native speakers do to detect words, followed by what research shows about how adults detect words in a new, unfamiliar natural language. Then, we describe English and Russian, our methodology, results, discussion, and conclusion.

2. Background

2.1 Babies and the speech stream

The current study investigates adults, but we will briefly consider the L1 developmental literature as it demonstrates the kinds of processes used to segment the speech stream in the absence of an existing language. Such processes may also be available in adults, bearing in mind that adults may have a greater processing capacity and access to their L1 mechanisms and representations.

At 10½ months, babies exposed to English are able to apply to fluent speech phonotactic information (language-specific restrictions on combinations and positions of sounds) such as aspiration to distinguish 'night rates' as opposed to 'nitrates' (Jusczyk, Hohne & Bauman 1999). At 9 months old, babies prefer listening to new words with the phonotactic properties of the language to which they were exposed, either Dutch or English (Jusczyk et al. 1993) or just Dutch (Friederici & Wessels 1993). A study by Mattys and Jusczyk (2001) showed that English 9-month-olds preferred listening to novel words embedded in a passage where words CC edges signalled word boundaries.

Jusczyk, Houston, and Newsome (1999) demonstrated that at 9 months old, babies exposed to English also listened significantly longer to two-syllable words with strong-weak stress rather than weak-strong words; this was independent of syllable weight (Turk et al. 1995) and likely arises from the predominant strong-weak pattern in English. This (trochaic) bias was demonstrated earlier by 7½-

month olds' detection of words with strong-weak stress, such as 'kingdom' vs. weak-strong stress such as 'guitar' in passages they listened to after listening to such words in isolation. Sensitivity to weak-strong was observed later, at 10½ months (Jusczyk, Houston & Newsome 1999). This points to use of a Metrical Segmentation Strategy (MSS) where in English a stressed syllable often begins a new word (Cutler & Carter 1987; Cutler 1990; Cutler 1994).

These and other studies suggest that babies become attuned to the phonetics, phonotactics, and prosody of their language and generalize this knowledge from exemplars to new sequences between eight and ten months, before they attach meanings to words.

Relevant to the present study is research on how adults segment the speech stream in their native language. For example, Cutler and Norris (1988) showed that adults rely on both the MSS and on phonotactic information (McQueen 1998). Thus, are adults still able to segment the speech stream of an unfamiliar language?

2.2 L2 learners and the speech stream

Like babies acquiring their L1, to acquire an L2, the learner must become attuned to metrical, phonetic, and phonotactic patterns of the input. There are clearly differences between these populations. All L2 learners have already acquired at least one language, whose phonological properties have been abstracted from the input and mentally represented. Older learners are cognitively more mature and presumably much better equipped to solve problems and to deal with abstract concepts (Mitchell et al. 2019: 84). And for such learners, exposure often occurs in the classroom where the learning process may be explicit and draw on metalinguistic skills. For adults, explicit instruction is typical but does not preclude the possibility of implicit learning, much like babies acquire language without awareness of their own acquisition processes and without demands on central attentional resources (Ellis 2009: 3). We know from studies from the 1980s of non-classroom 'naturalistic' adult learners, most of whom were immigrants and some of whom had little formal education in their L1s, that implicit acquisition occurs (see summary in Vainikka & Young-Scholten 2011). We next summarize the key findings on segmentation by L2 learners who accumulated a good amount of experience with the target language including through instruction.

With respect to phonotactics, Altenberg and Cairns (1983) showed that English L1/German L2 advanced learners, most of whom started learning the L2 at or before age 12 but some later, were affected by legal sequences in English. This was evident during a timed lexical decision task requiring them to decide if words were possible in English (e.g., 'slien') or in German (e.g., 'pflok'). Unlike English monolingual controls who accepted only words with English phonotactics, L2 German participants accepted words with English and German phonotactics as possible English words. Similarly, a study by Weber and Cutler (2006) on highly proficient German speakers of English who had been learning English as a foreign language for about 15 years with a mean exposure age of 11 years, had slower reaction times and a higher number of misses when they had to spot an English word such as [list] from a sequence which yielded a clear phonotactic boundary in English but not in German, e.g., [far﬩list]. They were also affected by a clear boundary in the German but not in the English condition, e.g., [gois﬩list]. English monolingual controls were only influenced by 'no boundary' in the English condition. Altenberg (2005) showed that Spanish learners of English who had been learning the L2 for 5.1 years since the age 17.2 also drew on L1 phonetic knowledge for how they made use of the Spanish glottal stop in English segmentation, e.g., correctly segmenting 'a nice man' not as 'an ice man'. However, they struggled with the use of aspirated stops for segmentation, e.g., they segmented 'chief's cool' as 'chief school' because of the absence of aspirated stops in Spanish.

With respect to prosody, studies by Archibald (1992, 1993) showed that adult Polish and Hungarian post-puberty learners of English were greatly affected by various L1 stress placement strategies. Hungarian speakers tended to stress the first syllable of English words, e.g., 'agenda', whereas Polish speakers tended to stress the penultimate syllable, e.g., 'cabinet'. Archibald also found that these learners were sensitive to the operation of stress by lexical class in English; that is, nouns were (incorrectly) stressed on the first syllable, e.g., 'horizon' instead of 'horizon', while verbs were stressed on the final syllable, e.g., 'astonish' instead of 'astonish'.

These studies showed that adults are affected by their L1 word detection strategies in their L2 segmentation. Even after they have accumulated abundant L2 experience, the L1 continues to bias their listening. Is this inevitable, particularly for those exposed to a new language after puberty, after the end of a critical or sensitive period? Do adults demonstrate segmentation strategies beyond those in their L1s? This is a question (among others) first exposure studies have been aiming to answer.

2.3 First exposure studies

There is little research on the segmentation abilities of adults who are complete L2 beginners. In this section, we discuss what we know about study participants who receive only minimal input, without explicit instruction, in an unfamiliar language, similar to L1 children's exposure. Such studies are typically referred to as 'first exposure' studies.

Some studies have been carried out on artificial languages; in fact, the earliest were exclusively on these (e.g. Aslin et al. 1998; Linzen & Gallagher 2017; Saffran, Aslin & Newport 1996; Saffran, Newport & Aslin 1996; Yang & Givón 1997). Although these studies are beneficial in allowing the researcher complete control over the input presented to learners, the trend has since been to use natural languages (see Carroll 2014:114). These have greater ecological validity as results are more generalizable to real-life language acquisition scenarios. In using natural languages, researchers have tended to measure and manipulate input in various ways to answer specific questions. Most such share the goal of determining how the L1 and target language interact during exposure, and to identify what implicit learning mechanisms the learner brings to the process of learning a new language. A key advantage of this method is that it abstracts away from individual differences in the ability to engage with input and benefit from explicit language instruction.

Studies show that adults can segment words in an unfamiliar language from the speech stream for different L1/L2 pairings and under different study designs. However, unlike babies, who first segment their native language efficiently after 10½ months of exposure, the amount of input required for segmentation in first exposure studies may be far less.

Input is designed for implicit learning, and amount ranges from one exposure to many hours. Gullberg et al. (2010) and Gullberg et al. (2012) set the amount of input in advance, in minutes, while Carroll (2012, 2014) provided exposure until certain criteria were met. For Rast (2008) and Shoemaker and Rast (2013), input involved hours over a number of weeks, no manipulation of input but instead exposure in an intensive Polish class following the communicative approach, without explicit instruction. Polish words were recognized by French speakers after 6½ hours of instruction.

In her work, Carroll found that Anglophone participants segmented, memorized, and retrieved German names which were cognate (*Oskar*) and non-cognates (*Otto*) after hearing them just a few times.

Using another study design, Gullberg et al. (2010) showed that segmentation was possible after as little as seven minutes of exposure to a narrated audiovisual weather report and that learners generalized knowledge to words not in the input. Their Dutch participants recognised disyllabic Mandarin words, provided their meanings, and generalized certain phonotactic information about monosyllabic Mandarin to words which they had not encountered in the input. That is, they identified which words were possible Mandarin words and which were not, in violation of Mandarin syllable structure. The seven minutes of their exposure to Mandarin, might, however, have been supplemented by participants' ambient exposure to the language, e.g., from listening while dining on or ordering Chinese food, from the media or from overheard conversations among Mandarin-speaking students and immigrants (Lim 2016). This does not question Gullberg et al.'s (2010) findings about participants' generalization abilities but only about the amount of exposure required. Generalization has been found in other studies where there was no ambient exposure because the language was an artificial one. Linzen and Gallagher (2017) in their study showed that adult English native speakers rapidly generalized target word sounds to novel sounds after as little as one exposure to a list of five words containing these sounds. Participants discriminated words which appeared in the input from words which did not appear in the input and had non-generalizable properties. Participants also started to differentiate words which appeared in the input from words which did not appear in the input and generalized properties only after two or more exposure to the list. These studies, all on adults, demonstrate that generalization can take place rapidly and suggest that this occurs at the start of exposure a new language. The ability to make phonological generalizations seems to be a fundamental property of language acquisition regardless of the age of the learner and adults' faster rates of generalization and segmentation may reflect their superior statistical learning abilities (Arnon 2019).

Whether the studies involve a few trials, seven minutes, or six hours of exposure to an unfamiliar language, their results indicate an astonishing ability for the detection of words by adults after minimal aural input which cannot be solely explained *via* the transfer of properties of the L1. The findings of first exposure studies certainly confirm what is expected: learners easily detect words which share characteristics of words in their L1. What studies also indicate is that adult listeners go beyond their L1 in segmentation in their analysis of novel language input. This turns out to interact with other linguistic and non-linguistic variables. For instance, words which are stressed are recognized better than words which are unstressed (Rast & Dommergues 2003; Rast 2008). There is a preference for longer words when segmenting. In Gullberg et al. (2012), disyllabic words were segmented more accurately than monosyllabic words. In Carroll's (2014) study of German names, participants segmented those with up to seven syllables better than shorter names. These findings are consistent with studies on the effect of distributional properties on segmentation in artificial languages. For example, according to Saffran, Newport, and Aslin (1996) in one study, words with more than one syllable with higher word-internal transitional probabilities were easier to detect in the speech stream in comparison to monosyllabic words with only word-external transitional probabilities.

Frequency of target words in the input to which participants are exposed may also play a role, but this is unclear. Gullberg et al. (2012) demonstrated that participants identified frequent words after as little as seven minutes of exposure when they appeared eight times in the Mandarin input, but not words which only appeared twice. But Rast (2008) and Shoemaker and Rast (2013) did not find significant differences between high- and low-frequency words in the Polish input to French speakers.

These studies point to robustness of findings in a cross-linguistic context given the involvement of different language pairs. There is more to investigate about the impact of phonological cues on segmentation by first exposure participants along the lines of what is described above in L1 and L2 acquisition. To comply with other studies on first exposure and with the ecological validity, the study discussed in this chapter involved aural exposure to Russian for adults unfamiliar with the language to examine their word segmentation abilities. As in previous studies, participants were unaware of the real purpose of the study to increase the chances that they would be implicitly learning.

3. Research questions

The study aimed to answer the following research questions:

i. Does participants' ability to detect Russian words increase over time?
ii. Are participants more accurate in detecting patterns of Russian phonotactics which exist in English due to transfer than those which exist only in Russian?
iii. Are participants more accurate in detecting Russian words with a strong-weak stress pattern due to transfer of MSS, than words with a weak-strong pattern?
iv. Do participants show a preference for disyllabic over monosyllabic words because the previous research has shown that longer words are segmented better than shorter words?
v. Can participants generalize phonotactic properties of words heard in the input to new words because previous research found evidence of generalizations after first exposure?

3.1 Russian

Russian has flexible word order, rich inflectional morphology, and marks case and agreement. All target words in our study were actual Russian nouns but masculine to control for case-related phonological variation. The nouns were in the nominative and accusative cases whose inflection does not change; they always end with a consonant as opposed to feminine and neuter nouns and other cases. It thereby enables us to simultaneously evaluate learning based on L1 transfer, and learning based on induction by the same participant.

Russian was the target language because like English, it allows a variety of consonant clusters and initially stresses nouns; unlike English, Russian allows consonant clusters which are not found in English and has frequent word-final stress. A Russian onset can contain between zero and five consonants (Halle 1959). Only word-initial two-member clusters, not all of which are possible in English, were included in our stimuli. These are be divided into four categories based on Sonority Sequencing Principle (SSP) and Minimal Sonority Distance (MSD):

1. clusters with rising sonority and MSD = 2 (e.g., *dl'ia* [dlʲa] 'for')
2. clusters with rising sonority and MSD = 1 (e.g., *kniga* [ˈknʲigə] 'book')
3. clusters with plateau sonority or MSD = 0 (e.g., *pchela* [ptʃeˈla] 'bee')
4. clusters with reverse sonority or MSD = −1 (e.g., *lba* [lba] 'GEN.SG forehead')[1,2]

Russian stress assignment resembles English in that each lexical word has one syllable which bears primary stress. There have been many attempts to explain stress patterns in Russian, and this is still under debated. Some categorize Russian with languages with unpredictable or 'free' stress where stress is stored with words in the lexicon and phonological properties of a word have no influence (see Zaliznjak 1977, 1985; Archibald 1994). Others claim that Russian has an iambic foot (Halle and Vergnaud 1987; Melvold 1990; Alderete 1995; Crosswhite 2001) which accounts for stress on a word-final syllable in multi-syllabic words being more common than initial stress. For instance, Crosswhite et al. (2003) showed that mono-morphemic words, e.g., [navʲek] 'forever', were stressed on the final syllable 90% of the time, followed by stress on medial syllable at 9%, with initial stress on only 1% of words. Here Russian differs from English whose disyllabic nouns are more likely to have initial stress. Evidence from Sereno (1986) and Kelly and Bock (1988) (both as cited in Guion et al. 2003: 406) suggests that disyllabic English nouns are stressed on the first syllable 73% of the time (Sereno) and 94% of the time (Kelly & Bock).

4. Methodology

4.1 Design

The study took place in a quiet room over four consecutive days during which the same procedure was followed each day with an input phase and then testing phase. The three tasks involved, one of which had two versions, are described

---

1. See Selkirk (1984) for explanation what SSP is.
2. See Broselow & Finer (1991) for explanation what MSD is.

below. On the first and second days, participants listened to input about 'music' and took the first version of a task, and on the third and fourth days they listened to input on 'university life' and took the second version of a task. Two other tasks were always the same. On the final day, participants also completed a language history questionnaire adapted from Gullberg and Indefrey (2003) to collect bibliographical data, e.g., about their age, gender, place of birth, residence, and knowledge of other languages.

A laptop and good-quality, comfortable headphones with a self-adjusting headband and cushioned ear-pads were used. Participants were not told the language was Russian to avoid biasing their listening. This ensured that participants did not explicitly recruit any partial knowledge of the target language, though due to the screening process, it is extremely unlikely that participants had this knowledge. The identity of the language was only revealed at the end. The participants, stimuli, input phase, and testing tasks are described next.

4.2 Participants

Twenty-nine students from Newcastle University, UK were recruited through an advertisement that specified a study was looking for native English speakers without knowledge of Slavic languages to take part in a linguistic experiment, the aim of which was to investigate how foreign languages are learned. To be eligible, participants had to confirm no knowledge of Slavic languages. The advertisement also mentioned that participants would be thanked with a £10 Amazon voucher. None reported a hearing or language impairment.[3] All were native speakers of English, but one participant was English-Welsh bilingual from birth. The mean age was 23 years and 3 months. Cantonese, Mandarin Chinese, French, German, Japanese, Korean, Spanish, and Portuguese were reported as L2s and in a few cases L3s.

4.3 Stimuli

All stimuli (144 words) used in this experiment were monosyllabic and CCVC in structure or disyllabic and CCV.CVC or CCVC.CVC in structure. Stimuli were checked by a native English speaker to make sure they did not resemble existing English words. The stimuli were used to create four experimental conditions to answer the five research questions above on phonotactics (with native and non-native categories), stress (strong-weak and weak-strong categories), word length

---

[3]. Two participants reported that they had a learning difficulty, but their results were not excluded.

(monosyllabic and disyllabic words), and generalization (targets, generalizable distractors, non-generalizable distractors).

4.3.1 Target stimuli

Forty-eight Russian nouns were targets; see Table 1 and Table 2. These were used in the input phase (described next) and in the testing phase, and words were selected to create experimental conditions as follows.

The phonotactic condition comprised words with onset consonant clusters (CC type) divided into words with native and non-native phonotactics (24 words in each category). The native category tested the effect of pre-existing knowledge of the L1 (English). The non-native category tested the extent to which participants had assimilated Russian phonotactics. The native list ($n=24$) had eight types of onset clusters frequent in both English and Russian: *kl-, bl-, gl-, sm-, sl-, pl-, kr-, gr-*. The non-native list ($n=24$) contained eight onset clusters frequent in Russian but absent in English: *hl-, kn-, sv-, ʃt-, tv-, ʃk-, zv-, sr-*.

Table 1. Target words with native phonotactics

Phonotactic condition = Native					
Monosyllabic words		Disyllabic words			
		Strong-weak words		Weak-strong words	
IPA	Latin script	IPA	Latin script	IPA	Latin script
[kɫik]	klik	[ˈklʲevʲɪr]	klever	[klaˈtʃok]	klochok
[blʲef]	blef	[ˈblʲinʲɪk]	blinnik	[blʲɪzʲˈnʲets]	bliznec
[glas]	glaz	[ˈglʲænʲɪts]	glianec	[glaˈtok]	glotok
[smʲesʲ]	smes'	[ˈsmʲenʲʃːɪk]	smeschik	[smʊˈglʲak]	smugliak
[slux]	sluh	[ˈsʲlʲitək]	slitok	[slaˈvarʲ]	slovar'
[plof]	plov	[ˈplʲedʲɪk]	pledik	[plaˈtok]	platok
[krax]	krah	[ˈkrolʲɪk]	krolik	[kraˈvatʲ]	krovat'
[grom]	grom	[ˈgruʃːɪk]	gruzschik	[graˈfʲin]	grafin

The word length condition investigated the impact of this on segmentation with 8 monosyllabic words in one category and 16 disyllabic words in another for each native and non-native phonotactic condition.

The stress condition investigated if participants were relying on their L1 English prosody, or using Russian stress patterns. It contained 16 disyllabic words divided into two categories of 8 words with initial stress (strong-weak) and 8 words with stress on the second syllable (weak-strong) for each phonotactic condition.

Table 2. Target words with non-native phonotactics

		Phonotactic condition = Non-native				
Monosyllabic words		Disyllabic words				
		Strong-weak words		Weak-strong words		
IPA	Latin script	IPA	Latin script	IPA	Latin script
[xlʲep]	hleb	[ˈxlopʲits]	hlopec	[xlaˈpok]	hlopok
[knʲelʲ]	knel	[ˈknʲigəm]	knigam	[knʲaˈzʲok]	kniazek
[svʲet]	svet	[ˈsvʲitək]	svitok	[svʲɪˈnʲets]	svinec
[ʃtat]	shtat	[ˈʃtopər]	shtopor	[ʃtʊrˈval]	shtyrval
[tvʲɪt]	tvid	[ˈtvorək]	tvorog	[tvaˈrʲets]	tvorec
[ʃkaf]	shkaf	[ˈʃkolʲnʲɪk]	shkolnik	[ʃkodʲɪk]	shkodik
[zvuk]	zvyk	[ˈzvonaˈrʲ]	zvonar'	[zvaˈnok]	zvonok
[srok]	srok	[ˈsrubʃʲːɪk]	srubschik	[srasˈtok]	srostok

4.3.2 *Generalizable distractors*

These were 48 test words not present in the input, which had properties generalizable to target words. This tested whether participants could generalize phonotactic properties of words heard in the input to new words; see research question 5. These words were used, along with non-generalizable new words (see below), as distractors (*n* = 96), for testing hypotheses based on research questions i–iv.

Generalizable words were selected and distributed evenly across experimental conditions in the same way as the targets and had word-initial two-member clusters, e.g., target word [plof] and generalizable distrator [plaʃ]; see Table 3 and Table 4. There were 24 items in each phonotactic condition, and for each condition, 8 monosyllables and 16 disyllables. The disyllabic condition had 8 words with a strong-weak stress pattern and 8 with a weak-strong stress pattern.

4.3.3 *Non-generalizable distractors*

Additional distractors were 48 words not in the input. These contrasted with targets and generalizable distractors due to non-generalizable properties. They tested participants' responses to phonotactic properties which could not be generalized; see research question v. These were distractors in the 96 words addressing research questions i–iv. The 48 distractors were selected and evenly distributed across experimental conditions in the same way as the targets and generalizable distractors. Stimuli were evenly divided into two phonotactic conditions. The native phonotactic condition contained 24 Russian words which are phototactically legal in both English and Russian. Initial clusters were: *sk-, tr-, br-, dr-, fl-, fr-, sp-, sn-*. The non-native phonotactic condition contained 24 items which

Table 3. Generalizable distractors with native phonotactics

Monosyllabic words		Disyllabic words			
		Strong-weak words		Weak-strong words	
IPA	Latin script	IPA	Latin script	IPA	Latin script
[klat]	klad	[ˈklapən]	klapan	[klʊˈbok]	klubok
[blat]	blat	[ˈbludik]	bludik	[blaˈtʃok]	blachok
[glupʲ]	glub'	[ˈglazʲɪk]	glazik	[glaˈgol]	glagol
[smok]	smog	[ˈsmʲeʒʲːʲɪk]	smezhik	[smarˈtʃok]	smorchok
[s⁽ʲ⁾lʲisʲ]	sliz'	[ˈslonʲɪk]	slonik	[s⁽ʲ⁾lʲɪzʲˈnʲak]	slizniak
[plaʃ]	plasch	[ˈplotʲɪk]	plotik	[plaˈmbʲɪr]	plombir
[krʲik]	krik	[ˈkrovnʲɪk]	krovnik	[krʲɪˈkun]	krikyn
[grʲasʲ]	griaz'	[ˈgroxət]	grohot	[grɪˈzun]	gryzyn

Table 4. Generalizable distractors with non-native phonotactics

Monosyllabic words		Disyllabic words			
		Strong-weak words		Weak-strong words	
IPA	Latin script	IPA	Latin script	IPA	Latin script
[xlor]	hlor	[ˈxlʲupʲɪk]	hlupik	[xlʲɪˈvok]	hlevok
[knʲot]	knet	[ˈknutʲɪk]	knutik	[knʲi ʒʲːʲɪk]	knizhik
[svot]	svod	[ˈsvoraˈt]	svorot	[svʲɪˈstok]	svistok
[ʃtuk]	shtyk	[ˈʃturmən]	shturman	[ʃtiˈrʲok]	shtyrek
[tvʲil]	tvil	[ˈtvʲistər]	tvistor	[tvʲorˈdos]	tverdoz
[ʃkʲif]	shkiv	[ˈʃkʲipʲɪr]	shkiper	[ʃkaˈlʲar]	shkoliar
[zvʲerʲ]	zver'	[ˈzvʲozdəm]	zvezdam	[zvaˈnʲets]	zvonec
[srif]	sryv	[ˈsrʲestʃɪk]	srezchik	[sramʲɪk]	sramik

were either non-existent but legal Russian or other language words whose onsets included infrequent CC Russian phonotactics. Three words violated sonority: *rt-*, *lʒ-*, *lg-*, and one word had a sonority plateau *ptʃ-*. Because we wanted to include more words, there were four onsets illegal in Russian and English: *mp-*, *gb-*, *nk-*, *ht-*. The non-generalizable distractors are presented in Table 5 and Table 6.

Table 5. Non-generalizable distractors with native phonotactics

Monosyllabic words		Disyllabic words			
		Strong-weak words		Weak-strong words	
IPA	Latin script	IPA	Latin script	IPA	Latin script
[skas]	skaz	[ˈskupʃːik]	skupschik	[skaˈkun]	skakun
[trʲelʲ]	trel'	[ˈtrʲepʲɪt]	trepet	[ˈtravnʲɪk]	travnik
[brak]	brak	[ˈbratʲɪk]	bratik	[brʊˈsok]	brysok
[dropʲ]	drob'	[ˈdrotʲɪk]	drotik	[drʊˈzok]	druzhok
[flʲus]	flus	[ˈflotʲɪk]	flotik	[frʲɪˈgat]	fregat
[spʲex]	speh	[ˈsposəp]	sposob	[sparˈnʲik]	sparnik
[sʲnʲek]	sneg	[ˈsʲnʲimək]	snimok	[snaˈʃːik]	snoschik
[prut]	prud	[ˈprʲibɨlʲ]	probyl'	[praˈʃif]	proshiv

Table 6. Non-generalizable distractors with non-native phonotactics

Monosyllabic words		Disyllabic words			
		Strong-weak words		Weak-strong words	
IPA	Latin script	IPA	Latin script	IPA	Latin script
[mpar]	mpar	[ˈmpovər]	mpovar	[mpaˈrʲik]	mparik
[gbʲit]	gbit	[ˈgbagʲet]	gbager	[gbɨˈnom]	gbinom
[nkʲib]	nkib	[ˈnkomak]	nkomak	[nkaˈmʲin]	nkamin
[xtʲex]	hteh	[ˈxtʲerʲɪk]	hterik	[xtaˈnok]	htonok
[rtutʲ]	rtut'	[ˈrtovʊn]	rtovun	[rtʲɪˈʃːɪˈk]	rtischek
[lʒets]	lzhec	[ˈlʒivən]	lzhivon	[lʒeˈmud]	lzhemud
[lgatʲ]	lgat'	[ˈlgunʲam]	lguniam	[lgaˈnʲiʃ]	lganish
[ptʃak]	pchak	[ˈptʃɪvʲer]	pchiver	[ptʃɪˈlʲak]	pcheliak

4.4 Input phase

Two lists of 48 different sentences were constructed around the 48 targets, with each target used once in a sentence. Sentences contained a minimum of four and a maximum of six words with the target in sentence-medial position and preceded and followed by words of three to five syllables. Gomez (2002), in a study on the learning of an artificial language, showed that even short pauses can cue a word boundary, so in the present study, the sentences were recorded without pauses between words, and none of the words received a focal accent. Each target word appeared after a word ending with [n], [m], [l], [t], [oj], or [ij] because, in conjunction with the first segment of the targets, this resulted in a word boundary in both English and Russian. We examined all words in the input and boundaries between words to confirm that there were no phonotactic clusters anywhere else in sentences which were in the target words.

For an independent measure of participants' attention, 20 English-Russian shared words were embedded in the materials.[4] It was assumed that if participants paid attention to the input, they would notice these words, recognizing them through L1 representations being triggered. Two lists were created, one containing words about music, for example [ˈlʲirʲɪkə] 'lyrics' and the other words about university life, for example [stuˈdʲent] 'student'. Words from each list were used to record two sets of sentences. The sentences about music were interspersed into the first set of 48 sentences containing targets and generated an audio recording 3:31 minutes long. The second set of sentences about university life were interspersed within another set of 48 sentences with targets, resulting in an audio recording 3:40 minutes long.

Participants were exposed to the input phase twice each day over four consecutive days resulting in exposure to eight instances of target words during 27 minutes of total exposure to Russian by the end of the fourth session. Exposing participants to input over four consecutive days examined segmentation abilities over time. As mentioned in the design section above, on the first and second days, participants listened to input about music, and to input about university life on the third and fourth days.[5]

4.5 Tasks

The three tasks tested participants individually after each input phase in this order: word recognition, forced-choice task, and shared words identification. Participants took the relevant version of the shared words identification task on days one and two and three and four respectively. The word recognition and the forced-choice tasks were always the same.

---

4. 'Shared words' refer to words common between English and Russian which are loanwords in both languages rather than cognates. While some call such words cognates (e.g., Carroll 1992: 93) we use this term instead since these words are not genetically related but rather have other ultimate and intermediate origins.

5. This does not include exposure through testing.

4.5.1 *Word recognition task*

This task addressed research questions i–iv by examining if participants could detect target words they had heard in the input phase, as opposed to distractor words. This task also addressed research question v by examining if participants had assimilated knowledge of phonotactic patterns they had heard in the input and generalized this knowledge to new items.

Similar to the procedure described in Gullberg et al. (2012), participants sat approximately 60 cm from a computer screen and the experimental list of audio files was played via headphones, one at a time. The experiment started with the presentation of a screen with the instructions indicating that the participant would listen to 144 words presented to them one by one and if they thought they had heard the word before, they needed to press 'z' on the keyboard, otherwise they should press 'm'. 'Z' and 'm' were chosen for ergonomic reasons, being the farthest left and farthest right letter keys on the bottom row the keyboard. A white fixation dot appeared at the centre of the screen for the duration of each sound file. This was followed by presenting on the screen the number of trials (1–144) to motivate the participants by letting them know how many trials remained, and a green letter 'z' on the left-hand side of the screen, and a red letter 'm' on the right-hand side of the screen for up to four seconds. They were given four seconds to respond. Upon a keypress, the participant heard a beeping noise.

The word recognition task contained all 144 stimuli, 48 of which were target items (requiring a 'z' response) and 96 of which were distractors (generalizable and non-generalizable) (requiring an 'm' response).

4.5.2 *Forced-choice task*

The primary motivation for running this task was because it was anticipated that the results from the word recognition task might show only limited sensitivity due to being confounded by individual biases, e.g., some participants may exhibit a negative response bias, pressing 'm' (word not recognised) for an overwhelming majority of trials, making their data difficult to analyze (see results section for further discussion).

Each participant listened to 48 pairs of items presented one by one. Just as the word recognition task, this task aimed to address research questions i–iv by examining which of two items in each pair they had heard in the input. If participants thought they had heard the first word, they were asked to press 'z', and to press 'm' if they thought it was the second word. Participants were asked to respond as fast as possible, and if they failed to respond within four seconds, the program moved to the next item. Forty-eight pairs of sound files consisted of the list of targets from the input on the one hand, and the list of generalizable distractors, which were matched in phonotactics, word length, and stress. For instance, the generalizable counterparts to the targets *klik* [kɫik], *klever* ['klʲevʲɪr], and *klachok* [kla'tʃok] were *klad* [klat], *klapan* ['klapən], and *klubok* [klʊ'bok], respectively.

Research question v about generalization abilities was not addressed by this task because asking whether participants generalized phonotactic properties of words heard in the input to new words by treating generalizable distractors similarly to targets is the same as asking about performance on targets, which is what research question i addressed. Moreover, the successful learning of the targets on this task would hinder our ability to investigate subtle manipulations of the distractor items. Such relatively subtle effects would only be apparent in a familiarity measure such as a word recognition task, where generalizable distractors are not competing with targets because they do not occur in pairs.

4.5.3 Shared words identification task

This task started with instructions on the screen which were the same as in the word recognition task with the only difference being that there were only 20 words. The test items included 10 shared words from the audio recording and 10 shared words not in the input as distractors. For example, *bariton* [bərʲɪt'on] 'baritone' and *pianino* [pʲɪanʲ'inə] 'piano' were included in the input, and *robot* ['robət] 'robot' and *telefon* [tʲɪlʲɪ'fon] 'telephone' were not. This task took no longer than two minutes to complete.

For all tasks, the presentation of the sound files was randomized, and the sound files played sequentially by the software identically for each participant on all four days. Both tasks were created using experimental software *OpenSesame* version 3.1.6 Jazzy James (Mathôt et al. 2012).

5. Results

Research questions i–v generated the following five hypotheses.

i. H1: Participants' accuracy on words from the input will increase with number of sessions.
ii. H2: Participants will be more accurate in detecting patterns of Russian phonotactics which exist in English than those patterns which are new / exist in Russian.
iii. H3: Participants will be more accurate in detecting Russian words with a strong-weak stress pattern.

iv. H4: Participants will be more accurate in detecting Russian disyllabic words than Russian monosyllabic words, given that it is easier for them to compute word internal transitional probabilities of disyllabic words.
v. H5: If participants have assimilated the phonotactic properties of Russian, they will treat generalizable distractors as possible targets because they have the same phonotactic properties, while non-generalizable distractors will not be treated as such.

The word recognition task had an unbalanced design (more distractors than targets) making it prone to negative response bias, e.g., some participants with a tendency to correctly reject words could achieve high accuracy because they would be correct for most of the distractors, which constituted more items than targets. We applied an analytical method to control for this bias and employed *Signal Detection Theory* (SDT) for the word recognition and shared words identification tasks (Green & Swets 1966). The forced-choice task and the shared words identification task were not prone to response bias, and the dichotomous response variable "accuracy" with the values "correct/incorrect" was modelled using a mixed-effect logistic regression utilising the package *lme4* (Bates et al. 2015). A mixed-effect logistic regression was chosen because mixed-effects models are considered superior to traditional analyses based on quasi-F tests in their ability to model variation due to random factors and deal with missing values (Baayen et al. 2007; Jaeger 2008).

To perform the SDT analysis, indices of sensitivity and discriminability, such as d', *beta, A'*, and c, were calculated using the *psycho* package (Makowski 2018) in R software (R Core Team 2013). For the analysis of the word recognition task data, D-prime (d') was the parametric measure of sensitivity most used among all such indices. According to Stanislaw and Todorov (1999), it can be difficult to interpret particular values of d' due to use of standard deviations in its computation. The following interpretation of d' values is commonly used: a zero value of d' signals that participants can discriminate between a signal (target) and a noise (distractor) at a chance level (50%); larger values signal good discriminability. For example, $d' = 4$ signals excellent discriminability (at 100%), and negative values mean that participants performed below the level of chance. According to Azzopardi and Cowley (1998), a value of $d' = 0.5$ corresponds to approximately 60% accuracy, and $d' = 1.5$ to about 75% accuracy.

On the word recognition task, participants' responses varied from 0 to 1 so the limits on the y-axis range from 0 to 1. The analysis of accuracy started by calculating the numbers of hits, misses, false alarms, and correct rejections based on all stimuli (48 targets and 96 distractors). The data were aggregated and grouped anew according to hypotheses (stated above) based on our research questions (i–v), including relevant variables (such as session, phonotactics, stress, word length, and generalization) which produced new d' values each time an analysis was run. ANOVA analyses were conducted with these d' values using the *afex* package (Singmann et al. 2015). Last, but not least, the calculation of d' does not model variation among items because the formula involves overall rates of true/false positives/negatives. Though it is not ideal that we lost the ability to model by-item variation, we felt it was more important to model response bias, as this is likely to have a greater impact on findings.

For the forced-choice and shared words identification tasks, mixed-effect logistic regressions modelled the effect of each condition (session, phonotactics, stress, and word length) on response (1 = correct word / shared words identified, 0 = incorrect word / shared words not identified).[6] The initial random effects structure included by-subject and by-item intercepts for all condition variables. Standard procedures outlined by Baayen et al. (2007), involving the comparison of nested models using the ANOVA command, were used to determine the maximal random effects structure and the significance of the fixed effects.

5.1 Shared words identification task

Recall this task was to ensure that participants paid attention to the input during the sessions and an increase in accuracy over sessions is an indication that participants paid attention to the properties of the input. Accuracy in detecting shared words was analysed. Two mixed-effect logistic regression models were fitted with accuracy as the dependent variable and subject and item variables as random factors. The first model compared the first session to the second, while the second model compared the third session to the fourth because participants listened to different input with shared words and completed different tasks. The results of the first model indicated that accuracy was higher on the second day ($M=70\%$) than on the first session ($M=63\%$) with a significant effect of the second session ($OR=1.45$, $p<.05$, 95% CI [1.09, 1.93]). The results of the second model indicated that accuracy was higher on the fourth day ($M=75\%$) than on the third session ($M=66\%$) with a significant effect of the fourth session ($OR=1.71$, $p<.05$, 95% CI [1.28, 1.71]). The mean accuracy percentages are presented in Figure 1. This allows us to conclude that our participants were paying attention to the input.

---

6. Only condition "session" is relevant to shared words identification task.

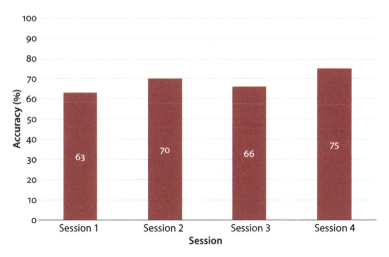

Figure 1. Shared words identification task: Mean percentage of accuracy scores across sessions

5.2 Participants increasing ability to detect words

H1 predicted that participants' accuracy on words from the input would increase with number of sessions. The results support this hypothesis. D-prime scores by session are in Figure 2, which shows evidence for participants' detection of words after a single session and an improvement in d' over sessions. A one-way ANOVA was conducted with d' scores as a dependent variable and session number as an independent variable to investigate this. The ANOVA identified a main effect of session ($F(3,75) = 12.44$, $p < .001$, $\eta_p^2 = 0.33$). A planned pairwise comparison showed a statistically significant increase from the first to second sessions ($F(3,75) = 12.44$, $p = .05$) with the mean $M = 0.20$ on the first session, and $M = 0.36$ on the second session. There was no significant increase in d' from the second to third sessions ($F(3,75) = 12.44$, $p = .86$) with $M = 0.40$ on the third session. Critically, there was a significant difference in d' between the third and fourth sessions ($F(3,75) = 12.44$, $p = .04$) with $M = 0.57$ on the fourth session, the highest score among all four sessions. There was a statistically significant difference in d' between the first and third sessions ($F(3,75) = 12.44$, $p < .001$) and between the second and fourth sessions ($F(3,75) = 12.44$, $p < .001$). That is, there was an improvement over time with only a comparison between the second and third sessions not being significant. The value $d' = 0.57$, which participants scored on the fourth session, corresponds to about 64% accuracy. Importantly, performance was above chance on all sessions, even on the first day.

Accuracy for the forced-choice task, by session, is shown in Figure 3, where there are moderate increases in accuracy over time with $M = 49\%$ on session 1,

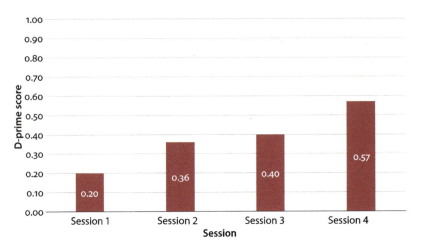

Figure 2. Word recognition task: D-prime scores for each session

$M = 51.3\%$ on session two, $M = 52.1\%$ on session three, and $M = 56.7\%$ on session four. A mixed-effects logistic regression modelled accuracy as the dependent variable and session as an independent variable (indicator coded) and indicated a significant effect of the fourth session ($OR = 1.4$, $p < .01$, 95% CI [1.19, 1.62]), not for the second session ($OR = 1.10$, $p = .21$, 95% CI [0.94, 1.29]), and only a marginally significant effect for the third session ($OR = 1.14$, $p = .09$, 95% CI [0.97, 1.33]).

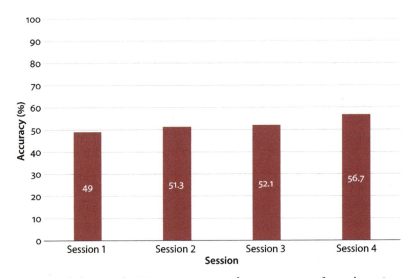

Figure 3. Forced-choice task: Mean percentages of accuracy scores for each session

5.3 Accuracy in detecting Russian/English phonotactics vs. Russian-only

H2 predicted that participants would be more accurate in detecting patterns when they exist in both Russian and English, than those which are Russian-only. For the word recognition task, d' on words with native English phonotactics ($M = 0.35$) was higher than that on words with non-native phonotactics ($M = 0.12$). This effect was identified as significant in an ANOVA ($F(1, 25) = 14.64$, $p < .001$, $\eta_p^2 = 0.37$). Figure 4 presents d' values for phonotactic condition on this task.

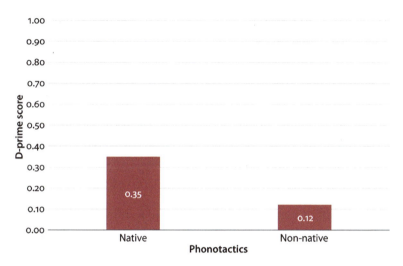

Figure 4. Word recognition task: D-prime scores for phonotactic condition

For the forced-choice task, accuracy on words with non-native phonotactics was higher ($M - 53.3\%$) than accuracy on words with native English phonotactics ($M = 51.2\%$), yet a mixed-effect logistic regression model showed the difference was not significant ($OR = 1.08$, $p = .57$, 95% CI [0.82, 1.45]). The mean percentages of accuracy scores for the phonotactics condition on the forced-choice task are presented in Figure 5.

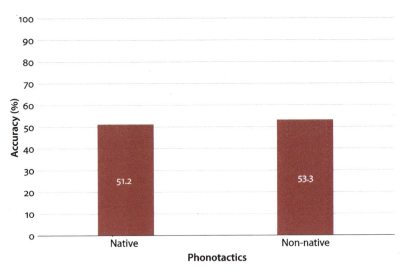

Figure 5. Forced-choice task: Mean percentages of accuracy scores for phonotactics condition

5.4 Accuracy in strong-weak vs. weak-strong stressed Russian words

H3 predicted greater accuracy in detecting Russian words with strong-weak stress. For the word recognition task, d' on words with weak-strong stress ($M=0.30$) was higher than for strong-weak stress ($M=0.25$), but not significantly so ($F(1,25)=0.44$, $p=.51$, $\eta_p^2=0.02$). For the forced-choice task, accuracy on words with weak-strong stress ($M=57.2\%$) was higher than on words with strong-weak stress ($M=48.6\%$). The results of a mixed-effect logistic regression model for strong-weak stress demonstrated a trend towards significance ($OR=0.70$, $p=.06$, 95% CI [0.48, 1.01]).

5.5 Participants preference for disyllabic over monosyllabic words

H4 predicted that participants would be more accurate in detecting disyllabic words than monosyllabic Russian words given that it is easier for them to compute word internal transitional probabilities of disyllabic words. For the word recognition task, accuracy on disyllabic words was $M=0.28$ and on monosyllabic words $M=0.25$, but an ANOVA identified this difference to be not significant ($F(1,25)=0.28$, $p=.60$, $\eta_p^2=0.01$). For the forced-choice task, accuracy on disyllabic words was $M=52.8\%$, and on monosyllabic words $M=51.2\%$, a non-significant difference ($OR=1.07$, $p=.64$, 95% CI [0.79, 1.46]).

5.6 Participants generalization of phonotactic properties

H5 predicted that if participants have assimilated Russian phonotactic properties, they would treat generalizable distractors as possible targets due to the same phonotactic properties as in the input, while they would not think non-generalizable distractors were possible targets. If participants select generalizable stimuli as targets, there would be a lower d' because they would have found it hard to discriminate between input targets and generalizable distractors due to the same phonotactics. If participants do not treat non-generalizable stimuli as targets, there would be a higher d' because they have discriminated between non-generalizable stimuli and targets based on unfamiliar phonotactics.

To test this, we calculated d' scores for generalizable and non-generalizable stimuli by using their rates of false alarms and misses, and adding values of hits and misses from targets.[7] The results (presented in Figure 6) showed that d' on non-generalizable stimuli ($M = 0.63$) was higher than that for generalizable stimuli ($M = 0.19$). An ANOVA analysis identified this difference as significant ($F(1,27) = 83.19$, $p < 0.001$, $\eta_p^2 = 0.75$). This shows that participants were not inclined to treat targets and generalizable words differently, whereas they treated non-generalizable distractors as non-targets.

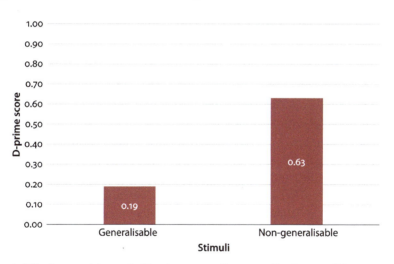

Figure 6. Word recognition task: D-prime scores for generalization condition

---

7. Without hits and misses, it would not be possible to calculate d'.

6. Discussion

6.1 Session

The results of the word recognition task showed a clear improvement in accuracy scores across four sessions. This is consistent with other studies which showed that increasing the amount of input correlates positively with participants' improved accuracy (Rast & Dommergues 2003; Rast 2008, 2010; Gullberg et al. 2010; Gullberg et al. 2012; Carroll 2014). Gullberg et al. (2012) found an effect of segmentation of frequent words in the input (8 vs. 2 input occurrences) after 7 minutes of exposure. We did not investigate the effect of frequency-within-session: each target occurred once during input phases (3:31 and 3:40 minutes) which occurred twice before testing, leading to about 7 minutes of exposure to Russian per session. Instead, we investigated cumulative exposure over four sessions. Our results are consistent with Gullberg et al.'s (2012) for frequency albeit with a different experimental design. By the end of the second session, our participants had accumulated nearly 14 minutes of exposure to Russian and had heard target words 4 times. A significant effect of detecting targets was observed in the second session showing a high level of participant response as well to 4 occurrences in 14 minutes over two days, similar to Gullberg et al.'s (2012) 8 occurrences in 7 minutes. In our study, however, there was a lower ratio of "frequent" to "infrequent" words, i.e., 4 occurrences of targets over 2 sessions rather than 8 occurrences of targets over 2 sessions. Gullberg et al. (2012) found that the accuracy of participants after a one-time seven-minute exposure where there were 8 instances of target words was 55%, which closely corresponds to the d' value on the second day of our study ($d'=0.36$), about 57%.

Our study is unique in having looked at the word detection abilities over four sessions, revealing that participants detected words better from the first to second, from second to third, and from third to fourth sessions. Our participants were about 64% ($d'=0.57$) accurate at spotting target words among distractors by the final day. Recall that Gullberg et al. (2012) had a double exposure group for whom target words occurred 16 times, and at 60% accuracy. We still need to explain why the accuracy in the word recognition task in our study is slightly higher than that in Gullberg et al.'s (2012) despite half the amount of exposure to target words. These results may be the outcome of our within-subject study design where all participants took part in all input and testing sessions over the four days. This meant they had additional exposure to targets while taking the tasks; participants heard one instance of a target in a word recognition task and one more instance in a forced-choice task on each of four days leading to 8 instances of exposure to targets at testing, which were interspersed among distractors. A study by Davis et al.

(2009) showed that new words learnt the night before testing became more solid in participants' memory. Participants had faster reaction times to words learnt the night before testing as opposed to control words which were learnt on the same day. Moreover, Gullberg et al. (2012) utilised a between-subject design, meaning that half of the participants were in the single exposure group and half in the double exposure group, and weak learners may have been allocated by chance to the double exposure group, making the learning rate of that group lower.

Our results also show that the effect of session was more pronounced in the word recognition than in the forced-choice task. For the former, the effect was already present after the first session ($d'=0.20$, which corresponds to about 54%), as well as throughout all subsequent sessions. In contrast, accuracy in the forced-choice task on the first day was 49%, i.e., slightly below chance, and slowly increased, becoming marginally significant at the third and significant at the fourth session. Given these differences, we need to consider what their source is. For both task types, the 4 second time-out was intended to limit participants' ability to consciously focus on aspects of the words' structure. However, the stimuli in the forced-choice task differed minimally, most often by a single consonant in a syllable coda, e.g., [kɫik] versus [klad]. Knowing that only one was the target, participants could have more consciously focused on the varying portion of the word, and compared their phonotactics resulting in a task that drew more on explicit than implicit learning. In comparison, the word recognition task drew on implicit knowledge. The instructions for this task did not draw participants' attention to why some words were less plausible; participants were merely instructed to indicate which words they had heard previously. Differences between the two tasks notwithstanding, we can still conclude that implicit learning has taken place. This is plausible if we consider frameworks which suggest that explicit representations only emerge after implicit learning has taken place, e.g., Karmiloff-Smith's (1995) Representational Redescription approach. Nonetheless, it should also be noted that we might want to place the two tasks at different locations along an implicit-explicit continuum.[8] That said, a wholly implicit task would ideally not make the participant aware that they were being tested on word learning, and that would also mean testing participants only once.

---

8. A reviewer asked what distinguishes "first exposure" studies apart from the studies that involved minimal, incidental exposure to an unfamiliar language where learning occurs without any intent to learn. Hulstijn (2013:1) describes "incidental learning" as acquisition of a word or expression without the conscious intention to commit the element to memory – in such studies participants are informed of neither the learning target nor that they will be tested later in the experiment. First exposure studies, at least ours, are an example of incidental learning, although we admit that after the first session participants knew how they would be tested, but not on what or for what purpose.

6.2 Phonotactics

In light of the above, it is not surprising that our participants relied more on their native English phonotactic constraints than Russian phonotactics when detecting words in the word recognition task. This is consistent with the previous research on the effect of L1 phonotactic cues for speech segmentation in psycholinguistic tasks which measured the on-line performance of highly proficient L2 learners who appeared to be activating their knowledge of L1 phonotactics when listening to an L2 they are proficient in (Altenberg & Cairns 1983; Weber 2000; Weber & Cutler 2006). It is also consistent with the first exposure studies by Rast and Dommergues (2003) and Rast (2008) which showed that learners were more accurate in repeating words in a new language if they contained a segment or a cluster in their L1. The results of the forced-choice task showed that words with Russian-only phonotactics were slightly – but not significantly – preferred over words with English-only phonotactics, and this could have involved some explicit learning. This was not the case in the word recognition task so it could be due to working memory load. That is, in forcing participants to compare two stimuli, the forced-choice task required participants to temporarily represent, maintain and process two-word forms which may have overwhelmed participants. In addition, this process may have been complicated by the need to maintain non-English word forms, which limited participants' ability to recruit L1 phonotactic knowledge. By maintaining non-English word forms, our participants might have adopted a strategy of accepting the words which sounded "least English", thus selecting more targets with non-English phonotactics. Kellerman's (1979) *psychotypology* may shed some additional light on this. Kellerman proposes that language learners can have assumptions about differences and similarities between source and target languages and argues that L2 learners may treat similar constructions in the two languages with scepticism, leading to avoidance of them and attending instead to differences. This process seems to involve some level of conscious analysis of typology on the part of the learner (Rothman 2015). For example, in our study, participants could have noticed that clusters such as *kn-*, *zv-*, *tv-* do not "sound right" in English, so they must belong to the new language. Moreover, they could have noticed that the language which they listened to sounded as if it belonged to the Slavic language group which coincides with the actual typology (Russian is the Slavic language). A study by Skirgård et al. (2017) further illuminates this possibility. They used a large sample of participants from all over the world who listened to audio clips from 78 different languages in the online Great Language Game and had to guess which language it was using a multiple-choice format. There was much confusion in deciding among Slavic languages, yet here another study by Kirk et al. (2013) shows listeners can distinguish between a Germanic and a Slavic language.

6.3 Stress

There was a trend towards significance for forced-choice task for weak-strong stressed words to be better recognised than strong-weak stressed words. There was no such trend for the word recognition task. This means that the hypothesis that strong-weak words would be segmented better than weak-strong words was not supported. In fact, the opposite effect was observed: participants were more accurate on the forced-choice task in detecting words with weak-strong stress, e.g., [klaˈtʃ ok] was preferred over [ˈklʲevʲɪr] and [knʲaˈzʲok] over [ˈknʲigəm]. This is surprising, as it is not consistent with previous perception studies of L1 or L2 learners. For example, studies of babies found a strong role for the MSS (e.g., Cutler & Norris 1988; Cutler 1990; Cutler & Butterfield 1992; Jusczyk, Houston & Newsome 1999; Cutler 1994; Turk et al. 1995). For L2 adults, studies suggest a role for the MSS at least at non-ab initio levels (e.g., Archibald 1992, 1993). Our results instead suggest that during first exposure, participants attend to weak-strong stress. This may stem from the analysis of Russian which is claimed by some researchers to have an iambic foot (Halle & Vergnaud 1987; Melvold 1990; Alderete 1995; Crosswhite 2001; Crosswhite et al. 2003). Again, that such results were observed in the forced-choice task but not the word recognition task could be due to what we have discussed above in relation to this task, and here because weak-strong stress is different from the L1, it attracts attention.

6.4 Length of syllables within a word

Word length was not a factor affecting word detection albeit there was a trend towards significance in disyllabic words being recognised better than monosyllabic words. Not finding a clearer effect is surprising given its importance in relevant studies in all three learner categories: in babies' segmentation (e.g., of English, in Johnson & Jusczyk 2001), in adults' segmentation of artificial languages (e.g., Saffran, Aslin & Newport 1996; Saffran, Newport & Aslin 1996; Aslin et al. 1998), and in natural language first exposure studies. For the latter, Gullberg et al. (2012) found that Dutch speakers recognized Chinese disyllabic words significantly better than monosyllabic words, and Carroll (2014) found higher success rates with longer words (six syllables) than shorter words (four or five syllables). Rast (2010) found participants were better at translating longer words (three to six syllables) than shorter words. However, Rast and Dommergues (2003) and Rast (2008) found no effect of word length (from one up to six syllables) on French learners' ability to repeat Polish words, results which may reflect a task effect. In our study we used online perception tasks, while Rast and Dommergues (2003) and Rast (2008) asked participants to repeat target words after hearing them in sentences and the effect they observed may be due to production constraints. We have some evidence of learners' heightened sensitivity to longer words, echoing what Dommergues and Segui (1989) found in their study that monosyllabic words presented more processing problems than disyllabic words. Finally, it could be that we would have found a word-length effect if we had also included longer words, e.g,. trisyllabic and longer.

6.5 Generalization

One of the few first exposure studies which has investigated generalization abilities in phonology is Gullberg et al. (2010) who found that Dutch participants were able to generalize properties of Mandarin to novel words after seven minutes of exposure. We wanted to know whether our participants would be able to generalize the phonotactics of Russian to words not encountered in the input when the novel words shared phonotactic properties with targets they had heard. The results from our study are similar. The word recognition task showed that d' index of sensitivity to generalizable distractors was significantly lower (participants struggled to discriminate generalizable stimuli from targets) than the index on non-generalizable distractors (participants did not confuse non-generalisable stimuli for targets). Our results also corroborate Linzen and Gallagher's (2017) which showed that adult English speakers after as little as one exposure to a passage in an artificial language rapidly generalized patterns from target words to novel sounds. Our findings, taken together with these, demonstrate that adults can make and apply phonological generalizations from input to novel words after brief exposure to either natural or artificial languages.

7. Conclusion

Babies demonstrate the ability to convert the continuous stream of sound into discrete meaningful units (the words of the language) before they associate them with meanings. Extensive research shows that they respond to various properties of language such as the sound patterns of their own names and allophonic, phonotactic, prosodic, and distributional cues, as well as the interaction of phonotactics and stress. Our study has extended what we know about adults' first exposure to natural languages by looking at a new language pair, English and Russian, and by looking at the cumulative effect of input using two measures of participants sensitivity to phonotactic patterns (i.e., stress and word length cues) while ensuring that participants were actually paying attention to the input by utilising a shared words identification task. A robust finding of our study is that after only around 21 minutes of exposure to aural input in an unfamiliar language, adults generalized phonotactic information from words heard during the input to novel examples with the same licit Russian phonotactics.

The exposure in our study was separated only by days, and our findings point to long-term maintenance of statistical-phonological information after a brief exposure, perhaps not entirely unlike what Carroll (2014) has shown for retention of new words after two weeks without further exposure.

We found that participants recognized isolated target words – without instruction – which they heard embedded in sentences. We also found an influence of participants' L1 phonotactics, similar to what researchers such as Gullberg et al. (2010), Gullberg et al. (2012), Carroll (2012, 2014), and Shoemaker and Rast (2013) have shown. Surprisingly, our metrical stress results do not tally with others, and we suspect this may be due to how implicit vs. more explicit learning influences word detection after first exposure.

One might, however, argue that the segmentation abilities observed in our study, and others cited in first exposure studies, stem from participants' auditory short-term memory capacity which enables them to analyze the speech stream, assimilate possible word forms, and recognize them again after a short delay (Li & Cowan 2014). Our findings suggest that participants do not merely store phonological chunks in memory which are activated on hearing the item. Our generalization results provide evidence against this view in that participants demonstrated systematic and creative linguistic behaviour in going beyond the input they had heard. We argue that our results are due to an ability present at birth, genetically determined, to acquire the phonology of natural languages, an ability which does not diminish across the lifespan. In fact, the finding that adults show sensitivity to the speech stream of a new language after matter of minutes in comparison to babies who require months of exposure, suggests we are underestimating the abilities of adult L2 learners. In addition to the capacity to generalize, there is evidence that new phonological representations are not always constructed according to L1 patterns. For example, English metrical patterns were not applied. This finding potentially indicates the role of linguistic universals which override the characteristics of the L1.

Whether and how this relates to the further acquisition of a new language remains an open question; "above chance performance is very different from successful L2 acquisition", as Gullberg et al. (2012: 259) are careful to point out. Yet documentation of abilities, however modest, represents the earliest steps in acquiring a new language and calls for considerably more research. For instance, in addition to what we have already highlighted with respect to the possible influence of implicit vs. explicit learning processes, it would be interesting to design a longitudinal study with longer successive exposure to a target language by controlling its exposure from the moment of first encounter. By doing this, we would be able to see how the L1 and universals interact.

References

Alderete, J. 1995. Faithfulness to prosodic heads. Unpublished manuscript, University of Massachusetts.

Altenberg, E. P. 2005. The perception of word boundaries. *Second Language Research* 21(4): 325–358.

Altenberg, E. P. & Cairns, H. S. 1983. The effects of phonotactic constraints on lexical processing in bilingual and monolingual subjects. *Journal of Verbal Learning and Verbal Behavior* 22(2): 174–188.

Archibald, J. 1992. Transfer of L1 parameter settings: Some empirical evidence from Polish metrics. *Canadian Journal of Linguistics* 37(3): 301–339.

Archibald, J. 1993. *Language Learnability and L2 Phonology: The Acquisition of Metrical Parameters*. Dordrecht: Kluwer.

Archibald, J. 1994. A formal model of learning L2 prosodic phonology. *Second Language Research* 10(3): 215–240.

Arnon, I. 2019. Statistical learning, implicit learning, and first language acquisition: A critical evaluation of two developmental predictions. *Topics in Cognitive Science* 11(3): 504–519.

Aslin, R. N., Saffran, J. R. & Newport, E. L. 1998. Computation of conditional probability statistics by 8-month-old infants. *Psychological Science* 9(4): 321–324.

Azzopardi, P. & Cowey, A. 1998. Visual pattern and motion detection in a hemianopic subject. *Journal of Cognitive Neuroscience* Suppl. 14.

Baayen, R. H., Davidson, D. J. & Bates, D. M. 2007. Mixed-effects modelling with crossed random effects for subjects and items. *Journal of Memory and Language* 59(4): 390–412.

Bates, D., Maechler, M., Bolker, B. & Walker, S. 2015. *Linear Mixed-Effects Models Using Eigen and S4*. (R Package Version 1.1-8). <http://CRAN.R-project.org/package=lme4>

Broselow, E. & Finer, D. 1991. Parameter setting in second language phonology and syntax. *Second Language Research* 7(1): 35–59.

Carroll, S. E. 1992. On cognates. *Second Language Research* 8(2): 93–119.

Carroll, S. E. 1999. Putting 'input' in its proper place. *Second Language Research* 15(4): 337–388.

Carroll, S. E. 2001. *Input and Evidence: The Raw Material of Second Language*. Amsterdam: John Benjamins.

Carroll, S. E. 2012. First exposure learners make use of top-down lexical knowledge when learning words. In *Multilingual Individuals and Multilingual Societies*, K. Braunmüller, C. Gabriel & B. Hänel-Faulhaber (eds), 23–45. Amsterdam: John Benjamins.

Carroll, S. E. 2013. Introduction to the special issue: Aspects of word learning on first exposure to a second language. *Second Language Research* 29(2): 131–144.

Carroll, S. E. 2014. Processing 'words' in early-stage SLA: A comparison of first exposure and low proficiency learners. In *First Exposure to a Second Language: Learners' Initial Input Processing*, ZH. Han & R. Rast (eds), 107–138. Cambridge: CUP.

Crosswhite, K. 2001. *Vowel Reduction in Optimality Theory*. London: Routledge.

Crosswhite, K., Alderete, J., Beasley, V. & Markman, V. 2003. Morphological effects on default stress placement in novel Russian words. In *Proceedings of the 22nd West Coast Conference on Formal Linguistics*, G. G. Tsujimura (ed.), 151–164. Somerville MA: Cascadilla Press.

Cutler, A. 1990. Exploiting prosodic probabilities in speech segmentation. In *Cognitive Models of Speech Processing: Psycholinguistic and Computational Perspectives*, G. T. Altmann (ed.), 105–121. Cambridge MA: The MIT Press.

Cutler, A. 1994. Segmentation problems, rhythmic solutions. *Lingua* 92: 81–104.

Cutler, A. & Butterfield, S. 1992. Rhythmic cues to speech segmentation: Evidence from juncture misperception. *Journal of Memory and Language* 31(2): 218–236.

Cutler, A. & Carter, D. M. 1987. The predominance of strong initial syllables in the English vocabulary. *Computer Speech & Language* 2(3–4): 133–142.

Cutler, A. & Norris, D. 1988. The role of strong syllables in segmentation for lexical access. *Journal of Experimental Psychology* 14(1): 113–121.

Davis, M. H., Di Betta, A. M., Macdonald, M. J. & Gaskell, M. G. 2009. Learning and consolidation of novel spoken words. *Journal of Cognitive Neuroscience* 21(4): 803–820.

Dommergues, J-Y. & Segui, J. 1989. List structure, monotony, and levels of processing. *Journal of Psycholinguistic Research* 18(3): 245–253.

Ellis, R. 2009. Implicit and explicit learning, knowledge and instruction. In *Implicit and Explicit Knowledge in Second Language Learning, Testing and Teaching*, R. Ellis, S. Loewen, R. Erlam, J. Philp & H. Reinders (eds), 3–26. Bristol: Multilingual Matters.

Friederici, A. D. & Wessels, M. I. 1993. Phonotactic knowledge of word boundaries and its use in infant speech perception. *Perception & Psychophysics* 54(3): 287–295.

Gomez, R. 2002. Variability and detection of invariant structure. *Psychological Science* 13(5): 431–436.

Green, D. S. & Swets, J. A. 1966. *Signal Detection Theory and Psychophysics*, Vol. 1. New York NY: Wiley.

Guion, S. G., Clark, J. J., Harada, T. & Wayland, R. 2003. Factors affecting stress placement for English nonwords include syllabic structure, lexical class, and stress patterns of phonologically similar words. *Language & Speech* 46(4): 403–427.

Gullberg, M. & Indefrey, P. 2003. *Language Background Questionnaire. Developed in The Dynamics of Multilingual Processing*. Nijmegen, Max Planck Institute for Psycholinguistics. <https://www.researchgate.net/publication/343180501_Gullberg_Indefrey_Language_Background_Questionnaire_English_2003/link/5f1a9584299bf1720d5fd848/download> (7 July 2019).

Gullberg, M., Roberts, L. & Dimroth, C. 2012. What word-level knowledge can adult learners acquire after minimal exposure to a new language? *International Review of Applied Linguistics* 50(4): 239–276.

Gullberg, M., Roberts, L., Dimroth, C., Veroude, K. & Indefrey, P. 2010. Adult language learning after minimal exposure to an unknown natural language. *Language Learning* 60(s2): 5–24.

Halle, M. 1959. *The Sound Pattern of Russian: A Linguistic and Acoustical Investigation*. The Hague: Mouton.

Halle, M. & Vergnaud, J. R. 1987. *An Essay on Stress Current Studies in Linguistics*. Cambridge MA: The MIT Press.

Hulstijn, J. H. 2013. Incidental learning in second language acquisition. In *The Encyclopedia of Applied Linguistics*, Vol. 5, C. A. Chapelle (ed.), 2632–2640. Chichester: Wiley-Blackwell.

Jaeger, T. F. 2008. Categorical data analysis: Away from ANOVAs (transformation or not) and towards Logit Mixed Models. *Journal of Memory and Language* 59(4): 434–446.

Johnson, E. K. & Jusczyk, P. W. 2001. Word segmentation by 8-month-olds: When speech cues count more than statistics. *Journal of Memory and Language* 44(4): 548–567.

Jusczyk, P. W. 1997. *The Discovery of Spoken Language*. Cambridge MA: The MIT Press.

Jusczyk, P. W., Friederici, A. D., Wessels, J. I., Svenkerud, V. Y. & Jusczyk, A. M. 1993. Infants' sensitivity to the sound patterns of native language words. *Journal of Memory and Language* 32(3): 402–420.

Jusczyk, P. W., Hohne, E. A. & Bauman, A. 1999. Infants' sensitivity to allophonic cues. *Perception & Psychophysics* 61(8): 1465–1476.

Jusczyk, P. W., Houston, D. M. & Newsome, M. 1999. The beginnings of word segmentation in English-learning infants. *Cognitive Psychology* 39(3–4): 159–207.

Karmiloff-Smith, A. 1995. *Beyond Modularity: A Developmental Perspective on Cognitive Science*. Cambridge MA: The MIT press.

Kellerman, E. 1979. Transfer and non-transfer: Where we are now. *Studies in Second Language Acquisition* 2(1): 37–57.

Kelly, M. H. & Bock, J. K. 1988. Stress in time. *Journal of Experimental Psychology: Human Perception and Performance* 14(3): 389–403.

Kirk, N. W., Scott-Brown, K. C. & Kempe, V. 2013. How well can listeners distinguish dialects and unfamiliar languages? Paper presented at the *54th Annual Meeting of The Psychonomic Society*. Toronto, Canada.

Li, D. & Cowan, N. 2014. Auditory Memory. In *Encyclopaedia of Computational Neuroscience*, D. Jaeger & R. Jung (eds), 236–238. New York NY: Springer.

Lim, R. 2016. First Exposure to Mandarin in Newcastle: Does Ambient Language Input Matter? MA thesis, Newcastle University.

Linzen, T. & Gallagher, G. 2017. Rapid generalization in phonotactic learning. *Journal of the Association for Laboratory Phonology* 8(1): 1–32.

Makowski, D. 2018. *Psycho*. (R Package Version 0.3.4). <https://CRAN.R-project.org/package=psycho>

Mathôt, S., Schreij, D. & Theeuwes, J. 2012. OpenSesame: An open-source, graphical experiment builder for the social sciences. *Behaviour Research Methods* 44(2): 314–324.

Mattys, S. J. & Jusczyk, P. W. 2001. Phonotactic cues for segmentation of fluent speech by infants. *Cognition* 78(2): 91–121.

McQueen, J. M. 1998. Segmentation of continuous speech using phonotactics. *Journal of Memory and Language* 39(1): 21–46.

Melvold, J. L. 1990. Structure and stress in the phonology of Russian. PhD dissertation, MIT.

Mitchell, R., Myles, F. & Marsden, E. 2019. *Second Language Learning Theories*. New York NY: Routledge.

Pienemann, M. 1999. *Language Processing and Second Language Development: Processability Theory*. Amsterdam: John Benjamins.

Pienemann, M. 2007. Processability theory. In *Theories in Second Language Acquisition: An Introduction*, B. VanPatten & J. Williams (eds), 137–154. Mahwah NJ: Lawrence Erlbaum Associates.

R Core Team. 2013. *R: A Language and Environment for Statistical Computing*. R Foundation for Statistical Computing. <http://www.R-project.org/>

Rast, R. 2008. *Foreign Language Input: Initial Processing*. Clevedon: Multilingual Matters.

Rast, R. 2010. The role of linguistic input in the first hours of adult language learning. *Language Learning* 60(2): 64–84.

Rast, R. & Dommergues, J-Y. 2003. Towards a characterisation of saliency on first exposure to a second language. *EUROSLA Yearbook* 3: 131–156.

Rothman, J. 2015. Linguistic and cognitive motivations for the Typological Primacy Model of third language (L3) transfer: Timing of acquisition and proficiency considered. *Bilingualism: Language & Cognition* 18(2): 179–190.

Saffran, J. R., Aslin, R. N. & Newport, E. L. 1996. Statistical learning by 8-month-old infants. *Science* 274(5294): 1926–1928.

Saffran, J. R., Newport, E. L. & Aslin, R. N. 1996. Word segmentation: The role of distributional cues. *Journal of Memory and Language* 35(4): 606–621.

Schwartz, B. D. & Eubank, L. 1996. What is the 'L2 initial state'? *Second Language Research* 12(1): 1–5.

Selkirk, E. 1984. On the major class features and syllable theory. In *Language Sound Structure*, M. Aronoff & R. T. Oehfle (eds), 107–136. Cambridge MA: The MIT Press.

Sereno, J. A. 1986. Stress pattern differentiation of form class in English. *Journal of the Acoustical Society of America* 79: S36.

Shoemaker, E. & Rast, R. 2013. Extracting words from the speech stream at first exposure. *Second Language Research* 29(2): 165–183.

Singmann, H., Bolker, B. & Westfall, J. 2015. *Afex: Analysis of Factorial Experiments*. R Package, Version 0.14–2. <https://CRAN.R-project.org/package=afex>

Skirgård, H., Roberts, S. & Yencken, L. 2017. Why are some languages confused for others? Investigating data from the Great Language Game. *PLoS ONE* 12(4): e0165934.

Stanislaw, H. & Todorov, N. 1999. Calculation of signal detection theory measures. *Behavior Research Methods, Instruments, and Computers* 31(1): 137–149.

Turk, A., Jusczyk, P. W. & Gerken, L. 1995. Do English-learning infants use syllable weight to determine stress? *Language and Speech* 38(2): 143–158.

Vainikka, A. & Young-Scholten, M. 1994. The early stages in adult L2 syntax: Additional evidence from Romance speakers. *Second Language Research* 12(2): 140–176.

Vainikka, A. & Young-Scholten, M. 1998. The initial state in the L2 acquisition of phrase structure. In *The Generative Study of Second Language Acquisition*, S. Flynn, G. Martohardjono & W. O'Neil (eds), 17–34. Mahwah NJ: Lawrence Erlbaum Associates.

Vainikka, A. & Young-Scholten, M. 2011. *The Acquisition of German Introducing Organic Grammar*. Berlin: De Gruyter Mouton.

Weber, A. 2000. The role of phonotactics in the segmentation of native and non-native continuous speech. In *Proceedings of SWAP, Workshop on Spoken Word Access Processes*, A. Cutler, M. McQueen & R. Zondervan (eds), 143–146. Nijmegen: MPI for Psycholinguistics.

Weber, A. & Cutler, A. 2006. First-language phonotactics in second-language listening. *The Journal of the Acoustical Society of America* 119(1): 597–607.

Yang, L. & Givón, T. 1997. Benefits and drawbacks of controlled laboratory studies of second language acquisition: The Keck second language learning project. *Studies in Second Language Acquisition* 19(2): 173–193.

Zaliznjak, A. 1977. *Grammatičeskij Slovar' Russkogo Jazyka (Russian Grammatical Dictionary)*. Moscow: Russkij Jazyk.

Zaliznjak, A. 1985. *Ot Praslavjanskoj Akcentuacii k Russkoj [From Old Russian to Modern Russian Accentuation]*. Moscow: Nauka.

Input and evidence in the acquisition of syntactic structure

CHAPTER 9

Speech modifications and the Processability Theory hierarchy
Some observations on word order in Swedish L1 and L2 input

Gisela Håkansson
Lund University | Linnaeus University

This study explores to what extent there is a difference in input in L1 and L2 Swedish regarding word order. Swedish is a V2 language with only one constituent preceding the tensed verb. This phenomenon is acquired in different ways by L1 and L2 learners. L1 learners produce V2 without errors around the age of two years whereas L2 learners experience long-lasting problems with the postverbal placement of the subject. The reason for this difference is not fully understood. This study set out to investigate the characteristics of the ambient language in the two acquisition conditions. The results reveal a lot of variation but also differences in the input which suggest that 'input simplification' is not always helpful.

Keywords: V2, subject-verb inversion, Swedish, L1 acquisition, L2 acquisition, input, Processability Theory

1. Introduction

In this Festschrift, I thought it fitting to honour Susanne Carroll's inspiring work on input (see Carroll 2001 for example) by returning to a mystery that has been hanging over me for many years. Why are there such differences between first language (L1) and second language (L2) learners in the acquisition of Swedish syntax? Can input shed any light?

Swedish is a Germanic language with simple verbal morphology and less simple nominal morphology. The word order in declarative main clauses is verb-second (V2). This means the verb is always in second position, whereas the subject can either be before or after the verb in declarative main clauses. If the subject is in initial position, the verb has to follow immediately after, SVX. If another element is in initial position, the verb comes directly after and the subject follows the verb, XVS. The choice between SVX, often labelled canonical word order, and XVS order, known as inverted word order, is governed by principles of information structure, and both orders are frequent.

In a sociolinguistic study of adult spoken Swedish in different contexts – informal speech, formal debate, interviews, radio newscasters, and radio commentators – Jörgensen (1976) found the two syntactic possibilities to have an almost equal distribution (approximately 60% SV(X) versus 40% XVS). These proportions were about the same in formal and in informal speech. The only context where a preference higher than 60% for SV(X) declaratives was noted in Jörgensen's (1976) study was in the newscasting on Swedish radio, where about 80% of the sentences had the subject as the first sentence element. Newscasting is characterized by formal and well-planned language, where the information structure is straightforward.

In the acquisition of word order, a striking difference has been found. L1 children produce V2 (both SVX and XVS) as soon as they use multiword utterances. In contrast, L2 learners favour the SVX order, and XVS appears to be so problematic that it is "almost never produced fully target like" (Platzack 2001: 371). Instead, they use the ungrammatical structure XSV.

No explanation has been suggested for this difference. Why do young L1 children get the verb-second constraint right from the beginning and continue to use it, while L2 learners have to struggle for a long time before they learn it? Does it have to do with differences in input to L1 and L2 learners?

2. Simplified registers

In the 1970s, there was an outburst of studies focussing on characteristics of the language that learners were exposed to. The modifications of speech when addressing someone with lower language proficiency were discussed as examples of 'simplified' registers in L1 contexts as well as in L2 contexts (e.g., Corder 1977; Ferguson 1981; Hatch 1983; Meisel 1980; Snow 1972). In the L2 context, two types were identified: Foreigner Talk, and its classroom version Teacher Talk. Teacher Talk refers to the speech used by teachers in second language classrooms, where in the beginning, the language of instruction is only known by the teacher. In this context the aim for the teacher is twofold: to be understood and to serve as a language model for the learners. Teacher Talk properties have been described in several languages e.g., Czech (Henzl 1979), English (Chaudron 1988; Wesche & Ready 1985), French (Wesche & Ready 1985), German (Henzl 1979), Swedish (Håkansson 1987), and, more recently, Spanish (Dracos 2018).

Most studies of speech modification describe a complexity continuum with 'simplified' registers placed at one end of the continuum and 'true' languages with complex features at the other end. The interaction with L1 and L2 learners is characterized by slow speech rate, short utterances, and few subordinate clauses, whereas faster speech rate, longer utterances, and more subordinate clauses are associated with interaction between adult native speakers (Corder 1977; Costa et al. 2008; Hatch 1983; Larsen-Freeman 1985; Meisel 1980; Wesche & Ready 1985).

Few studies go beyond the perspective of general simplification and examine language-specific structures in Teacher Talk. There are individual studies reporting language-specific modifications, for example Henzl (1979) on teachers using fewer verb inflections in Czech when addressing beginner learners, Dracos (2018) on the overuse of Spanish subject personal pronouns to L2 learners, and Håkansson (1987) on underuse of inverted word order to beginning Swedish L2 learners.

2.1 Does 'simplification' help acquisition?

It is an empirical fact that people modify their speech when addressing learners – but does it help acquisition? Is there any evidence that the properties of simplified registers are beneficial to language acquisition? For child-directed speech (CDS), it has been claimed that it is "well designed as a set of language lessons" (Snow 1972:561), and that "if we wanted to design the optimal exposure for language acquisition, it would probably look very much like Baby Talk" (Ferguson 1977:233). In L2 acquisition, an indirect relationship has been suggested; if we can show that adjustments promote comprehension, we can deduce that linguistic adjustments help acquisition (Long 1985:378).

Different views on simplification have been discussed in the literature on language acquisition. A phonetic aspect of CDS is the hyperarticulation of vowels (e.g., Kuhl et al. 1997). This has been assumed to help infants identify the phonemes, and function as a teaching device (Uther 2007). But the opposite has also been claimed, that features in CDS cannot be of help for the child's understanding of adult speech (e.g., Cristia & Seidl 2014; Eaves et al. 2016). Furthermore, Martin et al. (2015) demonstrates that mothers' speech in fact is less clear to infants, and that infants face more variability than in adult speech. Finally, Benders (2013) suggests that the changes in vowel quality have nothing to do with teaching of language, but it is a side effect of showing affection and originates in parents' smiling when addressing infants.

Another proposal is that simplification is not primarily intended as facilitating language acquisition but aligning to the learners' speech diminishes the differences between the interactors, which in turn leads to increased cooperation in communicative situations (Costa et al. 2008; Shatz & Gelman 1977). Studies on interactions with comprehension checks, repetitions, clarification requests etc. (e.g., Long 1985) have demonstrated that it is easier for L2 learners to comprehend a message if the interaction is modified. But other studies have shown that too much interactional modification, for example during book-reading, may be overwhelming and block the child's interest (Chang & Luo 2020). Similarly, too much help with labelling slows down early language development (Silvén et al. 2003). The evidence for the usefulness of modifications is contradictory, to say the least. In some situations, simple structures are easier to comprehend and acquire, but too much simplification can make it harder to process the message. Some learners are helped by getting more than one chance to grasp the message through repetitions and reformulations of structures used in the target language, whereas others get bored.

2.2 Canonical word order against text cohesion

When it comes to word order in simplified registers, canonical word orders dominate in speech addressed to learners (Larsen-Freeman & Long 1991: 119). On the other hand, there is also a tendency for topics to occur in the beginning of the utterance and to be more salient (Wesche 1994: 227). For English, these two preferences can be combined – canonical word order and initial topic. But the teacher of Swedish faces a choice; *either* to use canonical word order, *or* to have a topic in the beginning. Swedish syntax does not allow both canonical word order and initial topic. Topic in initial position demands subject-verb inversion.

The initial place is not only used to make topics salient, but also to connect clauses to each other. Connective devices such as *then* and *later* help interpretation of temporal relationships, and *therefore, because, since,* and *so that* support causal and conditional relations. Coherence in a text is beneficial to reading, particularly when learners have little background knowledge. Experimental studies comparing participants reading texts that are more or less coherent show that readers are better at recalling the content if the text contains cohesive devices (McNamara et al. 1996; Reichenberg 2000). For Swedish, this implies inverted word order (XVS). Example (1a) illustrates a causal relation, and Example (1b) a temporal relation.

(1) a. Därför   hamnade det mycket vatten i Nilen
       Therefore came   it much   water in Nile-DEF
       'Therefore a lot of water came into the Nile'
    b. Då   kunde inte jägare och samlare vara kvar där
       Then could not hunters and gatherers stay   there
       'Then the hunters and gatherers could not stay there'

When young Swedish readers (14 years) were given different versions of texts, with or without cohesive devices, the coherence of the text was found to increase comprehension so that more coherent texts were better understood (Reichenberg 2000).

Thus, it can be questioned whether the use of canonical word order really makes the language easier to understand. For Swedish, it is at the same time a simplification, reducing the variation of word order, and a difficulty, omitting the cohesive devices between sentences (McNamara et al. 1996; Reichenberg 2000).

2.3 Canonical order and developmental stages

Processability Theory (PT) (Pienemann 1998, 2015) predicts five stages of the development of morphosyntax in a second language. These stages have been empirically tested and found to hold for Swedish as a second language. All L2 learners go through the same stages if they learn Swedish, with teaching or with no teaching (Håkansson 1998), in Sweden or in Australia (Håkansson & Norrby 2010). The only difference is the speed of acquisition. The underlying assumption is that L2 learners go through stages where the mechanisms for processing the second language grammar are created incrementally. There is a universal order in which morphosyntactic phenomena emerge in the learner's production. The explanation lies in the architecture of the human language processor, which works as a guide to and a constraint on language learning. Learners can only acquire what they can process, and the processing procedures are acquired in an implicational order. PT relates to Levelt's (1989) model of language production, in particular the part of the model that deals with the grammatical encoding of a message. The learner's route to the target language is interpreted as a development of processing procedures needed to handle grammatical structures. The procedures are automatized and make it possible for the speaker to handle communicative situations in real time: to interpret what others say, and to plan and produce utterances at the same time. For adult native speakers, these procedures operate automatically, but language learners must develop them step-by-step. For main clause word order, three stages are found: canonical SVO (Stage 2), topicalization without subject-verb inversion (Stage 3, ungrammatical), and topicalization with subject-verb inversion (Stage 4). Table 1 gives an idea of the place of subject-verb inversion in relation to the other word orders in the development of Swedish as a second language. The subordinate clause procedure will not be discussed here, but it is placed at Stage 5 to make the table complete.

Simplification is not mentioned in relation to these developmental stages. Rather, learners are gradually complexifying their grammar through the development. SVO is the first word order to emerge (Stage 2), and it can be described

Table 1. Processability hierarchy for Swedish (to be read from bottom-up; Pienemann 1998)

Processing procedures	Outcome: Swedish syntax
Stage 5: Subordinate clause procedure	Subordinate clause word order
Stage 4: S-procedure	Topicalized element + inversion
Stage 3: Phrasal procedure	*Topicalized element + SVO
Stage 2: Category procedure	(canonical) SVO
Stage 1: Lemma access	Chunks, single constituents

as a canonical word order, in contrast to the subject-verb inversion. Subject-verb inversion is acquired rather late, at Stage 4 (out of the five syntactic stages). Between these two stages we find the ungrammatical word order of Stage 3, with a topicalized item and canonical SVO word order. This means that the learners use text cohesion but not subject-verb inversion. Learners stay at this ungrammatical stage for a longer or shorter period, depending on the context of learning. It does not seem to help if learners have the Stage 4 structure (subject-verb inversion) in their first language, but they use topicalized items with canonical word order even if this is ungrammatical in their first language. For example, inversion is reported to be the most difficult structure to learn in L2 Swedish by Swiss German speakers, despite their having the same structure in German (Naumann 1997). Another example of the preference for canonical word order comes from an imitation task, where Swedish L2 learners of German changed the inverted order into noninverted order, by replacing the adverb with a proper name (Sayehli 2013: 103). When asked to repeat a German sentence with an initial adverb (*Morgen* 'tomorrow'), some learners changed the adverb *Morgen* in (2a) into a proper name (Morgan), thus changing the meaning but keeping a grammatical Stage 2 sentence. The original meaning of the sentence was about what Lena was doing tomorrow, but it was changed into the person Morgan meeting Lena's mother. The outcome was a grammatical sentence with canonical word order.

(2) a. ORIGINAL: Morgen   kann Lena Mama treffen
              Tomorrow may   Lena mother se
              'Tomorrow Lena may meet Mother'
    b. IMITATION: Morgan kannst treffe Lena's Mama
              'Morgan can meet Lena's Mother'

Other suggestions by these learners were the names Magnus (for *Morgen* 'tomorrow') and Dan (for *Dann* 'then'). This behaviour, changing the initial adverb into a person's name, suggests that the learner is more comfortable with PT Stage 2 with canonical word order, than Stage 3 with a preposed adverb or Stage 4 with subject-verb inversion, even when they have the same Stage 4 order in their first language.

Furthermore, some clinical populations are known to have problems with inversion. Topicalization without inversion is one of the diagnostic features of monolingual Swedish children with language impairment (Håkansson 2017; Håkansson & Nettelbladt 1993, 1996). Agrammatic Swedish patients with Broca's aphasia sometimes have the same problem with inversion (Månsson & Ahlsén 2001). On the surface, their production of word order looks identical to that of L2 learners (Armon-Lotem et al. 2015; Paradis 2010).

The PT predictions are based on the cognitive capacities of the individual learner, and the relationship between input and output is still very unclear. When it comes to children with language disorders and agrammatic patients, it is unlikely that their problems have to do with input. It is possible that they are more like the processing problems of L2 learners (Håkansson & Nettelbladt 1996; Platzack 2001).

3. The acquisition of Swedish grammar

3.1 L1 acquisition

Research on the acquisition of Swedish as a first language has a long tradition, from the diary study of Bolin and Bolin (1916) to the corpora collected by projects at Stockholm University (Lange & Larsson 1977), Gothenburg University (Plunkett & Strömqvist 1992), and Lund University (Håkansson & Nettelbladt 1993, 1996). Most work has been descriptive. Analyses have concerned various phenomena, such as semantic roles, morphology, negation, and relative clauses. Very few studies have analysed the acquisition of the V2 word order in main clauses, possibly since this is an early acquisition with no known problems. The first project focusing on main clause word order was the Lund project (Håkansson & Nettelbladt 1993, 1996) where production of word order in L1 children, L2 children, and children with language impairment was compared. The results revealed a difference between an early and unproblematic development of V2 word order in L1 children on the one hand, and the problems with V2 in L2 children and children with developmental language disorder on the other hand. The early acquisition of word order in L1 children has been confirmed by other studies (e.g., Josefsson 2003; Platzack 2001; Santelmann 2003). Example (3) illustrates word order variation in a conversation between Markus, 23 months, and his father.

(3) Markus 23 months (CHILDES database)

   a. Father: Va   har Totte där?
                 What has Totte there?
                 'What has Totte got there?'

   b. Markus: Hammaren   *har han*
                  Hammer-DEF has he
                  'He has the hammer'

   c. Father: Jaha, han ska bygga nånting
                 yes, he will build something
                 'Yes, he is going to build something'

   d. Father: och när han ska bygga så *tar*   han på sej sina blåa byxer
                 and when he will build so takes he   his blue pants
                 'and when he is building he puts on his blue pants'

   e. Markus: Snickebyxer
                  carpenter pants
                  'carpenter pants'

   f. Father: Ja, de e snickebyxer
                 Yes, it is carpenter pants
                 'yes, it is carpenter pants'

   g. Father: Plankan *har han* lagt   på en pall
                 the plank has he placed on a stool
                 'He has placed the plank on a stool'

In the conversation between Markus and his father, there is a variation between canonical and inverted word order. Of the 5 declarative main clauses in this extract (i.e., (3b, c, d, f, g)) three have inverted word order (i.e., (3b): *hammer has he*; (3d): *so takes he*; (3g): *the plank has he*) and two have the SV order (i.e., (3c): *he will*; (3f): *it is*). This indicates that inverted order is not something that is avoided in early conversations between adult and child. It is interesting that topicalization of the object seems to emerge before topicalization of adverb. One reason may be that children do not talk about time before the age of two. Markus has a couple of examples when he is 22 months where he uses the adverb *där* 'there' in initial position (*där gubben* 'there the man'), but it is difficult to hear if he uses the copula *är* 'is' or if he says *där gubben*.

To conclude, the grammatical development of L1 Swedish shows no relationship to the PT developmental stages. After the one-word and two-word utterance stages, the children develop Stages 2 (SVO) and 4 (XVS) simultaneously, around the age of two years. They rarely produce topicalized sentences without inversion – this sentence type is characteristic of children with language impairment.

3.2 L2 acquisition

Research in Swedish as a second language started in the 1970s (e.g., Hammarberg & Viberg 1977; Hyltenstam 1977). It was soon observed that word order was the most difficult to learn, irrespective of mother tongues. Hammarberg & Viberg (1977) studied 18 learners with ten different languages, from five different language families: (i) Indo European: English, Greek, Persian, Polish, Spanish; (ii) Finno-Ugrian: Finnish, Hungarian; (iii) Semitic: Arabic; (iv) Turkish; and (v) Japanese. Hyltenstam (1977) analysed data from 160 learners, with 35 different languages. The acquisition of V2 was the most striking problem. Many studies focussed on the gradual acquisition of word order, and tried to establish developmental stages (e.g., Bolander 1988; Colliander 1993; Håkansson & Nettelbladt 1993, 1996; Hyltenstam 1977). In stark contrast to the error-free acquisition in L1 children, subject-verb inversion turned out to be the major stumbling block for L2 learners. In Pienemann & Håkansson (1999), results from 14 research projects on L2 Swedish (both morphology and syntax) were grouped together and analysed through the PT framework. Apart from some gaps in the data, the development of L2 Swedish could be explained within PT. Later studies have collected data from the different PT stages and evidence for all stages have been found (e.g., Eklund Heinonen 2009; Glahn et al. 2001; Schönström 2014).

Summarizing L1 and L2 acquisition, studies have shown that L1 children use the target subject-verb inversion in topicalized clauses as soon as they produce multiword utterances (Josefsson 2003; Plunkett & Strömqvist 1992; Platzack 2001; Santelmann 2003) whereas L2 learners follow the predictions of PT and use the ungrammatical subject-verb order in topicalized clauses (Hammarberg & Viberg 1977; Håkansson & Nettelbladt 1993; Hyltenstam 1977; Pienemann & Håkansson 1999; Schönström 2014).

3.3 Input

Slow speech rate, short utterances, and few subordinate clauses have been suggested to be typical to the interaction with L1 and L2 learners, whereas faster speech rate, longer utterances, and more subordinate clauses are associated with interaction between adult proficient speakers (Corder 1977; Hatch 1983; Larsen-Freeman 1985; Meisel 1980; Wesche 1994; Uther et al. 2007). This view on simplified registers has given rise to the impression that modified input to infants and adults is similar (e.g., Corder 1977; Uther et al. 2007).

What about word order? Earlier studies of the word order of input to L1 children demonstrate stable V2 patterns in the adult speech. There is a variation between different positions of the subject and the verb and both SVX and XVS are common (Josefsson 2003; Waldmann 2008). In the only longitudinal study on Swedish Teacher Talk in the classroom, there was a striking lack of subject-verb inversion in the beginning, and a clear change from canonical word order to more and more inversion (Håkansson 1987: 35). This phenomenon had not been observed before and motivated a closer examination of L2 input along with a comparison to what L1 learners are exposed to.

4. Present study: Teacher Talk narrative to L1 and L2 listeners

The focus of this study is about the extent to which input to Swedish L1 speakers and L2 learners may vary in terms of SVX and XVS word order. In order to answer this question, two research questions have been formulated:

RQ1: To what extent does word order vary between narratives directed to L1 speakers and L2 learners?

RQ2: Can the teacher's modifications be related to the learners' developmental stage of Processability Theory?

Based on earlier research of word order in input (Håkansson 1987; Larsen-Freeman & Long 1991: 119), it can be expected that teachers prefer canonical word order in speech to L2 learners. But there is also the opposite expectation, that teachers would use more inversion. The tendency for topics to occur early in speech to foreigners (Wesche 1994: 227), together with the positive effect of connective devices (McNamara et al. 1996; Reichenberg 2000), suggest that there would be more inverted clauses addressed to less proficient listeners, i.e., L2 learners. To explore whether speakers vary the use of inversion to different listeners in a systematic way, a study was set up to compare how the same person retells a narrative to L1 speakers and L2 learners.

4.1 Participants and data collection

Nine teachers of Swedish as an L2 participated in the study. They were teaching adult immigrants in intensive courses of Swedish at various educational institutions. The criteria for inclusion in the study were: (i) The teachers were experienced L2 Swedish teachers (mean length of experience 14 years); and (ii) The learners had a multitude of different L1s, so Swedish was the only language the teacher could use for communication in the classroom. The learners were at an intermediate level of Swedish with between 250 and 500 hours of Swedish lessons before the data collection took place. The teachers were familiar with the learners, having taught them 5–6 hours per day for a couple of months.

The instruction for the teachers was to read a written text, memorize it, and then put the paper away. They first told the story to their own group of learners and then to an adult L1 speaker of Swedish. The task was arranged as a listening task, and the learners were given questions to answer on the content.

For the text to be reasonably interesting to adults, both to the L2 learners and to L1 speakers, a story from the Nordic Folklore was chosen. The text was a legend about how a giant helped in building Lund Cathedral for the monk Saint Lawrence. The giant and the monk made a deal that the giant would build the cathedral, and the monk had to find out the name of the giant before the cathedral was finished. Otherwise, the monk had to give up his eyes to the giant. This kind of myths around building of churches are common in Scandinavia.

5. Results

The teachers' two versions of narratives were audio-recorded and transcribed. The proportions of canonical and inverted word orders in declarative sentences were calculated. The analyses revealed a small, but consistent difference between the version to the L1 speaker and the version to the L2 learners. The proportion of inverted word order in the original written text was 50%. That was almost the same proportion as the teachers used to the L1 speakers, 49% (range 39%–58%). The proportion of inversion was lower in the versions to the L2 learners, 41%, (range 31%–50%). Despite large individual variation, it is striking that all nine teachers used fewer sentences with inversion in speech directed to L2 learners than in the same story told to L1 speakers. Three of them had higher proportion to L1 listeners than in the original version of the text.

Table 2 displays some of the examples, where the same teacher is modifying their speech to L2 learners:

Table 2. Examples from the narrative to L1 speakers and to L2 learners

To L1 speakers	Modifications to L2 learners

1a. Och så dök det upp en jätte
    and so came it up a giant
    'and a giant appeared'
	1b. Och en hemsk jätte visade sig
	    and a terrible giant appeared
	    'and a terrible giant appeared'

Table 2. *(continued)*

To L1 speakers	Modifications to L2 learners
2a. *Innan kyrkan var färdig så måste* before the church was finished so had *han veta* he to know 'Before the church was finished, he had to know'	2b. *Han måste komma på jättens namn* he had to find out the giant's name 'He had to find out the giant's name'
3a. *Nerifrån marken kom det* from under the ground came it 'It came from under the ground'	3b. *Det kom nerifrån* it came from under 'It came from under'
4a. *Rasande rusade han ner i kryptan* enraged ran he down in the crypt 'Enraged he ran down the crypt'	4b. *Och han rusade ner, in i kryptan* and he ran down, into the crypt 'And he ran down, into the crypt'
5a. *Så blev han mindre och mindre* so became he smaller and smaller 'Then he became smaller and smaller'	5b. *Han blev mindre och mindre* he became smaller and smaller 'He became smaller and smaller'

Table 2 depicts two versions of the same sentence, one with inverted word order (the a-versions) and one with SV word order (the b-versions). Importantly, they are both grammatically correct. The difference is that the a-versions have connective devices which trigger obligatory subject-verb inversion to fulfil the V2 rule. The connective devices are connecting adverbs (*så* 'so', *då* 'then'), a subordinate clause (*innan kyrkan var färdig* 'before the church was finished'), a prepositional phrase (*nerifrån marken* 'from the ground'), and a present participle (*rasande* 'enraged'). These devices are combining elements and signal the cohesion with the foregoing context. In the b-versions, there are no such relationships between the sentences; each sentence stands alone.

Let us look at some examples in (4) and (5) from the teacher A.K. who used 58% XVS to L1 speakers and 43% to L2 speakers, omitting temporal and causal connectors.

(4) a. Lars ropade: Finn! Då   blev   jätten   arg
       Lars called: Finn! then became giant-DEF angry
       'Lars called out: Finn! Then the giant became angry'
    b. Lars ropade: Finn! Jätten   blev   arg
       Lars called: Finn giant-DEF became angry
       'Lars called out: Finn! The giant became angry'

Example (4a) is addressed to an L1 speaker, and the adverb *då* 'then' makes a temporal and causal connection between the sentences, emphasizing that the giant became angry when Lars called his name. In Example (4b), there is not such an explicit connection.

The next example contains a causal adverb in the version to the L1 speaker in (5a), but not to the L2 learner in (5b).

(5) a. och därför kände han sig bedrövad när han gick
       and therefore, felt he sad when   he went
       'Therefore, he felt sad when he went'

    b. munken   han var helt   bedrövad
       monk-DEF he was totally sad
       'the monk was totally sad'

In Example (5b), there is no explanation as to why the monk was sad, but the learners had to figure it out themselves. Importantly, both versions are grammatically correct. The only difference is that the (5a) has a connective device which triggers obligatory subject-verb inversion, whereas the (5b) does not signal cohesion explicitly and has no inversion.

We do not know the impact of these modifications. Did the subject-verb word order make it easier for the learners to grasp the story? Or did the lack of cohesive element instead contribute to making it more difficult? The answers to the comprehension questions varied a lot, both within and between the nine groups. The analysis of the relationship between learners' answers and teachers' modifications gave no indication about whether the word order was important or not. Instead, features such as slow speech or fast speech with many repetitions seemed to facilitate the comprehension. The proportions of SVX and XVS not only represent word order, but also textual cohesion. In monologues of the telegram reading type on radio, a SVX dominance is expected since the telegrams are not connected but read one-by-one (Jörgensen 1976), whereas narrative texts are characterised by cohesion and sentences are connected by temporal and causal links. In Swedish, these links most often are placed in the sentence-initial position and therefore they result in subject-verb inversion. When the explicit causal and temporal links are not there and the relations are only implicit, the story is harder to understand (Reichenberg 2000), which means that the Teacher Talk strategy of not using inversion goes against making the message clearer.

Is there any connection to Processability Theory? Adverbs in first position and subject-verb inversion are characteristic of PT Stage 4, so the teachers' under-use of inversion could be interpreted as an avoidance of this PT stage.

6. Relation to PT

When addressing the L2 learners, the teachers omitted many cohesive devices. They used more of PT Stage 2 SVO sentences to L2 learners than to L1 speakers. Were they aligning to the learners' PT Stage of development, to decrease the difference and reach cooperation (Costa et al. 2008; Shatz & Gelman 1977)? When looking at the data from the learners, this does not seem plausible. Not a single example from the teachers can be related to PT Stage 3, which was what most learners used in their answers. Some examples are given in (6):

(6) a. Efter   han   måste   lämna   sina   ögon
       After   he   must   give   his   eyes
       'Then he must give his eyes'
       Correct: Sedan *måste han* lämna sina ögon
                  'Then *must he* give his eyes'

   b. När   han   står   i   en   backen   han   hör   att   någon   sjunga
      when   he   stands in   a   hill-DEF he   hear   that   someone sing
      'when he is standing on the hill he hears someone singing'
      Correct: När han står i en backe *hör han* någon sjunga
                 'When he is standing on a hill *hears he* somone sing'

   c. Då   Lars   förstod   att   det   var   jättefru
      Then   Lars   understood   that   it   was   giant wife
      'Then Lars understood that it was the giant's wife'
      Correct: Då *förstod Lars* att de var jättens fru
                 'Then *understood Lars* that it was the giant's wife'

The use of canonical word order by the teacher and the avoidance of cohesive devices do not stop the learners from using topicalization together with canonical order, i.e., the ungrammatical XSV word order.

7. Discussion

Important differences have been found in L1 and L2 acquisition of Swedish and some of these differences are reflected in the input. Even though both CDS and Teacher Talk use shorter utterances there is a difference in the use of the language-specific subject-verb inversion. The same difference turns up when we compare teachers addressing L2 learners and addressing adult L1 speakers. Regarding the first research question about word order in narratives addressed to L1 speakers and to L2 learners, the results revealed a small but steady difference. All the nine teachers used more inversion to L1 speakers than to L2 learners. The narrative about the giant Finn is stripped of many cohesive devices in the learner versions, which may make the text difficult to follow (McNamara et al. 1996; Reichenberg 2000). Underuse of cohesive elements makes a narrative monotonous and repetitive.

The difference is clear, but it is less clear why this happens. Assuming that the intent is to teach properties of the language (cf. Eaves et al. 2016: 3), it seems odd that the teachers use less subject-verb inversion with learners than with L1 speakers when retelling the same story. They do not exploit the possibility of using the inverted word order, which is exactly the structure the learners need to hear. One can speculate on whether the modified input provided by the teachers in the present study is in fact facilitating language acquisition or if it is, on the contrary, interfering with it. How can the teacher support the learner by not giving full access to the language-specific structures in the target language? If learners form their hypotheses about the target language based on the language they encounter, it is important to give the accurate variation in the input.

It is possible this is only relevant to the Swedish situation. The possibility of avoiding language-specific word order patterns and still using a grammatically correct structure may be one example. Maybe the teacher is not concerned with the teaching of these structures at all, but only striving to promote as much comprehension as possible in a communicatively difficult situation, having to address listeners in a language of which they do not have full understanding.

With respect to the second research question about the relationship between teacher modifications and the learners' developmental stage of Processability Theory, the answer is negative. Judging from the responses on the comprehension questions, most learners have at least some examples from Stage 3, illustrating topicalization without inversion. This clause type is never used by the teachers, who are always using grammatical sentences, either from Stage 2 (SVO) or from Stage 4 (Inversion). This means that the learners use word order patterns that are never provided in the input. The teachers avoid cohesive devices, but the learners use them, and get the word order wrong.

8. Conclusion

This study has generated more questions than answers, and it is uncertain whether it has shed any light of the role of input in the acquisition of Swedish subject-verb inversion. There is a difference between L1 and L2 acquisition of word order, and a difference between the word order in the input, and this study sshows that there is also a difference in the same teacher's use of word order in addressing adult L1 speakers and L2 learners. But is the difference in input related to the differences in outcome? L2 learners use ungrammatical clauses that are never found in the input. Do they hear too few examples of V2? Do they need a critical mass? If so, then the teachers are using the wrong strategy, depriving the learners of what they most need, and at the same time not creating the positive cooperative mood of alignment by reducing the differences. Future research is required to investigate this issue.

References

Armon-Lotem, S., de Jong, J. & Meir, N. (eds). 2015. *Assessing Multilingual Children. Disentangling Bilingualism from Language Impairment*. Bristol: Multilingual Matters.

Benders, T. 2013. Mommy is only happy! Dutch mothers' realisation of speech sounds in infant-directed speech expresses emotion, not didactic intent. *Infant Behavior and Development* 36(4): 847–862.

Bolander, M. 1988. Is there any order? On word order in Swedish learner language. *Journal of Multilingual and Multicultural Development* 9(1–2): 97–113.

Bolin, I. & Bolin, M. 1916. De två första årens språkutveckling hos en svensk flicka [The two first years' language development in a Swedish girl]. *Svenskt Arkiv för Pedagogik* 4:159–223.

Carroll, S. E. 2001. *Input and Evidence. The Raw Material of Second Language Acquisition*. Amsterdam: John Benjamins.

Chang, C.-J. & Luo, Y.-H. 2020. A longitudinal study of maternal interaction strategies during joint book-reading in Taiwan. *Journal of Child Language* 47(2): 401–417.

Chaudron, C. 1988. *Second Language Classrooms*. Cambridge: CUP.

Colliander, G. 1993. Profiling second language development of Swedish: A method for assessing L2 proficiency. In *Problem, Process, Product in Language Learning*, B. Hammarberg (ed.), 32–47. Stockholm: Stockholm University, Department of Linguistics

Corder, S. P. 1977. 'Simple codes' and the source of the second language learners' initial heuristic hypothesis. *Studies in Second Language Acquisition* 1: 1–10.

Costa, A., Pickering, M. J. & Sorace, A. 2008. Alignment in second language dialogue. *Language and Cognitive Processes* 23(4): 528–556.

Cristia, A. & Seidl, A. 2014. The hyperarticulation hypothesis of infant-directed speech. *Journal of Child Language* 41(4): 913–934.

Dracos, M. 2018. Teacher talk and Spanish subject personal pronouns. *Journal of Spanish Language Teaching* 5(1): 1–15.

Eaves Jr., B. S., Feldman, N. H., Griffiths, T. L. & Shafto, P. 2016. Infant-directed speech is consistent with teaching. *Psychological Review* 123(6): 758–771.

Eklund Heinonen, M. 2009. Processbarhet på prov. Bedömning av muntlig språkfärdighet hos vuxna andraspråksinlärare [Processability in Tests. Assessment of Oral Language Proficiency in Adult Second Language Learners]. PhD dissertation, Uppsala University.

Ferguson, C. 1977. Baby talk as a simplified register. In *Talking to Children: Language Input and Acquisition*, C. Snow & C.A. Ferguson (eds), 209–235. Cambridge: CUP.

Ferguson, C. 1981. 'Foreigner talk' as the name of a simplified register. *International Journal of the Sociology of Language* 1981(28): 9–18.

Glahn, E., Håkansson, G., Hammarberg, B., Holmen, A. & Hvenekilde, A. 2001. Processability in Scandinavian second language acquisition. *Studies in Second Language Acquisition* 23(3): 389–416.

Håkansson, G. 1987. Teacher Talk: How Teachers Modify Their Speech When Addressing Learners of Swedish as a Second Language. PhD dissertation. Lund: Lund University Press.

Håkansson, G. 1998. Modern times in L2 Swedish. Syntax and morphology in formal and informal acquisition of Swedish. In *Views on the Acquisition and Use of a Second Language. EuroSLA 7 Proceedings*, L. Diaz & C. Perez (eds), 39–50. Barcelona: Universitat Pompeu Fabra.

Håkansson, G. 2017. Typological and developmental considerations on Specific Language Impairment in monolingual and bilingual children: A Processability Theory account. *Language Acquisition* 24(3): 265–280.

Håkansson, G. & Nettelbladt, U. 1993. Developmental sequences in L1 (normal and impaired) and L2 acquisition of Swedish. *International Journal of Applied Linguistics* 3(2): 131–157.

Håkansson, G. & Nettelbladt, U. 1996. Similarities between SLI and L2 children. Evidence from the acquisition of Swedish word order. In *Children's Language*, Vol. 9, C. Johnson & J. Gilbert (eds), 135–151. Mahwah NJ: Lawrence Erlbaum Associates.

Håkansson, G. & Norrby, C. 2010. Environmental influence on language acquisition: Comparing second and foreign language acquisition of Swedish. *Language Learning* 60(3): 628–650.

Hammarberg, B. & Viberg, Å. 1977. The place-holder constraint, language typology, and the teaching of Swedish to immigrants. *Studia Linguistica* 31(2), 106–163.

Hatch, E. 1983. Simplified input and second language acquisition. In *Pidginization and Creolization as Language Acquisition*, R.W. Andersen (ed.), 64–86. Rowley MA: Newbury House.

Henzl, V. 1979. Foreign talk in the classroom. *IRAL* 17(2): 159–167.

Hyltenstam, K. 1977. Implicational patterns in interlanguage syntax variation. *Language Learning* 27(2): 383–411.

Jörgensen, N. 1976. *Meningsbyggnaden i talad svenska*. [*Sentence Structure in Spoken Swedish*]. Lund: Studentlitteratur.

Josefsson, G. 2003. Input and output: Sentence patterns in child and adult Swedish. In *The Acquisition of Swedish Grammar*, G. Josefsson, C. Platzack & G. Håkansson (eds), 95–133. Amsterdam: John Benjamins.

Kuhl, P.K., Andruski, J.E., Chistovich, I.A., Chistovich, L.A., Kozhevnikova, E.V., Ryskina, V.L., Stolyarova, E.I., Sundberg, U. & Lacerda, F. 1997. Cross-language analysis of phonetic units in language addressed to infants. *Science* 277(5326): 684–686.

Lange, S. & Larsson, K. 1977. Studier i det tidiga barnspråkets grammatik [Studies in Early Child Grammar]. PhD dissertation, Stockholm University.

Larsen-Freeman, D. 1985. State of the art on input in second language acquisition. In *Input in Second Language Acquisition*, S. Gass & C. Madden (eds), 433–444. Rowley MA: Newbury House.

Larsen-Freeman, D. & Long, M. H. 1991. *An Introduction to Second Language Acquisition Research*. London: Longman.

Levelt, W. J. M. 1989. *Speaking: From Intention to Articulation*. Cambridge MA: The MIT Press.

Long, M. H. 1985. Input and second language acquisition theory. In *Input in Second Language Acquisition*, S. Gass, & C. Madden (eds), 377–393. Rowley MA: Newbury House.

Månsson, A-C. & Ahlsén, E. 2001. Grammatical features of aphasia in Swedish. *Journal of Neurolinguistics* 14(2–4): 365–380.

Martin, A., Schatz, T., Versteegh, M., Miyazawa, K., Mazuka, R., & Dupoux, E. 2015. Mothers speak less clearly to infants than to adults: A comprehensive test of the hyperarticulation hypothesis. *Psychological Science* 26(3): 341–347.

McNamara, D. S., Kintsch, E., Butler Songer, N. & Kintsch, W. 1996. Are good texts always better? Interactions of text coherence, background knowledge, and levels of understanding in learning from text. *Cognition and Instruction* 14(1): 1–43.

Meisel, J. M. 1980. Linguistic simplification. In *Second Language Development: Trends and Issues*, S. W. Felix (ed.), 13–40. Tubingen: Gunter Narr.

Naumann, K. 1997. Svenska som främmande språk i Schweiz [Swedish as a foreign language in Switzerland]. In *Svenskans beskrivning* 22, G. Håkansson, L. Lötmarker, L. Santesson, J. Svensson & Å. Viberg (eds), 318–334. Lund: Lund University Press.

Paradis, J. 2010. The interface between bilingual development and specific language impairment. *Applied Psycholinguistics* 31(2): 227–252.

Pienemann, M. 1998. *Language Processing and Language Development: Processability Theory*. Amsterdam: John Benjamins.

Pienemann, M. 2015. An outline of Processability Theory and its relationship to other approaches to SLA. *Language Learning* 65(1): 123–151.

Pienemann, M. & Håkansson, G. 1999. A unified approach towards the development of Swedish as L2: A processability account. *Studies in Second Language Acquisition* 21(3): 383–420.

Platzack, C. 2001. The vulnerable C-domain. *Brain and Language* 77(3): 364–377.

Plunkett, K. & Strömqvist, S. 1992. The acquisition of Scandinavian languages. In *The Crosslinguistic Study of Language Acquisition*, Vol. 3, D. Slobin (ed.), 457–556. Mahwah NJ: Lawrence Erlbaum Associates.

Reichenberg, M. 2000. Röst och kausalitet i lärobokstexter. En studie av elevers förståelse av olika textversioner [Voice and Causality in Textbooks. A Study of Students' Comprehension of Different Versions of Swedish Texts]. PhD dissertation, Göteborg University.

Santelmann, L. 2003. The acquisition of Swedish wh-questions. In *The Acquisition of Swedish Grammar*, G. Josefsson, C. Platzack & G. Håkansson (eds), 261–305. Amsterdam: John Benjamins.

Sayehli, S. 2013. Developmental Perspectives on Transfer in Third Language Acquisition. PhD dissertation, Lund University.

Schönström, K. 2014. Visual acquisition of Swedish in deaf children. *Linguistic Approaches to Bilingualism* 4(1): 61–88.

Shatz, M. & Gelman, R. 1977. Beyond syntax: The influence of conversational constraints on speech modifications. In *Talking to Children: Language Input and Acquisition*, C. Snow & C.A. Ferguson (eds), 189–198. Cambridge: CUP.

Silvén, M., Ahtola, A. & Niemi, P. 2003. Early words, multiword utterances, and maternal reading strategies as predictors of mastering word inflections in Finnish. *Journal of Child Language* 30(2): 253–279.

Snow, C. 1972. Mothers' speech to children learning language. *Child Development* 43(2): 549–565.

Uther, M., Knoll, M.A. & Burnham, D. 2007. Do you speak E-NG-L-I-SH? A comparison of foreigner- and infant-directed speech. *Speech Communication* 49(1): 2–7.

Waldmann, C. 2008. Input och output. Ordföljd i svenska barns huvudsatser och bisatser [Input and Output. Word Order in Swedish Children's Main and Subordinate Clauses]. PhD dissertation, Lund University.

Wesche, M.B. 1994. Input and interaction in second language acquisition. In *Input and Interaction in Language Acquisition*, C. Gallaway & B.J. Richards (eds), 219–249. Cambridge: CUP.

Wesche, M.B. & Ready, D. 1985. Foreigner talk in the university classroom. In *Input in Second Language Acquisition*, S. Gass & C. Madden (eds), 89–114. Rowley MA: Newbury House.

CHAPTER 10

Varieties of DP recursion

Syntax, semantics, and acquisition

Ana T. Pérez-Leroux[1], Yves Roberge[1], Diane Massam[1],
Susana Bejar[1] & Anny Castilla-Earls[2]
[1] University of Toronto [2] University of Houston

> Our objective is to shed light on recursion through an exploration of the L1 development of four DP structures in English. Since recursion is in narrow syntax, there is no reason to expect asymmetries between constructions but specific formal differences between structures might make acquisition of certain forms more difficult, and there may be differences according to meaning classes. We report a study targeting possessives, comitatives, locatives, and part-whole expressions, each with 2-level embedding. The results reveal statistically significant effects of age and condition, with no interaction. Possessives and comitatives develop earlier than locatives and relatives, and are also more productive for adults. These results help us to delineate the domain of recursion and formulate a credible developmental scenario.

Keywords: acquisition, syntax, recursion, English

1. Introduction

The main theme of this paper is how children acquire syntactically complex aspects of grammar, specifically, recursive NP modification. Complexity is a topic that has received a lot of attention in linguistic research from theoretical linguistics but has not been carefully scrutinized in language acquisition studies. Complexity can be approached from widely differing angles. For instance, on the psycholinguistic side, we can study the computational demands of various representational alternatives in cases of ambiguity (Roeper et al. 2020). Or one can ask, more controversially, whether some languages are grammatically more complex than others (Newmeyer & Preston 2014). Here we look at complexity from the dual perspective of L1 acquisition and syntactic representations.

1.1 Background and context

Let us start from the most basic, uncontroversial observation. Children start out with structurally simple linguistic expressions and, with time, their internal grammar becomes gradually more elaborate before reaching the relative steady state that constitutes their adult grammar. Studying the development of grammatical competence in children, for us, boils down to tackling the "representational problem, [...] the problem of how the learner comes to have a representational system of a particular type, one capable of encoding certain constructs" (Carroll 2001: 236). As for the grammar itself, we focus on the "simplest computational operation [...] binary set formation" (Chomsky 2020: 9), called Merge in the Minimalist framework. More specifically, we concentrate on one of the natural consequences of binary set formation; namely, that it can apply to two entities of the same nature, resulting in what is called a recursive structure. Since there is a single operation Merge, we are left with something of a paradox: there is no *a priori* reason to assume that some instances or subcases of Merge are more complex than others, yet it is iterative applications of Merge that make a construction cumulatively more elaborate, and therefore potentially more complex, than a simpler one.[1]

Here we ask two general research questions, both concerning the children's development of recursive DPs, that is DPs that contain a modifier that likewise contains a DP that contains a modifier, also containing a DP. The first question is about structures; more specifically: Are all forms of recursive modification equally comparable? Are structurally *atypical* forms of recursion (i.e., Saxon genitive *'s*, which is both left-branching, and dependent on case marking) more difficult than those that follow the primary parameters of the language? The second question is about differences between children and adults. If not all forms of recursive modification are equal, are they comparable in children and adults in terms of relative difficulty of different types of structure?

Before attempting to provide answers to these questions (Section 5) on the basis of the results of the study we present in Sections 3 and 4, we devote the rest of this section to provide more precise definitions for the key terms we use and,

---

1. Some conceptions of Merge assume derivational differences. For instance, Chomsky (2020) states that: "one subcase of Merge might be simpler than another in the way it functions.... EM [external merge] and IM [internal merge]. To apply EM, we must search all of WS [the work space]: the Lexicon (which is huge) and all objects previously constructed (a set that can grow without limit as constructions become more complex). To apply IM, we search only a single object, a vastly simpler process." However, the EM vs. IM contrast is not pertinent to the cases we discuss here. Similarly, Chomsky (2004) and others have differentiated between set Merge (introducing complements and specifiers) and pair Merge (introducing adjuncts). Again, this is not a contrast we manipulate in our investigation, so we set it aside.

in Section 2, we describe in detail the various DP structures that serve as the basis for our experiment.

1.2 Merge and recursion

To consider the question of whether some structural configurations are more complex than others, let us examine the basic operation that creates structures. The binary set formation operation Merge creates a new object {X, Y} from two already existing objects (X and Y), such as lexical items or previously created syntactic objects. Stated differently:

(1) Merge: X, Y → Z where Z = {X, Y}

Recursive outputs are naturally created by repeated applications of Merge but, of course, not all repeated applications of Merge result in recursive structures. Some variation exists in the literature regarding the definition of recursion, so it is important to state specifically how we use the term in the rest of this chapter. Our focus is on what children need to learn, namely, which phrases can recur, given that some forms of embedding are not recursive in some languages. Roeper and Snyder (2005) cite the case of possessive *-s* in German; another case of a non-recursive rule at the word level is noun-noun compounding in Romance. Thus, we adopt the definition below from Widmer et al. (2017: 801).

> Syntactic recursion, as we understand it here, is present whenever a grammar can freely embed a phrase XP inside the same phrase XP, and – unlike recursion in the general mathematical sense – also assigns a structure of embedding with categories and relations that are repeated at each level to the resulting expression: an XP_n is recursively embedded into an XP_{n+1} iff the distributional properties of XP_n and the relationship between XP_n and XP_{n+1} are the same for all n, and there is no grammatical restriction on the value of n.

In other words, a recursive structure is composed of an XP embedded in an XP, involving at least 3 XPs of the same type (e.g., an XP that modifies an XP that itself modifies a head X), and a single semantic relation between X and the XPs.[2]

---

2. In the context of this paper, we refer to the types of semantic relations connecting the head Noun and the modifiers as *notional relations* to reflect the fact that each relation expresses a connection of a specific nature while remaining general in its exact definition. The relations express the notions of *possession, location, accompaniment,* and part-whole relations as expressed by so-called relational nouns (*box of x, king of x,* etc.). We use the term *marker* to refer to the different ways the notional relations can be expressed: prepositions, linkers, genitives, etc. In Di Sciullo's (2015) terminology, our cases all involve indirect recursion which she defines as the recursive merger of X mediated by a functional category F.

The requirement for there to be no restriction on the value of *n* means that if a language limits modification to 1-level for specific markers then the 1-level structure generated is not the result of recursion.[3] This is illustrated in (2) and (3), with intended constituency represented with brackets:

(2) [The man [with the baby [with the toy car]]]

(3) [The man [with the baby [in the stroller]]]

In (2), a recursive DP, there is level-1 and level-2 modification and the same marker *with* (expressing a comitative relation); we refer to these as self-same recursive DPs. The DP in (3) is similar to the one in (2) but two different notional relations are involved, expressed by two different markers (comitative *with* and locative *in*).

Note that recursive structures can be linearly identical to non-recursive structures. Most multiply modified DPs are ambiguous because there are two attachment points for the modifiers beyond level-1: another level-1 attachment or a level-2 attachment. The DP in (2) always refers to the man that has the baby but (minus the bracketing) is ambiguous as to who has the toy car, the man or the baby. Obviously, given a richer (pragmatic) context, the ambiguity is not problematic. Syntactically, the two readings are based on two different structures, so compare (2) – recursive modification – to (4) – sequential modification – a non-recursive structure:

(4) [The man [with the baby] [with the toy car]]

Returning to the complexity issue in L1 development, we consider more elaborate DPs such as (2), (3), or (4) to be more complex than less elaborate ones such as (5).

(5) [The man [with the baby]]

What we aim to determine is whether complexity is an issue in development and one of the ways to determine this is to try to find out if more complex DPs are more difficult for children (and indeed for adults as well). In fact, previous research has shown that recursive structures are difficult for children in a variety of languages and constructions. In child English for instance, recursive possessive

---

3. Widmer et al. (2017: 800) provide an example from Russian where expansion beyond level-1 of adjectivized nouns (to express possession) is disallowed:

i. (*Ivan-ov-a/Ivan-a)   mam-in-a   kniga
    (*Ivan(M)-adjz-SG.F/Ivan(M)-GEN.SG mother(F)-adjz-SG.F book(F)
    '(Ivan's) mother's book'

(such as *Bobby's friend's toy car*) and PP (as above) structures are rare in production, and difficult to understand (Limbach & Adone 2010; Roeper 2011); more on this in 2.2. But what is the nature of the difficulty? As we have noted, such structures are the result of multiple applications of Merge, a basic operation.

One way to elucidate the nature of the difficulty created by the complexity of these structures is to compare different recursive structures. In Bejar et al. (2020:16) we raise the possibility that "because recursive iterations of Merge can result in different varieties of recursively embedded output structures, some structural elaborations [may] turn out to be more complex than others." Here we explore this possibility in some detail in an experimental study involving four types of recursively modified DPs, presented in Section 3.

2. Recursive DPs in English and their acquisition

The structures at the center of this paper entail the modification of a head Noun by another Noun, the function of which is to restrict the denotation of the Noun to a specific referent. We first look at the structures involved and what we know so far about their development in L1 acquisition.

2.1 On modification

To illustrate modification and its function, let's say you need to tell someone about a phone. You can of course simply say *the phone*, but you may also need to facilitate communication by saying, more specifically, *the phone on the table* or *the phone with a red case* or *Alex's phone* or *Alex's friend's phone* and so on and so forth. As we have seen, progressively more elaborate DPs expressing various notional relations can be created by the application of a Merge.

Although we limit our investigation to Nouns modifying Nouns, the notional relation connecting them can be expressed through a variety of syntactic means. This is important as while we may want to target modification of N by PP in our study, it is very possible that our participants might have recourse to other types of markers. *The phone on the table* is also *the phone that is on the table*; in both cases, *the phone* and *the table* are linked by the same notional relation.[4] In our contexts, we can limit this variety to three main constructions: PP (6), Saxon genitive (7), and Relative Clause (RC) (8).

---

4. Relative clauses clearly represent an alternative arguably more complex way to express the relations. Although we did not target them in our study, they do appear in the responses provided by our participants.

(6) PP modifier construction[5]

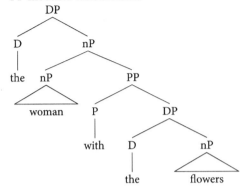

(7) Saxon genitive[6]

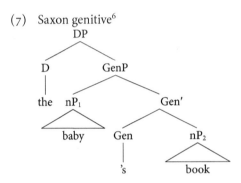

---

5. There are two widely adopted structures for NP-PP recursion, namely modificational selection (Cinque 1999) and adjunction (e.g., Ernst 2002). They both involve the same patterns of recursion so we present the more traditional representation of adjunction.

6. Because of the nature of our research questions, we focus on the Saxon genitive as an expression of the notional relation of possession but there are other means to express it in English: *the car's safety record* or *the safety record of the car*.

(8) Relative Clause

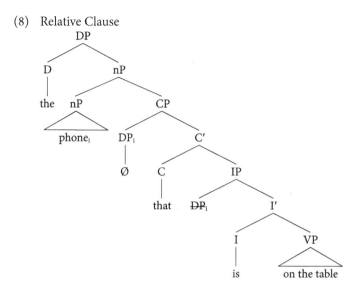

The three constructions above can be iterated to create the recursive structures that we are likely to encounter in our results; however, we can safely assume that very young children do not immediately produce such complex DPs, even though all that is needed to do so is Merge and lexical knowledge of the markers required to express the intended notional relation. What can the learning challenge be? First, the fact that these are cases of modification, not complementation, immediately suggests that semantic bootstrapping cannot be invoked as a facilitator. Complementation involves an s-selection relation between the head and the complement, which serves as the basis for the syntactic bootstrapping hypothesis (Gleitman 1990), the idea that the learning of, for instance, specific verb meaning is facilitated by the selectional contexts in which the verbs appear. The construction of a VP through applications of Merge thus includes information available in the input that can in turn participate in the learning of how to construct VPs, or as Gillette et al. (1999: 171) put it:

> The findings bolster the considerable accumulating evidence that lexical and syntactic knowledge in the child, far from developing as separate components of an acquisition procedure, interact with each other and with the observed world in a complex, mutually supportive, series of bootstrapping operations whose outcome is a lexicalized grammar.

As an example, a transitive verb must appear with a complement in order to satisfy its semantic properties. But the modification relations expressed in the four DPs above do not involve s-selection: the nouns *man* and *baby* have no selectional properties that can be satisfied by the PPs with which they appear in our examples. A possessive or locative modification serves to restrict the denotation of the head Noun it modifies and for this reason it makes sense to assume that much of the learning that needs to take place concerns the various components that make up those relations. It follows that some differences can potentially exist in their development in young children's grammars.

Finally, on the structural side, the DPs expressing the four notional relations we target are formed identically – two instances of self-embedding mediated by a marker – so it is highly unlikely that, if differences are found in our results, they could be attributed to syntactic reasons. Nonetheless, Saxon genitives involve left-branching recursion, for which some initial production evidence in Pérez-Leroux et al. (2012) indicates the possibility of delay (relative to PP recursion). In addition, given current analyses of Saxon genitive nominals, it can be shown that level-2 embedding for these structures (in contrast to level-1) involves immediate same label recursion in the left branch (i.e., a genitive DP is embedded in the specifier of a genitive DP). Such same label recursion has been seen as dispreferred, if not disallowed (e.g., van Riemsdijk 2011). It would thus not be surprising to observe differences in our results between POSS and the other three conditions, which would mean that something extra must be learned by children for the Saxon genitive. If, however, POSS develops similarly to the other structures, then we can assume that the syntax of recursion is robust in child grammar and that potential complexity issues must be attributed to other factors.

2.2 Acquisition of NP recursion in English

In the first few years of life, children use primarily simple, unmodified nouns. Experimental work shows children avoid modification and produce underinformative descriptions (Davies & Katsos 2010; Nadig & Sedivy 2002; among others). According to Nadig and Sedivy (2002: 33) children understand the contextual requirements of modification, but at times fail to incorporate "common-ground information (or any potentially constraining information) ... because of its complexity."

Recursive structures, containing iterative embedding as defined above, appear in use only after substantial development. They seem virtually absent in spontaneous or narrative language samples. Eisenberg et al.'s (2008) study of NP elaboration in typically-developing English children reports only double use of adjectives but not of PP modifiers. In their data, simple PP or RC modification is only used in narratives by about 60% of children in their sample. Roeper and Snyder (2005) was the first study to directly investigate recursive structures in child language. These authors report that young children do not use recursive possessive genitives and seem to have substantial difficulties comprehending them. A wealth of subsequent experimental work confirms difficulties in a range of languages (Roeper 2011; Amaral et al. 2018).

(9) Mother: What is Daddy's Daddy's name?
    Sarah: Uh.

(Roeper 2011: 68)

The referential demands associated with recursive modification are unlikely to arise frequently in natural language use. Pérez-Leroux et al. (2012) designed an elicitation task to compare how often children succeeded at combining three nouns into an NP unit, depending on whether they involved recursively embedded structures (comitative PPs and possessive DPs) versus coordination. The children in their study, aged 3 to 5, were at ceiling in the production of prosodically integrated three-NP coordinates. In contrast, about half of them were unable to produce recursive targets. One third of them produced utterances with 1-level embedding; whereas only the remaining 17% of the children produced target-like double embedding (Pérez-Leroux et al. 2012). Given this asymmetry in their data, Pérez-Leroux and colleagues concluded that embedding is more demanding than coordination, which suggests that it is not narrow syntax that is at issue. Their results also uncovered a second asymmetry. The 15 children who produced at most phrases with one level of embedding were evenly divided between those who could produce only genitives, only PPs or both types of embedding. In contrast, they found an asymmetry for children who produced recursive embedding: 7 out of 8 children used only PPs; the eighth child (a 3-year-old) used only genitives.[7] On the basis of these results, they argued that the data supports the view that recursive embedding may involve a separate learning step beyond that of learning a single level of embedding, as Roeper and Snyder (2005) had initially suggested in their discussion of cross-linguistic variation in the forms of recursion. They also suggest the possibility that possessive -*s* recursion may be harder for children to learn than PP recursion.

A recent study by Giblin et al. (2018) implemented the elicitation of recursive possessives by means of a truth value judgement task supplemented by elicitation: children were prompted with a false level one modification prompt (*Big Bird's blanket got dirty*), which children enthusiastically rejected and often supplied a second level modification structure (*no, Big Bird's cat's blanket got dirty*). Their participants included a single 3-year-old, 17 children in the 4-year-old group, and

---

7. "Simple cases of the genitive and PP construction are acquired concurrently, but a developmental asymmetry arises for level-2 embedding. The evidence suggests genitive recursion is considerably harder than PP recursion. By the age tested, several children have mastered second-level PP recursion but not second-level genitive." Pérez-Leroux et al. (2012: 310).

8 children in the 5-year-old group. The youngest child produced a single recursive NP, while the majority of the children managed to produce recursive responses. Nonetheless, a full 20% of the children failed to do so. The increased opportunity to produce recursive possessives (4 tokens instead of 3) and the changes in method, which included both direct priming of the structure in the prompt question, in addition to pragmatically compelling motivation for elaborating a complex NP (rejecting a previously incorrect utterance), had a clear impact on baseline performance; possessive recursion seems to be not as constrained as in the initial results. Nonetheless, the question remains unresolved as to the apparent asymmetries between genitives and comitatives. For that purpose, we need to compare the emergence of the structures in children at the moment in which they start to use recursive modification productively.

3. English recursion study

With this background in place, we can now turn to the study itself. We ask two main questions: (1) Is recursive modification comparable in children and adults, in terms of relative difficulty of types of modification? and, (2) Are structurally 'atypical' forms of recursion (i.e., Saxon genitive) more difficult than those that follow the primary parameters of the language? In other words, we are trying to determine whether difficulties (if any) with recursive structures are structural or not, and if they are not, then what could be their source.

3.1 Participants

Child participants ($n=71$) were typically developing children recruited from preschools and daycares in Upstate New York (Fredonia) and the Greater Toronto area. There were 25 four-year-olds ($M=4;06$); 25 five-year-olds ($M=5;04$), and 21 six-year-olds ($M=6;05$). Adult controls were 13 adults from the same communities.

3.2 Task

Recursive DPs were elicited by means of a referential prompt (*which x...?*). A picture and story context established multiple contrasting referents: for example, one item had dogs next to trees and next to houses, and trees next to and far from houses (see Table 1 row 3). The goal of such a complex set up was that the optimal answer to the prompt question (i.e., *which dog is barking?*) would relate the three classes of elements, dogs, trees, and house: *the dog next to the tree next to the house*. The trials belonged to one of four conditions, defined accord-

Chapter 10. Varieties of DP recursion   255

ing to the type of notional relations linking the nouns and their modifiers: 6 trials each for comitatives (*with*), locatives (*in/on/next to*), and relational nouns (*of*). The relational condition could elicit right-branching (PP) or left-branching structures, whereas possessives were expected to be uniformly left-branching. To improve the balance between the number of left branching and right branching forms, we included 7 possessive -*s* trials. In order to mitigate boredom, the test included 18 additional question trials of various other types (pronouns, multiple wh-questions, adjectives), for a total of 43 trials. The trials were organized in two random orders, and individual children were randomly assigned to one of the two orders of presentation.

Table 1. Examples of the four conditions in the recursive elicitation task

Possessives

What flew away?
The clown's monkey's balloon.

Comitatives

Which girl has the large ice cream?
The girl with the dog with a hat.

Locatives

Which dog is barking?
The dog next to the tree next to the house.

Table 1. *(continued)*

Relational nouns	
On which box is the mouse sitting? On the box of cans of tomatoes.	

Children additionally received two standardized language tests (CELF, PPVT-IV), a standard non-word repetition task (Dollaghan & Campbell 1998), and the Non-Verbal Scale of the Kauffman Assessment Battery for Children Second Edition (KABC-II; Kaufman & Kaufman 2004). These measures showed that the children were in the typical range for these standard developmental tests. We also used those measures to verify whether the acquisition of recursive structure was linked to general vocabulary, knowledge of grammar, and cognitive development. For children, the elicitation task lasted between 20–25 minutes, but the entire test battery took between 1.5 to 2 hours.

4. Results

All data were transcribed and coded for referential accuracy, syntactic form, including levels of embedding (from single noun to two levels of modifier embedding), and grammatical mechanism employed for phrasal embedding (possessive -*s*, PP, or relative clause). To be classified as a recursive target, responses had to contain the target noun (i.e., *the dog*) followed by the two target modifiers (*next to the tree* and *next to the house*) in a nested configuration. That is, we did not count as target recursive responses other referentially appropriate entries (such as *the dog in the middle*) or phrases that contained the target elements but not in a doubly embedded configuration (such as *the dog is next to the tree, and the tree is next to the house*) (for further details on methodology and coding system, see Pérez-Leroux et al. 2018a, 2018b).

To address the first question, we first consider overall frequencies of target responses per age groups and conditions. Overall relative degree of difficulty of varieties of nominal recursion across groups would be evidence that structural or semantic differences between conditions represent a specific learning challenge. Figure 1, representing the average frequency of targets per group per condition, reveals three core observations.

First, we note that children are not as successful as adults, and second, that within the children, 4- and 5-year-olds perform similarly and are not as successful as 6-year-olds. Third, we note that the possessive and comitative DPs are not fun-

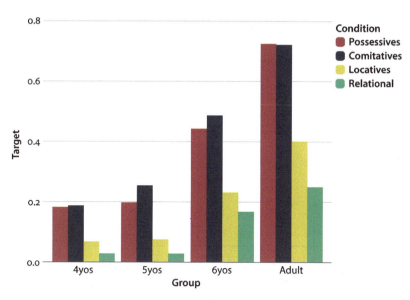

Figure 1. Mean individual proportion of target responses per condition per group

damentally different from each other, but clearly easier than the locative and relational DPs, for all groups. The data was entered into a generalized linear mixed effect (logit) model fit by the maximum likelihood method (Adaptive Gauss-Hermite Quadrature, nAGQ = 0), using the binomial distribution. Fixed effects were age group, and syntactic condition and participants were entered as random effects. Adding the interaction between group and condition did not contribute to the model. In fact, it decreased the fit of the model to the data (AIC = 1850.2, relative to the model without the interaction, which obtained AIC = 1836.7). The details of the best model (no interaction) are presented in Table 2.

The question of the relative difficulty of the various types of recursive modification is thus clearly answered. There are differences between the four notionally-defined types of modification, but these differences are comparable across age groups.

We next explore how measures of memory, vocabulary, and general language relate to individual children's ability to produce recursion. Table 3 summarizes the most promising predictors among all measures.

All the language measures were highly intercorrelated. To avoid collinearity, we followed an incremental variable selection process in building a series of linear models with individual proportion of target responses as the dependent variable, and the external measures as additive predictors. The best model ($F(2,68) = 41.77$, $p < .001$, adjusted $R^2 = 0.538$) showed small but highly significant contributions of both age (Est = 0.007, $t = 4.1$, $p < .001$), and the word structure subtest of the CELF

Table 2. Generalized linear mixed effect models with response (target/non-target) as a binary dependent variable, with condition and age group as fixed effects and participants as random effects. Formula: Target ~ Agegroup + condition + (1 | participant)

Fixed effects*	Estimate	SE	z	p
(Intercept)	−1.560	0.232	−6.71	< .001 ***
Agegroup5yos	0.219	0.304	0.721	0.471
Agegroup6yos	1.571	0.303	5.182	< .001 ***
AgegroupAdult	2.558	0.343	7.445	< .001 ***
ConditionLocatives	−1.370	0.172	−7.954	< .001 ***
ConditionPossessives	−0.160	0.145	−1.100	0.271
ConditionRelationals	−2.055	0.1973	−10.416	< .001 ***

* 2092 observations, 84 participants, AIC = 1836.7

Table 3. Correlation between external measures and individual proportion of target recursive responses (method = Pearson)

Construct	Measure	Correlation to recursion targets
General language	CELF_WS	0.662
Age	Age in Months	0.650
Receptive vocabulary	PPVT	0.635
General language	CELF_SS	0.602
Memory for sentences	CELF_Sent	0.582
Expressive vocabulary	CELF_EV	0.418
Memory	KABC_Hand	0.385

(Est = 0.021, t = 4.4, p < .001). As Figure 2 shows, after five years and 4 months, all children produce some form of recursion or another, and we see a rapid growth in productivity, for all conditions. However, the measures of general development including vocabulary, memory for patterns, and sentence repetition, do not account for much of this growth.

Last, we turn to the structural question. These results so far indirectly address the question of whether type of structure (atypical s vs. PPs) determines acquisition, since children seem to make no notable contrast between possessives and comitatives. However, the analysis of overall targets does not distinguish by structural type of response. For this, we need to focus on the structural analysis of the data. For target responses, our coding system isolated the grammatical markers used to connect the modifiers. Some target responses were structurally consistent,

Chapter 10. Varieties of DP recursion **259**

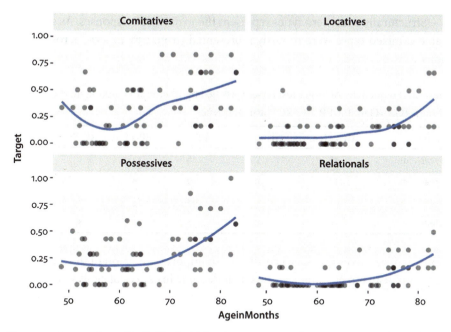

Figure 2. Scatterplots of individual children's proportion of target responses for each condition. The locally fitted smooth lines are used to represent overall age changes per condition

using the same marker for both levels (i.e., self-same embedding in the sense of Widmer et al. 2017). Examples of these consistent types are provided in (10):

(10) Genitive: Elmo's sister's basketball. (EN001, 4;00)[8]
    PP: The girl with the dog with the hat. (EN301, 6;00)
    RC: The one that the mom is holding that has the flowers in her hand.
     (EN031, 5;02)

Other target responses, instead, were produced by a combination of two different markers as in (11), which nests a possessive within a relative clause.[9]

(11) The one that Elmo's sister is holding (EN015 5;08)

---

8. There were four examples with the genitive configuration but missing 's, which we counted among this category:
    i. Elmo sister ball (EN047 5;11.5)
    ii. The clown's monkey... balloon (EN309 6;02.0)
    iii. Uh, the clown monkey balloon. (EN025 5;10.8)
    iv. The fireman little kid kite (EN011 4;03.3)
9. As pointed by a reviewer, this was also observed in Merx (2016) and may thus be a significant acquisition phenomenon.

Structurally consistent types represent the majority of responses. As shown in Table 4, mixed types were robustly represented (from 25% to 42%, across conditions).

Table 4. Frequencies of target responses classified by whether the linking markers were of same (Gen-Gen, PP-PP, RC-RC) or mixed types

Group	Gen-Gen	Gen-other	PP-RC	PP-PP	RC-RC	Total
4-year-olds	27	3	16	22	5	73
5-year-olds	29	7	19	28	5	88
6-year-olds	61	7	68	34	6	176
Adults	59	9	37	58	8	171

Consistent genitives (gen-gen) constitute an important portion of the data, about one third of all targets. These counts include some instances of genitives that were produced in response to the relational condition. When we consider each condition separately, we see that the genitive condition mostly elicited true-to-type target responses, i.e., the responses where level-1 and level-2 embedding reflect the same relationship and grammatical link, or self-same embedding, as in Widmer et al.'s definition (i.e., *s-s* for possessives, and P-P for the other conditions). For adults, all target responses to the possessive condition were gen-gen. For children, these made up about 85% of all target (95 out of 112 tokens). In comparison, same preposition responses were less robustly represented. Here we consider only COM (which targeted the preposition *with*) and REL (which targeted *of*). For adults, half of all COM targets (39 out of 78) were linked by two instances of *with*. For children, it was a bit less (41%, or 20 out of 49). In the relational noun condition, participants gave lower rates of targets among all conditions. This is in part because speakers used a more diverse set of connectors, including genitives, other prepositions, and compounding, which was not included among embedding strategies because the linked categories were not DPs, and our project was designed to explore phrasal recursion. For adults, 4 out of 10 of all target responses were *of-of*, and for children, 2 out of 7 targets. This means that when we consider how often the strict lexical type is produced relative to all target responses (by our definition), the genitive structure is actually more consistent than either comitative *with* or relational *of*.

Nonetheless, to answer our second question, the issue is not how often a given self-same type is used relative to another, but how many children succeed (or not) at showing mastery of one recursive type vs. the other. To answer that question, individual analyses are in order.

With our methodology and across all conditions, 17 out of the 71 child participants failed to produce any form of recursive modification, of any structural types. Five additional children produced several doubly-modified structures but these were not recursive iterations of the same type. We cross-tabulated the remaining individual participants according to what structural types they were able to produce, and presented this in the form of a Venn-Euler diagram, with intersections including children who produced more than one type. As shown in Figure 3, most of these 54 children were using multiple recursive configurations (36 of them had both target possessives and PPs). Only 10 children had only a single iterative type: 1 had only RCs, 2 only PPs and 7 only genitives.

Here we see that the asymmetry seems to run in the other direction, with iterative possessives in the advantage.

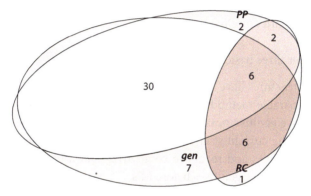

Figure 3. Venn-Euler diagram of children who produce one or another form of recursive configuration

Clearly, the genitive delay observed in the 2012 pilot study is not replicated using the same methodology, once the number of trials increases. For a clearer comparison to the 2012 data, we limit our comparison to the same age groups (4- and 5-year-olds), and conditions (possessive and comitatives). Table 5 presents this direct comparison between studies.

The individual analysis of the current data finds no developmental delay with the recursive genitive construction: At the relevant ages, and given sufficient opportunities to produce these complex structures, the majority of children in the current study fall within the Both or None category.

Table 5. Individual analysis comparison of results for 4- and 5-year-olds' production of recursive genitive and recursive possessive targets

		None	Gen	Com	Both
Pérez-Leroux et al. (2012)	4-year-olds ($n=16$)	15	0	1	0
	5-year-olds ($n=14$)	8	0	6	0
Current study	4-year-olds ($n=25$)	10	5	1	9
	5-year-olds ($n=25$)	7	8	3	7

5. Discussion and conclusion

Our results offer three basic observations:

1. Different structures have similar developmental timelines. With more stimuli and a comparable method, the asymmetry between recursive comitative PPs and recursive genitive possessors observed in Pérez-Leroux et al. (2012) disappears. In the current study, we observe that most children are using both recursive genitives and recursive comitatives, but a handful of children are able to use recursive genitives before PPs.
2. Similar structures can yield differences in performance. Adults and children produced targets at different rates across conditions that are expressed by structurally comparable options (such as comitative PPs and locative PPs).
3. There is no interaction between adult and child rates of target responses across conditions. This indicates that specific conditions do not add to the learning challenge. In the present study, adult responses of recursive DPs are not at ceiling, but children's target responses are a fraction of these. The gap closes a bit for the older children. Nonetheless, no specific semantic type or structural type seems to be developing later or at different rates, as far as our data can show.

These observations generally undermine the possibility of a structural account of children's difficulties with recursion. On one hand, speakers, both children and adults, are not disadvantaged by the structurally distinct possessive -s, which contrary to the preliminary work in Pérez-Leroux et al. (2012), is now on a par with recursive comitative PPs, both on the overall rates of success, as well as on an individual basis. This answers our second question. On the other hand, there are differences between the conditions, which suggest speakers are more likely to rely on recursive possessives and comitatives to describe objects in complex scenarios, rather than in terms of their location, or part-whole relationships. In answer to our first question then, there are differences between constructions, but these differences are not structural. Interestingly, the results here match those of other languages, as shown by a review of results in other languages, related to the present study (Pérez-Leroux & Roberge 2018).

These observations suggest that a purely structural explanation for the challenge presented by the development of recursion is not available. We might therefore turn to the domain of processing or interpretive complexity, for an account. What, then, is "difficult" about recursion, for children?

To learn a recursive configuration the child must first acquire the simple relation and its associated marker (e.g., comitative *with*). The child would then have to figure out which forms allow self-same iteration in the target language (i.e., *the girl with a dog with a hat*). Not all forms of embedding allow iteration. Pérez-Leroux et al. (2020), in a study on the L1 acquisition of German possessive recursive DPs, show that while German possessive *-s* is very common, children are not tempted to overgeneralize it to recursive configurations. Li et al. (2020) suggest that productivity, defined in the sense of which types of nouns enter into the possessive relation, is a necessary condition for generalization to the recursive level.

In other words, level-1 input must provide sufficient evidence that Saxon genitive *'s*, for instance, is the most general tool to express the concept of possession (in English, but not in German). The Saxon genitive can then be used recursively (extended to level-2). On this view, productivity of level-1 embedding (or its statistical signature) is a trigger for acquisition of recursion of that configuration. This view is compatible with work that integrates grammar building and statistical learning (Yang 2016).[10] We know that human babies are powerful statistical learners and that they transform the output of statistical learning into symbolic representations (Marcus et al. 1999).

---

10. A reviewer pointed out that another option would be to incorporate into the labeling algorithm the information that certain nodes are recursive. Roeper (2011: 80) states that "in effect it would be a method whereby recursive nodes could look different from non-recursive ones which in turn would fit the claim we make that the acquisition path for recursion involves a critical step beyond recognition of the basic syntactic category." Yet another option, articulated in Boeckx (2014), turns this scenario on its head, positing a "densely recursive" syntax that is filtered by legibility at the interface (2014: 90). For Boeckx the syntax itself is feature-free and the only accessible properties of lexical items are their edge features, which license Merge. All other properties of lexical items (e.g., syntactic category) are emergent from labeling and interpretive procedures at the interfaces. On this view, the acquisition path for recursion would require a stage where certain structures are unlabelable/illegible at the interfaces and then a critical step that makes them labelable/legible.

Beyond such realization, the most obvious challenge for children pertains to real-time deployment of target structures, of serializing the hierarchical structure into proper chunks that can express the given relations. Some previous findings associate emergence of recursion with working memory, as in Arslan et al. (2017), who found this at the clausal level, and Pérez-Leroux et al. (2018b) who found this for PPs. In the present data, sentence repetition, a measure of verbal memory, had a strong positive correlation with ability to produce recursive targets, as did other standardized measures of development. However, our data does not offer proof that a participant's ability for sentence repetition adds to their ability to produce recursive structures, beyond what is accounted for by age and general language ability. Thus, our present results are compatible with but not indicative of a role for changes in processing capacity in children in the emergence of the ability to produce DP recursion.

In sum, our findings support the view that the grammar required to produce recursive structures is part of narrow syntax, but that the development of recursion is constrained by experience and productivity and that its use is dependent on third factor considerations (processing) or, as Carroll (2005: 80) puts it: "even seemingly "simple" grammatical phenomena may embody complex structural knowledge and be instantiated by a plethora of diverse cues."

Funding

The research reported here benefited from funding by the Social Sciences and Humanities Research Council of Canada (grant 435-2014-2000 on the development of DP complexity in children to Pérez-Leroux and Roberge)

Acknowledgements

This paper greatly benefited from the comments of two anonymous reviewers and of the editors. We thank our collaborators on this project: J. Brunner, T. Roeper and P. Schulz; and our research assistants: E. Pettibone, G. Klassen, E. Hall, K. Bamba, O. Marasco, J. Jaffan, N. Docteur, M. Elliot, M. Sanjeevan, A. Cournane, B. Wan, A. Yoh. R. Rusnyak, S. Harrington, A. McCandless, N. Da Silva, K. Antonsen, and R. Kermani.

References

Amaral, L., Maia, M., Nevins, A. & Roeper, T. (eds). 2018. *Recursion in Brazilian Languages and Beyond*. Cambridge: CUP.

Arslan, B., Hohenberger, A. & Verbugge, R. 2017. Syntactic recursion facilitates and working memory predicts recursive theory of mind. *PLOS ONE* 12(1): e0169510.

Bejar, S., Massam, D., Pérez-Leroux, A. T. & Roberge, Y. 2020. Rethinking complexity. In *Syntactic Architecture and its Consequences, I: Syntax Inside the Grammar*, A. Bárány, T. Biberauer, J. Douglas & S. Vikner (eds), 15–24. Berlin: Language Science Press.

Boeckx, C. 2014. *Elementary Syntactic Structures: Prospects of a Feature-Free Syntax.* Cambridge: CUP.

Carroll, S. E. 2001. *Input and Evidence: The Raw Material of Second Language Acquisition.* Amsterdam: John Benjamins.

Carroll, S. E. 2005. Input and SLA: Adults' sensitivity to different sorts of cues to French gender. *Language Learning* 55(S1): 79–138.

Chomsky, N. 2004. Beyond explanatory adequacy. *Structures and Beyond: The Cartography of Syntactic Structures*, Vol. 3, Adriana Belletti (ed.), 104–131. Oxford: OUP.

Chomsky, N. 2020. Fundamental operations of language: Reflections on optimal design. *Cadernos de Linguística* 1(1): 1–13.

Cinque, G. 1999. *Adverbs and Functional Heads: A Cross-Linguistic Perspective.* Oxford: OUP.

Davies, C. & Katsos, N. 2010. Over-informative children: Production/comprehension asymmetry or tolerance to pragmatic violations? *Lingua* 120(8): 1956–1972.

Di Sciullo, A. M. 2015. On the domain specificity of the human language faculty and the effects of principles of computational efficiency: Contrasting language and mathematics. *Linguíftica* 11(1): 28–56.

Dollaghan, C. & Campbell, T. F. 1998. Nonword repetition and child language impairment. *Journal of Speech, Language, and Hearing Research* 41(5): 1136–1146.

Eisenberg, S. L., Ukrainetz, T. A., Hsu, J. R., Kaderavek, J. N, Justice, L. M. & Gillam, R. B. 2008. Noun phrase elaboration in children's spoken stories. *Language, Speech, And Hearing Services in Schools* 39(2): 145–157.

Ernst, T. 2002. *The Syntax of Adjuncts.* Cambridge: CUP.

Giblin, I., Zhou, P., Bill, C., Shi, J. & Crain, S. 2018. The spontaneous eMERGEnce of recursion in child language. In *Proceedings of the 43rd Annual Boston University Conference on Language Development*, M. M. Brown & B. Dailey (eds), 270–285. Somerville MA: Cascadilla Press.

Gillette, J., Gleitman, H., Gleitman, L. & Lederer, A. 1999. Human simulations of vocabulary learning. *Cognition* 73(2): 135–176.

Gleitman, L. 1990. The structural sources of verb meaning. *Language Acquisition* 1(1): 3–55.

Kaufman, A. S. & Kaufman, N. L. 2004. *Kaufman Assessment Battery for Children*, 2nd ed. Circle Pines MN: AGS Publishing.

Li, D., Yang, X., Roeper, T., Wilson, M., Yin, R., Kim, J., Merritt, E., Lopez, D. & Tero, A. 2020. Acquisition of recursion in child Mandarin. In *Proceedings of the Annual 44th Boston University Conference on Language Development*, M. M. Brown & A. Kohut (eds), 294–307. Somerville MA: Cascadilla Press.

Limbach, M. & Adone, D. 2010. Language acquisition of recursive possessives in English. In *Proceedings of the 34th Annual Boston University Conference on Language Development*, K. Franich, K. M. Iserman & L. L. Keil (eds), 281–290. Somerville MA: Cascadilla Press.

Marcus, G. F., Fernandes, K. J. & Johnson, S. P. 1999. Rule learning in 7-month-old infants. *Science* 283(5398): 77–80.

Merx, M. 2016. The Production and Comprehension of Recursive Possessive and Preposition Phrases of Dutch Children and Adults. BA thesis, University of Groningen

Nadig, A. S. & Sedivy, J. C. 2002. Evidence of perspective-taking constraints in children's on-line reference resolution. *Psychological Science* 13(4): 329–336.

Newmeyer, F. J. & Preston, L. B. (eds.) 2014. *Measuring Grammatical Complexity*. Oxford: OUP.

Pérez-Leroux, A. T., Castilla-Earls, A., Béjar, S. & Massam, D. 2012. Elmo's sister's ball: The problem of acquiring nominal recursion. *Language Acquisition* 19(4): 301–11.

Pérez-Leroux, A. T., Peterson, T., Bejar, S., Castilla-Earls, A., Massam, D. & Roberge, Y. 2018a. The acquisition of recursive modification in NPs. *Language* 94(2): 332–359.

Pérez-Leroux, A. T., Castilla-Earls, A., Bejar, S., Massam, D. & Peterson, T. 2018b. Strong continuity and children's development of NP recursion. In *Recursion in Brazilian Languages and Beyond*, M. Maia, L. Amaral & A. Nevins (eds), 182–200. Cambridge: CUP.

Pérez-Leroux, A. T. & Roberge, Y. 2018. A way into recursion. In *UMOP 41: Thoughts on Mind and Grammar (T.O.M. and grammar): A Festschrift in Honor of Tom Roeper*, B. Hollebrandse, J. Kim, A. T. Pérez-Leroux & P. Schulz (eds), 109–122. Amherst MA: GLSA.

Pérez-Leroux, A. T., Y. Roberge, A. Lowles & P. Schulz. 2020. Structural diversity does not affect the acquisition of recursivity: The case of possession in German. *Language Acquisition* 29(1): 54–78.

Roeper, T. 2011. The acquisition of recursion: How formalism articulates the child's path. *Biolinguistics* 5(1–2): 57–86.

Roeper, T., Maia, M. & França, A. I. 2020. Old story, new results and analyses: An eye-tracking and ERP evaluation of a classical ambiguity involving the attachment point of relative clause and prepositional phrase modifiers. *Cadernos de lingüística* 1(1): 1–24, 9 Jul. 2020.

Roeper, T., & Snyder, W. 2005. Language learnability and the forms of recursion. In *UG and External Systems: Language, Brain and Computation*, A. M. Di Sciullo (ed.), 155–169. Amsterdam: John Benjamins.

van Riemsdijk, H. 2011. An Element-theoretical approach to cohesion and repulsion in syntax. Paper presented at *New Perspectives on Language Creativity: Composition and Recursion*. Montreal, Canada.

Widmer, M., Auderset, S., Nichols, J., Widmer, P. & Bickel, B. 2017. NP recursion over time: Evidence from Indo-European. *Language* 93(4): 799–826.

Yang, C. 2016. *The Price of Linguistic Productivity: How Children Learn to Break Rules of Language*. Cambridge MA: The MIT Press.

Proper name index

A
Abutalebi, J. 20
Acquaviva, P. 55, 58–60, 63, 67
Adone, D. 249
Ågren, M. 121
Ahlsén, E. 232
Alderete, J. 198, 217
Alexandre, N. 125
Allen, P. 129
Altenberg, E.P. 193–194, 216
Amaral, L. 253
Antelmi, D. 61
Archibald, J. 194, 198, 217
Arencibia Guerra, L. 69–70
Armon-Lotem, S. 232
Arnon, I. 196
Aronoff, M. 57
Arslan, B. 264
Aslin, R.N. 195–196, 217
Azzopardi, P. 207

B
Baayen, R.H. 207–208
Bartning, I. 121
Bates, D. 207
Bates, E. 56, 61
Bauman, A. 192
Bayley, R. 131
Bazalgette, T.O. 63–64
Beckman, M.E. 145
Bejar, S. 11, 249
Benati, A. 57, 61
Benders, T. 228
Beniak, É. 7, 119, 121–122, 126–127, 129–130, 137–138, 140–141
Bianchi, G. 56–57, 61, 88
Biberauer, T. 55, 63–66
Bittner, D. 93, 97
Bock, J.K. 198
Boeckx, C. 83, 263
Bolander, M. 234
Bolin, I. 232
Bolin, M. 232
Boloh, Y. 54

Borges, J.L. 20
Bottari, P. 61–62, 93
Bradlow, A.R. 148, 150
Brandl, A. 146–147, 155
Broselow, E. 198
Brown, R. 40, 48
Burt, M.K. 33
Butterfield, S. 217

C
Cacciari, C. 58–59
Cairns, H.S. 193, 216
Campbell, T.F. 256
Canale, M. 120, 123–124, 139
Cantone, K.F. 69
Caprin, C. 61, 76
Carroll, L. 20
Carroll, S.E. 1–5, 7–11, 22, 37–38, 40, 47, 54, 67, 97, 99, 141, 157, 165, 185, 191–192, 195–196, 204, 214, 217, 219, 226, 246, 264
Carter, D.M. 193
Caselli, M.C. 61–62, 76
Castilla-Earls, A. 11
Castonguay, C. 127
Chalkley, M.A. 63
Chang, C.-J. 229
Chaudron, C. 227
Chini, M. 55–59, 61–62
Chomsky, N. 11, 18–19, 23, 30, 48, 63–64, 246
Cinque, G. 250
Cipriani, P. 61
Clahsen, H. 20, 30, 35
Clopper, C.G. 150
Colliander, G. 234
Conley, R. 148
Corbett, G.G. 54, 57, 66–67, 81
Corder, S.P. 24–25, 227–228, 234
Cornips, L. 96
Corteen, E.M. 90
Costa, A. 228–229, 239
Cowan, N. 219
Craft, J. 149, 156, 158
Cristia, A. 228

Crosswhite, K. 198, 217
Cutler, A. 193–194, 216–217

D
Davies, C. 252
Davis, M.H. 214
De Houwer, A. 26, 112
De Martino, M. 61
de Villiers, J.G. 17
de Villiers, P.A. 17
Dieser, E. 94
Di Sciullo, A.M. 247
Dollaghan, C. 256
Dommergues, J.-Y. 196, 214, 216–218
Dracos, M. 227–228
Dressler, R. 6
Dressler, W.U. 57–58
Dulay, H.C. 33, 40
duPlessis, J. 35–36, 38
Dyson, B.P. 41

E
Eaves Jr., B.S. 228, 240
Eichler, N. 61–62, 69, 94, 96, 111
Eisenberg, S.L. 252
Eklund Heinonen, M. 234
Ellis, R. 162–164, 178, 186, 193
Ernst, T. 250
Estebas-Vilaplana, E. 145
Eubank, L. 192
Ezeizabarrena, M.-J. 70

F
Face, T.L. 145
Faussart, C. 54
Felix, S.W. 23, 25
Ferguson, C. 227–228
Ferrari, F. 61
Fey, S. 62
Finer, D. 198
Flege, J.E. 145
Fodor, J.A. 22
Fodor, J.D. 2
Friederici, A.D. 192

Frota, S. 164

G
Gallagher, G. 195–196, 218
Gallego, M. 148
Garcia, F.I. 70
Gass, S.M. 162
Geeslin, K. 151
Gelman, R. 229, 239
Giblin, I. 253
Gillette, J. 251
Givón, T. 195
Glahn, E. 234
Gleitman, L. 251
Göksel, A. 170
Gomez, R. 203
Goo, J. 163
Granfeldt, J. 96
Green, D.S. 207
Gregg, K. 40
Guasti, M.T. 61, 76
Gudmestad, A. 151
Gudmundson, A. 59
Guilfoyle, E. 41
Guion, S.G. 198
Gullberg, M. 9, 191–192, 195–196, 199, 205, 214–215, 217–219

H
Hager, M. 61–63, 69–72, 77, 80, 96, 110
Hair, J.F. 179
Håkansson, G. 10–11, 41, 227–228, 230, 232, 234–235
Hakuta, K. 25
Halle, M. 198, 217
Hammarberg, B. 234
Harley, B. 120, 122–124, 137–139
Hatch, E. 227–228, 234
Hauser-Grüdl, N. 69
Heidolph, K.E. 92–93
Henriksen, N. 144–145, 156
Henzl, V. 227–228
Herron, C. 8, 165, 167, 185–186
Hohne, E.A. 192
Holmberg, A. 64
Hopp, H. 98
Housen, A. 168, 184
Houston, D.M. 192–193, 217
Hracs, L. 1–2
Hualde, J.I. 145
Hulk, A. 89, 96

Hulstijn, J.H. 163, 186, 215
Hyltenstam, K. 234

I
Ibernon, L. 54
Indefrey, P. 199
Ivanova-Sullivan, T. 63

J
Jaeger, T.F. 207
Jakubowicz, C. 54
Jansen, V. 61–62
Johnson, E.K. 217
Josefsson, G. 10, 232, 234–235
Jusczyk, P.W. 191–193, 217
Jörgensen, N. 227, 238

K
Kaltsa, M. 89, 96, 110
Karmiloff-Smith, A. 215
Karst, Y.N. 145
Katsos, N. 252
Kaufman, A.S. 256
Kaufman, N.L. 256
Kehoe, M. 89
Kellerman, E. 216
Kelly, M.H. 198
Kerslake, C. 170
Kewley-Port, D. 148
Kirk, N.W. 217
Köpcke, K.-M. 92–93, 106
Köylü, Y. 8
Kornfilt, J. 170
Krashen, S.D. 162, 164
Kuhl, P.K. 228
Kupisch, T. 5–6, 57, 61–62, 69, 71, 75, 88–89, 93, 96

L
Lado, R. 24
La Morgia, F. 112
Lampitelli, N. 60–61
Lange, S. 232
Lapkin, S. 120, 122, 139
Larsen-Freeman, D. 228–229, 234–235
Larsson, K. 232
Law, A. 64
Lee, S. 8
Leeman, J. 8, 166–167, 185–186
Lemmerth, N. 98
Leonard, L.B. 62

Leopold, W.F. 25
Levelt, W.J.M. 230
Li, Daoxin 263
Li, Dawai 219
Li, S. 163, 187
Lightbown, P.M. 169
Lim, R. 196
Limbach, M. 249
Lindauer, M. 93, 107
Linzen, T. 195–196, 218
Lleó, C. 89
Long, M.H. 8, 162–164, 166–167, 185, 228–229, 235
Longobardi, G. 64
Loporcaro, M. 57
Lowenstamm, J. 54–55, 60, 66
Luk, J. 145
Luo, Y.-H. 229
Lyster, R. 163, 165

M
MacDonald, D. 40
Mackey, A. 162
MacWhinney, B. 63, 92–93
Makowski, D. 207
Månsson, A.-C. 232
Maratsos, M.P. 63
Marcus, G.F. 263
Martin, A. 228
Massam, D. 11
Mathôt, S. 206
Matsuura, H. 145
Matthews, S. 70
Mattys, S.J. 192
McNamara, D.S. 229–230, 235, 240
McNeill, D. 21, 23, 47
McQueen, J.M. 193
Meisel, J.M. 1, 4–5, 11, 22, 26–27, 32–34, 37–38, 44–45, 48, 67, 97–99, 111, 227–228, 234
Melvold, J.L. 198, 217
Mennen, I. 7, 144, 149, 156
Merx, M. 259
Miller, G.A. 21–22
Miller, M. 30
Mills, A.E. 63, 92–94, 107, 110
Mitchell, R. 193
Montrul, S. 88–89, 98–99
Mougeon, F. 7, 127–128
Mougeon, R. 7, 119–122, 124, 126–130, 137–141

Müller, N. 5, 38, 61–62, 69, 89, 94–95, 110–111
Muysken, P. 35

N
Nadasdi, T. 119, 122, 126, 128, 138
Nadig, A. S. 252
Naumann, K. 231
Nettelbladt, U. 232, 234
Newmeyer, F. J. 64, 245
Newport, E. L. 195–196, 217
Newsome, M. 192–193, 217
Nibert, H. J. 145–146, 155
Nishi, K. 148
Noonan, M. 41
Norrby, C. 230
Norris, D. 193, 217

O
Ono, L. 179
Opitz, A. 90

P
Padovani, R. 58–59
Palmeri, T. J. 148
Paradis, J. 232
Pavlovitch, M. 25
Pechmann, T. 90
Perdue, C. 44
Pérez-Leroux, A. T. 11–12, 252–253, 256, 262–264
Pérez-Pereira, M. 89
Pérez-Tattam, R. 83
Phakiti, A. 180
Pica, T. 162, 179
Picallo, C. M. 65
Pienemann, M. 10, 41, 169, 192, 230–231, 234
Pierrard, M. 168, 184
Pierrehumbert, J. B. 145
Pillunat, A. 71
Pirvulescu, M. 125, 138
Pizzuto, E. 61–62, 76
Platzack, C. 227, 232, 234
Plunkett, K. 232, 234
Poeppel, D. 42–43
Polinsky, M. 88, 99
Preston, L. B. 245
Prévost, P. 43–46
Prieto, P. 145

Q
Quilis, A. 145

R
Rankin, J. 61
Ranta, L. 165
Rasmussen, J. 148–149
Rast, R. 9, 191–192, 195–197, 214, 216–219
Ready, D. 227–228
Reeder, P. A. 61
Rehner, K. 7, 120, 124–126, 128, 131–132, 137–138
Reichenberg, M. 229–230, 235, 238, 240
Rizzi, S. 57, 61
Roberge, Y. 11, 263
Roberts, I. 63–65
Rodina, Y. 89, 110
Roeper, T. 245, 247, 249, 252–253, 263
Ronjat, J. 25
Roseano, P. 145
Rothman, J. 89, 216
Ruberg, T. 94, 97, 107
Russell, W. 59

S
Saffran, J. R. 195–196, 217
Saito, K. 144, 163
Sankoff, G. 141
Santelmann, L. 232, 234
Saussure, F. de. 19, 25
Sayehli, S. 231
Schiller, N. O. 92
Schlyter, S. 98–99
Schmeißer, A. 69–70
Schmidt, L. 145
Schmidt, R. 164
Schönström, K. 234
Schwartz, B. D. 34, 162, 191
Schwartz, M. 81, 97, 110
Schwichtenberg, B. 92
Sedivy, J. C. 252
Segui, J. 218
Seidl, A. 228
Sekerina, I. A. 63
Selkirk, E. 198
Sereno, J. A. 198
Serianni, L. 59
Shatz, M. 229, 239
Sheen, Y. 165

Shoemaker, E. 9, 191–192, 195, 197, 219
Silvén, M. 229
Singmann, H. 208
Skirgård, H. 216
Slobin, D. I. 23, 47
Smith, F. 21–22
Smith, N. 64
Snow, C. 227–228
Snyder, W. 247, 252–253
Spada, N. 169
Sprouse, R. A. 34
Stahnke, J. 5, 75
Stanislaw, H. 207
Steinmetz, D. 90
Stern, C. 17, 30, 93–94, 110
Stern, W. 17–18, 30, 93–94, 110
Stoehr, A. 88
Strömqvist, S. 232, 234
Sullivan, K. P. 145
Swain, M. 2, 120, 122–123, 139
Swets, J. A. 207
Szagun, G. 93–94, 98, 106, 110

T
Tagliamonte, S. 131
Tauroza, S. 145
Terrell, T. D. 164
Teschner, R. 59
Thornton, A. M. 55–59, 61, 80
Todorov, N. 207
Tomasello, M. 8, 29, 165, 167, 185–186
Trimble, J. 145–146, 148, 155–156
Truscott, J. 162
Tsimpli, I. M. 41
Tuite, K. 66
Turk, A. 192, 217

U
Unsworth, S. 89, 96, 110
Uther, M. 228, 234

V
Vainikka, A. 191, 193
van der Linden, E. 96
VanPatten, B. 162
van Riemsdijk, H. 252
Vergnaud, J. R. 198, 217
Viberg, Å. 234

W
Waldmann, C. 10, 235
Weber, A. 194, 216
Wegener, H. 94, 97
Wesche, M. B. 227–229, 234–235
Wessels, M. I. 192
Westergaard, M. 89, 110
Wexler, K. 42–43
White, L. 43–46
Widjaja, E. 2

Widmer, M. 247–248, 259–260
Willis, E. W. 145
Windsor, J. W. 2
Witzel, J. 179
Wode, H. 34

Y
Yang, C. 263
Yang, L. 195
Yilmaz, Y. 8–9, 165

Yip, V. 70
Young, R. 131
Young-Scholten, M. 9, 191, 193

Z
Zaliznjak, A. 198
Zampini, M. 148–149
Zárate-Sández, G. 146, 155
Zubin, D. 92–93, 106

Subject index

A
ablative 186–187
acquisition problem 22–23, 28, 32, 37, 39, 46
acquisition theory 16, 19, 22–23, 26, 29, 33, 37, 41, 43, 64
adjunct 246
adjunction 250
Adjunction parameter 36
adjusted target language use (ATLU) 179
age of onset (AoO) 97–99
agreement 44–46, 57, 60, 62–63, 82, 90–92, 96, 105, 109, 197 (*see also* gender agreement, number agreement)
Albanian 96–97
ambiguity 103, 245, 248
Anglophone 119–120, 130, 195
Arabic 44, 169, 187, 234
artificial language 9, 195–196, 203, 217–218
aspect 44
attention 148, 164, 168, 172, 184, 186, 204, 208, 215, 217, 219
attentional resources 168, 193
Autonomous Induction Theory 1
awareness 94, 163, 186, 193

B
behaviourist 24
bilingual:
    balanced bilingual 62, 125
    bilingual first language (L1) acquisition 17, 26, 62
    early bilingual 89
    early sequential bilingual acquisition (eL2) 6, 90, 94, 97–99
    late bilingual 88–89, 98
    simultaneous bilingual acquisition (2L1) 6, 23, 25–26, 90, 94, 96, 98–99
    successive bilingual acquisition (cL2) 25
    unbalanced bilingual 67
bootstrapping 22, 251 (*see also* semantic bootstrapping, syntactic bootstrapping)
boundary tone 8, 144–150, 152, 155, 157–158
brain imaging 48

C
Cantonese 199
case 6, 66, 81, 89, 91, 93, 197
    accusative case 91, 103, 197
    case-marking 97, 103, 246
    dative case 103
    nominative case 91, 103, 197
case study 5–6, 25, 88–89, 109
Catalan 96
child bilingualism 25
child-directed speech (CDS) 3, 10, 93, 228, 239
CHILDES 233
Chinese 217
clarification request 8, 164, 229
classifier 2
cognate 2, 195, 204
cognitive turn 4, 16, 18–19, 26, 32, 39
cognitive-interactionist 162–163
coherence 229–230
cohesive device 229–230, 239–240
comitative 11, 245, 248, 253–256, 258, 260–263
complement 141, 246, 251
complementation 11, 251
complexity 7, 11–12, 41, 64–65, 141, 228, 245, 248–249, 252, 263–264 (*see also* grammatical complexity)
comprehension 48, 157, 228–230, 238, 240
comprehension task 9, 173, 176–177
conceptual representation 1
connective device 229, 235, 237–238
contrastive analysis (CA) 24, 42
controlled first exposure language learning (CFELL) 2–3 (*see also* first exposure)
correction 2, 157, 185
corrective feedback (CF) 8–9, 162–168, 172, 174–177, 180–188
correct rejections 207 (*see also* Signal Detection Theory (SDT))
cross-linguistic 26, 29, 36, 54, 187, 197, 253
cross-linguistic influence (CLI) 88–90, 96, 98
cross-sectional 44, 144
cue:
    allophonic cue 218
    contextual cue 7
    distributional cue 218
    gender cue 88, 97, 106, 112
    intonational cue 145, 148
    morphological cue 6
    morpho-phonological cue 97
    phonological cue 6, 57–58, 63, 80, 93–94, 97, 197
    phonotactic cue 191, 218
    prosodic cue 191, 218
    semantic cue 6, 92, 95
    structural cue 89, 91–92
    syntactic cue 6, 58–61, 82–83
cue-based 72, 80–81
Czech 227–228

D
declarative 8, 144, 146–148, 150–156, 226–227, 233, 236
declension class 5, 54–55, 57–58, 60, 63, 66–69, 71–74, 79–83
developmental problem 5, 23, 39–40, 43

developmental psycholinguistics   4, 16, 21–23, 39, 46, 48
developmental sequence   31, 36, 40
developmental stage   11, 37, 69, 98, 123, 169, 230, 233–235, 240
dialect   19, 145–153, 155, 157 (see also macrodialect)
dialect identification   150
diary study   232
discriminability   207
discursive frequency   7, 118, 121
dislocations   1
distributional learning   46
dominant language   6, 69, 112, 123–124
Dutch   34, 89, 96, 192, 195, 217–218

E
ecological validity   9, 195, 197
embedding   245, 247, 252–253, 256, 259–260, 263
English   1, 6–11, 31, 34, 36, 66, 88–90, 96–97, 99–103, 110, 112, 119–120, 122–128, 138–139, 144–151, 155, 157, 162–163, 165, 169–170, 191–194, 196–202, 204, 206, 211, 216–219, 227, 229, 234, 245, 248–250, 252, 254, 263
evidence   2–3, 5, 8–9, 12, 31–32, 35, 37–38, 43–46, 48, 66, 83, 90, 94–95, 99, 126, 157, 162–166, 168, 181, 184–186, 197–198, 209, 218–219, 228–229, 234, 251–253, 256, 263 (see also negative evidence, positive evidence)
explicit:
    explicit correction   8, 165, 185 (see also correction)
    explicit instruction   7–8, 144, 146, 148–150, 152–153, 156–158, 165, 193–195 (see also instruction)
    explicit knowledge   163, 178, 186
    explicit learning   216, 219–220
    explicit teaching   156
exposure   2–4, 6–10, 26, 29–30, 38, 41, 45, 47, 67, 69, 90, 97–101, 109, 112, 118–119, 122, 124, 126–127, 131–132, 138–140, 145, 148, 157, 172, 175, 179, 184, 188, 191–197, 204, 214–220, 228 (see also controlled first exposure language learning (CFELL), first exposure)
external merge (EM)   246 (see also Merge)
eye-tracking   48, 98

F
facilitate   8, 11, 157, 162–164, 169, 228, 238, 240, 249, 251
factor weight   131, 133–135
false alarms   207, 213 (see also Signal Detection Theory (SDT))
Feature Economy (FE)   64–65, 68
feedback   2, 157, 164–168, 173, 177, 185–186 (see also corrective feedback)
feminine   55–61, 72–73, 76–79, 90–95, 97, 104–106, 108–112, 124, 137, 197
Finnish   97, 234
Finno-Ugrian   234
first exposure   9–10, 90, 97, 191–192, 194–197, 215–219 (see also controlled first exposure language learning (CFELL))
focal accent   203
focus   144, 147, 150, 152
for-to infinitive   1
forced-choice (task)   9–10, 204–205, 207–212, 214–217
Foreigner Talk   227
form-meaning   168, 184
Francophone   7, 118–132, 134, 137–141
French   1, 7, 25, 31, 36, 44, 54, 57, 66, 95–96, 118–132, 137–139, 141, 165, 167, 169, 187, 195, 197, 199, 218, 227
French immersion   120–124, 126, 129, 131, 139
French as a Second Language (FSL)   7, 118–121, 125–128, 130, 132, 134–139, 141
Full Competence Hypothesis   42
Full Transfer hypothesis   34, 38

G
gender:
    gender agreement   29, 54, 57, 61, 63, 94, 96, 110, 166
    gender assignment   54, 59, 61, 66, 68, 88–90, 93, 95, 98, 103–104, 106–107, 111
    gender feature   5, 54–55, 57, 60–61, 63, 67–68, 71, 73, 80–83
    gender marking   6, 54–55 80–83, 89–96, 98–100, 103–112
    (see also feminine, masculine, neuter)
generative   3–4, 18, 36–37, 39, 42–43, 47–48, 63
genitive   247, 252–254, 259–262 (see also Saxon genitive)
German   4–6, 16, 25, 27–28, 30–36, 38–39, 41, 44–45, 54, 62, 67, 69–71, 88–103, 109–112, 169, 187, 193–196, 199, 227, 231, 247, 263
Germanic   217, 226
grammatical complexity   11, 41, 65–66 (see also complexity)
grammatical theory   1, 26, 36–37, 39, 42, 46
grammaticality judgment   167
Greek   96–97, 234

H
head-final   32, 34–35, 38
head-initial   30, 35, 38
Headedness parameter   36
Hebrew   97
heritage language (HL)   6, 88–89, 97, 99, 109–110, 112
heritage speaker (HS)   6, 88–90, 98–100, 146, 151, 155, 157
hierarchical   28–30, 32, 35, 264
hits   207, 213 (see also Signal Detection Theory (SDT))
Hungarian   194, 234
hybrid system   48

I
ideal speaker-hearer   4, 18–20
implicit:
    implicit acquisition   193

Subject index

implicit corrective feedback 163 (*see also* corrective feedback)
implicit instruction 146 (*see also* instruction)
implicit knowledge 4, 23, 163, 178, 186, 215
implicit learning 193, 195, 197, 215
incidental exposure 215
incidental learning 215
Indo European 234
inductive learning 22, 37–38, 46, 48
infinitive 130, 186 (*see also* for-to infinitive)
information structure 10, 227
innate 4, 22–24, 46–47, 63–64
input 2–5, 9–10, 22, 30, 41, 46–47, 59, 64–65, 67, 97–98, 122, 124–126, 131, 140, 148, 152, 162–164, 168–169, 176, 184, 193–201, 203–206, 208–209, 213–214, 218–219, 226–227, 232, 234–235, 239–241, 251, 263
Input Generalization (IG) 64–65, 68, 95
instruction 7–8, 24, 128, 144, 146, 148–153, 156–158, 162–165, 191, 193–195, 219, 227, 236 (*see also* explicit instruction, implicit instruction)
instructional treatment 169, 177, 187
Interaction Hypothesis 164
interface 89, 263
intergroup hierarchy 120, 125–126, 132–133, 135–137
interlanguage 156
internal merge (IM) 246 (*see also* Merge)
interrogative 28, 145, 150, 152, 155 (*see also* wh-question, yes-no question)
intonation 7–8, 144–152, 155–158
Italian 5–6, 44, 54–63, 66–73, 76–83, 89, 96, 169, 187
item-based learning 97
iterative 11, 246, 252, 261

J
Japanese 8, 166–167, 169, 185, 187, 199, 234

K
knowledge consolidation 168
knowledge internalization 168, 184
knowledge modification 168, 184
Korean 199

L
language acquisition device (LAD) 22, 26, 29–32, 36, 39, 48
language balance 55, 67
language dominance 69, 89, 96, 125
language impairment 199, 232, 234
language processor 2, 47, 230
language-making capacity (LMC) 23–24, 26, 33
Last-Member Principle 92, 111
learnability theory 2
learning mechanisms 2–3, 22, 43, 47, 195
learning problem 1–4, 7, 11, 47, 141
lexical decision task 193
L2 Intonation Learning theory (LILt) 7, 149, 156–157
linguistic theory 3, 11, 18, 21–22, 26, 29, 39, 41–42, 46
loanword 59, 90, 204
locative 8–9, 11, 162–163, 167–170, 172–179, 184, 186–188, 245, 248, 251, 255, 257, 262
longitudinal 6, 30, 44–45, 48, 69, 88, 93–94, 220, 235

M
macrodialect 8, 146–148, 150–153, 155–157 (*see also* dialect)
macroparameter 64–65
macro-processes 168, 184
majority community 120, 137
majority language 6, 89–90, 99, 109–110, 112, 118
Mandarin 36, 195–197, 199, 218

markedness 5, 64–65, 67–68, 81, 89, 123
masculine 55–63, 73, 76–79, 90–95, 97, 104–106, 108–112, 197
mean length of utterance (MLU) 31, 62, 67, 69–70, 102
Merge 11, 246–247, 249, 251, 263 (*see also* external merge (EM), internal merge (IM))
mesoparameter 64–65
Metrical Segmentation Strategy (MSS) 193, 197, 217
microparameters 64–65
Minimal Sonority Distance (MSD) 198
Minimalist 36, 63, 246
minority community 121–123, 137
minority language 6, 99, 110, 112
misformation 179
misses 194, 207, 213 (*see also* Signal Detection Theory (SDT))
Missing Surface Inflection Hypothesis (MSIH) 43–46
modality 44
modeling 157, 177
models 5, 8–9, 20, 42, 162–168, 172–174, 176–177, 180–188, 192, 207–208, 257–258
modification 11–12, 168, 184, 227–229, 235–238, 240, 245–246, 248–249, 251–254, 257, 261
modifier 246, 250, 256
monolingual 6, 17, 26, 31, 55, 61–63, 67, 81, 88–90, 93, 95–96, 98–100, 109–111, 125, 194, 232
Monosyllabic Place Holders (MPHs) 62
multilingualism 69
multiple-choice 162, 168, 170–171, 178–184, 186, 216

N
nanoparameters 64–65
Natural Approach 164
naturalistic 6, 24, 48, 88, 93, 163, 193
negation 165, 167, 232

negative evidence 3, 8, 37, 162–166, 181, 184–185
neuter 90–92, 94–96, 104–112, 197
Norwegian 89
noticing 40, 163, 168
number 2, 5–6, 30, 44, 55, 57, 59–62, 66, 68, 80–82, 91, 103, 172, 175
　　number agreement 29, 62, 166–167
　　number feature 55, 57, 62–63
　　number marking 71, 80
　　(see also plural, singular)

O
omission 5, 54–55, 61–63, 69, 71, 73, 75–77, 79–82, 93, 98, 103–108, 111
oral picture description 162, 167–168, 171, 178–184, 186
overgeneralization 76, 94, 96, 98, 111–112

P
parameter 5, 30, 35–38, 41, 55, 63–68, 246, 254
　　parameter hierarchy 55, 63–67
　　parameter taxonomy 55, 65, 68
　　parameterized 5, 36, 38, 46
　　parameter (re)setting 1, 5, 37–38, 64
　　Parameter Theory 30, 35, 37, 41
　　parametric 37, 63–65 (see also Adjunction parameter, Headedness parameter, Proper Government parameter, principles and parameters, V2 parameter)
part-whole 245, 247, 263
perception 3, 7, 144–146, 148–150, 155, 158, 217–218
Persian 234
person 7, 30, 44–46, 66, 130, 231, 235

phonotactic 9–10, 191–195, 197, 199–208, 211–213, 215–216, 218–219
plural 5–7, 40, 55–56, 58–62, 66, 71–73, 76–78, 91, 97, 103, 108, 118, 121, 130, 135–136, 140, 170
Polish 17, 81, 97, 194–195, 197, 218, 234
Portuguese 44, 199
positive evidence 3, 8, 163–166, 168
possessive 11, 90, 103, 245, 247–248, 251–256, 259–263
primary linguistic data (PLD) 22–23, 26, 28–30, 32, 37–38, 47, 64–65
priming 254
primitives 1
principle 19, 22–23, 26, 30–33, 35–36, 41–43, 46, 48, 63–64, 68
principles and parameters 36, 64 (see also principle, parameter)
Processability Theory (PT) 10–11, 230–235, 238–240
processing 2–3, 5, 11, 23, 32–33, 41, 45, 47, 64, 90, 163, 168, 192, 218, 230–232, 263–264
　　processing procedures 7, 10, 230–231
　　processor 2, 47, 169, 230
production 9, 11–12, 48, 68, 72, 75–77, 79–80, 98, 144, 146, 149, 156, 158, 162, 164, 167–169, 171–172, 174–175, 177, 184–185, 218, 230, 232, 249, 252–253, 262
production task 9, 174–175, 177
prompt 165, 167, 253–254
Proper Government parameter 36
property problem 22
prosodic 7, 150, 191, 218
prosody 144, 191, 193–194, 200

Q
quality:
　　of errors 111
　　of exposure 3
　　of input 67
quantity:
　　of exposure 3
　　of input 67

R
raising 30–32, 35, 43
recast 8, 165–167, 185
recursion 11, 245–248, 250, 252–254, 256–258, 260, 262–264
　　recursive modification 12, 246, 248, 253–254, 257
　　recursive structure 11–12, 247–249, 251–252, 256, 264
reflexive 1, 123, 137–138, 141
reformulation 165–166, 174, 229
relational nouns 11, 247, 255–256
relative clause (RC) 232, 249, 251–252, 256, 259–260
reliability coefficient 179
repetition 146, 166–167, 185–186, 229, 238, 256, 258, 264
representational problem 1, 11, 246
Romance 34, 60, 67, 94, 96, 110–111, 247
Russian 9–10, 61, 81, 94, 97, 99, 191–192, 197–202, 204, 206–207, 211–214, 216–219, 248

S
saliency 48
salient 30, 229
Saxon genitive 246, 249–250, 252, 254, 263
segment 9–10, 92, 191–193, 195, 204, 216
segmentation 2, 9, 191, 193–197, 200, 204, 214, 216–217, 219
semantic bootstrapping 11, 251 (see also bootstrapping)
semantic roles 232
Semitic 234
sensitivity 95, 97, 191, 193, 205, 207, 218–219
sequential modification 248
shared words identification task 204, 206–209, 219
Signal Detection Theory (SDT) 207 (see also correct rejections, false alarms, hits, misses)
simplification 226, 228–230
simplified registers 227–229, 234
singular 5–6, 45, 55–60, 62, 66, 71–73, 76–78, 90–91, 103, 107, 121, 130
Slavic 199, 216–217

Subject index

sociolinguistic   123, 129, 141, 150, 227
Sonority Sequencing Principle (SSP)   198
Spanish   7–8, 36, 44, 57, 59, 83, 89, 96, 98, 144–158, 166–167, 169, 185, 187, 194, 199, 227–228, 234
specifier   246, 252
speech stream   191–193, 195–196, 219
stagnation   6, 88, 90, 99–100, 104, 109, 112
statistical learning   196, 263
stress   57, 59, 166, 193–194, 196, 198–200, 206, 208, 217–219 (see also strong-weak stress pattern, weak-strong stress pattern)
strong-weak stress pattern   9, 192–193, 197, 199–203, 206, 212, 217 (see also stress, weak-strong stress pattern)
Structure Building Hypothesis   41
structure dependency   29
subject-verb inversion   34–35, 229–232, 234, 237–240
subordinate clause   28, 31–32, 34–36, 38, 228, 230–231, 234, 237
suppliance in obligatory contexts (SOC)   179
surface position   29
Swahili   36
Swedish   10–11, 226–236, 238–240
syllable weight   59, 192

T

syntactic bootstrapping   251 (see also bootstrapping)

T

Teacher Talk   10, 227–228, 235, 238–239
tense   30–32, 44, 226
third person plural (3PL)   7, 118, 120–122, 130–131, 134–140
topic   229, 235
topicalization   1, 166–167, 185, 230, 232–233, 239–240
transfer   24, 33–34, 37–38, 149–150, 156, 196–197
transitional competence   25, 33
trigger   16, 23, 25, 30, 37–38, 40, 59–60, 204, 237–238, 263
truth value judgement task   253
Turkish   8–9, 34, 97, 162–163, 165, 168–172, 177–180, 184, 186–188, 234

U

underspecification   6, 91, 93, 95
unified (acquisition) theory   4, 17, 23, 41
unilingual   120, 122–123
universal grammar (UG)   5, 22–23, 29–33, 35–38, 43, 47–48, 63–64
universal   1, 22–23, 29–30, 40, 46, 219–220, 230
usage-based   29, 31
utterance identification task   151

V

V2 parameter   38

verb placement   4, 16, 27, 31, 33, 39
verb-second (V2)   10, 28–29, 31–34, 37–38, 226–227, 232, 234–235, 237, 241
visual information processing   2
vocative   108

W

weak language   54, 62, 67, 69, 79, 83
weak-strong stress pattern   9–10, 191–193, 197, 199–203, 212, 217 (see also stress, strong-weak stress pattern)
Welsh   199
wh-question   8, 144–147, 149–157, 255 (see also interrogative)
word learning   2, 215
word order   7, 10–11, 30–33, 35, 38, 41, 145–147, 152, 197, 226–241
word recognition task   9, 205–207, 210–218

Y

yes-no question   8, 28, 144–157 (see also interrogative)
Yiddish   36

Z

Zweitspracherwerb italienischer und spanischer Arbeiter (ZISA)   44–45